Jesus, a Life

Michele —
May these reflections
be food for your journey.

Regards,
Dan

Jesus, a Life

Daily Reflections
on the Gospel of Luke

Daniel Plasman

Jesus, a Life
Daily Reflections on the Gospel of Luke

Copyright © 2015 by Daniel Plasman

Scripture passages are the author's translation.
Photographs included in this book are by the author and are the exclusive, copyright-protected property of the author.

Printed in the United States of America

First Printing, 2015

ISBN-10: 1505958032
ISBN-13: 978-1505958034

dplasman@aol.com
www.danielplasman.com

For my grandchildren:
LAINA, BEN, NOLAN, EMILY, and CAROLINE

When you welcome a child, you welcome me.
JESUS

INTRODUCTION

This book is about Jesus. More specifically, these reflections are about the Jesus we discover in Luke's gospel. Beginning with the first verses of the opening chapter of Luke and ending with the last verses of the closing chapter, there are 365 reflections in all—one for each day of the year, if you choose that pace.

These reflections are intended for people who know almost everything there is to know about Jesus, as well as for those whose only familiarity with Jesus is a vague sense that he lived a long time ago and probably had a beard and wore sandals.

These ponderings are written for those who turn to the Bible more faithfully than to their smartphones, as well as for people surprised to learn that Luke is located in the New Testament between Mark and John. This collection is meant for people who are spiritual but not religious, for people who are religious but not spiritual, and for those who are both or neither.

Pastors, preachers, youth group leaders, and Bible study facilitators will benefit from reading these reflections, as will white-collar and blue-collar workers, truck drivers, office administrators, techies, rock musicians, cashiers, and those in any other occupation you can imagine, including college students, stay-at-home parents, and retirees.

This collection is for people who deeply love Jesus, God, and the church, but it's more purposely directed toward those who've given up on all three because of the harm authority figures and religious institutions have inflicted on them. This is a long list that includes those who've been devalued, discouraged, and denounced because of their gender or gender expression, their life experiences, their marital status, their ethnicity, their race, their addiction, their disability, their sexual orientation, their politics, their doubts, or their questions.

My hope is that you will find something in this book that sparks your interest and feeds your soul. If my reflections affirm some of your views on Jesus and the life he lived, good. If you find yourself at times disagreeing with me, that too can be good. Either way, please feel free to let me know (dplasman@aol.com).

With a few exceptions, each titled meditation begins with my paraphrase based on several English translations, including the New Revised Standard Version, the Common English Bible, and the New Century Bible, as well as the Greek New Testament. The result is a fluid reading of Luke that is contemporary and accessible.

Whether you are reading your way through this book alone or sharing the journey with someone, I hope you will find the question at the end of each reflection an opportunity for additional pondering, and maybe even some discussing. If so, then you've fulfilled my intent and you have my deepest gratitude.

What prompts you to begin this journey through Jesus, a Life?

THE GOSPEL

An Internet search of the word *gospel* produces more than two hundred million links. Sometimes it appears as an adjective: gospel choir, gospel church, gospel music, or gospel radio. Other times, *gospel* is used as a noun, as in this Wikipedia definition: "A gospel is an account, often written, that describes the life of Jesus of Nazareth."

The word *gospel* derives from the Greek word from which we get our English word *evangelism*. *Gospel* also relates to a combination of two Old English words of several centuries ago: *god*, meaning "good" and the German *spel*, meaning "talk" or "tale." *Godspell*, the smash-hit musical on the life of Jesus based on Matthew's gospel, opened on Broadway in 1971.

Where does all this dictionary searching lead us? Most simply to this: The gospel is the good tale, the good talk, the good story. Said another way, the gospel, as the Greek suggests, is the good news. This good news is the story of Jesus—who he was, what he said, what he did, and what he means for people today.

The New Testament contains one gospel message written by four gospel writers: Matthew, Mark, Luke, and John. We know little about the writers themselves. Unlike some authors today who are more popular than the books they write, the gospel writers are secondary to the story they tell. Their message is what counts, and that message, evident even in a quick read, reveals that they set out with their descriptive brushes to paint a portrait of one called Jesus of Nazareth, who lived more than two thousand years ago in what is now Palestine.

You might want to double-check my findings. Depending on the search engine, the word *Jesus* generates close to three-quarters of a billion links. The only other "religious" name inhabiting cyberspace that has more links—over a billion—is the name *God*.

What's the most recent good news you have heard?

1

ACCORDING TO LUKE

These reflections center on the story of Jesus according to Luke. The word *according* has within it the Latin word *cordus* or *cor* from which is derived our English word *heart*. The story of Jesus is gathered, compiled, arranged, and written from the heart of Luke, just as Matthew, Mark, and John wrote from their hearts. It's widely believed that Mark's gospel was written first and that Matthew and Luke borrowed heavily from Mark, along with introducing material not found there. None of the gospel writers claims the voice of God whispered the exact words that compose their work.

Luke was probably a non-Jew, writing about a Jewish rabbi from Nazareth. He wrote to a non-Jewish audience nearly fifty years after Jesus died. Though Luke doesn't identify himself in the gospel story, many scholars believe he is the beloved physician mentioned by name in Paul's letter to the Colossians. Luke, who also authored the New Testament book the Acts of the Apostles, was probably not an eyewitness to Jesus.

Each gospel has particular emphases unique to the writer. In this case, Luke has a passion for outsiders, for non-Jews in the first-century world. Many of the stories Jesus tells and many of the locales Jesus visits include people who don't belong or adhere to the Jewish traditions.

Luke also has a heart for minority groups and those on the bottom rung of the social ladder; these include the sick and the poor, lepers and outcasts, Samaritans, and especially women. Given the culture of the time, Luke seeks to portray women in the best possible light. Luke's Jesus is always challenging social customs that diminish a woman's status.

Luke's Jesus models new ways for people to relate to one another in which walls and barriers are dismantled, the downtrodden are lifted up, exploitive powers are brought low, forgiveness is the norm, and mercy extends to all.

This is God's story—the Gospel according to Luke.

What adjective would you use to describe Jesus?

AN ORDERLY ACCOUNT
Luke 1:1-4

We are beneficiaries of those who have put into words the life and teachings of Jesus, some of whom were eyewitnesses to him. After much study and careful investigation, I've decided to do the same for you, dear Theophilus, so that you may know the true story about the One we follow.

+

Though each of the four gospels tells the story of Jesus, stylistic differences abound. Matthew, for example, begins with a seventeen-verse genealogy that traces Jesus' family tree through Joseph back to the patriarch Abraham. Mark begins with an adult Jesus receiving baptism in the Jordan River. John introduces the story of Jesus with a theological prologue: "In the beginning the Word existed; this Word was with God and was God."

Luke, however, gives his reason for writing before launching into the story. Substantiating his credentials as a careful historian, Luke begins the greatest story ever told by asserting his own research and reliability. Though he is not an eyewitness to Jesus, as a second- or third-generation member of the Christian community, Luke asserts that the stories passed on to him are trustworthy and life-changing. Only after careful investigation of these accounts does Luke set out to write his record.

Luke writes for the benefit and edification of a Christian named Theophilus, a name meaning "friend of God." Where Theophilus lives and what he does, we're not told. In all probability, he is a believer in the early church and representative of a community of believers Luke feels needs further instruction in the faith. Luke commits himself to retelling the story of Jesus so one individual and a particular community will be inspired by the life Jesus lived.

Even with all our technology, the means and methods of storytelling haven't changed much. From one person to another, the story weaves its influence—thread by thread. Storytelling best conveys the deepest truths of human existence. Stories have power like nothing else in this world.

Who's been most influential in shaping your story?

BROKEN PLACES
Luke 1:5-7

When Herod was the king in Judea, there was a priest named Zechariah, who belonged to the priestly section of Abijah. Zechariah was married to Elizabeth, a distant relative of Israel's first priest, Aaron. Both were decent and holy people, living according to God's commandments. However, they were childless, because Elizabeth couldn't conceive, and both were getting on in years.

+

Compared to the royal power of Herod, Zechariah and Elizabeth are little people living on the weak side of clout. The adjectives describing this aged couple speak volumes about their character. They are decent and holy, righteous and blameless, meticulously following the commandments of their tradition. To watch them is to witness holiness on legs.

Weighing heavily on their hearts, however, is a sorrowful burden, a broken place. With their fruitful, childbearing years behind them, these law-observing Jews remain a family of two. Few stigmas in biblical times carried more reproach than childlessness. What people wondered aloud cut deeply: "What have they done to displease God? Why is God punishing them? Too bad about Zechariah and Elizabeth, such nice folks!"

Childlessness proves problematic in other ways, too. If Zechariah dies first, who will care for Elizabeth? Who will preserve the names of the departed parents if there are no children, especially no son?

It's hard to imagine how many prayers this childless couple uttered in a lifetime. So many petitions and supplications seemingly ignored! If they were bitter and resentful in the autumn years of their lives, who could blame them?

Luke chooses his adjectives with great care. Zechariah and Elizabeth are decent and holy, nobly accepting what they can't change, faithfully observing what their religion requires of them. They never turn against God. "The world breaks everyone," Ernest Hemingway writes in *A Farewell to Arms*, "then some become strong at the broken places."

Where are you experiencing a broken place?

DIVINE COINCIDENCE
Luke 1:8-11

One day, as Zechariah was performing his priestly duties at the temple in Jerusalem, he was selected among the priests to enter the sanctuary of God and burn incense. While many people were praying outside, suddenly an angel of God, standing near the altar of incense, appeared to Zechariah.

+

Hebrew priests carried out many tasks. They offered morning and evening incense, kindled the fire on the altar in front of the temple, served as butchers in the slaying of animals for sacrifice, and cleaned up the ashes after the flames died out. In addition to these ceremonial duties, priests examined cases of leprosy and various maladies, determining who was permitted to enter the house of worship. Thousands of priests were available to perform these functions. A division or section of priests was chosen to do so each week.

This particular week, the turn falls to the section of Abijah. Each day of the week, priests from the order are selected to perform specific tasks, including burning incense in the Holy Place. Since there are many priests, it is unlikely that one will be chosen more than once in his lifetime for this honor. As the lot falls and divine coincidence comes into play, it is the privilege of the aged priest Zechariah to execute the task. On this day an angel appears.

How do we explain such an encounter? How do we understand the orchestration of being in the right place at the right time? Is it merely the luck of the draw? A twist of fate? The convergence of random odds? Did Zechariah go to work that day with a "feeling" that something life-changing might happen?

All we know is that in the course of faithfully performing his duties, by just showing up as he has done for dozens of years, Zechariah meets an angel of God. Divine mystery enshrouds an aged priest while he is carrying out his tasks.

It's hard to say how and when a rendezvous like this occurs. Perhaps it happens most frequently to persons doing the routine things of life in faithful ways.

When did an encounter with something mysterious stop you in your tracks?

Mount Carmel Cemetery, Hillside, IL

HEALTHY FEAR
Luke 1:12

When Zechariah saw the angel, he was overcome with fear.

+

Sometimes the biblical writers use the word *fear* in the same way we use the words *reverence* and *honor*. "The fear of God is the beginning of wisdom, and the knowledge of the Holy One is insight" (Proverbs 9:10). "These are the commandments that your God charged me to teach you . . . so you, your children, and your children's children may fear God" (Deuteronomy 6:1-2). "Let the earth fear God; let the people of the world stand in awe of God" (Psalm 33:8).

As a member of the priestly order, Zechariah is no stranger to feelings of reverential awe. He lives and breathes it. What overwhelms him now, however, is the more commonly understood notion of fear. Zechariah is afraid, scared of what he sees, fearful of what this encounter might mean.

Zechariah's thoughts may have flashed back to Moses, who, when he asked to see God's glory, was told, "You can't see my face, for no one who sees me will live" (Exodus 33:20). Unaware of the surprise visitor's identity, Zechariah may be wondering to himself, "Am I beholding the face of God? Will I live to tell about it?"

Perhaps Zechariah displays all the physiological manifestations of distress: sweaty palms, a racing heart, legs turning to mush. In any case, Luke wants us to know that this aged priest, who has already spent a lifetime dealing in the business of God, is terrified at what he now sees.

Two human tendencies are difficult to avoid. When we whittle God down to our size, we fashion a deity of our own making. When we relegate God to an interstellar black hole of insignificance, we end up having no use for a God so far away. In either case, there is nothing to be afraid of, but nothing to revere either. Developing a healthy fear of both dangers—and a healthy awe for God—is an ongoing spiritual quest.

When did you last experience a fear of the unknown?

DIVINE DELAYS
Luke 1:13

The angel said to Zechariah, "Don't be afraid; God has heard your prayer. Elizabeth will give birth to a son, and you'll name him John."

+

This is the first time in Luke's account that someone receives the assurance "Don't be afraid." It won't be the last. Similar soothing words are addressed to Mary when she encounters an angel, to the shepherds when they receive the news of Jesus' birth, and to the bewildered visitors at the tomb on Easter Sunday. "Don't be afraid. Have no fear. All is well."

The mysterious messenger is quick to get to the point. This is not a reprimand or a rebuke. The earnest prayers of the elderly couple have been heard and answered.

Though we don't know how long Zechariah and Elizabeth had prayed for a son, we can be reasonably sure they offered their petitions early in their marriage and continued such prayers into advanced age. For twenty, thirty, forty years or more, they directed a singular prayer to heaven without seeing fruition.

Centuries earlier, another childless couple—Isaac and Rebekah—faced a similar situation. "Isaac prayed to God for his wife, because she couldn't conceive. God answered his prayer and Rebekah became pregnant" (Genesis 25:21). The implication is that God's answer to Isaac's prayer was immediate. A reading of the entire passage, however, reveals a more accurate timeline. Isaac was forty when he married, forty when he began to pray for a son. He was sixty when Rebekah became pregnant. That's twenty years of praying! Two decades of waiting for God! A quarter of a lifetime adjusting to divine delays! Maybe unanswered prayers aren't necessarily disregarded prayers.

Do we fare as well in the constancy of prayer, or succumb to the forces of attrition? Zechariah and Elizabeth remind us that on the anvil of life's long delays, character is hammered and shaped.

For what have you stopped praying?

GREAT EXPECTATIONS
Luke 1:14-17

The angel said, "You will be glad, and many will rejoice when your son is born, for he will be great in God's eyes. He must never drink alcohol. The Holy Spirit will fill him even before he is born. He will help many in Israel turn to God. Empowered by Elijah's spirit, he will direct the hearts of parents to their children, and the disobedient to the sources of wisdom. He will prepare a people for God."

+

Six great promises accompany the announcement of this birth: joy and gladness will come to his parents; people will celebrate his arrival; greatness will accompany him; the Holy Spirit will find a home in him; he'll bring the wayward back to God; and with a style reminiscent of Elijah, John will heal relationships between parents and children, while turning many to God.

Few births are accompanied by as many promises. Old Zechariah must have grabbed the nearest chair as the promises kept coming—his own boy, like Elijah, a blessing to the nation!

Oh, the dreams we dream for our children!—that they get into a good preschool, excel above their peers, possess athletic prowess or academic acumen, get into the college of their choice, settle into a rewarding career, find a suitable partner, have children who will have children of their own. These are not unimportant concerns, yet they pale in comparison to the promises about John.

God has plans for John—big plans—a destiny that Zechariah and Elizabeth are privileged to know long before their child takes his first lungful of air. Like some who came before him and like others who will come after him, John will bring to his time and place an outpouring of God's deepest desires for the world.

John is destined for a greatness that has little to do with power, status, wealth, or prestige, but everything to do with being a conduit through which God will act. John will set the stage for an even greater arrival.

What do you imagine as your unique calling?

9

SUSPENDED DISBELIEF
Luke 1:18

Zechariah said to the angel, "How can this be true? I'm an old man, and my wife isn't young either."

+

When given the message, Zechariah doubts the messenger. He is, after all, a man with both feet firmly planted in reality. He may have been born at night, but it wasn't last night!

Life follows certain rules and nothing disrupts those fixed certainties. Stub your toe and pain follows. Inch too close to the flame of a temple candle and skin burns. Rack up decades on the calendar and childbearing potential faces impossible odds.

Wise people learn to accept life's matter-of-fact realities. Mature people come to terms with life as it is. One learns to adjust and downsize expectations. Better to live with a healthy sense of what's reasonable than to expect too much. Be sane and be safe.

Zechariah's temporary disbelief falls well within the range of appropriate human responses. He's in good company. Centuries earlier, a 100-year-old Abraham and a 90-year-old Sarah balked at the angelic news of their childbearing capabilities. No wonder Zechariah, a professional man of prayer, gives the angel a quick lesson: gerontology trumps obstetrics every time. Right?

Maybe prayer's power has nothing to do with one's faith or lack of it. God's sheer readiness and willingness to act on our behalf doesn't depend on the reasonableness of our expectations.

What makes you most doubtful?

STRUCK SPEECHLESS
Luke 1:19-20

The angel replied, "I am Gabriel, and I am near to God so I've been sent to give you this message. But because you don't believe it will come true, you won't be able to speak until the day these things happen."

+

So much for introductions! "I'm Gabriel, and by the way, you're going to be speechless for nine months." Though angels are frequent subjects in biblical stories, only two are named: Michael, whose name means "who is like God," and Gabriel, whose name means "God is my might." Michael's role, described in the books of Daniel and Revelation, was that of a heavenly enforcer who fought those who dared to oppose God. Gabriel, on the other hand, was primarily a messenger of good news. Michael displayed the justice of God; Gabriel, the mercy of God. Michael overthrew; Gabriel built up.

Zechariah requests a sign, a confirmation of the angel's promise. Gabriel is prepared to fill the order and strikes Zechariah speechless. The one whose vocation and livelihood depend on offering supplications and intercessions on behalf of worshippers is unable to use his most valued commodity—his voice.

In the speechless months that follow, perhaps Zechariah finds himself meditating more, contemplating more, giving thanks more. When the one thing most needed is suddenly removed, it's possible to discover an openness and dependency on God we never knew we had.

What did you learn when something important was no longer available?

BODY LANGUAGE
Luke 1:21-23

The people wondered why Zechariah was taking so long in the sanctuary. When he finally came out and was not able to talk, they realized he had seen a vision. He kept motioning with his hands, unable to speak. When his time of service in the temple ended, he returned home.

+

It was customary, after the priest completed his duties inside the temple, that he would emerge and offer the following blessing to the worshippers waiting outside: "God bless and keep you; may God's face shine on you and be gracious to you; God is present so you may have peace" (Numbers 6:24-26).

When Zechariah finally emerged but was unable to speak, the crowd concluded he had seen a vision. How did they know that? Were there physical clues in addition to his inability to speak? Did Zechariah's face glow? Did his eyes reveal what his voice couldn't? Did a mystical aura surround him? Were they able to piece together clues like an ancient game of charades? Somehow, the message was facilitated without words. By Zechariah's body language alone, the temple worshippers perceived the presence of divine activity.

Body language—who I am minus my words. Turn off the volume. No spoken words. No articulation of faith. No carefully crafted double talk to explain away contradictory behaviors. If I could offer nothing but gestures and motions, I wonder what people would see and conclude.

How would you mime an apology or show forgiveness?

DIVINE GAZE
Luke 1:24-25

Soon, Elizabeth conceived and stayed indoors for five months. She said, "God has done this by looking favorably on me and removing the stigma I've endured among my people."

+

Considering how thrilled Elizabeth is to learn of her pregnancy, we might wonder why she chooses to remain in seclusion (literally, "to hide herself") for five months. Is her self-imposed privacy an attempt to avoid further reproach from neighbors and busybodies who would have a hard time believing a woman her age could conceive? Is her decision to remain behind closed doors a wife's attempt to support a husband still struggling with his recent disability? Perhaps solitude takes her into deeper meditation and leads to a fuller prayer life.

Whatever the reason for Elizabeth's secrecy, she refuses to gloat publicly over her motherly status. The humble yet ready acceptance of her new condition contrasts with Zechariah's initial disbelief and doubt. As often happens in Luke's gospel, a woman emerges as the model recipient of God's good news.

Like her Hebrew ancestors Sarah, Rachel, and Hannah, Elizabeth bursts into joyous praise over the favor shown her. God's gaze is fixed on her. She's the focused object of divine concern.

Elizabeth isn't usually included among the Bible's towering figures. She didn't lead a nation through the Red Sea, slay a giant, or win a strategic battle. Yet, her quiet acceptance of God's gaze teaches us a lesson about the stuff from which saints are fashioned. What separates saints from the rest of the world isn't their innumerable works of righteousness or their holy deeds stacked end to end; it's their daily awareness of the divine gaze, the moment-to-moment reality that they are objects of God's concern.

Who models Elizabeth in your life?

MARY
Luke 1:26-27

Six months into Elizabeth's pregnancy, God sent the angel Gabriel to the Galilean town of Nazareth, to a young woman named Mary who was engaged to Joseph, a descendant of King David.

+

Like Elizabeth, Mary (whose name means "bitterness" or "beloved") is the recipient of an angelic announcement. Why Mary is chosen for this visitation instead of another Jewish girl, we don't know. To suggest she possesses a deeper spirituality is mere speculation. What Mary brings is of far less concern than God's good pleasure to choose her.

Unlike Elizabeth, who prayed a lifetime for a child, recently engaged Mary has on her mind more pressing matters. There's a wedding to plan, a guest list to compile, and a thousand other details to manage.

Mary is a favorite subject of paintings, songs, poems, sculptures, and jewelry. She's been the inspiration for artists for two millennia. The subject of Mary, however, has served as a theological landmine keeping Roman Catholics and Protestants at arm's length. By ascribing to her saintly perfection, the former elevate Mary to near God-like status. By downplaying her unique holiness, the latter reduce Mary to a mere incubator for the Jesus-fetus.

Luke is content to keep the details of Mary's life in the shadows, giving us only the essentials. Mary lives in the Galilean town of Nazareth, located along a major trade route frequented by foreign merchants and Roman soldiers. She's betrothed, or engaged, to Joseph, a descendant of King David. The betrothal period could last as long as a year.

Most Bible translations use the word *virgin* when describing Mary. Biblical scholars will never find agreement as to whether Mary was a virgin or merely a young girl or an unmarried woman—or all three. When people ask me, I say, "Whatever." And I don't intend that as a flippant answer. Whatever the real situation was, God used it in ways human beings could never have imagined. There's no shortage of good news in that fact!

What qualities do you imagine in Mary?

14

Mount Carmel Cemetery, Hillside, IL

FAVORED STATUS
Luke 1:28-30

The angel Gabriel appeared to Mary and said, "Greetings! God's favor is with you." But Mary was stressed out by this angelic message and wondered about the implications. The angel reassured her, "Don't be afraid, Mary. God is with you."

+

Mary has good reason to be stressed out. Some of her ancestors also received "God's favor," and their fate was nothing to envy. Sarah and Abraham knew favored status and had to leave the old neighborhood and head for a land somewhere beyond the horizon. Isaac's favored status got him tied to an altar with a knife blade inches from his throat. Favored Joseph was thrown into a pit before being sold to a caravan headed for Egypt. Moses, the favored Hebrew in Pharaoh's house, spent forty years on the lam hiding in the desert of Midian.

Favored status sent the Hebrews wandering in the Sinai wilderness. Eventually, it was Samson's favored status that buried him under the rubble of his Philistine captors. Satan saw Job's favored status and used it to justify all manner of torture that went far beyond waterboarding.

The favored nation was carried off to the land of their Babylonian conquerors. Jeremiah, a favored prophet called to speak God's word, got nothing but grief and throughout his life did more weeping than laughing. (The same could be said for every prophet's mother!)

Mary knows her people's history. She's well aware of the costs incurred by those on whom God's favor rested. She probably has a good hunch where "favored status" might take her.

What's the hardest thing you ever had to do for a higher cause?

JESUS
Luke 1:31-33

"Mary, you will become pregnant and give birth to a son. You will name him Jesus. He will be great, and people will call him God's son. God will give him the authority of his ancestor David. He will rule God's people forever, and his influence will never end."

+

These verses contain three Old Testament references, each one used by Luke to link with the history, traditions, hopes, and expectations of the Hebrew people: "God will give you a sign. Look, the young woman is with child and will bear a son and name him Immanuel" (Isaiah 7:14). "God said to me, 'You are my son; today I've begotten you'" (Psalm 2:7). "David will establish a family for my name, and I will establish forever his influence. I will be a father to him, and he will be a son to me . . . Your house and influence will be made sure forever; your throne will be established forever" (II Samuel 7:13, 14a, 16).

The Hebrew name for Jesus is "Joshua," meaning "Yahweh saves." Jesus' name is not associated with earthly royalty or political powers. In those days, it was as common a name in Hebrew circles as are the names Matt and Jason today. Luke attaches no meaning to the name Jesus; however, Matthew offers this clarification: "He will save his people from their sins."

The name denotes the purpose and clarifies the mission. Jesus—the exalted one—still in the womb of his mother, will point the way to wholeness and life.

What does your name mean?

THEOLOGICAL BIOLOGY
Luke 1:34-37

Mary said to the angel, "How can this be? I don't know a man in that way." The angel explained, "The breath of the Holy God will be involved and make this happen. Your child will be holy; he will be called God's son. Your aunt Elizabeth, who once was childless, also became pregnant with a son six months ago. Nothing is impossible with God.

+

Gabriel's encounter with Mary is known as the "Annunciation." According to Luke, the angel announces to Mary what is about to happen. Notice the absence of any questions put to Mary, such as: "Will you do this? Will you collaborate with God? What do you think of this crazy scheme?" In biblical stories, God seldom asks people if they're up to the task. Mary stands in a long line of chosen ones for whom the call of God comes not as a question but as an invitation.

Orthodox believers exalt Mary's virginity as an all-important necessity, suggesting that if she isn't a virgin, then Jesus isn't of God. At the opposite end of the theological spectrum, others, dismissive of Mary's virginity, hold to the conviction that the natural universe has no room for miraculous interventions on God's part.

The focus in the story isn't the reproductive equipment of either Mary or Joseph. There will be no final exam requiring one to answer the question "Was Mary a virgin?" The Annunciation is an announcement about *God*. This God, who at the dawn of the world created from the formless void, who formed a nation when it wasn't yet a people, who promised childless senior citizens offspring, who brought back a remnant from exile when the rest of the world had written them off, is the same God who brings about this birth.

This is *God's* story, not Mary's. Human life isn't the mere product of biological necessity, but the arena of God's mysterious involvement.

When have you felt overshadowed by a power beyond yourself?

LET IT BE
Luke 1:38

Mary said, "I'm God's servant; let things work out as you say they will." Then the angel left her.

+

What would have happened if Mary had said, "Thanks, but no thanks. I'll take a pass"? Would God have chosen another Jewish girl? Would the angel Gabriel have moved on to another address?

Did Mary have to agree for God's plan to progress? Did the drama of God's plan teeter on a teenage girl's reply? If God's plan had fallen through, was there a default option?

Here's another way to look at it. Does an airline flight or a passenger train need me to get on board for it to reach its destination? Clearly, it does not. Whether I get on board or stay at the terminal isn't going to determine whether United Airlines or Amtrak reaches its destination. The question is this: Will I choose to be a part of the journey or not?

Mary's reply isn't a consent that gives God the permission to proceed. Mary's nod isn't a green light that guarantees the salvation vehicle will arrive on time. Mary's answer is a purposeful alignment of her life with God's desire. What God will do, God will do, whether Mary is a willing participant or not.

Life's choices often come down to our saying Yes or No. Yes, I will accept this unexpected news, this turn of events, this unforeseen shift in plans—or I won't. Yes, I'll explore this wild possibility, this unforeseen scenario—or I won't. Saying Yes to the plans of uninvited angels, as Barbara Brown Taylor (*Gospel Medicine*) suggests, doesn't mean we do so without hesitation; it simply means we're willing to go forward and move ahead anyway.

Where did your last Yes to an unplanned future lead you?

WOMB WANDERINGS
Luke 1:39-45

After a time, Mary headed to a town in the countryside and stayed at the home of Zechariah and Elizabeth. When Elizabeth was greeted by Mary, the child kicked in her womb. Elizabeth gushed loudly, "You're a blessed woman, and so is the child inside you. I'm amazed that the mother of my God comes to me. As soon as I heard the sound of your voice, the child inside me kicked for joy. Indeed, you're blessed for believing that God will fulfill everything told to you."

+

Luke tells the story of two births, two advents, side by side. In the opening chapter, he writes as much about Elizabeth as he does about Mary. Both births happen against a backdrop of pessimistic odds—one woman is too old and the other is too young. Both mothers-to-be are paired with silent partners—Zechariah's silence comes by angelic decree, and Joseph's by a minor role with no speaking part in Luke's script.

It's tempting to want the characters to say more and play larger parts. The characters tell the story, but ultimately, the story isn't about them. The story is God's through and through. If the main thing is always the main thing, then the main thing is always the transformational power of God to enter the messiness of life and create anew.

Ordinary people are thrust into roles larger than they would ever have dreamed of playing if left to their own imaginations. God takes nobodies and makes somebodies. God accepts the insurmountable odds and beats the house, calling forth people the world largely ignores.

Elizabeth's pronouncement to Mary is liberation for both women. The elder ends her five-month, self-imposed seclusion and confirms for Mary all that the angel Gabriel has said. It's enough to make an unborn do a somersault.

When were you thrust into a role you hadn't planned on?

MAGNIFICAT (I)
Luke 1:46-50

Mary said, "My soul magnifies God, and my spirit rejoices in the One who saves me and looks favorably on my lowliness. From now on people will call me blessed. The Holy One has done great things for me. Mercy is on those who worship God."

+

Commonly known by the first word of the Latin rendering of Mary's song, the *Magnificat* is a remarkable statement of faith in the God who acts on behalf of the voiceless, powerless, and defenseless. Of the four gospel writers, Luke alone records Mary's hymn of praise and portrays her as a speaking participant in the birth stories.

Mary's song divides into two parts. The first has the feel of a mother's lullaby. In these verses, Mary gives thanks to God for her personal blessings: "*My* soul magnifies God . . . *my* spirit rejoices in the One who saves *me* . . . people will call *me* blessed . . . God has done great things for *me*." Mary acknowledges that God has treated her with favor and grace. Future generations will acknowledge her because through her, God has chosen to work.

Mary sings, offers praise, and gives thanks. Mary's prayer is a personal testimony to a life transformed by God. Mary is in touch with the rhythm of a disciple's life and responds with full-throated gratitude.

Mary is a model for all of us—not only for women. She reminds us of the folly of putting our trust in things and institutions that can't deliver, in lesser gods who fail to make good on their promises.

When was the last time your trust was misplaced?

MAGNIFICAT (II)
Luke 1:51-56

"God's arm is strong and has scattered the proud who trust in themselves. God has brought down the powerful from important places, and lifted up the humble. God has filled the stomachs of the hungry, and sent away the rich with nothing. God has been merciful to the people of Israel, just as God promised to Abraham and his descendants forever." After three months, Mary returned to her home.

+

The second half of Mary's prayer has endured a variety of labels: a war cry, a political platform, a revolutionary's manifesto, even a subversive tract. Mary's prayer moves beyond the personal and private into the reality of God's great reversals. What starts as a lullaby is now laced with landmines.

Borrowing again from her ancestors, Mary uses imagery uttered by Moses (Exodus 15:1-18) and Deborah (Judges 5:1-31) and David (Psalms 33, 47, 136). The great deeds of God are declared in the past tense as works already accomplished in the life and history of Israel. However, as past actions, they are experienced in the present and will continue in the future. What God has done, God is doing, and God will continue to do.

If we find ourselves among the world's humble, hungry, and poor, Mary's *Magnificat* is powerful assurance of a God who sides with the oppressed and one day will turn the tables. However, if a proactive God troubles our status quo sensibilities, then we tend to spiritualize Mary's radical message and fashion to our liking a domesticated God.

No doubt, it is from their parents—especially their mothers—that John and Jesus learn the radical nature of living into God's ongoing transformation of the world. From their parents, they learn of God's deep connection with those who suffer disconnect. From their parents, they learn that God won't let things sway forever in favor of the rich and powerful. From their parents, they learn of the God who stands in solidarity with the weakest and most vulnerable.

Where have you seen the great reversals of God?

A GIFT
Luke 1:57-66

When Elizabeth gave birth to her son, her neighbors and relatives rejoiced because of God's goodness. Eight days later, they prepared to circumcise the child. Everyone thought they were going to name him Zechariah after his father. But Elizabeth said, "His name will be John." They said to her, "No one in your family is named John." Then they motioned to Zechariah to find out what name he wanted to give the child. Zechariah wrote down, "His name is John." Everyone was amazed. At that moment, Zechariah was able to speak, and he thanked God. The neighbors talked about all these things, wondering aloud, "What exactly will this child become?" It was apparent that God's hand was with him.

+

Most births are greeted with great joy. However, in regions of China and India, and in some other developing nations, the birth of a girl brings deep sorrow. This was true in the ancient world, too. Biblical scholar William Barclay (*The Gospel of Luke*) reminds us that in Palestinian villages, the occasion of a birth brought out local musicians. If the newborn was a boy, the musicians played joyously. If the baby was a girl, the music stopped and the musicians walked away.

Festivities surround this birth. The fact that an elderly couple welcomes into the world a son makes it a double blessing. Following their religious customs, eight days after the birth, Elizabeth and Zechariah take their child to the local synagogue to be circumcised by a rabbi. The rite of male circumcision reminded all Jews of the covenant God made with the patriarch Abraham in Genesis 17, a promise sealed in the cutting of male foreskin (Abraham, by the way, was ninety-nine!).

During the rite of circumcision, the son was given a name. It's odd that folks expected the son to be named Zechariah Jr. Sometimes sons were named after their fathers, but not always. The name John is an abbreviation of "Jehohanan" which means "Jehovah's gift."

The fact that John was a gift eventually loosens his father's tongue as well as the tongues of everyone else who couldn't keep quiet.

Who has been a gift to you?

23

BENEDICTUS (I)
Luke 1:67-75

Then Zechariah, inspired by the Holy Spirit, imagined the future. "Blessed be Israel's God, who has looked favorably on us and has set us free. God gave us a mighty savior from David's family, so we will be delivered from enemies who hate us, just as the ancient prophets predicted. God was merciful to our ancestors and has remembered the promise made to our forefather Abraham, that, being freed from our enemies, we might serve God without fear, being holy and righteous."

+

What tickled your throat, tongue-bound Zechariah, and moved you to blurt out your benediction?

What did your tired eyes see, old man, prompting you to offer your blessings?

What did you smell, seasoned priest of holy rites, moving you to utter this invocation?

What did you touch with crooked, arthritic hands, causing you to call upon the God of Israel?

What did you hear in your God-imposed silence, telling you now is the time to speak?

Who is this God, so active and alive, described by your well-placed verbs?

Who is this Holy One looking favorably on these people and redeeming them?

Who is this Benevolent Deity raising up a mighty savior about whom holy prophets dreamed?

Who is this Source of all things who shows mercy and remembers the promise sworn to Abraham?

May the Holy Spirit inspire us, too, Zechariah, to see God's fingerprints on the world, to give witness to God's ways, to testify to the dynamism of God's being!

Blessed be God!

Who is most in need of your blessing today?

BENEDICTUS (II)
Luke 1:76-79

"And you, my son John, will be known as the prophet of the Most High. You will prepare God's ways, to give knowledge of salvation to God's people by the forgiveness of their sins. By God's loving mercy, a new day will break upon us, giving light to those in darkness who are threatened by death, and to guide our feet along peaceful paths."

+

Did you know, blessed father Zechariah, all that your son would do? Could you foresee, first-time father, all that awaited this prophet of the Most High? Was it clear to you, priest-after-Abijah, all that Jesus' forerunner would say? Were you disappointed, husband of Elizabeth, that John was not the Messiah?

Will you be one of the sinners he baptizes in Jordan's muddy waters? Will you be there among the crowds he calls a brood of vipers? Are you guilty, like the rest, of fleeing the wrath to come? Are your tree roots the ones he'll have in mind when he warns of the axe's edge?

Moreover, what of the dawn from on high that will break upon us? And the light to those who sit in darkness and death's shadows? And the guiding of our feet into the way of peace? Did you imagine the infant in your arms as one like a reborn Samuel or a new Isaiah?

Touch his tender skin with your wrinkled flesh, old man. Smell his newborn innocence and inhale his eight-day beauty. Look into his moistened Hebrew eyes and see the ways of the One to whom he points. Look long enough and you will see also the platter on which his severed head soon enough will rest.

What hopes and dreams did your parents have for your future?

TRANSITIONS
Luke 1:80

The child John matured—physically and spiritually. Eventually, he went into the wilderness until it was time for him to preach publicly to Israel.

+

Though John's birth is uniquely announced to his parents and accompanied by prophetic songs of praise, he undergoes all the normal developmental patterns of childhood. Luke's description is similar to what we know of others in Israel's history: "The boy Samson grew and God blessed him" (Judges 13:24). "The boy Samuel continued to grow in stature and in favor with God and people" (I Samuel 2:26). Luke gives no details concerning John's childhood and adolescence. He'll appear again in the third chapter, all grown up and fully engaged in the ministry of preaching and baptizing at the Jordan River.

With this single verse, Luke makes a transition in the story. Elizabeth and Zechariah, righteous and blameless before God, have filled their roles in the divine drama and aren't heard from again. Another set of parents, Mary and Joseph, are prepared now to continue the story. John recedes into the background to make room for another birth. John's light dims so that Jesus' light will shine.

The biblical parents hear God's voice and live in response to that calling. Did they always act with certainty? Did they always walk with confident strides? If we could ask them, "Did you know exactly what God wanted you to do?" they would probably shrug their shoulders, suggesting that absolute clarity is less important than following divine hunches.

Annie Dillard (*The Writing Life*) reminds us there is no shortage of good days; it is good lives that are hard to come by. How one defines a good life depends on who's doing the defining. However, if Elizabeth and Zechariah and son John are any indication, the good life—shaped by holy habits—is a faithful response to God's gracious call.

How do you define "the good life"?

BEHIND THE SCENES
Luke 2:1-3

During his rule, Emperor Augustus gave the order for a census of the world. This was the first census taken while Quirinius was governor of Syria. All Roman citizens and subjects went to their hometowns to comply.

+

An old world map hanging in Emperor Augustus' office carried this heading: *Orbis Terrarum, Imperium Romanum:* "All the world subject to Roman rule." Who could argue? One world capital, Rome. One official language, Latin. One absolute ruler, Caesar. Rome makes the rules. Rome builds the roads. Rome collects the taxes. Rome conducts the head count.

Not all historians agree that Augustus Caesar issued a worldwide census. There is documented evidence, however, that censuses periodically occurred in the region of Palestine, including Syria. One such census occurred nearly eight years before the birth of Jesus, around the time Quirinius was governor.

Clearly, Luke wants it known that the birth of Jesus is set on the stage of world history while other world events are taking place. Luke's introduction to Jesus' birth raises several implicit questions: Is Caesar or Jesus king? Does a census-taking emperor or the Creator of the universe shape history? Does ultimate power reside in Rome or in the City of God? Whom will the world remember: Quirinius or Jesus?

Luke's account of Jesus' life, ministry, and mission, beginning with his birth, is the gospel writer's answer to these questions. Nations, governments, heads of state, powerful potentates, and population counters—with or without their knowledge—become useful instruments in the hands of God to bring about a more just and fair world.

When have you felt God working "behind the scenes" in your life?

THE JOSEPH OPTION
Luke 2:4-5

Complying with the census, Joseph went from the Galilean town of Nazareth to the city of David, called Bethlehem, because he was a descendant of King David. He traveled with Mary, to whom he was betrothed. She was pregnant.

+

Joseph suddenly appears in the biblical narrative. A minor character playing a supportive role, Joseph speaks no words. We could easily conclude that Joseph's only purpose in the story of Jesus' birth is to get a very pregnant Mary to Bethlehem on time.

However, a more complete character sketch of Joseph emerges in the opening chapter of Matthew's gospel. Joseph and Mary were betrothed to each other—engaged, but with legal implications. Jewish law contractually bound them together, though they still lived in the homes of their respective parents. Sexual activity between them was forbidden until the wedding. When Mary tells Joseph she's pregnant and he's not the father, Joseph takes the high road and is prepared to go back to the rabbi and void the betrothal contract, sparing Mary public humiliation and possible punishment, including stoning.

Then comes a dream in which an angel explains to Joseph that God is at work in this messy situation; by taking Mary as his wife, Joseph will acknowledge this divine activity. What happens next is one of the most amazing miracles in the Bible: Joseph agrees. Going against conventional wisdom, laying aside his wounded manhood, re-evaluating his sense of right and wrong, refusing to punish the one he loves, Joseph opts for the twofold responsibility of husbandhood and fatherhood. He marries his pregnant fiancée.

Joseph reminds us that religious legalism has its limits. Doing what we have a right to do, and doing it to others when they're guilty of something, often puts us in conflict with the power of love. Faced with more than one option, Joseph redefines what it means to be a moral person, where love is at the center and religious customs, conventions, and legalities lie on the periphery. No doubt, Joseph will end up modeling and teaching this option to Jesus every chance he gets.

When did someone act like a Joseph to you?

28

DELIVERY TIME
Luke 2:6-7

While Mary and Joseph were in Bethlehem, she gave birth to her first son and wrapped him in strips of cloth. She laid him in a feed trough because there wasn't any room for them in the inn.

+

Luke gives no details about Mary's labor. We don't know whether it was quick and easy or a struggle that lasted for hours. Other details are lacking as well. How much did Jesus weigh? What did he measure from head to toe? Was he born with thick dark hair? Were there any features of Joseph—any at all—found in Jesus' face? Luke gives us only the delivery basics: she gives birth, wraps him in strips of cloths (just like his Hebrew ancestors Samson and Samuel), and places him in a feed trough.

Though none of the gospel writers includes the presence of animals at Jesus' birth, Christmas cards and nativity scenes seem incomplete without them. If indeed Jesus was born in a stable, it's not a stretch to imagine a variety of animals present, along with swarming fleas and dung piles. Animals or not, this delivery is anything but the antiseptically clean experience of first-world, modern-day births. No gowns or gloves, no mouth-covering masks, no sterilized instruments.

Nobody of importance is there either. No political attaché standing outside. Not a staff aide from Quirinius's office checking on things. No reporter from the Bethlehem bureau writing copy. If God wanted the world's attention, you'd think there would have been a thousand better places than in this poverty-stricken region for Jesus to be born. Nevertheless, here it is, somewhere outside an unnamed inn, in a cattle shed, in an all but unnoticed corner of the Roman Empire. Maybe this is just the beginning of how Jesus shatters our expectations.

When did you last experience holiness in an unexpected place?

29

SHEPHERDS
Luke 2:8-14

While shepherds were in the area tending sheep, an angel of God appeared, and the glory of God radiated around the shepherds, causing them great fear. The angel said, "Don't be afraid; I'm bringing you joyous news. A savior is born today in the city of David; he is God's anointed one. You will find a baby wrapped in strips of cloth and lying in a feed trough." Suddenly a multitude of angels appeared praising God, "Glory to God in heaven, and peace on earth to all people."

+

Though we idealize them in Christmas pageants and can't imagine a children's performance without them, shepherds were not A-list people. Shepherds were at the bottom of the social ladder, and the prevailing opinion about them at the time of Jesus' birth was a negative one. The reason was simple enough. Shepherds took care of sheep, often belonging to someone who could afford a flock, and the work was dirty. There was nothing glamorous about keeping watch over a flock by night, especially on hillsides far from home. Because shepherds' work required that they accompany sheep for extended periods, the religious authorities regarded them as outsiders—unclean and unfit.

Yet, in the Old Testament, some important figures started out as shepherds. Before he was called to lead the slaves out of Egypt, Moses tended the flock of his father-in-law in Midian. King David started out as a shepherd, and later wrote, "God is my shepherd, I lack nothing" (Psalm 23:1). Prophets often used shepherd imagery: "God will feed them like a shepherd, and gather the lambs in God's arms" (Isaiah 40:11). "I'll raise up shepherds who will care for them; they won't be afraid or be dismayed, nor will any get lost" (Jeremiah 23:4). By the time of Jesus' birth, however, a shepherd's stock was at an all-time low.

If we update the Christmas story, who would take the place of first-century shepherds today? Whom do the religious gatekeepers and spiritual authorities deem unclean and unfit? Imagine the "dirtiest" people in the world and you're probably close. By the way, later in his life, in John's gospel, Jesus calls himself the "good shepherd."

Where would you go to find shepherd-like people?

FIELD TRIP
Luke 2:15-20

When the angels left, the shepherds talked it over: "Let's go to Bethlehem and see if this is true." They made the trip and found Mary and Joseph, and the baby in the feed trough. Then they shared what the angels had told them about this child, and everyone was amazed. Mary embraced their message and thought often about the implications. The shepherds returned, glorifying and praising God for all they had experienced.

+

Luke seems to suggest that the shepherds immediately headed for Bethlehem once the angels departed, almost as a reflex response. Maybe it happened exactly that way, but maybe not. The shepherds have obligations to consider. What will they do with the owner's sheep entrusted to their care? Considering it's no small task to herd a flock from one locale to another, should they take them along or leave them behind?

Perhaps they need time to process what they have just experienced. Late nights and little sleep (or sour wine) can do strange things to the human mind. Did they all see and hear the same thing? Do any of them express the slightest hesitation to go and see for themselves? Luke suggests nothing holds them back. To Bethlehem they go, and just as the angel said, they find the newborn wrapped in long strips of cloth.

The humble and rustic adornments of the makeshift nursery apparently don't diminish their enthusiasm. Perhaps these uneducated and unlearned herders of sheep know that one greater than Caesar and his army lies before them this night. If so, then it's those outside the loop of influence, those never asked for their vote, much less their opinion, who are the first to witness this birth.

What was the last hunch you impulsively followed?

ACCORDING TO THE LAW
Luke 2:21-24

After eight days, the child was circumcised and named Jesus. When it was time for purification according to their religious customs, Mary and Joseph brought their son to the temple in Jerusalem because all firstborn males had to be dedicated to God. They also offered a small sacrifice, as was required.

+

Jesus was born a Jew. His parents were Jews. Eight days after his birth, like all Jewish male infants, Jesus was circumcised and given a name. Forty days after his birth, Mary and Joseph observed the rite of purification and presented Jesus in the temple.

According to the laws found in the book of Leviticus, after giving birth to a son, a woman was considered ceremonially unclean for a period of forty days (eighty days if she had given birth to a daughter). During this time, she wasn't permitted to enter the sanctuary. Upon submitting to the rite of purification, the mother was fully restored to the worshipping congregation.

At the end of the purification rite, parents offered a sacrifice, most likely purchased from temple vendors. Typically, parents gave a lamb for a burnt offering and a pigeon for a sin offering. If this proved too costly, two doves or pigeons were substituted. Dirt poor, Mary and Joseph offered a pair of birds.

Though Luke doesn't mention it, Mary and Joseph were likely responsible to pay a redemption fee to the priest. According to Hebrew tradition, every firstborn son was presented to God and dedicated for temple work at the appropriate age. However, a redemption fee of several small coins paid to the priest could exempt the child from official temple duties in future years. There were no freebies in the first-century temple system.

By recording the observance of the Jewish rituals of circumcision and purification, and implying that of redemption, Luke reminds us that Jesus' family follows the holy customs. Jesus stands in continuity with his faith traditions. In later years, when Jesus challenges his own people, he will do so as an insider, steeped from birth in God's ways.

What family traditions do you continue to observe?

ISRAEL'S COMFORT
Luke 2:25-26

During this time, there was a man in Jerusalem named Simeon who was devoutly good. Inspired by the Holy Spirit, he longed for a sign of comfort for the Hebrew people. The Holy Spirit revealed to him that he wouldn't die before he saw God's chosen one, the Messiah.

+

We know next to nothing about Simeon. Whether he's a member of the professional clergy or a layperson isn't entirely clear. Like many in the biblical story, Simeon walks into the drama, plays his role, and leaves the stage forever.

Like Zechariah before him, Simeon is described as righteous and devout, a faithful observer of the religious traditions. Here is a good man who has been patiently waiting for the consolation and comfort of Israel that would come with the arrival of the Messiah. Exactly what "Messiah" meant varied widely. Some believed that the Messiah would be a warrior figure ushering in the past glories of the nation. Others believed that through this chosen and anointed one, God would intersect the world with cataclysmic powers.

In contrast, a minority group known as the "Quiet of the Land" longed neither for military uprisings nor for cosmic upheavals. Rather, they committed themselves to a life of prayer and a posture of watchful waiting. They knew not when or how, but were convinced that God would one day comfort the faithful. They leaned on the hopes of the ancient prophet: "Comfort, comfort my people" (Isaiah 40:1). "Sing for joy and rejoice, O heavens and earth; break into song, O mountains! God has comforted us and will have compassion on the suffering" (Isaiah 49:13).

Simeon stands in a long biblical line of those whose hopes and dreams, uttered in a lifetime bathed with prayer, take on flesh later rather than sooner. Though we seldom see it this way, the dividends of old age sometimes exceed the promises that accompany youth.

What are the advantages of old age?

LIGHT AND GLORY
Luke 2:27-32

Moved by the Spirit, Simeon entered the temple. When Mary
and Joseph brought Jesus to do what was customary, Simeon
took the infant in his arms and thanked God, saying, "Now
I can die in peace, for my eyes have seen your salvation
prepared for all, revealing light to the nations and glory to
God's people."

+

In every way, Mary and Joseph followed the customs of their faith
tradition. The presentation of an infant was a common practice. Jesus was probably one among many babies brought by parents to
receive a blessing from the temple priests.

Luke doesn't tell us what Simeon sees in this baby or in the
parents that confirms for him that this particular infant is God's
chosen one. Maybe Simeon's heart skips a beat. Maybe he feels a
twinge he can't ignore. Maybe there's a voice whispering inside his
head, "Pssst, Simeon, this is the One I told you about." Whatever
Simeon hears or feels, his wrinkled hands and crooked fingers cradle
the newborn to his chest.

Simeon isn't interested in Jesus' physical features. He doesn't seem
to care what the boy looks like or which parent he most resembles.
Simeon's concern at this moment is with God's activity. In this baby,
God will bring light to the nations and glory to a people.

Drawing again on themes from Isaiah, Luke understands God's
comfort and consolation extending to the world. Though God's
glory will shine upon those who can trace their existence back to
their Hebrew forebears, it won't be limited to a people, a nation, a land,
or even a hemisphere.

What have you learned from the wisdom of the elderly?

SOUL PIERCING
Luke 2:33-35

Mary and Joseph were amazed at what Simeon said. Then he blessed them and said to Mary, "This child will cause the falling and the rising of many in Israel. He will be a clarifying sign, exposing the inner thoughts of many people. Not even your own soul will escape sadness."

+

How does Simeon know all this? What do his tired old eyes see in Mary's newborn that hints of "the falling and rising of many in Israel"? How is Simeon able to discern in this baby a sign by which inner thoughts are exposed? Nothing in the world was different because of this birth. Caesar was still in charge. Rome's army still occupied the land.

Though Simeon will never experience the public ministry of Jesus, he hasn't a doubt about Mary and Joseph's boy and the mission Jesus will fulfill. Cataracts or not, Simeon clearly discerns that Jesus will bring a crisis of choice. Lives will fall or rise because of him. Decisions for or against him will be made. Commitments to follow or oppose, to turn toward or to turn away will affect individuals, families, even nations.

Mary won't escape the sword-piercing pain. She will witness the suffering her son soon enough will bear at the hands of the privileged and powerful. But some of her pain will result from the choices Jesus himself makes—decisions to subordinate family ties to a deeper connection with those who walk with him; determination to leave home and carpentry shop in favor of building spiritual families that transcend blood ties; commitment to self-sacrifice rather than self-preservation; preferences for the least, the last, the lost, and the lonely, regardless of the cost. Soon enough, Mary will realize that the only way to keep her son is to give him away, to give him to the world.

Where is your deepest pain today?

ANNA
Luke 2:36-38

In the temple that day was also an elderly prophet named Anna, the daughter of Phanuel, of the tribe of Asher. Her husband had died after seven years of marriage, and now she was eighty-four. She never left the temple but worshipped, fasted, and prayed night and day. She praised God and spoke about the child Jesus to all who were looking for the deliverance of Jerusalem.

+

Her name means "joyful one," yet there is little about Anna's life that suggests her years have been joy-filled. Luke notes she is eighty-four. The Greek, however, can be translated in such a way as to suggest she has been a widow for that many years. If so, then Anna is past her one-hundredth birthday.

Despite the hardships that a widow was forced to endure, Anna remains a spiritual fixture in the temple. The temple is her home—spiritually and physically. In the temple area, she fasts and prays. In the Court of Women, she longs and hopes for Israel's Messiah, a deliverer who will usher in God's dream for the world. Like Simeon, her prophetic counterpart, Anna tenaciously believes in a faithful and dependable God. In her brittle bones, she knows God won't fail to make good on God's promises.

Like Simeon and Elizabeth and Zechariah, Anna represents the aged presence of faithful Jews and devout worshippers whose trust and hope in God doesn't waver, and whose active prayers eventually bear fruit. Though none of these devout folks will witness the full fruition of Jesus' ministry, to behold him in his infancy is enough.

Again, the birth and infancy narratives remind us of the God who is pleased to use a troupe of ordinary and seemingly unimpressive persons to accomplish divine purposes. Nobody of power and prestige is here—just poor people of the land, a vulnerable young couple, and a pair of senior citizens. Given the assignment, most of us might have written a different version of the story.

What elderly person has had the greatest influence on you?

Jaipur, India

HOME-GROWN
Luke 2:39-40

When they completed everything their tradition required, Mary and Joseph returned to Nazareth. Jesus grew and matured, becoming wise in life and in the things of God.

+

Having observed their customs, rituals, and religious obligations, Mary, Joseph, and Jesus return home to familiar environs. Once again, Luke wants us to know that Jesus was born into the flow of Jewish history and raised in the tradition of the Hebrews.

Of the next thirty years, save for his visit to the temple at the age of twelve, we know nothing about Jesus' life. None of the gospel writers reveals anything about the formative years of Jesus' childhood, adolescence, or young adulthood. The things Jesus excels at, what he struggles with, his preferences, his inclinations—all the stuff that fills the biographies of great persons—receive in the gospel accounts no attention at all. Not a word.

These omissions reveal something about the gospel books themselves. Matthew, Mark, Luke, and John didn't set out to record a factual and historical biography of the life of Jesus. They write as if disinterested in the decades between Jesus' birth and his public ministry.

Luke, in particular, emphasizes the fact that Jesus doesn't emerge from the womb fully equipped and pre-assembled. Jesus is as human as any infant, as human as any adolescent, as human as any teenager. Like all human beings, Jesus requires nature's gift of time to develop and mature.

Jesus grows and becomes strong. He learns to sit up, crawl, walk, and run. His bone density increases. He conquers the alphabet and learns to read. He develops hair under his arms. He experiences puberty. Fully human was he.

What difference does it make that Jesus experienced all the issues of growing up?

38

LEFT BEHIND
Luke 2:41-45

When Jesus was twelve, he accompanied his parents to Jerusalem for the festival of the Passover. When it was time to return home, Jesus remained in Jerusalem without his parents' knowledge. Assuming that Jesus was in the group of travelers accompanying them, Mary and Joseph traveled for a day. When they looked for Jesus among their relatives and friends but didn't find him, they returned to Jerusalem.

+

Though accounts of angelic choruses and predictions of Jesus' future fill the second chapter of Luke, the gospel writer never strays far from reminding us of Jesus' Jewish roots. Law and ritual, tradition and custom play as important a role in Jesus' life as do extraordinary events.

Luke alone records this story of Jesus. We know nothing else about his life between birth and the beginning of his public ministry at age thirty. Jews annually observed three religious holidays in Jerusalem: the feasts of Passover, Tabernacles, and Pentecost. Every Jewish male living within fifteen miles of Jerusalem was required to attend the observances in that ancient city. That both Joseph and Mary annually make the three-day journey from Nazareth, nearly ninety miles to the north, is a testament to their deep piety.

After the event, the Nazareth contingency of neighbors and friends heads home, but Jesus isn't with them. Surprisingly, his absence goes unnoticed for an entire day. Because women traveled in one group and men in another, it's reasonable that Mary assumed Jesus was in the company of Joseph, who, in turn, assumed he was with Mary. In either case, Jesus is separated from his parents. We can easily imagine the sinking feeling that accompanied them on their trek back to Jerusalem.

For the first time, physical separation frays this parent/child relationship—Jesus is in one place, his parents in another. It is also the first instance of "soul piercing" foreseen by Simeon. The familial bonds will continue to separate so that Jesus can establish a greater family held together with ties stronger than bloodlines.

What do you imagine Mary and Joseph thinking as they hunt for their child?

I MUST BE
Luke 2:46-50

After three days, Mary and Joseph found Jesus in the temple having discussions with the religious teachers, who were amazed at his understanding and responses. When his parents saw him, they were astonished and his mother said, "Child, why have you treated us like this? We've been worried sick about you." He said to them, "Why were you searching for me? Don't you know I must be in my Father's house?" But they didn't understand what he was saying.

+

A twelve-year-old holding his own with seasoned intellectuals in most circumstances would elicit from proud parents: "Our son, the honor student!" However, any initial parental pride suggesting approval quickly fades as Mary voices her anxiety. At this point in the interaction, there's not a parent who doesn't side with Mary.

Jesus' reply sets the tone for his public ministry, still some eighteen years away. Jesus' first words recorded by Luke indicate an awareness of his relationship to God. He claims for himself what angels and prophets have already proclaimed. Jesus' connection with his Divine Source indicates a shift in allegiance and a re-ordering of priorities, an acknowledgment neither parent is fully ready or able to understand. Again, the parent's soul is pierced.

Several translations of Jesus' response to his parents' anxiety are possible: "I must be in my Father's house" or "I must be about my Father's business." Both renderings suggest that Jesus begins to understand an undeniable compulsion, the necessity of a greater cause, the bending toward a new obligation.

Soon enough, hard choices will emerge, leaving family behind. Security and ease will be exchanged for a way of living that includes standing with the poor, befriending those pushed away by the dominant culture, and risking one's own safety by challenging a status quo that casts too many aside.

That his parents don't understand what Jesus is saying is probably evidence enough that, at this moment, God's grace is actively present.

When were you left speechless by someone's determination to do the right thing?

OBEDIENT ONE
Luke 2:51-52

Then Jesus went home with his parents to Nazareth and was obedient to them. His mother thought about these things for a long, long time. With each passing year, Jesus grew wise. God was with him, and people respected him.

+

After his temple experience, life for Jesus returns to normal. He goes home. He takes his place in the family. The years go by. Approval, both divine and human, rests on him.

Jesus isn't shipped off to theological boot camp. He isn't placed in a gifted class for boys with messianic leanings. There is no biblical account that he cures his neighbor's sick dog or rescues his pet hamster from the grip of death. None of the gospel writers suggests Jesus lives out his formative years as a precocious wonder kid, dazzling onlookers with early displays of deific powers. (Some non-biblical accounts—books that never made it into the Bible—do record such stories of Jesus.)

When chores need tending, Jesus does them. When rooms need cleaning, Jesus cleans them. When water needs hauling, Jesus hauls it. When animals require feeding, Jesus feeds them.

With the end of Luke's second chapter, we hear no more of Joseph. Legend suggests he died at a relatively early age, but no biblical record confirms this. Mary never assumes the spotlight she held in the beginning of this chapter. The role she now plays is a minor one.

Like others we have met in this chapter, Joseph and Mary arrive on the scene and take up their God-given roles. Humbly—at times haltingly—they offer their lives to God. With no clear idea where they are going or what God is calling them to do, they obey. Not sure of the big picture, they remain faithful in the details as much as they know how. Their lives are less a competition with God than a submission to a new way of being.

What was the best year of your growing up?

POWER BROKERS
Luke 3:1-2

Fifteen years into the rule of Tiberius Caesar, Pontius Pilate governed Judea, Herod ruled Galilee, Herod's brother Philip ruled the region of Ituraea and Traconitis, and Lysanias ruled Abilene. Annas and Caiaphas served as high priests in Jerusalem. During this time, the word of God came to John, son of Zechariah and Elizabeth, in the wilderness.

+

When we last left John (in Luke 1), he was a young man in the wilderness, growing strong in the spirit. He's still there, but ready now to launch his public ministry.

The world which John will confront is ruled by men of unrivaled and unmatched power. They are history makers. Some—Pilate, Herod, Annas, and Caiaphas—will appear again in Luke's gospel and play significant roles in opposing the ministry of Jesus. Others—Tiberius, Philip, and Lysanias—are mentioned here, but never again by Luke.

Unlike his political and religious contemporaries, John's power doesn't originate in Rome's palace or Jerusalem's temple, but in God. To this desert dweller, the word of God arrives. God chooses to speak not to the power brokers of the mighty Roman Empire, but to a wilderness-toughened prophet.

Like Jeremiah, Hosea, Micah, and other Old Testament prophets before him, John doesn't begin his prophetic activity until God breaks the silence. Far removed from the seats of power and institutional influence, John is prepared to move from obscurity to notoriety.

We might second-guess God's choices. Why didn't the word of God come to someone closer to hierarchical power? A cabinet member in Pilate's administration or a high priest in the temple, divinely appointed to work on the inside to set the stage for the Messiah's arrival, might have proven a more efficient candidate. Or not.

Luke's story, however, isn't about what humans are capable of doing on their own for God. The real story points to God, whose call comes to unlikely recipients; because of them and the call they receive, the world is forever changed.

What "little person" do you know who has made a difference?

ROAD WORK
Luke 3:3-6

John went to an area near the Jordan River, proclaiming a baptism of repentance for the forgiveness of sins, as the prophet Isaiah had written, "The voice of one announcing in the desert: 'Prepare the way of the Lord, make the paths straight. Fill every valley, lower the mountains and hills, straighten what's crooked, and smooth the rough places. Eventually, everyone will see God's work in the world.'"

+

Fresh from his divine call and empowered by the word of God, John emerges from his desert home to preach at the Jordan River a message of baptism and repentance. Like the Old Testament prophets, John asserts that humanity's stubbornness has caused a rift in the relationship with God. Only repentance—an about-face, a turning away from sin, a turning toward God—can restore the relationship. John's notion of repentance isn't a ceremony of ritual cleansing but a moral alteration, a radical shift in living. To grow, one needs to change.

Luke connects John's ministry to the words of Isaiah 40. In biblical times, when a king prepared to visit a region, he sent ahead a messenger to prepare the road over which the king would travel. John, the new messenger, exhorts his listeners to prepare the way for the Messiah's arrival by leveling the obstacles and removing the hindrances in their lives so that society itself will undergo a transformation.

The path of Jesus' way is straightened when mountains of stubborn pride are humbled, when boulder-sized obstacles are removed, and when crooked hearts bent on corruption are made straight. This way of wholeness (closely linked with "salvation" in the Greek), envisioned by the prophet Isaiah and announced by John, is God's intention for all creation.

The lives we're intended to live aren't necessarily the ones with which we start out. Who we are isn't necessarily dictated by where we've been. John moves us toward the One who is to come, toward the One who has the power to change us into what we're meant to be. On the roadways of life, we're all works in progress.

Where in your life is roadwork underway?

43

HARD-CORE
Luke 3:7-8a

John said to all who came to be baptized, "You're nothing but snakes in the grass! Who warned you to flee the coming wrath? Do the right things that show your repentance."

+

Italian sculptor Augusta Rodin (1840–1917) chiseled a statue of John the Baptist and named it "John the Precursor." The long-haired, bearded prophet poses stark naked. His lean, muscular body shows no evidence of any fat. His mouth open and his right arm gesturing, the sculpted figure appears to be haranguing all who come within earshot of his fire and brimstone.

And what a message it is! If the Messiah is coming, then hearts need turning, behaviors need changing, lives need rehabbing, unjust systems and structures need dismantling. Only repentance will do, but how does one define it? Feeling sorry? Having remorse? Wishing the past could be rewritten? What are the fruits worthy of such repentance?

Though Alcoholics Anonymous claims no particular religious affiliation, one of the best definitions of repentance and the fruit produced by it comes from AA's Twelve Steps. Integrated into these steps are the concrete repentant acts of acknowledging, admitting, amending, and remaining "awake." A person acknowledges his or her powerlessness over a substance, and that a greater power is needed to bring wellness. A man admits to himself and to others how his behavior and addiction have affected relationships. A woman commits herself to make amends to those she has harmed. One resolves to remain awake and aware through prayer to and meditation upon the higher power and source of strength that brings life.

Two thoughts: (1) It's been said that a typical AA meeting often looks more like the church than the church. If you've been to both, you might agree. (2) It's no surprise that John was so hard on his audience; hard-core repentance is not for the faint of heart.

When was your most significant experience of repentance?

NO BLOOD EXEMPTIONS
Luke 3:8b-9

"Don't say, 'Abraham is our ancestor.' Listen, God is able to make children of Abraham from these stones. Right now the axe is lying at the root of the trees, and every tree that doesn't produce good fruit will be cut down and burned up."

+

Nothing about John is subtle or nuanced. Like a bloodhound with its nose to the trail, John can smell foulness long before anyone else gets wind of it. He doesn't cajole his listeners with a smile, and he's not interested in winning them over with a hearty slap on the back.

Surprisingly, like moths to a porch light, the crowds can't stay away. The curious and the questioning, the critics and the committed, sinners public and sinners private, all came out to hear him. Likewise, proud ones with pedigrees traced to father Abraham stand before the prophet. John saves his harshest words for those who trust in their bloodlines as a way to curry favor with the Almighty. It's as if John is cautioning, "Don't count on it. These rocks will have a better future than you if you fail to repent. Your precious family roots won't save you either. The axe is sharp, and fruitless trees make good kindling. Don't hide behind traditions stripped of their spirituality. Don't imagine all will be well by simply quoting chapter and verse of the sacred writings. Don't think that attending Dr. Eloquent Voice's church is enough, either. And if you hope that wrapping yourself in your country's flag is what God desires, then obviously you haven't talked to God lately."

John's message is as direct as his delivery system; the relationship between faith and fruit, belief and behavior is inseparable. Surveys don't always bear this out, however. Pollster George Gallup once conducted research to determine what effect spirituality has had on the behavior of Americans who considered themselves religious. His survey found little difference in ethical behavior between the churched and the unchurched. He concluded that religion, as practiced by Americans, does little to change morality. John the Baptist would have something to say about that.

Assuming Gallup's survey is accurate, how do you explain the results?

SOCIAL CONSCIENCE
Luke 3:10-11

People asked John, "What are we supposed to do?" John answered, "Whoever has two coats must share with one who has none; and whoever has food must do the same."

+

The crowd wants to know, "Tell us what to do. Bring it down to a practical level. What's expected of us?" John obliges. The fruit-bearing life is as simple as giving a coat to one who has none and food to one who is hungry. Take care of the less fortunate. The haves cannot forget the have-nots. Contentment and happiness aren't possible until everyone has enough. The two-coat person shouldn't sleep well until the coatless person's dilemma is addressed. Those with full cupboards can't truly enjoy their meal until everyone has enough to eat.

Maybe some in the crowd were hoping to hear a more palatable message, something along the lines of: "If you really want to know what bearing fruit looks like, then say a little prayer every day" or "If your conversations aren't sprinkled with a healthy dose of 'God spoke to me,' then you're not on the right track" or "The religious life is best summed up in knowing where you will end up after death."

Instead, John's answer contains an undeniable social bent. Take care of the needy. Look out for your neighbor. Work for a more equitable society. Level the playing field. Sometimes that will mean a coat to the coatless or a bag of groceries to the hungry. Other times it will mean changing unjust structures that keep the oppressed marginalized. Start where you are, then go where you never imagined going.

Some might conclude that such advice bears little resemblance to a proper "religious" answer. John omits saying anything about prayer or whether his preference is hymns or praise songs. At the top of the list are concrete acts of justice carried out by those with aroused social consciences—a hint of what Jesus, John's cousin, will also endorse.

How would John fit in at most churches today?

KEEP IT FAIR
Luke 3:12-14

Even tax collectors came to be baptized and asked John, "What are we supposed to do?" He answered them, "Collect no more than the fair amount." Soldiers also asked him, "What about us?" He said, "Don't extort money from anyone by threats or trumped-up charges, and be satisfied with your wages."

+

Tax collectors or soldiers—it's hard to say who received the most hate mail. Tax collectors were first-century pyramid schemers who shamelessly took advantage of Rome's insatiable appetite for more revenue. Some tax collectors, themselves Jews, gathered taxes at a higher rate than Rome demanded and pocketed the difference. With underlings and junior apprentices to work the system, tax collectors built considerable net worth. John has a message for them: "Keep your jobs, but play fair. Don't line your pockets by collecting more than Rome demands."

The soldiers likely were Jewish enforcers of King Herod's policies, perhaps working as temple police to ensure the peace. Like tax collectors, these men were viewed with contempt for benefiting from Roman occupation by betraying their own people. John has a message for them: "Keep your jobs, but play fair. Don't line your pockets by intimidating those who can't defend themselves."

John refuses to divorce the godly life from the ethical life. In God's vision for the world, our social connections must undergo a change. The old way of doing business simply will not do. People can't be ignored, cheated, or bullied. Not only must individuals change; entire societies are called to transformation.

The repentant life isn't lived in stratospheric realms but in daily-life particulars. The heart of the repentant beats in the everyday. We participate in God's holiness when we stop seeing people as commodities for our personal gain. We give up power and control over others so that we might be set free to serve.

What does John's message compel you to do?

WARM-UP ACT
Luke 3:15-17

Everyone was excited and wondered whether John might be the Messiah. John responded, "I baptize you with water, but One more powerful than I is coming. I'm not worthy to untie his sandals. He will baptize you with the Holy Spirit and fire. He will clean the grain on the threshing floor with a winnowing fork and gather wheat into his barn, but he will burn the chaff with a raging fire."

+

Since the time of the Hebrew prophet Malachi (the last book of the Old Testament), an eclipse covered the land—not the solar or lunar variety, but an eclipse of divine revelation. For four centuries, God chose not to speak. Deity opted for a self-imposed moratorium on communication. God went into hiding. Of course, it could be argued that God's people refused to hear anything that God was trying to say.

All that changes when John takes the stage. He speaks God's word. He announces God's intentions. He does so with such conviction that all who were still hoping for a rescuing Messiah hope John is the one.

John, however, isn't the Messiah, but the forerunner. He's not the Word, but the voice speaking the word. He's not the main event, just the warm-up act. John isn't the Christ, but he points to the One who is. Steeped in humility, John considers himself unworthy to remove even the sandals from the Messiah's feet.

In a final sermon, John foretells the Messiah's powerful work. What John cleanses outwardly with Jordan's water, the Messiah will cleanse inwardly with the Holy Spirit and fire, causing a separation like chaff from wheat.

The human tendency is to look beyond ourselves and make chaff-identifications by pointing to those persons and perspectives that seemingly oppose God's purposes. However, the unquenchable fire burns within each of us, feeding on the oxygen of our own denials of God's ways. If it burns hot and long enough, one day even chaff-producing persons like us will find wholeness.

When were you most aware of God's silence?

PRISON PROPHET
Luke 3:18-20

Every chance he got, John proclaimed God's message to all. But King Herod, whom John had criticized for marrying his brother's wife, Herodias, and because of other evil things he had done, arrested John and threw him in prison.

+

There were many Herods in the New Testament era. Herod the Great, who was part Jewish, ruled when Jesus was born. Following his death, his realm was divided between three sons: Archelaus, Herod Antipas, and Herod Philip. Herod the Great fathered other sons, but not all of them lived long lives. Their father was suspicious of any who might rival his power and was not above arranging the premature death of family members.

Antipas threw John in prison because the prophet criticized the king's marriage to Herodias. Given the complexities of this dysfunctional royal family, the exact details are messy and unclear. This much we know: Herod Antipas married the wife of his brother (also named Herod) who lived as a private citizen in Rome. The marriage was a breach of Jewish law that prohibited a man from seducing the wife of his brother. Neither Herod Antipas nor Herodias were bothered by what the law stated, but John the Baptist wasn't about to ignore it. He spoke truth to power and paid the price of imprisonment near the Dead Sea. According to Matthew and Mark, eventually Herod Antipas, granted the wish of his dancing stepdaughter, prompted by her mother, and beheaded John.

If John had preached nice spiritual sermons of self-improvement, he might never have seen the inside of a prison or lost his head. He would have made many friends. He could have been Herod's personal spiritual advisor. He might have written best-sellers and traveled the lecture circuit. But he didn't. How dare John suggest that neither spiritual transformation nor social transformation can happen without the other!

Who are the prophetic truth-tellers today?

BAPTISMAL WATERS
Luke 3:22a

John baptized everyone who came to him, including Jesus.
While Jesus was praying, the sky opened up and the Holy
Spirit came down on him in the form of a dove.

+

We can imagine Jesus saying to his cousin, "John, you've done a
tremendous job of preparing the way for me. You've jump-
started a spiritual awakening that enables people to see what God is
doing in the world, and many have responded. Thanks much, John, I
couldn't have reached this point of departure without you. I'll take over
from here."

Christian doctrine and tradition teaches that Jesus lived a life of
sinless perfection, a life without and apart from sin, the spotless Lamb.
Why, then, does Jesus seek to be baptized? Maybe what the church
teaches about Jesus' sinlessness isn't what Jesus understands about
himself. Maybe it hasn't yet occurred to Jesus that he's any different
from his contemporaries or exempt from their condition. On the other
hand, perhaps Jesus simply submits to the irresistible urge to identify
with the people he's come to know and love—those burdened with life
in an occupied land who've given up hope for anything better to come,
who've come to realize they're fresh out of options with no resources
of their own.

If Jesus truly wanted to be one of us—to be human—what better
way to identify with the mess and mud of the world than to stand in
line with those ready to submit themselves to the baptismal waters of
the Jordan River? In the words of church father Irenaeus, "Jesus
became what we are in order to make us what he is."

Then Jesus prays, and like a poet, Luke describes the heavens
stirring and the Spirit descending in dove-shaped form. Perhaps Luke
is mindful of the prophet Isaiah's God-directed plea, "Tear open
the heavens and come down" (Isaiah 64:1). Clearly, God is up to
something, and that something is the disclosure of a vision lived out in
the life of Jesus.

When have you been aware that God was present with you?

DIVINE PLEASURE
Luke 3:22b

A voice from heaven said, "You're my son, the Beloved One;
I'm pleased with you."

+

Though Matthew, Mark, and Luke all record a voice speaking from
heaven, there is no reason to believe that an audience of eaves-
droppers is able to hear it. The voice comes to Jesus alone.

Jesus isn't the first in the biblical tradition called God's son. The
title was given at various times to the entire nation of Israel: "God says
to Israel, 'You're my firstborn son'" (Exodus 4:22). At royal
coronations, kings throughout Israel's history were reminded of their
special relationship to the Divine: "You're my son, and I am your
father" (Psalm 2:7). Even Adam, the firstborn of Genesis, is noted in
Jesus' genealogy as the "son of God" (Luke 3:38).

Echoes of this baptismal voice resonate in the moving
Suffering Servant passage of Isaiah 42:1: "Here's my servant, the one
I uphold, my chosen who delights me. My spirit is in him; he'll bring
forth justice to the nations."

Drenched by the waters of the Jordan River, Jesus is the newest
and fullest recipient of God's good pleasure, the one upon whom all
blessings flow, the Beloved One, God's child. However, Jesus' sonship
is meant to be shared, a relationship of belonging meant to be conferred on a wider family. The writer John says as much: "Anyone who
is open to Jesus and embraces the Jesus life becomes a son or daughter
of God, a new family not connected through bloodlines or human
fashioning, but by God's sheer delight" (John 1:12-13).

When have you heard that you were God's beloved child?

51

THIRTY-SOMETHING
Luke 3:23a

Jesus was about thirty years old when he began his ministry.

+

The numerical parallels between the onset of Jesus' ministry and that of other biblical figures are worth noting. The Old Testament patriarch Joseph was thirty years old when he entered the service of the Egyptian pharaoh. Jesse's youngest son, David, began his kingship over Israel when he was thirty years of age. At thirty years, the sons of Kohath were deemed ready to begin their priestly duties in the tent of the tabernacle. In the thirtieth year, Ezekiel heard the word of God and began to prophesy to the exiles.

When Jesus "was about thirty years old," his private life gave way to his public ministry. Whether by divine nudge or human instinct, or a combination of the two, Jesus leaves the comfort and familiarity of family in favor of a life without home.

Jesus doesn't begin his work before he is ready. He is schooled in the traditions, customs, and rituals of his Jewish heritage. He learns the Hebrew scriptures and memorizes large portions. He listens to the voices of the prophets. He worships in the synagogue. He prays the Hebrew prayers his ancestors prayed. With his family, he observes the holy days.

Thirty years might seem to us a long apprenticeship. If, as most scholars agree, his public ministry lasted only three years, then the ratio of preparation to actual implementation is a staggering ten-to-one.

Maybe this is another way Luke reminds us that Jesus comes from within the history and heritage of his people, not from outside them. Before he could begin, Jesus had much to learn, much to digest, and much to appreciate about God's ways.

What was the longest training period you had to go through?

FAMILY TREE
Luke 3:23b-38

Jesus was the son (as most believed) of Joseph, son of Heli, son of Matthat, son of Levi, son of Melki, son of Jannai, son of Joseph, son of Mattathias, son of Amos, son of Nahum, son of Esli, son of Naggai, son of Maath, son of Mattathias, son of Semein, son of Josech, son of Joda, son of Joanan, son of Rhesa, son of Zerubbabel, son of Shealtiel, son of Neri, son of Melki, son of Addi, son of Cosam, son of Elmadam, son of Er, son of Joshua, son of Eliezer, son of Jorim, son of Matthat, son of Levi, son of Simeon, son of Judah, son of Joseph, son of Jonam, son of Eliakim, son of Melea, son of Menna, son of Mattatha, son of Nathan, son of David, son of Jesse, son of Obed, son of Boaz, son of Sala, son of Nahshon, son of Amminadab, son of Admin, son of Arni, son of Hezron, son of Perez, son of Judah, son of Jacob, son of Isaac, son of Abraham, son of Terah, son of Nahor, son of Serug, son of Reu, son of Peleg, son of Eber, son of Shelah, son of Cainan, son of Arphaxad, son of Shem, son of Noah, son of Lamech, son of Methuselah, son of Enoch, son of Jared, son of Mahalalel, son of Kenan, son of Enosh, son of Seth, son of Adam, son of God.

+

If you managed to get through all the names, congratulations! Most people, even with the best of intentions, have neither the stamina nor the inclination.

Though both Luke and Matthew record Jesus' genealogy, differences are evident. Matthew places Jesus' family tree at the beginning of his gospel; Luke places it between Jesus' baptismal call and the wilderness temptations. Perhaps Luke is answering the question "Now that Jesus has been identified at his baptism as God's chosen one, is he qualified?" Jesus' unbroken lineage traced through Israel's history removes any doubt.

Another difference emerges when we place the two genealogies side by side. Names don't always match up. Where Luke lists Nathan, Matthew names Solomon. Luke identifies Jesus' grandfather as Heli; Matthew calls him Jacob. Some scholars conclude that Luke traces Jesus' line through Mary, while Matthew uses Joseph. Others contend that the legal heritage often includes different names than the physical or biological line.

Perhaps the most significant difference is that Matthew, starting with Abraham and ending with Jesus, works from the past to the present. Luke, beginning with Jesus and concluding with Adam, works from the present to the past. According to Luke, not only is Jesus connected to David and Abraham—significant leaders in Israel's history—but his lineage goes back to the first human being, even before Israel was called out from among the whole human race.

Jesus is proof that God doesn't give up on the world and abandon creation to fend for itself. Not only is Jesus the obedient and observant Jew; he is God's unique representative who lives out God's deepest passions for the entire world. Jesus transcends ethnicities, boundaries, and borders. He reaches beyond his own people and welcomes outsiders, a habit of welcome we will see practiced in Jesus' life.

What expectations does your family heritage place on you?

Downers Grove, IL

CLARIFICATION TIME
Luke 4:1-2

Jesus left the Jordan River area and followed the Holy Spirit's leading into the desert. For forty days, he battled the devil and ate nothing. Afterwards, he was famished.

+

Damp from his baptismal dousing and affirmed by his Divine Source, Jesus is led (Mark says "driven") by the Holy Spirit into the wilderness to do battle with forces beyond and within himself. The gospel writers identify these nefarious forces as the devil. Luke strategically places this temptation episode immediately after the high point of Jesus' baptism. Following affirmation at the Jordan River, Jesus wrestles with the growing awareness of his developing identity.

Before Jesus commences his ministry, he undergoes an extended time of clarification. He struggles with the questions: What will it mean to live out God's vision for humanity? How will this be accomplished? What methods are necessary? The answers to these questions find their shape in three temptations posed by the devil.

Here, Luke connects Jesus to past figures in Israel's history who underwent their own forty-day ordeals. Moses faced his forty days of testing on Mt. Sinai. Elijah endured his while hiding from King Ahab, who was intent on murdering him. Noah and his family survived forty days and nights of steady downpour. The entire nation of ex-slaves wandered forty years in the wilderness.

In the church year, the forty weekdays of Lent are a time for heightened self-examination and clarification as we participate in the life and suffering of Jesus. A discipline of forty days and forty nights— or however long it takes—can turn a life around.

What in your life needs further clarification?

HUNGER PANGS
Luke 4:3-4

The devil said to Jesus, "If you're the Son of God, command this stone to become bread." Jesus answered, "It is written, 'A person doesn't live by bread alone.'"

+

That Jesus has a conversation with the devil may cause some to dismiss this passage as a literary creation of primitive minds. Whether Jesus goes eyeball-to-eyeball with the devil or the temptations are mental struggles played out in his own mind, the issue for Luke is the same: How will Jesus demonstrate God's deepest longings for the world? What shape will his ministry take? If his recent baptism confirmed his embrace by God, then in what ways will that identity find expression?

Though Jesus is full of the Holy Spirit, his stomach is empty. What better time for doubts to arise? The devil doesn't deny that Jesus is chosen of God, but he uses the designation in a conditional clause: "*If* you are, then do this." The implication is obvious. Chosen ones of God don't go hungry. Kings don't suffer. God's appointed one shouldn't experience deprivation. Are you sure God has you covered? Can you trust the one who called you "my child"?

The temptation toward self-preservation will prove an alluring consideration for Jesus throughout his ministry and for his followers who will carry on his work. Can we ever be sure that God is with us? What could be more important than saving oneself from hardship and difficulty, from loss of influence, or from extinction itself? Companies and churches and families fret about this every day.

Jesus responds by quoting Deuteronomy 8:3, "A person doesn't live by bread alone, but by the word that comes from God's mouth." Physical bread alone isn't enough to sustain God's people. Survival is as much a matter of affirming our dependence on God and living out such dependence in obedience as it is about satisfying physical needs. As proven in our consumer-saturated culture, one can starve to death on bread alone. Bread alone has suffocating capacities. Bread alone can lead to malnutrition with deadly consequences.

Where do you feel the greatest hunger in your life?

TEMPTING VIEW
Luke 4:5-8

Then the devil led Jesus to higher ground and showed him all the nations of the world. He said to Jesus, "I'll give you all their power and glory and authority; it's been handed over to me, and I can give it to anyone I please. If you worship me, it will be yours." Jesus answered him, "It's written, 'Worship and serve God alone.'"

+

The scene shifts from a downward gaze at stone to a panoramic view of global domination. Jesus' second wilderness temptation (Matthew records it as his third) is an invitation to use his power and influence to establish a political empire.

The phrase "at once" has origins in the Greek word *stigme*, similar to another Greek word, *stigma*, which is used to describe the beatings and lashings Jesus received at his arrest and trial. Additionally, the verb translated "been handed over" is the same Greek verb used when Jesus later predicts that he will be "handed over" to the authorities intent on killing him. This temptation to usher in God's purposes without the stigma of suffering or the scandal of being handed over to executioners is a powerful one.

The tempter's promise closely resembles God's promise to Israel's kings—"Ask me, and I will give you the nations and all the earth. You will break them with a sword, and smash them to pieces like a potter's vessel" (Psalm 2:8-9)—though the devil fudges in his grandiose claim that the nations of the world are his to give.

Nonetheless, the suggestion that Jesus seize sociopolitical power —a power that can be used for much good—is again a temptation to avoid whatever pain and suffering lie ahead. Quoting Deuteronomy 6:13, Jesus resists the tempter's urgings. Constructing God on our terms and conditions is another form of idolatry.

What might be your most regrettable compromise?

GOD ABUSE
Luke 4:9-12

Then the devil took Jesus to the highest temple peak in Jerusalem and said, "If you're God's chosen one, throw yourself down, for it is written, 'God will command the angels to protect you,' and 'They will carry you so you won't smash your foot against a rock.'" Jesus replied, "It's also been said, 'Don't test God.'"

+

The tempter is no slouch. Borrowing from Psalm 91, he knows what the texts say. Again, the devil doesn't deny who Jesus is, but uses the conditional as if to say, "If you are who you say you are, then . . . defy death and come out a hero. What better way to capture people's attention and loyalty? Face it, people aren't attracted to losers. Bored minds don't tolerate three-point sermons. Play to their eyes. Throw yourself over the edge and let them witness how God will spare you.

"Oh, and no need to demonstrate your love by identifying with their pain. Take a leap right here and you won't even stub a toe. No need to be moved by the suffering of others. Cast yourself on angel wings. You're exempt from the messiness of humanity, Jesus. Everyone craves the immediacy of God. Give 'em what they want."

William Sloane Coffin (*Collected Sermons*) suggested, "So much that passes for spirituality is pure laziness." Perhaps this is the ultimate temptation for Jesus—to avoid the work of identifying with the world's suffering and to leave it up to God, or someone else. The implications for our own lives become abundantly obvious. Instead of getting our hands dirty and making a difference, how much easier (and more pious) it is to claim with spiritual certainty, "This is the way the world is because people deserve what they get. Winners earn their rewards and losers have no one but themselves to blame. That's how God works."

Jesus quotes Deuteronomy 6:16, which suggests that we abuse God whenever we hold God liable to promises God never made. The devil tries, but Jesus doesn't fall for it. Jesus never looks to God for protection, but leans on God for support.

With regard to growing into your better self, where are you the laziest?

UNTIL LATER
Luke 4:13

When finished tempting Jesus, the devil left and waited for an opportune moment.

+

The English word *opportune* is a combination of two Latin words: *ob*, meaning "toward," and *portus*, meaning "port" or "harbor." A ship sailing toward a harbor is heading for a suitable or convenient place. Failing to get Jesus to take shortcuts on the way, the devil begins to plan his attacks for a more suitable occasion. With time on his hands and a patient temperament, the tempter knows the lessons of waiting for a more convenient harbor of opportunity.

Jesus eventually performs many of the miracles suggested by the tempter. Soon, Jesus will alleviate the hunger of five thousand people, not by turning stones to bread, but by offering a few loaves and a pair of fish. Soon, he will cleanse lepers, raise corpses, give sight to the blind, and enable the lame to walk. Though he won't free-fall from the temple roof, he will wow his followers with other majestic displays.

The difference between the devil's temptations and Jesus' own choice to use his powers becomes clear when we realize that with each temptation, the devil attempts to get Jesus to avoid the reality of self-sacrifice in favor of embracing self-preservation. Each temptation is a shortcut to another way, an easier way, a less painful way—a way to avoid ushering in the world God intends.

Jesus will not seek to protect, avoid, or exempt himself from life's realities. St. Paul describes it this way: "Though Jesus was of God, he didn't regard equality with God as something to be exploited . . . he humbled himself and became obedient to the point of dying on a cross" (Philippians 2:6, 8).

For Jesus and all who, like him, seek to live out the reign of God in this world, the temptation to preserve and protect oneself is a powerful urge. The tempter—in all his, her, and its manifestations—always waits for the opportune moment.

What does a safe harbor look like to you?

Piazza della Rotonda, Rome, Italy

PRAISED BY EVERYONE
Luke 4:14-15

Inspired by the Spirit, Jesus returned to Galilee, where his popularity spread. He taught in the synagogues and everyone sang his praises.

+

Of the critical decisions facing Jesus at the onset of his public ministry, one holds geographical significance: Where, *literally*, should he begin? Fresh from surviving his desert ordeal, Jesus returns to familiar ground, the place of his upbringing, the northern region of Palestine called Galilee. Here, through word and deed, through call and conviction, Jesus' ministry gets underway.

Luke moves quickly from the temptations of Jesus to his ministry in Galilee, the first of three ministry locations. Later, Luke gives attention to Jesus' ministry on the way from Galilee to Jerusalem. Finally, there is his ministry in the city of Jerusalem itself, culminating in his suffering, death, and resurrection.

From the Hebrew word *gail* meaning "circle," Galilee was a fertile expanse surrounded by non-Jewish (Gentile) neighbors. Religiously more progressive than the traditionalists and hard-liners in Jerusalem, Galilean commoners were more receptive to new teachers, especially those who spoke out against the Roman oppressors. The first-century Jewish historian Josephus described the Galileans as a feisty and hearty lot, ready to follow any charismatic leader who promised to oust the Romans from their land. Indeed, Galilee was fertile ground.

As a traveling rabbi (teacher), Jesus has occasion to teach in synagogues. Word of his wisdom spreads quickly throughout the region. Jesus impresses his listeners and they respond favorably. All speak well of him. Everybody praises him. A good start for a local boy from the Galilean town of Nazareth.

Perhaps their adoration is a response to the Spirit working in Jesus. Or maybe, just maybe, they haven't heard enough from him yet to know any better. Soon enough that will change.

What potential dangers arise when all speak well of you?

AS WAS HIS CUSTOM
Luke 4:16

When Jesus returned to his hometown of Nazareth, he went to the synagogue on the Sabbath as he always did.

+

In Jesus' day, Nazareth boasted nearly twenty thousand inhabitants. Though overshadowed by the neighboring city of Sepphoris, a city later destroyed by the Romans, Nazareth was anything but a backwater place.

Nazareth held strategic importance for three reasons: Pilgrims journeying from the north traveled through Nazareth on their way to attend temple festivals in Jerusalem. Traders from Egypt with goods destined for Damascus and beyond found Nazareth a suitable stopover point. Finally, caravans from eastern locales throughout the Roman Empire left on Nazareth impressions of distant cultures.

Fresh from popular teaching campaigns that attracted growing public interest, Jesus heads home for Sabbath worship. In a typical synagogue worship service, someone would read the words found in the book of Deuteronomy, "Hear O Israel, God is one." This was followed by a time of prayer, then a reading from the Pentateuch (one of the first five books of the Hebrew Bible). More prayers and praises were offered, followed by thanks to God for the sacred writings. An attendant then would invite someone—a member or visitor—to read from the prophets. The scroll was read and time was allotted for teaching and comments on the text. The service ended with a time of praising God and offering prayers of thanksgiving.

As was his custom, Jesus attended synagogue services. Hometown traditions, religious rituals, holy habits—wrapped strand by strand into sacred fibers—strengthen the people who observe them. Some days, the long acquaintance with holy routines provides the necessary strength that a faltering faith, absent those routines, cannot.

What religious customs are part of your family life?

PICTURE PERFECT
Luke 4:17-19

Jesus stood up to read the scroll of the prophet Isaiah that
was handed to him. He unrolled it and found the place where
it is written, "The Spirit of God is with me, because God
anointed me to bring good news to the poor, to release those
who are bound, to give sight to the blind, to free those who
have been treated unfairly, and to proclaim the year of God's
favor."

+

A more cherished passage Jesus could not have read for the
hometown congregation. Every religious Jew longed for that glo-
rious day when God's anointed one would turn the tables and restore
to Israel the fortunes and freedoms of the past.

Isaiah 61 paints a portrait of God's future reality. The Spirit-
anointed one will bring reversals of misfortune and counter-revolutions
for those on the bottom of the social ladder. No more last-place
finishes. No more uneven playing fields. No more occupied lands. No
more home-away-from-home. No more afflictions of mind and
body. No more prisons for the innocent. No more death-row
sentences for the wrongly accused. This is the world God intends—
the "year of God's favor."

In the book of Leviticus, every fiftieth year is called the Year of
Jubilee, a time when all debts are forgiven, all properties restored to
their rightful owners, all slaves set free, all families reunited, all things in
all ways made right. Picture perfect! Though there is little evidence in
Israel's history that the Year of Jubilee was systematically observed, it
remained an ideal picture of God's intentions for the world.

As Jesus finishes his reading, it's doubtful there is a dry eye in the
house. Their home-grown boy has read well, and proud they are.
Picture perfect!

If God's intentions were fully lived out, what would the world look like?

64

ALL SPOKE WELL OF HIM
Luke 4:20-22

Jesus rolled up the scroll, gave it back to the worship leader, and sat down. Everyone stared intently at him. Then he said, "Today, what you've just heard is coming true." Everyone was impressed and amazed at his grace-filled words. They said, "Isn't this Joseph's son?"

+

Jesus sits down to assume the customary position of a rabbi ready to teach. The moment is one of heightened anticipation. All eyes and ears are riveted on him. Nobody coughs. Nobody moves. Nobody unwraps candy. How will Jesus interpret Isaiah's prophecy? What scribal authorities will he quote when commenting on the text?

Jesus doesn't fail to deliver. "Today, what you've just heard is coming true." His pronouncement is clear and certain. The one about whom Isaiah spoke now stands before them. He—Jesus—will bring good news to the poor, release to the captives, sight to the blind, freedom for the oppressed, and God's good favor.

Though Matthew and Mark place the story of Jesus preaching in his hometown synagogue closer to the middle of his ministry, Luke places it at the beginning. At the onset of Jesus' public life, Luke wants readers to note how Jesus understands his identity, his spiritual calling, and his ministry focus. Jesus stands in continuity with the Old Testament promises. God hasn't forgotten God's people. Prayers have not been ignored. Jesus' baptism was confirmation of his heavenly anointing, and now he's ready to align his work with Israel's deepest longing for redemption and deliverance.

All were impressed. Their hopes took a giant leap forward. Their prayers were being answered before their eyes. The future was knocking on their door and standing before them. "Could it be? We know his family! Is he the one to lift our poverty, to break our captivity, to open our eyes, to restore our freedom?"

What gracious words will you speak today?

SAYINGS
Luke 4:23-24

Jesus said, "I'm sure you will quote this proverb: 'Doctor, cure yourself!' and say to me, 'Do for us what you did in Capernaum.' Let me remind you, prophets are never accepted in their hometowns."

+

If Jesus had ended his message with "Today this scripture has come true in your hearing," he would have left the synagogue facing a tough decision about which dinner invitation to accept. They loved him, or at least they loved what they thought they had heard. But rather than bask in the adulation, Jesus ups the ante and continues his sermon.

Perhaps Jesus senses in their gratuitous response a narrow preoccupation that emphasizes *our* good news and *our* captivity and *our* deliverance. Jesus responds by quoting two ancient proverbs: "Doctor, cure yourself!" and "Prophets are never accepted in their hometowns."

In the first saying, Jesus makes known what he thinks they expect of him. Gently and poignantly, he accuses the synagogue folks of demanding of him miraculous healings to prove who he is: "If you're the real thing, do for us—your own people—what you did in Capernaum! Give us something to evaluate. Show us a sign, and make it a good one. Give us proof, and we'll believe." (Didn't Jesus just endure this temptation in the wilderness?)

The second proverb originates in Israel's own history. Her prophets, all of whom afflicted the comfortable and comforted the afflicted, were rejected; many—Isaiah, Jeremiah, Ezekiel, Amos, and Micah—were killed. The messengers who came to announce the year of God's "favor" experienced themselves as "out of favor" once their message was delivered.

More is at stake here than blindness and slowness of heart. Demand for additional substantiation, coupled with rejection of the messenger, confirms the all-too-human tendency of seeing only what we want to see and hearing only what we want to hear.

Where are your "comfortable" and "afflicted" points?

BEYOND THE BORDERS
Luke 4:25-28

"There were many widows in Israel in Elijah's day when there was no rain for three and a half years. Yet, Elijah was sent to none of those widows, except to one at Zarephath in Sidon. There were also many lepers with skin diseases in Israel during the time of the prophet Elisha, and none was healed except Naaman, the Syrian." When the people in the synagogue heard this, they were enraged.

+

In Elijah's day, there were many widows in Israel suffering from hunger due to a long drought. However, Elijah didn't provide the *Israelites* with a miraculous supply of flour and oil, or raise *their* dead sons. God sent Elijah beyond Israelite territory to a widow at Sidon.

During the time of Elisha the prophet, many in Israel were sick and ailing, but Elisha didn't heal the *Israelites* with miraculous gestures of wholeness. God sent him instead to a man named Naaman, commander of an enemy army, who lived beyond the borders in Syria.

The truth, obvious enough, must have stung. It wasn't the first time God chose to deal graciously with those beyond the borders of Israel, and, as Jesus' sermon indicates, it won't be the last.

They had come to the synagogue seeking confirmation of what they thought they knew about God: God is *our* God. God abides in *our* land. God takes *our* side. God waves *our* flag. God supports *our* way of life. But instead of confirming those assumptions, Jesus challenges them. In the tradition of Elijah and Elisha, Jesus does what every preacher who steps into the pulpit fears doing. He refuses to bless their notion of a partisan God. Jesus won't adopt a party line that smugly assumes *our* enemies are God's enemies. He treats outsiders as insiders.

Seldom do tempers flare when God is depicted as merciful and gracious toward *us*. As long as we see ourselves as insiders and others as outsiders, we're cozy with God. But expand God's concern to include those we would cross the street to avoid, or those who would wage war against our way of life, and that becomes a matter of an altogether different nature. It's enough to enrage us and keep us that way.

When was the last time God didn't come around to your way of thinking?

THE ESCAPE
Luke 4:29-30

The synagogue worshippers got up and drove Jesus to the hill on which their town was built. They were ready to push him off the cliff, but Jesus managed to escape and continued on his way.

+

No one bothers to wait for the benediction. Nobody makes a motion for a congregational vote. In an apparent act of unanimous spontaneity, the synagogue worshippers rush the speaker's chair and hustle Jesus out of town. So much for job security.

The word *drove* suggests in Greek, as it does in English, a hostile and aggressive action. Here's blind rage fueled by mob mentality: "No one comes on our home court and makes those accusations. Hometown son or not, nobody gets a free pass spouting that God's love is meant for people we can't stand!"

With dust funnels swirling behind them and Jesus securely in tow, the crowd reaches a suitable execution spot. The preacher has to die, and in all likelihood, he would have were it not for a bizarre and mysterious turn of events.

Jesus somehow "managed to escape." Huh? How's that possible? Nobody sees him walk away? Are we to believe the hilltop altitude gives them bigger problems than the preacher's message? Does their prolonged argument over who's going to push him off the cliff actually provide Jesus the opportunity to give them the slip?

The fact that Luke doesn't dwell on the logistics of the escape is reason enough to let the issue stand. The Sabbath crowd tries to kill Jesus. (Wait a minute, weren't executions unlawful on the Sabbath?)

Rather than pointing to a divinely orchestrated rescue operation, this near-death episode is a reminder that Jesus doesn't stay where his presence isn't wanted. He may arrive an unannounced visitor, but he doesn't remain an unwelcome guest. Yet, in spite of the treatment, Jesus doesn't invoke on them fire and brimstone. There might be a lesson there if we choose to see it.

When was the last time you roasted a preacher?

DEMON TERRITORY
Luke 4:31-34

Jesus went to the Galilean city of Capernaum and taught on the Sabbath. They were amazed at his teachings because he spoke with authority. In the synagogue, there was a man afflicted with a demon. He shouted, "Let us alone! What do you want with us, Jesus of Nazareth? Are you going to destroy us? We know you're the Holy One of God."

+

Again, we find Jesus teaching in a synagogue—this time at Capernaum, a village on the northern shore of the Sea of Galilee. People are astounded by his authority. If Jesus' Capernaum teaching is at all like his Nazareth lesson, he isn't content merely to quote past teachers but interprets the Hebrew scriptures in light of his self-understanding and mission. Jesus speaks with an authority unlike other rabbis.

The service soon turns into a shouting match as a man with a severe affliction cries out. The demon world was not an imagined world. It was believed that demons and unclean spirits caused all manner of malady: spiritual and physical blindness, paralysis, deafness, madness, even epilepsy. Demons were warlords of imprisonment, underworld thugs dealing in the wares of despair.

The demon recognizes Jesus and accuses Jesus of trespassing on the demon's turf: "You've got no business here, Jesus of Nazareth. Leave quietly and avoid trouble. Get out of my neighborhood, Holy One of God!" The demon speaks and gets it right. Jesus is one of God's own, and he's in the oppression-destroying business.

Really now, when was the last time you saw or heard a demon? Such a primitive story! Lest we dismiss this encounter because we no longer believe in a demon-infested world, we would be wise to acknowledge that though the terminology has changed, the destructiveness remains real. Maybe we don't call them demons, but they sure act like demons: shame-based despair, heartless competition, numbing addictions, an insatiable appetite for war, rules that favor the rich and keep the poor in their poverty. And that's just for starters. We could add to the list more demons than we can shake a stick at.

What demons do you see loose in the world?

69

DIVINE REBUKE
Luke 4:35-37

Jesus rebuked the demon, "Be quiet! Come out of him!" The demon threw the man to the ground and came out without harming him. The crowd was amazed, "What's this all about? He has authority and power to expel evil spirits!" Reports about Jesus spread everywhere.

+

Jesus doesn't choose this moment to practice his pastoral counseling skills, but if he had, he might have said to the madman, "Now, tell me exactly how you feel. Yes, you're angry. I hear defiance. Good, get it out. Where do you suppose that comes from? Where are you in the birth order of your siblings?"

Instead, Jesus takes on the chaos. As God's word subdued the Genesis void and brought order to the pre-creational chaos, Jesus subdues the belligerent madness on this day. "Be quiet! Come out!" The demon obeys.

Jesus' authority, evidenced in his preaching and teaching, is substantiated now by his control over the demonic world. Not only does Jesus teach; he confronts oppression. Not only does Jesus know scripture; he casts out demons. Not only does Jesus preach the good news; he ushers in the abundant life of God's transformational power.

The synagogue worshippers watching Jesus believe that before them stands one whose authority and power are obvious gifts from God. Only later, on other demonic battlefields, will witnesses accuse Jesus of sleeping with the devil.

This is the first miracle recorded in Luke's gospel. By placing himself in the presence of evil's demonic power, where the stakes involve issues of life and death, Jesus points to God's ultimate power over evil's domination. That these evil forces are the first to recognize the Holy One of God is one of the many ironies in Jesus' life.

Where does the Holy One of God confront your life?

JESUS, M.D.
Luke 4:38-41

After leaving the synagogue, Jesus went to Simon's house. Simon's mother-in-law had a high fever, and they asked Jesus if he could do something. Jesus stood next to her bed and rebuked the fever and it left her. Immediately, she got up and headed for the kitchen to serve them. A short time later, those who were sick with all kinds of diseases came to Jesus for healing. Demons also came out of many shouting, "You are the Son of God!" But he commanded them to be quiet, because they knew he was God's anointed one.

+

With growing popularity come growing demands. In settings both private and public, Jesus is surrounded by the sick and the infirm. Opinions about him begin to form. To some, he's a teacher with authority. To the demons, he's the Son of God. To the masses, he's the one who cures and heals. Luke says nothing about the faith of those who seek him out. These are stories about the healer more than they are about the healed.

We might wonder if Jesus recalled his wilderness temptations while performing medical triage. These are the sorts of people-pleasing things the devil tempted him to do in the wilderness. Jesus doesn't qualify his actions with the disclaimer "This isn't *all* that I'm about." Instead, he gives people what they seek and what they want. *The customer's always right. Find their itch and scratch it. If you heal it, they will come.* The likelihood that a healing frenzy might fuel erroneous expectations of his mission is evidenced in Jesus' need to silence any "Son of God" reports.

In the gospels, two Greek words are used for "miracle"—one is translated "act of power" and the other as "sign." As acts of power and signs, Jesus' miracles are not ends unto themselves but point to another reality. In the emerging presence of God's reign, neither demons nor disabilities, neither death nor oppressive poverty have the final say-so. Sometimes, words alone are enough; other times, words plus a powerful sign are necessary.

What miracles have you experienced?

RESISTING THE BOTTOM LINE
Luke 4:42-44

Early in the morning, Jesus went to a quiet place. The crowds found him and tried to prevent him from leaving. Jesus explained, "I must proclaim the good news of God's dream for humanity to other cities, too." He continued preaching in the synagogues.

+

For Jesus, the rhythm is a familiar one—time with the crowds, then time alone. Even Jesus needs balance. A life of meeting people's needs can quickly make one a slave to people's expectations. Likewise, a life of chosen detachment can make one aloof to the world's brokenness. Jesus needs both public engagement with people and private renewal with God.

Maintaining this rhythm requires of Jesus a vigilant resistance to the bottom line. With ever-increasing popularity, his venues are standing room only. Jesus is prime-time. As any CEO, church pastor, or head of television programming will tell you, it is impossible to resist the lure of numbers. Numbers don't lie. Filled churches must be doing something right. Ratings matter. Quality may be a worthy pursuit, but quantity pays the bills and keeps the shareholders happy.

The devil said as much in the wilderness of temptation. The bottom line is everything. Yet, when Jesus has the opportunity to pursue the bottom line, he chooses to resist it and heads for other locales. Jesus refuses to be the exclusive property of anyone.

Jesus lives by a single necessity. Though they plead for him to remain, he leaves the adulation of this crowd to pursue the most important thing: "I must proclaim the good news of God's dream for the world to other cities, too."

How do you maintain balance?

IF YOU SAY SO
Luke 5:1-5

One day while Jesus was standing by the Sea of Galilee, many people gathered to hear him teach. Jesus saw two boats on the shore and fishermen who were washing their nets. He got into one of the boats belonging to Simon (Peter) and told him to push off a bit from the shore. Then Jesus sat down in the boat and taught the crowds. When he finished speaking, he said to Simon, "Go into deep water and let down your nets." Simon answered, "Master, we've worked all night long but haven't caught a thing. Yet if you think it will help, I'll do as you say."

+

The Sea of Galilee was in the region where Jesus' teachings, healings, and exorcisms contributed to his growing popularity. The scene Luke describes was a common shoreline sight. After a night of fishing, no one went home until the nets were cleaned and, if necessary, repaired. One needed to disentangle the lead weights around the edges of the nets and mend any tears that may have occurred while hauling in a catch of fish.

It must have struck Simon as presumptuous that Jesus, raised in landlocked Nazareth, would instruct him to venture again into deep waters and cast his nets overboard. Prime fishing time had come and gone. The nets, washed and cleaned, were ready for tomorrow's possibilities. Besides, Simon had recent history to back him up; toiling all night, he hadn't caught a thing. Any unfished opportunities beckoned for another day.

At this moment, Simon has to make a decision. Either he can let the experiences of past failures determine his inaction, or at the risk of looking foolish and possibly failing again, he can cast his nets in deeper waters. His willingness to take Jesus' advice may have been nothing more than a tired angler's attempt to prove Jesus wrong. It also may have been the first evidence of new resolve. Sometimes, the remarkable gift hidden from our eyes lies just below the surface, waiting only for the exercise of our commitment.

When was the last time you ventured forth in spite of deep reservations?

Sorrento, Italy

CAREER CHANGE
Luke 5:6-10

When the fishermen lowered their nets, they caught so many fish that the nets began to rip. They called to their partners in the other boat to help them. In no time, both boats were full and became so heavy that they began to sink. When Simon saw it, he knelt and said to Jesus, "Go away from me, for I'm a sinful man!" The fishermen, including Simon's business partners James and John, the sons of Zebedee, were amazed at the amount of fish they caught. Then Jesus said to Simon, "Don't be afraid; from now on you will rescue people."

+

Luke is a master of details. The weight of the catch tests the strength of the nets. Many hands are required to haul them in. Two boats are needed to accommodate the load. The vessels begin to sink.

If Luke had ended the story with merely a descriptive detail of the catch, we might come away with several lessons. *Never give up, who knows when your fish will come in! Just keep at it; success will arrive before you know it! Past failures need not determine future results!*

Yet, something more profound is happening here, as witnessed in Simon's response. The overwhelmed fisherman drops to his knees and acknowledges his own unworthiness. No backslapping. No high fives. No fist bumps. Face-to-face with the power and mystery of the one responsible for this catch, Simon senses his own inadequacies. Aware of the gap between his own life and this holy man, Simon pleads for him to leave. Jesus reassures Simon and offers him a career change: "Soon, you will rescue people." Literally, "You will catch human beings alive," or "You will save them from danger."

So begins one fisherman's second career. Simon gets it right; he is unworthy. Perhaps what he experiences is similar to what one might experience when standing on the rim of the Grand Canyon at sunset—being overwhelmed at the sheer majesty of it all. How can anyone stand for long in the glory of such a moment? That we're affirmed in who we are and offered an invitation to join in Jesus' work is the most significant miracle in this story.

What does awe feel like to you?

75

LEAVING AND FOLLOWING
Luke 5:11

When they came to shore, they left everything and followed Jesus.

+

And just like that, they left everything and followed Jesus. Disinclined to sleep on it for a night, they left it all behind. Seeking advice from no one else, they abandoned their boats on the shore. With little regard for past investments made, they bet it all on one who said, "Don't be afraid." Caring nothing for inventory counts or customer obligations, they walked away to walk with another. Choosing not to put their own houses in order, they followed Jesus, who had no home. Knowing nothing but the fishing business, they opted for a mid-life career change. Giving little thought to friends and neighbors, they said goodbye and hit the road. Assuming no need to tend to his recovering mother-in-law, Simon followed the one who promised new fishing spots. Not concerned enough to stay behind with their father, James and John left Zebedee to fish alone.

And just like that, after bringing their boats to shore, they left everything and followed Jesus. Could it have been so easy to leave everything and follow him? Should one make life-impacting decisions because of the quantity of fish caught? How could they leave all and commit everything when they knew so little about him? What dreams were they dreaming about future rewards and greater successes? Had Jesus told them anything yet about sacrifices and sorrows and suffering?

These and a thousand other questions linger unanswered. Nevertheless, in their leaving everything and following Jesus, they demonstrate for us that in relinquishing our grip and losing our lives, we find the security and the life God intends for us.

What was the last decision you made that made sense to no one else?

76

THE TOUCH
Luke 5:12-14

In a nearby town, there was a man with leprosy. When he saw Jesus, he bowed down and pleaded, "Master, you can choose to make me well." Jesus touched him and said, "Yes, I choose to make you well." Immediately the leprosy left him. Jesus told him to keep quiet and instructed him, "Show yourself to the priest; then, as Moses commanded, make an offering for your cleansing as a testimony to your healing."

+

Few diseases in the ancient world were more devastating than leprosy. That leprosy was taken seriously is confirmed in Leviticus where the entire thirteenth and fourteenth chapters (116 verses!) are devoted to various symptoms, precautions necessary, purification rituals required, and priestly duties to safeguard the community.

Believed to spread by human contact, leprosy was the kiss of death—not always a physical one, but certainly the stigma a social death. Religiously and socially, lepers were outcasts and often forced to live in isolation from family and community. A leper's life was reduced to roadside begging and sharing the misery with other lepers.

One day a leper gets close enough to Jesus to speak with him, and professes his belief that Jesus has the power to cleanse him, if only he would so choose. Jesus responds by breaking a few dozen purity laws with a single act. He touches the leper, skin on skin, flesh on flesh.

The Levitical laws that Jesus breaches prescribed that purity and holiness were maintained through distance and separation from those deemed unclean, impure, and evil. Purity was kept when a healthy person avoided contact with a leper. On this day, however, Jesus redefines purity. In touching the leper, Jesus wants everyone to see what it means to live and act in holy ways. The sick and marginalized are more important to God than the laws established to keep healthy people clean.

To be holy and pure, is it not this? To touch the untouchable. To bring in the outsider. To befriend the lonely. To break a barrier and soothe a soul. Jesus touches him, and immediately the leprosy leaves; community is restored. God's dream for the world becomes real.

Who are modern-day lepers?

PHARISEES (I)
Luke 5:15-17a

Word about Jesus spread quickly. Large crowds gathered to hear him and receive healing. Jesus often took time to retreat to quiet places and pray. One day, Pharisees and legal scholars listened in while Jesus was teaching.

+

Jesus seeks solitude. Refreshment, refocus, and renewal are important self-care rituals, especially now that the eyes of the Pharisees and legal scholars are on him.

Even people who don't know much about the New Testament have a hunch that the Pharisees are not the good guys. A fuller understanding of Pharisees in Jesus' day, however, gives us a different picture. Pharisees were spiritual giants who lived and breathed obedience to God by keeping the law of God. They sought to live close to God, in the will of God, and near the heart of God.

In Jesus' day, the term *the law* was understood in three ways. First, it referred to the Ten Commandments given to Israel through Moses. Second, *the law* was also a catchword for the first five books of the Bible, traditionally known as the Books of Moses or the Pentateuch (literally, "the Five Rolls").

A third use of *the law* was related to oral laws. The oral laws were later elaborations of the Ten Commandments. What the "Big Ten" lacked in specificity, these later additions made up for in exhaustive detail rivaling the U.S. tax code. How much detail? One commentary on the law—the Jerusalem Talmud—contains 156 double-sided pages of elaborations on what it means to keep the Sabbath day holy. Think law on steroids.

The Pharisees and teachers of the law were huge fans of the oral laws. Yet, lest we scoff at their rule-keeping tendencies, there are worse things, especially in our narcissistic culture, than wanting to live a life pleasing to God.

How many of the Ten Commandments can you name?

PHARISEES (II)
Luke 5:17b

Now, the Pharisees and teachers of the law had come from every village of Galilee and Judea and from Jerusalem. God's power made it possible for Jesus to heal.

+

If the scribes and teachers lived and breathed to interpret the multi-layered dimensions of the law, the Pharisees sought perfection in keeping the laws. *Pharisee* means "separate one." Having noted the virtues of Pharisees in the previous reflection, for the sake of balance and full disclosure, let's seek to understand their shortcomings.

Committed to obeying the laws in every detail, the Pharisees separated themselves from ordinary people to follow meticulously all the commands of the law. They were saints with a single-minded passion of maintaining absolute obedience to God's law. However, as with doctors, lawyers, members of Congress, Wall Street bankers, professional athletes, and clergy, a few bad ones in the bunch can tarnish the image of the entire group.

Jesus often levied severe criticism on those Pharisees who were religious hypocrites. Some Pharisees were so determined to live the law that they showed little concern for the needs of widows, the poor, and the outcasts. Other Pharisees lived in such a way that their outward displays of piety bore little resemblance to their inward attitude. Certain Pharisees loved nothing more than to place the weighty demands of the law on the backs of those who were least able to keep them.

Yes, of the nearly six thousand Pharisees in Jesus' day, a few sullied the reputation of the entire group. As Luke will record in later passages, Jesus has no patience for any Pharisee who practices pseudo-spirituality. Some, as we will see, seek to entangle Jesus in theological debates as a way to discredit him. A few even plot to get him arrested. The vast majority, however, hope to deepen the spirituality of the nation. And what could be wrong with that?

Who is the most morally upright person you know?

THEIR FAITH
Luke 5:18-20

Some men arrived at the house where Jesus was teaching, carrying a paralyzed man on a bed. Because of the crowd, they couldn't get close to Jesus, so they climbed on the roof and removed some tiles, then lowered the bed through the hole. When Jesus saw their faith, he said, "Friend, your sins are forgiven."

+

What Luke fails to share with us is the heated discussion held with the local zoning board about ripping a hole in the roof. "What? You're going to put a hole where? Mike, what about liability? Bill, we can't risk a lawsuit! Do you know how easy it is to lose your footing? What about your back, John? Think of the property damage! Phyllis, do we have insurance for this kind of thing? Who's going to clean up the mess? What about the carpet? Jack, you've got something to say? Yes, I agree, let's assign this one to a committee and revisit the idea at our next meeting. Is there a motion to adjourn?"

In spite of it all, the plan succeeds. Even Jesus is impressed. He sees their faith, and their creativity, and their imagination, and their determination, and their stubbornness, and their persistence, and their refusal to let the world's No become their No. *Their* faith is the only faith Jesus observes. *Their* faith is the only faith Jesus mentions. *Their* faith—the faith of the bed-carrying friends, not the faith of the carried one—is the faith Jesus notices.

Can the faith of others, offered for and on behalf of someone, move God to act in benevolent ways? In Genesis 18, Abraham negotiated with God to spare *all* the inhabitants of Sodom should only ten righteous people be found in the city. The faith of one was offered to and received by God on behalf of others.

Perhaps what our world needs most is "go-between" people, intercessors who pray for and act on behalf of those unable to do so for themselves. Thank God for those willing to put holes in roofs so that God's wholeness can get through.

For whom do you pray without their knowing?

80

WHAT NERVE!
Luke 5:21

Then the scholars and religious leaders remarked to themselves, "Who does he think he is? Only God is able to forgive sins!"

+

That Jesus first forgives the sins of the paralyzed man, and that the Pharisees challenge his authority to do so, highlights the causal connection in the ancient world between sin and sickness: If you're sick, it's because you've sinned.

The Pharisees make it clear what's on their minds. They don't question Jesus' ability to heal, only his self-appointed authority to forgive sins. An itinerant wonder-worker is one thing; one who claims authority reserved for God alone is another.

Let's reconstruct the logic. Person A commits a wrongful act against person B. Who can choose to forgive person A? Only B can forgive A. Persons C, D, E, and F don't have the authority to forgive A because A's wrongful action wasn't directed at any of them. However, the Old Testament also teaches that God has the authority to forgive person A. "I am the One who blots out your transgressions for my own sake, and I will not remember your sins" (Isaiah 43:25). Therefore, if person C, D, E, or F claims an authority to forgive person A, such a claim is an affront to God because it assumes a right reserved only for God.

One more thing: If person C, D, E, or F exercises a right reserved only for God, such a person might be implying that something of God resides within him or her. That, too, opens one to the charge of blasphemy. In Leviticus 24, God said to Moses, "Take the blasphemer outside the camp and let everyone stone him. Anyone who blasphemes my name deserves death."

The religious experts know their biblical algebra and they know Leviticus. Jesus is a blasphemer.

What's the most outrageous forgiveness you've offered?

AWESTRUCK
Luke 5:22-26

Jesus knew what they were thinking and commented, "Why are you raising those questions? What's easier to say: 'Your sins are forgiven,' or 'Stand up and walk'? I will prove to you I have authority to forgive sins." Jesus said to the paralyzed man, "Stand up, take your bed and go home." The man stood up, grabbed his bed, and went on his way, thanking God. The crowd was awestruck: "We're at a loss for words!"

+

The Old Testament is rife with passages that promise blessings to the righteous and misfortunes to the unrighteous. "The righteous are like trees planted by rivers, yielding their fruit in season, and their leaves don't wither. They prosper in everything. The wicked aren't so, but are like chaff that the wind drives away" (Psalm 1:3-4).

The issue of suffering as the result of personal sin would seem settled were it not for the forty-two chapters preceding Psalm 1. Job, a righteous tree, is buffeted and driven like dandelion seeds in the wind, calling into question the relationship between personal suffering and sin.

Jesus' critics believe, as the ancients did, that suffering and sickness are the results of personal wrongdoing. The victim did something to deserve the malady. Before healing can come, sin has to go. Jesus argues with them on their own terms. "Tell me what's easier to say: 'You're forgiven,' or 'You're healed'?" The point is obvious to the Pharisees. If, as they believe, healing can't arrive without prior forgiveness from God, then any healing is proof of divine forgiveness. Therefore, if Jesus heals the man, like God he has also forgiven the man. The power of God in Jesus does both the forgiving and the healing. It is logic divine enough to send the best legal experts back to their law books.

When Jesus turns to the paralyzed man and announces that his sins are forgiven, perhaps the "sins" that are forgiven and removed and lifted are the attitudes and judgments placed on him by those who can't see him any other way. In that case, he's now free to walk away.

What do you believe about the connection between sin and suffering?

COLD CALL
Luke 5:27-28

One day, Jesus saw a tax collector named Levi sitting at the tax booth. Jesus said to him, "Follow me." Immediately, Levi got up, left everything, and followed Jesus.

+

Unlike the earlier enlistment of Peter, James, and John that occurred after the miraculous catch of fish, we don't know what, if any, prior contact Levi had with Jesus. Meeting Levi perhaps for the first time, Jesus makes a cold call and issues his invitation: "Follow me." Like the earlier disciples, Levi does exactly that.

Levi is a tax collector who works for a government that never saw a tax it didn't like. The Roman Empire was able to exert its will on occupied people through an organized system of collecting taxes. Every individual paid a set of taxes: a 10 percent tax on all grains, a 20 percent tax on wines and oils, and taxes on personal income. Additionally, taxes were levied on roads, marketplace items, axles on carts, and import and export transactions.

The Romans divided geographical regions into districts and assessed each district a specific tax amount. They then hired out the dirty work of collecting the taxes to those willing to work within the oppressive system. The system was rife with abuse. As long as Rome's assessments were paid, tax collectors could set fees at higher amounts and pocket the difference. The result was threefold: (1) tax collectors were never invited to business schools to lecture on "Ethics in the Workplace"; (2) a poor tax collector was an oxymoron; (3) tax collectors (often Jews who collaborated with the Romans) were less fondly regarded than professional athletes who turn their backs on hometown teams for bigger paychecks with rival clubs.

To this tax collector, Jesus says, "Follow me." God's transformations are good news not only for the poor and downtrodden, but for those on top of the heap as well. Of course, Levi doesn't take his tax booth with him. In light of his immediate response, it appears a trade-off he's willing to make.

What have you left behind in order to embrace a higher cause?

Granada, Nicaragua

INSTITUTIONALIZED SINNERS
Luke 5:29-30

Levi gave a dinner party for Jesus in his house. Also attending were many tax collectors and unsavory people. The religious leaders and scholars complained to Jesus, "Why do you eat and drink with tax collectors and sinners?"

+

It's one thing for Jesus to violate a Sabbath law or to walk around claiming a cozy relationship with God, but quite another thing to hang around with the wrong people, especially to share a meal with them. "Why do you eat and drink with tax collectors and sinners?" Jesus is guilty of laxity. He seeks out the presence and enjoys the company of those who aren't good enough to worship in the temple. That's enough to push the piety-conscious clergy over the edge, then and now.

The term *sinners* as used in Jesus' day has a different connotation than our understanding of the word. Today, we might collectively admit that, to a greater or lesser extent, we're all sinners. In the first century, however, sinners were those who failed to keep the holiness laws. Found primarily in Leviticus 17–24, the holiness laws outlined the necessary requirements for maintaining ceremonial and ritualistic purity. Those laws also provided regulations on topics as varied as farming, sexual relations, and fabric used in clothing.

In Jesus' time, there were sinners and non-sinners, those who failed to keep the holiness laws and those who followed them. Certain occupations deemed morally corrupt, like collecting taxes for an oppressive empire, automatically kept a person off the "non-sinner list." The list also included shepherds, because they couldn't keep the cleanliness codes to save their lives, and poor people, who couldn't contribute to the temple treasury. Today, some would add to the list the homeless, undocumented immigrants, and, of course, those whose sexual orientation or gender identity is outside the accepted norm. Some things never change. We still keep score of who's in and who's out.

What would association with the wrong people look like for you?

WELL AND SICK
Luke 5:31-32

Jesus answered, "Only the sick need a doctor, not those who are healthy. I'm here not to call good people to repent, but sinners."

+

We might expect Jesus to say, "Look, everyone needs a doctor from time to time. No one is exempt from the sin disease. All people are sick, whether they realize it or not. There's no such thing as a well person. Anyone who thinks about getting through this life and on to the next without me is a fool."

Jesus, however, does not take this opportunity to rip into the institutional/hierarchical/externalized/fossilized/elitist religious system to which some religious leaders have devoted themselves. In fact, the "healthy" and the "good" Jesus is referring to *are* the religious leaders. That's a compliment of the highest order.

In this teaching moment, Jesus resists laying out an either/or worldview. The "sick" and the "healthy" are embraced together—those who need treatment and those who don't. Jesus is saying to those who prefer the purity-by-separation way of living, "Okay, if you want to live that way, then live that way. If you think you're perfect, good luck trying to live up to that standard. You won't be happy. You'll be stressed out. You won't sleep well because you'll fret that someone else might be having a good time. You'll be more susceptible to peptic ulcers and high blood pressure, and you'll probably die a premature death. Your attitude will be so annoyingly self-righteous that others will reach for the doorknob whenever you walk into the room. But if that's the way you see it, then so be it. In God's house, there are more rooms than you can count, and there's even one for you. Now if you don't mind, I'd like to finish my meal."

What does wellness look like to you?

FASTING FROM FASTING
Luke 5:33-35

Then the religious leaders said to Jesus, "Disciples of John the Baptist often fast and pray like our followers do, but your disciples never miss a meal." Jesus replied, "You can't expect friends of the groom to fast when he's still with them, can you? The day will come when the groom will be taken away; that will be the time to fast."

+

Not wanting to drop the issue, the religious leaders continue their attack. "Look, Jesus, everybody knows that true representatives of God fast. We fast. John the Baptist fasted, and so do his disciples. Holy people fast. You and your disciples seem to ignore this discipline. Frankly, that concerns us. What do you have to say on the matter?"

It's a question asked from their own experience. The only required fast was the one that took place once a year on the Day of Atonement. These religious leaders, however, regularly fasted twice a week, usually from six o'clock in the morning until six in the evening on Mondays and Thursdays.

Jesus is no stranger to fasting; he fasted forty days in the wilderness of temptation. His reply to the criticism suggests that the issue centers on appropriateness and timing. When the bride and groom host the weeklong reception in honor of their wedding, it is not appropriate to take a pass on the food in favor of fasting. This is the time to honor the couple by eating and drinking. Anything less would be inhospitable.

The joy of the celebration is a gift we receive. Fasting is a discipline we offer in response to generosities given us. There's a time and place for each.

What's been your experience with fasting?

DO THE MATH
Luke 5:36-39

Jesus told a story: "No one tears a piece of cloth from a new garment and sews it on an old one; this will damage the new garment, and the new piece of cloth won't match the old. Likewise, no one pours new wine into old leather sacks; the new wine will burst the leather and spill out. New wine must be poured into new leather sacks. No one drinking aged wine wants new wine, but says instead, 'This aged wine is best.'"

+

Old ways are hard to give up. The simple solution is to adopt just enough new strategies to fix the old. The result is a win/win solution. We get to keep the familiar while we welcome the new.

Businesses do this all the time. Fast-food restaurants keep their fat-laden staples while adopting health-conscious salad menus too. Car makers keep gas-guzzling models but also offer a model or two you can plug in. The old is tweaked to accommodate the new.

The old system of separating the "clean" and the "unclean" won't do. The old way can't be fine-tuned, readjusted, or patched with the new. The issue is one of incompatibility.

Making room for the new while attempting to hang onto the old was an issue that plagued the early church. Many insisted on merely adding Jesus as a supplement to the established traditions, suggesting that Jesus *plus* something creates what God intends. Here are some ways (past and present) how the spiritual math works out:

Jesus + circumcision = church membership
Jesus + kosher foods = a religious diet
Jesus + speaking in tongues = mature Christianity
Jesus + heterosexual orientation = traditional values
Jesus + male gender = godly leadership
Jesus + free enterprise = God's economy
Jesus + military dominance = one nation under God

The math was faulty in Jesus' day. It's still faulty in our day.

Which equations do you feel are legitimate? Which ones are repulsive?

88

SABBATH SPAT
Luke 6:1-5

While Jesus was walking through a field on the Sabbath, his disciples plucked some heads of grain, rubbed them in their hands, and ate them. Some religious leaders said, "Why are you breaking the Sabbath law?" Jesus answered, "Haven't you read what David did when he and his companions were hungry? He entered God's house and ate the holy bread, designated for the priests only; then he shared it with his companions. Human beings take precedence over the Sabbath."

+

The tension between Jesus and the religious leaders in the previous chapter evolves into a full-blown controversy. The issue concerns appropriate Sabbath behavior. The Sabbath (meaning "rest") is the Hebrew day of worship. Sabbath observance begins at sunset on Friday and extends to sunset on Saturday. Sabbath roots go back to God's own day of rest after completing creation.

Specific Sabbath regulations and prohibitions appear throughout the books of Exodus, Leviticus, and Deuteronomy. Sabbath laws were serious matters, as evidenced in this command: "You must keep the Sabbath, because it is holy. Everyone who violates the Sabbath will be put to death; whoever works on the Sabbath will be cut off from the people" (Exodus 31:14).

The religious leaders accused Jesus' disciples of violating Sabbath laws because they helped themselves to a roadside snack. Though the laws mercifully permitted a hungry traveler to pluck heads of grain from another's property, the disciples crossed the line when they rubbed the heads of grain in their hands. This action, considered a form of work, was a clear violation of the Sabbath laws.

Jesus, however, reminds the Sabbath-watchers that even King David set aside a religious law in favor of meeting human need—the way God intended. This won't be the last time Jesus teaches his critics a Sabbath lesson.

How do you observe Sabbath rest?

A QUESTIONABLE HEALING
Luke 6:6-11

On another Sabbath, while Jesus was teaching in the synagogue, there was a man with a misshapen hand. The religious leaders watched to see whether Jesus would heal on the Sabbath so they might accuse him. Sensing their thoughts, Jesus said to the man, "Come here." The man approached Jesus. Then Jesus said to those watching, "Is it lawful to do good or harm on the Sabbath, to save life or destroy it?" No one answered, so Jesus said to the man, "Stretch out your hand." When he did, his hand was restored. Jesus' critics were furious and secretly plotted how they could undermine him.

+

The scene shifts from the cornfields to the synagogue, where Jesus is invited to teach. Luke quickly builds the tension. Suspicious eyes are watching. Accusations are forming. Jesus senses their thoughts. Will he break another Sabbath law by healing the man with a misshapen hand? Will he prove again to be a Sabbath-breaking rabbi?

Like an experienced storyteller, Luke builds the drama. Instructing the man to stand in the midst of the worshippers, Jesus asks the religious leaders whether one should do good or harm, save life or destroy it on the Sabbath. No neutral ground here. Even the decision to do nothing is a decision to do harm.

The Sabbath laws required behaving in one way; Jesus seeks another way. Jesus waits for an answer, but no one dares to give one. Jesus responds to the human misery in front of him in a compassionate act that causes the synagogue faithful to erupt. Furious (literally, "at their wits' end"), the religious leaders confer about how to handle Jesus when such problems arise again.

Some choose to believe that the real miracle here is the healing of the hand. Maybe so. But perhaps Luke merely uses the hand as a stage prop to demonstrate an even greater wonder: the miracle of legalism trumped by human need. If, in the face of human suffering, the decision to do nothing is no better than the decision to do harm, of how many harmful acts would Jesus find us guilty?

What has been your experience with a law standing in the way of justice?

THE TWELVE
Luke 6:12-16

Once Jesus went to a mountain and spent the night in prayer. The next day, he called his closest followers and chose twelve, whom he named apostles: Simon (Jesus named him Peter), and his brother Andrew, and James, and John, and Philip, and Bartholomew, and Matthew, and Thomas, and James the son of Alphaeus, and Simon (called the Zealot), and Judas the son of James, and Judas Iscariot, who became a traitor.

+

As a leader, Jesus seldom did what many leaders typically do. He didn't rely on opinion polls. He didn't write a book on successful leadership strategies. He didn't sit on an advisory board or run for public office. He shunned mass mailings and glossy brochures. He didn't build a website, open a Facebook account, or ever send a 140-character tweet. Yet, if the technology had been available, I imagine Jesus would have been a savvy communicator. I wonder: Mac or PC?

What Jesus does as a leader provides some clues to his identity and ministry. To begin with, he prays. He prays a lot. On good days, he prays. On bad days, he prays. The more his critics chirp, the more Jesus prays. The more the crowds swell, the more Jesus prays. The more the sick and afflicted require his time, the more Jesus prays. Sometimes he prays in marathon sessions, through the night, without sleep. Other times, he launches single-sentence prayers on the run.

Jesus attracted many followers and disciples. From the crowds, he chooses twelve to train as apostles—the "sent ones"—who will carry on his work after his death. Of this elite dozen, some are fishermen, one is a tax collector, and one will become a traitor. It's hard to know what skill set Jesus saw in them—perhaps only a readiness to learn what he was willing to teach. When the selection process is between availability and ability, Jesus opts for the former every time.

How do you practice availability?

ALL OF THEM
Luke 6:17-19

Jesus came down from the mountain and stood in an open area. Many followers and a large crowd of curious people from Judea, Jerusalem, and the coastal towns of Tyre and Sidon were waiting. They came to hear him and to be healed of their diseases. Even those afflicted with unclean spirits found wholeness. Many tried to touch him in hopes of a healing.

+

Jesus isn't content to remain on the mountain. A coming down always follows his going up. His popularity is growing. People from Jerusalem, ninety miles to the south, and from western cities on the Mediterranean Sea, suggesting a non-Jewish population, seek him.

Three groups are identified: The newly appointed twelve apostles form Jesus' inner circle. A large number of disciples, less intimately connected to Jesus, are around them. Finally, a great multitude gathers with interest, fascination, and curiosity.

Everybody wants to get close to Jesus. Everybody wants a piece of him. Some grasp his clothes. Some feel his skin. With each desperate touch, wholeness-delivering power is seemingly released like water from a hydrant. Jesus heals all of them. All of them, regardless of their background and citizenship. All of them, regardless of their lot in life. All of them, regardless of their depth or lack of faith. All of them, Jew and non-Jew, male and female, heterosexual and homosexual. All of them, the hyper-curious and the hypercritical. Everyone leaves affected.

It's a healing Woodstock, a healing World's Fair, a healing Olympics. One wonders whether the devil is looking on and musing over the sight, "You may have said No to me in the wilderness, Jesus, but this spot in Galilee will do just fine."

Lavishness rules the day. With reckless abandon, the life-changing graces flow as if pumped from a bottomless well. Nothing is measured and rationed, nothing meagerly calculated in droplet doses. The multitudes seek and feast on him until Jesus grants wholeness of body and mind. They go home freer and emotionally lighter than when they arrived, less oppressed by what others think of them. Healing comes.

In what ways have you received more of a good thing than you expected?

THE BLESSINGS
Luke 6:20a

Then Jesus spoke to his followers: "You are favored . . ."

+

The sayings of Jesus commonly known as the Beatitudes are one of the most treasured literary expressions in the world. Recorded also in Matthew's gospel where eight are listed, the Beatitudes in Luke comprise four sayings about poverty, hunger, sorrow, and persecution.

The Greek word from which we derive the word *beatitude* is *makarios*—a quality or condition attributed to Greek gods whose blissful state was believed to be independent of any random conditions in life. The blessedness to which these sayings point is deeper than any happiness we might enjoy when positive experiences come our way.

The Beatitudes are not instructions or commandments. We're not given a new set of behavioral patterns to follow. There is no directive to "go and do likewise." Jesus lays down no moral or ethical obligation, not a single "ought" or "should." These aren't *pre*scriptions for how to live, but *de*scriptions of people who have experienced God's favor.

The Beatitudes suggest a present and future dimension, an "already but not yet" reality. What God *will* bring about in transforming the social order is, in part, *already* happening. The poor, the hungry, the sorrowful, the persecuted are blessed and favored *now*, precisely because God's reign is breaking into the world.

How these sayings are received depends upon where one sits. Those on the top will tend to shove them into the genre of proverbial sayings—nice but hardly relevant. Those on the bottom will embrace them as a present claim and a future promise.

The Beatitudes remind us that we need not offer God something to receive a blessing. Rather, in our poverty, hunger, sorrow, and suffering, the blessing of God's fullness is ours already. Let's explore these Beatitudes and see how this is possible.

Where are you most blessed?

BLESSED POVERTY
Luke 6:20b

"You are favored by God if you're poor, because you're close to God's heart."

+

If you have any knowledge of the Beatitudes, you probably know them from Matthew 5. The gospel writers differ not only in the number of Beatitudes recorded, but in style, implication, and meaning. Nowhere is this more evident than in the saying about the poor. In Matthew's version, Jesus directs his words to the "poor in spirit." In this usage, the poor are the humble and devout who seek God. Through the ancient prophet, God speaks: "This is the person I notice: the one who is poor and contrite in spirit" (Isaiah 66:2).

In Luke's version, Jesus may be including the poor in spirit, but it seems a more specific condition is implied. The poverty of which Jesus speaks includes not merely a condition of the heart, but one of the wallet and bank account. This is an audience made up of mostly peasants and rural folks living under Roman domination. Life is hard. Scarcity abounds. Oppression is real. Most of these folks don't have enough to eat. They have no access to systems of power. They don't count, and that's about as poor as one can get.

How, then, are those in this poverty-infested condition favored? Their lives get noticed by God, and on them God's favored presence is pleased to rest. The poor might live at life's margins, but there are no margins in God's heart. That Jesus' ministry is to, for, and with the poor is the clearest indication of where God's deepest concerns abide.

A few statistics worth gnawing on: One in five people on the planet lives on less than a dollar a day. The top 1 percent of the world's richest people have a combined wealth equal to that of 60 percent of the world's population. Four hundred American billionaires control as much wealth as 150 million American citizens. Who is more able to recognize that the world belongs to God?

Where have you experienced the poverty of this Beatitude?

BLESSED HUNGER
Luke 6:21a

"You are one of God's own if you're hungry now; the time will come when you will be filled."

+

Numbers and statistics often numb our senses, but these are difficult to shrug off: According to the organization Bread for the World, nearly 15 percent of the world's population (925 million people) are hungry. Every day, almost 16,000 children die from hunger-related causes. That's one child every five seconds. Twelve children will die in the time it takes to read this meditation. Stretch that over a year and you wipe out the population of Maryland.

Matthew's version of this Beatitude reads, "Blessed are those who hunger and thirst for righteousness." A lot of good sermons encourage people to hunger and thirst for righteousness. I don't know if as many have been preached on hungering for food and thirsting for water.

The same questions come to mind here as with the previous Beatitude: What does Jesus mean? Is he downplaying their condition? Is he turning the hungry away from their plight in order to focus them on God's abiding presence? Are the hungry more holy, more God-sensitive than those who don't face such deprivations? How do the hungry ones in the crowd hear Jesus' words?

Throughout the Beatitudes, there's no mention of one's faith index or belief quotient or piety scale. None at all. What stirs God's heart to promising a more benevolent future are the conditions and circumstances one is called to endure in this life.

In his ministry, Jesus feeds the hungry rather than merely conferring a blessing on them. Global hunger and starvation have gotten worse since Jesus' time. In some religious circles, we haven't gotten past the "saving souls versus filling stomachs" discussion. Jesus is concerned with both, but more often than not, he opts to fill stomachs.

God grieves over our reluctance to put all our resources and brainpower into ending hunger on the planet. The real tragedy in our lack of will is that, in refusing to follow Jesus' lead, we miss the chance to deal with our own hungers.

In what ways are you hungry?

BLESSED SORROW
Luke 6:21b

"You are not forgotten by God if you're weeping now; one day you will laugh."

+

We might not know poverty and we might not know hunger, but all of us have experienced the reality of sadness and sorrow. We all weep. Tears are a staple ingredient in life's recipe, and they arrive from all directions. There are tears of loss and tears of regret, tears of unfulfilled dreams and tears of hopes dashed, even tears of anger.

Though we might not realize it, when we weep we're in the great company of biblical people for whom weeping was not foreign. The patriarch Jacob mourned when he was told the news of his son Joseph's supposed death. David mourned the death of his son Absalom. The Hebrew prophets cried out and mourned the inequities and injustices throughout the land. Peter mourned after denying he knew Jesus. Mary and Martha mourned the death of their brother Lazarus, and so did Jesus. Jesus also mourned the stubbornness of Jerusalem. When we weep, we find ourselves good company.

Most enduring lessons come through weeping. Though we might not see those lessons when our eyes are filled with tears, it's possible to grasp them in retrospect. After a tragedy, illness, or misfortune, we discover a deep awareness about ourselves and God. We become wiser, less judgmental, a friend of patience.

Weeping, however, doesn't always work that way. We can easily turn into bitter people rather than better people. Though the world's wisdom suggests we should avoid sorrow at all costs, Jesus reminds us that tears are vessels holding deeper lessons. The times our tears make us better are occasions to rejoice, to be glad, maybe even to laugh. Through it all, God does not forget those who weep.

When did your tears soothe your heart's ache?

96

Holy Door, St. Peter's Basilica, Vatican City

BLESSED REJECTION
Luke 6:22-23

"You're cared for by God when people hate you, exclude you, ridicule you, and attack your character on account of me. Be glad and content; a great reward is waiting for you. Remember, that's what the prophets' ancestors did to them."

+

Let's be clear: Jesus isn't talking here about any kind or every kind of persecution. This Beatitude is persecution-specific. It's the hatred, exclusion, ridicule, and defamation suffered because we seek to live in the manner of Jesus. In other words, when his life is the life we seek to embrace, the odds are good we'll get the same ill treatment he did. Standing with the lost, the last, the least, and the lonely is no guarantee the world will nominate you for sainthood, or even pat you on the back.

Rejection is a reaction we should anticipate, always. Therefore, a creed for such occasions might be to our benefit:

When faced with persecution's arrows, I'll find refuge in knowing such things Jesus predicted: "You'll be hated, excluded, ridiculed, and attacked."

I'll find comfort in the company of disciples and saints who, long before me, felt the sting of such suffering: of Abel slain by Cain, of Elijah chased by Ahab, of David pursued by Saul, of Mary Magdalene scorned by the self-righteous, of Paul imprisoned in Rome.

I'll not respond to hostility with more hostility or fuel hate with more hate. I'll remember the words of Jesus, who promised a reward great, not always in the present, but surely in what is yet to come.

Who has modeled for you how to endure under pressure?

OUAI! *(oo-ah-EE)*
Luke 6:24-26

Jesus issued a warning: "Woe to the rich; you've received your comfort. Woe to you who have it all; one day you'll be hungry. Woe to you who laugh now; the day will come when you'll cry real tears. Woe to you when everyone speaks glowingly of you; that's exactly how your ancestors treated false prophets."

+

We long to live in a world that's neat and orderly. We draw lines, connecting them to form boxes. In separate boxes, we put the haves and the have-nots, those who are in and those who are out, those blessed and those cursed. The labels help us sort things, determining where we stand and who stands with us or against us.

But what if good and evil, blessings and curses are mixtures within each of us, mixtures we can't fully separate? Aleksandr Solzhenitsyn observed, "The line between good and evil runs not only through nations, but through the heart of every individual." If one dares imagine oneself as a mixture of good and evil, of rightness and wrongness, then Jesus' "woes" find in each of us a target in the same way his blessings do.

In Greek, the word for *woe* is pronounced *"oo-ah-EE"* and is used as a curse, an expression of contempt. It's also used as an exclamation of grief. I'm the "blessed" person—poor, hungry, mournful, and reviled. I'm also the "woed" person—rich, full, laughing, befriended. Not one or the other, but simultaneously both.

The Beatitudes comfort the afflicted parts of me; the woes afflict the comfortable parts of me. They cut in order to heal; they cut in order to expose. God refuses to leave us alone.

Where is the woe currently heard in your life?

ALTERNATIVE LIFESTYLE
Luke 6:27-28

Jesus continued to teach: "Love your enemies, do good to those who hate you, bless those who curse you, pray for those who treat you badly."

+

Jesus dangles in front of us the impossible. Just love! Love everybody! The good, the bad, the ugly—love them all! Huh? Maybe Jesus says outlandish things and employs hyperbole because he knows anything less won't move us from the place we prefer to stand. Maybe his strategy is one of diminished expectations. If he can't get us to move a foot, perhaps with exaggerated statements he can get us to move at least an inch.

If loving one's enemies is beyond one's capacity, maybe loving the co-worker who's a constant irritation is within reasonable grasp. If loving my enemies is more than I can do, perhaps loving my neighbor who doesn't see the value in recycling plastic will come easier. If loving your enemies is not within your power, perhaps loving your alcoholic brother-in-law is.

I like this logic. It's a palatable strategy. Start with an unreasonable expectation to get us to attempt a less taxing one. Brilliant! And wrong. Jesus doesn't suggest the highest ideal so we can be satisfied with a lesser ethic. He means what he says. Love even those who hate you. Bless even those who curse you. Pray even for those who treat you horribly.

Maybe Jesus makes this statement not for the sake of the enemy alone, but for our sake too. Something happens to us when we love those whose actions toward us don't warrant our love. Something happens to us when we choose not to respond with hatred, cursing, and ill treatment. What happens is that we embrace an alternative lifestyle. We begin to take seriously Jesus' life. We move the world a little closer to the world God intends.

Which enemy do you find hardest to love?

RECIPROCITY BROKEN
Luke 6:29-30

"If anyone slaps you on the cheek, offer the other cheek as well. If anyone takes your coat, offer your shirt, too. Give to everyone who begs. If anyone takes away your stuff, don't ask for it back."

+

How do we break the cycle of needing to get even after we have been taken? How do we live in a way that reflects what God intends for our relationships? Turning the other cheek, giving the shirt off one's back, and unquestioningly helping those who ask are responses that don't come naturally. Ten thousand times—that's what it takes to make a new behavior a part of our being. Here are some revisions and updates to what Jesus said:

Break the cycle of reciprocity; a slap on the cheek doesn't require a return slap. Take the initiative and respond with a new way of interacting. Don't exchange insult for insult; you're better than that. You don't have to live passively; try to understand others. You might lose your shirt, but you'll never lose your dignity. Stop keeping score; life isn't about the win/loss column. Give to those who ask, and don't keep track. If you err, err on the side of generosity. Yes, it's a vulnerable way of life, but it's the only life worth living.

Don't expect others to return your generosity; however, they might surprise you. Sometimes you'll be taken advantage of, but the joke will be on them. Don't sing "poor old me" victim songs; you can choose how to respond. Bookkeeping is a good business practice, but don't use it for keeping track of wrongs done to you.

Act this way, and those determined to take advantage of you won't know what to do. Once you've disarmed them, you're making God's dreams real.

Which revision and update is toughest for you?

THE GOLDEN RULE PRAYER
Luke 6:31

"Treat others like you want others to treat you."

+

All religions claim a version of this. The ethic rings true for Christians, Jews, Muslims, Hindus, and nearly every faith tradition that seeks to put beliefs into daily practice. Treat others as you wish to be treated—the Golden Rule. It may be the one exhortation that keeps us from blowing up the world.

Lest we deceive ourselves and imagine that on our own we can live the Golden Rule, fourth-century bishop Eusebius of Caesarea offered this prayer:

> May I be an enemy to no one and the friend of what abides eternally. May I never quarrel with those nearest me, and be reconciled quickly if I should. May I never plot evil against others and if I should plot evil against one, may I escape unharmed and without the need to hurt anyone else. May I love, seek, and attain only what is good. May I desire happiness for all and harbor envy for none. May I never find joy in the misfortunes of one who has wronged me. May I never wait for the rebuke of others, but rebuke myself until I make atonement. May I gain no victory that harms one of my opponents. May I, insofar as I can, give necessary help to any friends and to all who are in need. May I never fail a friend in trouble. May I be able to soften the pain of the grief-stricken and give them comforting words. May I respect myself. May I always maintain control of my emotions. May I train myself to be gentle, and never anger others because of circumstances. May I not discuss the wicked or what they have done, but follow the steps of good people.

Which part of this prayer is hardest for you to embrace?

IMPARTIALITY ENACTED
Luke 6:32-36

"If you love those who love you, what's the big deal? Even the godless love those who love them. If you do good to those who do good to you, are you special? Even the despicable do that. If you lend to those who will pay you back, do you think you deserve attention? Money-grubbers will lend to anyone in order to get a return. But love your enemies, do good, and lend, expecting nothing back. Your reward will be great, and you'll be children of God. God is kind to the ungrateful and the wicked. Imitate God, who is full of mercy."

+

People who say they interpret the Bible literally, (a) don't; (b) do, but only selectively; or (c) have no idea of the implications of that claim. Lend and expect nothing back? That may work for pencils and trash bags but what about cars or home loans? Nobody takes this literally. God is kind to the ungrateful and wicked; therefore, we should show the same mercy to all? Does a biblical literalist conclude that if God shows lasting mercy to all people, then—ultimately and eternally and forever, in this life and the next—all people receive the same eternal fate?

Biblical faith wreaks havoc on our assumptions about God and the logic behind the universe. How should we think about all this? For starters, God is impartial. Divine love is generous love. In this world, there are saints and jerks, the grateful and the ungrateful, givers and receivers, lenders and borrowers, friends and enemies. God is kind to the whole sordid mix of humanity.

We're called to reflect God's love, showing no partiality and having no expectation that others will reciprocate in like fashion. Most days, this makes no sense at all. That's the truth, the gospel truth. Literally!

Who has a difficult time loving you?

WITHHOLDING JUDGMENT
Luke 6:37-38

"Do not judge, and you won't be judged in return. Do not condemn, and you won't be condemned in return. Forgive, and you'll be forgiven. Give, and you will receive a generous portion, densely compacted and spilling over into your lap. What you give will be what you get."

+

Let's have our sensibilities and traditional values shocked even more! In one fell swoop, Jesus erases the lines by which we keep others in check. If we don't judge or condemn, how can we evaluate behaviors?

We can't begin to interpret these verses unless we place them alongside other judging-related passages. For example, Jesus frequently instructs his disciples to use keen judgment when false prophets, re-sembling ravenous wolves, arrive in sheep's clothing (Matthew 7:15). Likewise, the disciples are frequently exhorted to practice vigilance against the multi-layered hypocrisy of some religious professionals. Judgment is necessary when choosing between the real and the bogus. We call this discernment, and it's a valuable virtue.

So, do we judge or don't we judge? Do we condemn or don't we condemn? Franciscan Richard Rohr (*The Good News According to Luke*) suggests that the answer depends on whether we're seeking to control people or discover the truth. Judging for the sake of slapping labels on people, reducing them to a subhuman existence, has no place in God's community. Such control techniques only serve to prop up our own sense of moral superiority. This kind of judging builds barriers instead of bridges. If you don't think so, consider these judgment-laden labels: welfare mom, illegal immigrant, left-wing, right-wing, radical feminist, white trash, tree-hugger, faggot.

Jesus summarizes his teaching in the boomerang effect: What we give will be the measure we get. In this life? Maybe, sometimes, occasionally, once in a while, sporadically. More likely, the reward is long-term and arrives in ways we don't expect.

What would it be like to go a day or two without judging anyone?

BLIND SPOTS
Luke 6:39-42

Jesus gave an example: "Can a blind person lead another blind person? Of course not! Won't both stumble and fall? A student isn't more important than the teacher, but everyone who is fully qualified will be like the teacher. Why do you see the speck of dust in someone else's eye but don't notice the log in your own? How can you say to a person, 'Let me remove the speck of dust in your eye' when you don't see the log in your own eye? Don't be a hypocrite! First remove the log in your own eye, then you'll see clearly to take the speck of dust out of your neighbor's eye."

+

Like parent, like child. Like teacher, like student. Like coach, like player. Not always true, but enough times it is. Those who serve as our models play an important role in shaping who we are and how we perceive the world. Good and bad habits, strengths and weaknesses often are passed on.

Jesus gives several illustrations related to blindness and vision correction. His use of the phrase "blind person" is a reference to those in the religious community (rogue religious professionals perhaps) who intentionally or unintentionally were leading people astray. What these blind leaders lack isn't mere eyesight, but the capacity for self-criticism. They can't see their own faults, and because of their ignorance, these faults are passed on to others.

With a comical illustration, Jesus more fully develops this self-criticism theme. Imagine, a person with a telephone pole in the eye trying to improve the vision of someone whose eye is impaled with a toothpick. It's as obvious as the eleventh commandment: "Thou shalt first remove the telephone pole in thine own eye before thou goest poking in thy neighbor's eye." It's not the flaw—the log or the speck—that counts against a person but the unawareness of flaws and the unwillingness to examine them that constitute blindness.

How did you feel the last time someone pointed out a flaw in you?

HORTICULTURAL LESSONS
Luke 6:43-45

"A good tree doesn't produce bad fruit, nor a bad tree good fruit. A tree is known by its fruit. Figs aren't gathered from thorns and grapes aren't picked from a bramble bush. Good people are all about producing goodness from their heart, but evil people only multiply evil. The heart produces both."

+

Eight lessons for avid gardeners and for those who occasionally just like to get their hands dirty:

Lesson #1 – Fruit (good and bad) develops over time. A disciple's maturity is never immediate or spontaneous; the dropout rate is a slow and steady attrition, influenced more by neglect than by a single event.

Lesson #2 – Though a good tree doesn't bear bad fruit, even good fruit will rot if left on the branches. Procrastination has caused many a withering. There's such a thing as the opportune time. Indecision and distraction can cause as much harm as any hailstorm.

Lesson #3 – Don't be fooled by images of perfect apple trees in seed catalogs. A tree's real test comes in eating the fruit. The marketing of faith deserves our attention, but form is no substitute for substance.

Lesson #4 – Don't expect to pluck peaches from a pear tree. Nature is quite insistent on that. Don't expect suspension of those laws just for your benefit. No amount of praying will change this lesson.

Lesson #5 – Even the best fruit trees appear dead during dormant months. That isn't the time to judge a tree. Trees, like people, need to practice self-care.

Lesson #6 – No matter how sweet the orange or delicious the grapefruit, some kids won't go near them with a ten-foot pole. Like God's love, some things can't be force-fed.

Lesson #7 – If you've ever witnessed TV preachers unashamedly hawking their wares and arm-twisting their viewers into sending checks, you know that nuts, like fruit, don't fall far from the tree trunk.

Lesson #8 – Prune! Prune! Prune! Get rid of the non-essentials. Live with less and have more. De-accumulate. Put it on Craigslist or eBay. Better yet, give it away. Live free.

Which lesson can you envision putting into practice?

BUILDING CODES
Luke 6:46-49

"Why do you respect me but don't follow my teaching? Someone who hears my words and acts on them is like the person who built a house with a deep foundation on rock. When a flood arose, the raging waters couldn't shake the house because it was solid. But the one who hears and doesn't act is like a person who built a house without digging a solid foundation. When the river rushed against it, immediately the house was ruined."

+

Sometimes it's difficult to distinguish between wise and foolish people. In this parable, both types of persons are receptive to Jesus' words. Each commits to the task of house building, and each must contend with the river's rising and the resulting floods. Regarding life's adversities, wisdom doesn't guarantee exemption and foolishness doesn't necessarily mean a greater exposure. Yet, at the end of the day, the house built on rock remains while the other is swept down the river.

Jesus' use of the word *rock* is laden with rich symbolic meaning, which many of his Jewish hearers would have noticed. "You've forgotten the rock that bore you and the God who gave you birth" (Deuteronomy 32:18). "My deliverance and my honor rest on God, my rock and refuge" (Psalm 62:7). "Trust God forever, for in God you have an everlasting rock" (Isaiah 26:4). To model Jesus' life is to step into the world fully secure that nothing can sweep us away.

Jesus ends his lengthy sermon reminding us that life will present us with many physical trials and emotional tests. Storms will rage. Winds will blow. Rivers will rise. Floods will saturate. Not even those committed to godly living can expect immunity. In and through it all, Jesus offers himself as a non-anxious presence.

What does a solid foundation look like to you?

THE CAPERNAUM CENTURION
Luke 7:1-3

After Jesus finished teaching, he went to the town of Capernaum. A Roman army officer, a centurion, had a highly valued servant who was deathly ill. When he heard Jesus was in town, he sent some of his Jewish friends to ask him to come and do a healing.

+

Capernaum was an important Roman outpost in Galilee, and this centurion is an important cog in the military machinery. His duties placed him in command of a hundred soldiers. Ancient historians were quick to laud and praise the reliability of these steady commanders.

It wasn't uncommon for a centurion to have several servants assisting in administrative details and household tasks. One of these servants is seriously ill. We shouldn't assume that the centurion's primary concern is the potential reduction of his workforce; "highly valued" suggests that the servant is honored and respected and dearly loved. This centurion cares about and cares for his servant.

Though he's a leader in the world's most powerful army, though he's surrounded by dozens of Roman gods and Greek deities, in a life-and-death situation this centurion turns to Jesus. This non-Jew, a foreigner and pagan who lives beyond the geographical borders and faith traditions of Israel, believes that Jesus can do what his lesser gods cannot.

Luke strings together a remarkable arrangement of events in Jesus' life. Rejected at his hometown synagogue, saddled with the charge of blasphemy, labeled a Sabbath-breaker, and viewed with rage by the "faithful," Jesus finds welcome and reception from an outsider.

It's a thematic thread Luke weaves throughout his gospel, a melody line that plays and replays throughout the life of Jesus —the boundaries of God's inclusive circle always expand, and never contract.

Who are the "outsiders" in your world?

SPEAK THE WORD
Luke 7:4-8

The centurion's Jewish friends said to Jesus, "This man is worthy of your time, for he loves our people and built the synagogue for us." So Jesus went with them, but when he was near the house, the centurion sent friends to him with a message: "Jesus, don't trouble yourself, for I'm not worthy to meet you or have you in my home. Just speak the word, and my servant will be healed. I, too, am a man with authority figures over me, and I'm in charge of soldiers. When I say to one, 'Go,' he goes. When I say to another, 'Come,' he comes. When I say to my servant, 'Do this,' he obeys."

+

The Jewish friends give a glowing report of the Roman centurion. Not only is he a good neighbor, but he even financed the construction of their synagogue. On the way to the centurion's home, Jesus meets a second entourage of spokespersons who convey four things. First, the centurion senses the inappropriateness of the situation; a non-Jew inviting a Jew to enter his house has the potential of being a defiling occasion for the Jew. Second, the centurion expresses his own unworthiness to stand in the presence of Jesus. Third, he acknowledges his belief that Jesus' spoken word has the capacity to heal, even from a distance. Fourth, he witnesses to the implicit authority by which Jesus engages the world.

This is the first time such faith appears in Luke's gospel. Up to this point, those experiencing wholeness in Jesus' presence actually see and touch him. Now this foreigner has faith enough to believe that the spoken word alone—uttered from a distance—has power to bring healing. For all who continue to seek a connection to this life-sustaining power, the good news is still the good news. The uttered word continues to heal.

How have you experienced a long-distance healing word?

SUCH FAITH
Luke 7:9-10

Jesus was impressed with what he heard from the centurion. "I haven't found this kind of faith anywhere in Israel," he said. When those who had been sent by the centurion returned to the house, they found the servant in good health.

+

This kind of faith. Jesus doesn't define or dissect it. For all we know, the centurion may have believed Jesus to be the latest miracle worker passing through town and nothing more. This kind of faith. No confession that Jesus is the Son of God, the second person of the Trinity, or the pre-existent Word present before the dawn of creation.

If we're looking for a textbook definition of faith, we might consider other places. But here are a few I keep close to my heart.

> If you follow your bliss, you put yourself on the kind of track that has been there all the while, waiting for you and the life that you ought to be living is the one you are living. (Joseph Campbell)

> What is decisive for all time is not how much we have believed, but that we have believed and followed Christ, however little we have understood about him. (Ernst Kasemann)

> To dare is to lose one's footing momentarily. To not dare is to lose oneself. (Søren Kierkegaard)

> God does not die on the day we cease to believe in a personal deity, but we die on the day when our lives cease to be illuminated by the steady radiance, renewed daily, of a wonder, the source of which is beyond all reason. (Dag Hammarskjöld)

> There are chances yet to be taken on the way to becoming free. (Ted Loder)

Which definition of faith resonates with you?

110

FUNERAL PROCESSION
Luke 7:11-13

Later, accompanied by his disciples and a large following, Jesus headed to the town of Nain, where a funeral procession was taking place. The dead man was the only son of a widow. When Jesus saw her, he was filled with compassion and said to the grieving mother, "Don't weep."

+

Jesus happens upon a funeral procession in the town of Nain, twenty-five miles southwest of Capernaum. The scene is mournful and tragic on several levels. The dead man's mother, in addition to being husbandless, is now without a son to care for her and carry on the family name.

Unlike the centurion who enjoyed a position of power and wealth, this woman knows neither. Not only is she grief-stricken; she is of all people most vulnerable—her son is dead and all means of support and security are dead with him. She has no voice and few rights. A bleak future is her only certainty.

Into the wailing and weeping Jesus walks as an unintended member of a funeral procession for a nameless corpse and a grieving mother. Jesus is emotionally affected (*compassion* literally means "to suffer with"). This isn't secondhand pity, a distant empathy, or a reflex response of consolation. Jesus claims a personal stake with the suffering one. He shares her sorrow. He bears her grief. He takes his place in the company of the weeping.

When a parent dies, the surviving children lose a piece of history. When a child dies, the surviving parents lose an unlived future. In the village of Nain, amid life's losses, we're reminded that Jesus chooses to walk with all who suffer.

Who has been a companion for you in times of suffering?

RISE!
Luke 7:14-17

Jesus got close enough to touch the open coffin, causing the pallbearers to stop. He said, "Young man, rise up!" The dead man did just that and began to speak. The people were afraid, yet they glorified God, declaring, "A great prophet is here! God has been good to us!" Reports about Jesus continued to spread.

+

Nine hundred years before this incident, the Old Testament prophets Elijah and Elisha performed strikingly similar miracles. Elijah raised the dead son of a Zarephath widow (I Kings 17), and Elisha restored to life the dead son of a Shunammite woman (II Kings 4). Luke wants his readers to know that Jesus stands in Israel's prophetic tradition, working signs and wonders. Luke's Jesus shares continuity with the long history of God's people. Jesus reveals the heart and nature of God, a revelation sown and grown in the soil of God's covenant with the Hebrews.

However, Jesus is more than a retooled version of the old. In Jesus, God's new reality breaks into the world and this new reality includes confronting the forces of death. Jesus touches the open coffin, seemingly ignoring the warning of Numbers 19:11 that "Those who touch a dead body will be unclean for seven days." Then Jesus utters the command, "Young man, rise up!"

If we hope to find here an example of robust faith, or any faith at all, we come up short. Luke tells us nothing about the faith of the mother or the faith of the pallbearers. No one asks Jesus to do anything. No one expects a confrontation with the powers of death. Faith is inconsequential here. It's the suffering of others that moves Jesus. In the world where God reigns, death doesn't have the last word, and not even the absence of faith can change that.

When have you experienced the power of life over death?

THE BAPTIST'S QUESTION
Luke 7:18-19

While John the Baptist was in prison, his disciples reported to him all that Jesus was doing. Curious about this, John sent two of them to Jesus with a question: "Are you the one we're expecting, or should we wait for another?"

+

Imprisoned by order of King Herod Antipas, John the Baptist makes a weighty inquiry. A prison cell can prompt an occupant to obsess on life's ultimate questions.

"Are you the one we're expecting, or should we wait for another?" These aren't mocking words, launched from Herod's holding tank and flung in the face of Mary's son. Perhaps there is a hint of desperation in the question, but that's to be expected from a prisoner in a cell with iron bars on the window.

"Are you the one we're expecting, or should we wait for another?" If Jesus is the Messiah, why is he taking so long to start the revolution? Nobody in Rome looks worried. Herod hasn't called for an emergency cabinet meeting.

"Are you the one we're expecting, or should we wait for another?" Could John have misunderstood? Did the warm-up act mistake the main event? Where's the fire and brimstone?

"Are you the one we're expecting, or should we wait for another?" Don't assume John's faith is evaporating because his days are numbered. Just a little confirmation is all he wants.

"Are you the one we're expecting, or should we wait for another?" John heard the reports from his own disciples. No details spared. A healing here, a wondrous deed there, a growing audience everywhere.

"Are you the one we're expecting, or should we wait for another?" John doesn't doubt that Jesus is doing these things. He just wants assurance this is what a Messiah is supposed to do. Is it a God-thing to care for the lost, the least, the lonely, the last? Then why is John still in prison? And why is Herod still in power?

What question would you most want Jesus to answer?

PROOF POSITIVE
Luke 7:20-23

When John's disciples found Jesus, they said, "John the Baptist sent us to find out, 'Are you the one we're expecting, or should we wait for someone else?'" Jesus answered their question, "Report to John what you witness: the blind see, the lame walk, the lepers are cleansed, the deaf hear, the dead are raised, the poor receive good news. Thank God for those who aren't threatened by this."

+

If one of today's world leaders had been consulted, the response to John's question might have taken a different direction.

Don't worry, John, my armies are amassing along the Mediterranean coastline and will embark for Rome from the ports of Caesarea, Joppa, and Sidon. I've called for a draft of all able-bodied men and women between the ages of eighteen and thirty-five. My twelve cabinet advisors and I are meeting daily in an underground war room. I'm not at liberty to disclose the exact location, but it's not far from the Qumran caves near the Dead Sea, an area you know well. I've named this military assault "Operation Liberation." Rest assured, John, this war is a bipartisan effort. God is on our side. The axis of evil will crumble. If necessary, we're prepared to deploy our weapons of messianic destruction, or, as we refer to them, the WMDs. If God is for us, who can be against us? Remember, John, peace through strength.

—*Your Master and Commander*

Jesus incorporates a different strategy, a life-giving affirmation: "Because of me, the blind see, the lame walk, lepers are cleansed, the deaf hear, the dead are raised, the poor receive the good news." What, no building maintenance? No budget appeals? No worship wars over hymns or praise songs? Lives are transformed, proving that personal and social wholeness is possible? Someone needs to get this news out!

What do you believe to be true about Jesus for your life?

JESUS' TRIBUTE TO JOHN
Luke 7:24-27

When John's messengers left, Jesus spoke to the crowd about him. "What did you expect to find in the desert—a reed shaking in the wind? What were you curious to see—someone dressed in plush robes? Look, those who put on fine clothing and live in the lap of luxury occupy palaces. What caught your attention—a prophet? Yes, and more than a prophet. This is what was written about him: 'I'm sending my messenger ahead to prepare the way before you.'"

+

Jesus asks three rhetorical questions which serve to remind people why they've gone out to hear John. Did they go into the wilderness to look at a reed shaking in the wind? A shaking reed along the Jordan River was a metaphor for a person easily swayed by the opinions of others.

Did they go into the wilderness to see someone dressed in soft robes, someone of royalty perhaps? In contrast, John wore a camelhair robe and subsisted on a diet of locusts and honey.

Did they go into the wilderness to see a prophet? Clearly, John was a prophet, but not just any prophet. John was the one whose arrival other prophets had predicted. Four hundred years earlier, God spoke through the prophet Malachi: "I'm sending my messenger ahead of you, who will prepare your way" (Malachi 3:1).

Jesus pays John a laudable tribute. John's the real thing. Not an ounce of phoniness about him. A person of tenacious conviction and focused determination, John lives a lean and sacrificial life preparing the world to recognize Jesus when he comes. John's earthly reward? A prison cell.

Where in your life are you seeking to live more faithfully?

GREATER THAN HE
Luke 7:28-30

"Listen, in this world no one outshines John; yet the least in God's community is greater than he." When people —including tax collectors—heard this, they acknowledged God's goodness because they had been baptized by John. By refusing the baptism John offered, the religious leaders and scholars, on the other hand, effectively rejected God's purposes.

+

After exalting John and his ministry, Jesus makes a statement that's difficult to understand. In his own way, John was great, but not as great as the least significant person who comes under Jesus' influence and actively seeks to bring about God's intentions for the world.

To understand this, it helps to recognize some differences between the two. John was called to point to the coming Jesus; Jesus was uniquely called to embody how God wants us to live. John's task was to prepare the way for another; Jesus' task was to walk the way of God for the world. The one was a signaler; the other was the one signaled. The death of one was a loss to all his followers; the death of the other was a gain for all who seek to live the way he lived.

Even the least of those who come under the life-changing influence of Jesus receive status as children of God's family. Those who were baptized by John—tax collectors and others of similar ilk—realized their own inability to bring about life-enhancing transformation. Those who refused John's baptism—the religious professionals who were convinced they had a monopoly on God—lived as though no one and nothing would ever cause them to change a thing.

The paradox is there if we choose to see it. Only by losing, do we win; only in our losses do we gain. John prepared the way; Jesus walked it.

What does experiencing a loss as a gain look like for you?

116

CHILDREN'S GAMES
Luke 7:31-35

"People today are like children sitting in the marketplace calling out, 'We played the flute for you, and you didn't dance. We wailed, and you didn't weep.' John the Baptist didn't eat bread or drink wine, yet you said he had a demon. I eat bread and drink wine, yet you say I'm a glutton and a drunk, a friend of tax collectors and sinners. I remind you, wisdom is vindicated by the wise."

+

They didn't listen to John and now they're not listening to Jesus. They didn't listen to the prophet and now they aren't listening to the one to whom the prophet pointed. Before Jesus stood the religious leaders and theological scholars, guardians of Israel's spiritual heritage. Some of them refused to listen. They refused to accept either John's baptism of repentance or Jesus' proclamation that God's dream for a new community was already taking shape. Some people are never satisfied.

Jesus is saying, in effect, "We—John and I—played the flute for you and you didn't dance, as one would dance with joy at a wedding. We cried out in mournful wails, and you didn't weep, as one would weep at a funeral. Why are you so stubborn? Why aren't you ever pleased with what you hear? You're never satisfied.

"John lived the austere life and you accused him of having devil issues. You wrote him off as a crazy man. Then, I come along and welcome all sorts of people—lonely people, lost people, people at the end of their ropes—and you call me a social slob and a drunken lush. What's with you? As far as it concerns John and me, we're damned if we do and damned if we don't.

"You wouldn't know good advice if it arrived at your door by registered mail. Maybe you should look around and see the proof right before your eyes. Because of me, the blind see, the lame walk, lepers are cleansed, the deaf hear, the dead are raised, the poor receive the good news. I give people a second chance, and as many chances as they need."

Where do you find your deepest dissatisfaction in life?

117

DINNER TIME
Luke 7:36-38

One of the religious leaders, a Pharisee, asked Jesus to eat with him. Jesus accepted, went to the man's house, and took a place at the table. A local woman—a known sinner—having learned that Jesus was eating there, brought a jar of expensive perfume. She knelt and wept as she washed Jesus' feet with her tears and dried them with her hair. Then she kissed his feet and poured the perfume on them.

+

The growing strain between Jesus and the religious leaders doesn't prevent a certain Pharisee from extending to Jesus a dinner invitation. Nor does the tension prevent Jesus from accepting it. We shouldn't suspect devious motives on the part of the host. He (later identified as Simon) simply wants an evening of good food and spirited discussion with Jesus.

Sharing a meal was a significant form of social acceptance in Jesus' day. One affirmed and confirmed friendships over meals. The meal also reflected social norms and practices. Those with whom you didn't associate beyond the home, you didn't invite to your dinner table.

An open porch or courtyard was the perfect place to catch cool breezes and relax around a sumptuous table. This explains how an uninvited guest finds her way in. This woman is a sinner, perhaps a prostitute or adulterer. Her indiscretions are known to the townspeople. Unable to withhold her devotion, she commits a physical (and sensual) act. With her tears, she washes Jesus' feet. With her flowing hair, she dries them. She kisses his calluses. She rubs ointment on his skin. She does what future worshippers will set out one morning to do . . . to a corpse . . . in a tomb . . . on Easter.

How did you feel the last time someone fussed over you?

118

Rome, Italy

HE WOULD HAVE KNOWN!
Luke 7:39

As the religious leader watched the woman washing Jesus' feet, he thought to himself, "If Jesus were a true prophet, he would know the dubious character of this woman touching him. We all know she's nothing but a sinner."

+

The host is offended, not only with the woman who crashed his party but with Jesus, who was far too at ease with the devotion she lavished on him.

Simon the Pharisee was right about many things; this woman violated all sense of religious propriety. In touching Jesus, she caused him defilement. By letting down her hair in public, she displayed immodesty. If Jesus were a real prophet, he would have protested graciously and sent her on her way. What good is a prophet if he doesn't recognize sin and call sinners to task when they're exposed? Like a bloodhound on the scent, Simon knows a sinner when he smells one. The conventional wisdom of the day labels this woman a definite sinner.

The wisdom of conventional religion is nothing if not decisively clear-cut and unambiguous. Conventional wisdom of any sort doesn't put up with loose ends. That may be why we opt for conventional wisdom more often than not.

Conventional wisdom says: The poor are lazy.
Conventional wisdom says: Not in my neighborhood.
Conventional wisdom says: God helps those who help themselves.
Conventional wisdom says: Close our borders to the south.
Conventional wisdom says: America, right or wrong.
Conventional wisdom says: We've got Middle East oil to protect.
Conventional wisdom says: Gays will fray the fabric of the family.

"If Jesus were a true prophet," Simon protests, "he'd know all about conventional wisdom." That much Simon seems to get right. Jesus is well aware of conventional wisdom, and has no use for it.

With which conventional wisdom do you agree?

SPEAKING IN PARABLES
Luke 7:40-43

Jesus said, "Simon, I've got a story just for you. A certain creditor had two debtors; one owed five hundred denarii, and the other fifty. When they couldn't pay, he canceled both debts. Which of the debtors was more grateful?" Simon answered, "I suppose the debtor who owed the most." Jesus replied, "You got that right."

+

From the Greek word *paraballein*, a parable is a story that pairs a theological truth alongside a seemingly unrelated object in order to make a point. Jesus tells parables for a specific reason. Rather than affirm what hearers think they know about God and how God should act in all circumstances, Jesus shatters assumptions to make a more poignant and startling claim about the ways of God. Reactions to Jesus' parables include confusion, wonder, awe, even outrage, but never indifference.

Two people owed money to a third individual. One debtor owed five hundred denarii; the other owed fifty. A denarius was roughly the equivalent of a day's wage. Five hundred denarii was a little less than a year and a half of wages; fifty derarii, less than a month and a half of wages. A staggering difference of which Simon undoubtedly took note.

The creditor cancels both debts, the big one and the little one. Jesus then asks a rhetorical question, which even a child could answer: "Which debtor will be more grateful and appreciative?" It's a setup by the Master Storyteller, and Simon doesn't anticipate it. He quickly answers correctly. Maybe Jesus nods and smiles slightly when he says, "You got that right." He knows the punch line is yet to come.

How has your understanding of God changed over time?

FAUX PAS
Luke 7:44-47

Jesus said to Simon, "Look at this woman. I entered your house and you didn't give me any water for my feet, but she washed my feet with her tears and dried them with her hair. You didn't greet me with a kiss, but from the time I came in, she hasn't stopped kissing my feet. You didn't anoint my head with oil, but she covered my feet with sweet perfume. Listen, all her sins are forgiven. Her love is great. A person who is forgiven little, loves little."

+

Though Simon the Pharisee is the host, it's the woman who extends to Jesus the gracious gestures and social courtesies. When guests entered a home, the host or the host's servant would remove the guests' sandals and wash their feet. Then the host would offer a greeting with the kiss of peace. Finally, a touch of sweet-smelling incense or a drop of olive oil was placed on each guest's head to complete the welcome. Whatever the reasons, Simon failed to extend to Jesus any of these courtesies.

Does the woman approach Jesus because she knows she's already received forgiveness, or does she come to Jesus hoping to receive forgiveness? It's not clear if Jesus means that because of her hospitality her many sins are forgiven, or that her hospitality is evidence of the forgiveness she has already experienced. Either way, her devotion is extravagant and lavish.

From the Latin words *extra*, meaning "extra," and *vagant*, meaning "wander," the English word *extravagant* literally means "to wander excessively." When one acts extravagantly, one does so without the confines of limits. Of all the charges levied against Jesus, the accusation that he offered extravagant welcome to outsiders and outcasts is one he never denied.

How might someone witness your extravagant welcome this week?

GO IN PEACE
Luke 7:48-50

Jesus said to the woman who had washed his feet, "Your sins are forgiven." Those at the table were offended: "Who does he think he is, forgiving her sins?" Then Jesus said to her, "Your faith has saved you. Go in peace."

+

Jesus forgives her sins and others object, "Just who does he think he is?" Rather than defend his authority, as he did in an earlier confrontation, Jesus directs his attention to the woman: "Your faith has saved you. Go in peace."

The only faith this nameless woman demonstrates is the hope that by approaching Jesus she'll find what she can't find anywhere else. This long-haired, perfume-carrying woman is dead to what the world offers. Her back against the wall, she has nowhere to turn but to this extravagant rabbi who has already healed and forgiven others. Fresh out of options, with nothing to lose because long ago the world labeled her a loser, she lays herself at Jesus' feet and finds herself in God's arms.

There is no indication that she speaks, not even a word. Silently, she offers her soothing and sensual act of worship. Soon, a tear forms in the corner of her eye, then another, and another. Like rivers they flow, witnessing to the sadness she knows. In her tears, Jesus reads her life.

Welcomed by God, forgiven by Jesus, she's told to "go in peace." Where now will she go with this newfound peace? Will she go back to a family that sees her as Jesus does? Will she muster the courage to sit in the women's section of the synagogue? Will she hold her head high while shopping in the marketplace, or will she backslide into her former life and old ways?

Where does anyone go after a life like hers? It's one thing to experience the welcome and forgiveness God offers, but quite another to receive it from others, free of residual blame and shame.

If Jesus said to you "Go in peace," where would you go?

MIXED COMPANY
Luke 8:1-3

Jesus traveled throughout the Galilee region, proclaiming the good news of how God was changing lives. The twelve disciples accompanied him, as well as women including Mary Magdalene (who had been healed from seven demons), Joanna (the wife of King Herod's steward Chuza), Susanna, and many other females who financially supported the group.

+

These verses offer valuable lessons about the makeup of the community traveling with Jesus and teach us something about the nature of biblical leadership. The close-knit community surrounding Jesus wasn't a "men's only" club. Those closest to Jesus included women. Alongside the twelve male disciples (also called apostles) are Mary Magdalene, Joanna, Susanna, and other women counted among the faithful. What new "family values" insights might we learn from married women, like Joanna, who left their husbands, perhaps their children, to hit the road with a popular Messiah?

Those traveling with Jesus made up a diverse economic and social mix. The group included working class fishermen and at least one from an aristocratic background. Levi was a former tax collector. Mary Magdalene was a former prisoner to seven demons.

Why did they choose to follow? One reason is that Jesus invited them to join him, and for some, their experience of healing and deliverance made it impossible for them to refuse. That's how spiritual leadership tends to work; we don't manufacture our calling as much as respond to an invitation that often arrives as a deep urge or gnawing passion.

Anyone who has ever been in leadership will take comfort knowing that Jesus had to deal with financial issues. There were bills to pay, lodging to secure, and food to purchase. This ministry reality makes Jesus a consoling companion to pastors, church treasurers, not-for-profit founders, and just about anyone who operates a worthy cause on two shoestrings. Early on, Jesus learned the wisdom of leaving the fundraising in the hands of a few capable women.

Where do you see mixed-gender leadership working effectively?

HOW GOD PLANTS SEEDS
Luke 8:4-8

People from all over came to hear Jesus. One day he shared this story: "A farmer scattered seeds. Some seeds fell on the path and were trampled; the birds eventually ate them up. Some seeds were thrown on rocks; as they grew, they died for lack of water. Some seeds were cast among thorns; as they grew, the thorns choked them. Some seeds landed on good soil, and when they matured, they produced a hundred times over. Anyone with ears should understand what I'm saying."

+

This parable also appears in Matthew and Mark. All three writers describe the farmer in similar fashion. The farmer is excessive and lavish, wasteful and careless. The farmer sows with a light grip, casting about and letting the seeds fall where the wind carries them. The farmer doesn't place the seeds in the soil—one seed, one hole—as much as fling them by handfuls. The farmer's aim is no better than that of a single-engine crop duster at three thousand feet.

The farmer shows no apparent concern for the various soil conditions that receive the seeds. A more conscientious farmer, mindful that seeds aren't cheap, would avoid paths hardened by a trafficking public. Even city folks know that seeds cast on rocks don't stand a chance of sprouting. What farmer doesn't first hoe the weeds before they rule the garden like neighborhood thugs? The adjectives fit well—the farmer is excessive, lavish, wasteful, and careless.

The farmer scatters seeds in the same way that God creates—profusely and indiscriminately. The farmer scatters seeds the same way God loves—abundantly and generously. So much muchness to God's heart! It's enough to drive a seed-counter crazy. The prize is an occasional hundredfold payoff. The price is experiencing failure three out of four tries.

Where do you experience God's muchness?

SECRET SEED
Luke 8:9-11

The disciples asked Jesus about the meaning of the story of the farmer and the seeds. Jesus said, "I'll tell you the secrets of how God operates in this world. For others, however, I'll use stories, so that even though they see, they won't perceive, and even though they listen, they won't understand. This is the meaning of the story: the seed is the word of God."

+

Why would Jesus withhold from the crowd secrets he readily shares with his disciples? Why would Jesus teach and preach in ways that obscure from the public truths revealed to his chosen ones? Why keep them guessing? Why the subtleties?

Some suggest that Jesus chooses to use parables precisely because his audience isn't able to understand them. If they aren't ready or willing to hear, why should Jesus waste his time? Others contend that parables hide his messianic claims, which, if openly revealed to the crowds, could morph into nationalistic expectations. Possibilities are found in both explanations.

What, then, is the secret to which Jesus refers—the secret of God's rule and reign? The secret is this: The seed is small. The seed is rejected. The seed is accepted. The seed is sown by God. The seed is God's gift and work. The seed is the word of God. The seed is sown on all types of soils. The seed is nurtured by some and strangled by others. The seed is hidden from the world once the soil covers it. The seed is lavishly tossed on the soil. The seed, though small, is able to produce a hundred times over. The seed—God's seed—is, of all living things, most vulnerable.

Vulnerability—the risk of being plucked up, devoured, trampled, choked, discarded, abused, ignored—is the risk Jesus accepts in living out God's intentions for the world. Considering the unpleasant consequences, it's a wonder he is willing to walk this way at all!

What seed is God growing in you?

SOIL LESSONS
Luke 8:12-15

"The seeds on the path are like those who've heard, but then the devil comes and takes away the word from their hearts so that they end up not believing. The ones on the rock are those who hear the word and eagerly receive it. However, they have no roots; their faith is short-lived, and when times get tough, they fall away. The seeds among the thorns are those who hear, but are choked by life's distractions; their fruit doesn't mature. But the seeds in the good soil are those who hear the word and receive it gratefully, and patiently bear fruit."

+

Most sermons preached on these verses emphasize the soil conditions. Are you hardened soil? Shallow soil? Thorny soil? Listeners are encouraged to cultivate the conditions that make for good soil where God's word can root and grow. The emphasis is placed on what *we* do or don't do to make ourselves more receptive to the seed.

Jesus, however, gives disproportionate attention to seed failure. Three of the four verses deal with the seeds' inability to take root and grow strong. Yet, the farmer doesn't stop sowing, and the failures don't prevent the good soil from producing abundant fruit.

What did this mean to early Christians suffering under Roman persecution? What did this parable mean for the disciples moments before their own deaths as martyrs? What does this fruit-in-spite-of-failure parable mean when an abundant harvest seems a dim hope? What keeps us going through long droughts and deep valleys?

Isn't it this? As the seed, Jesus was despised and rejected, trampled and choked. He was buried in the earth, then lived as a new presence among his followers. Martin Luther observed that Jesus' seed-like life was lived as a mystery in a way that can neither be known nor felt, but only believed and trusted. As a seed he began, eventually becoming the vine, inviting us to be the branches, together abiding.

When was the last time you experienced unexpected fruit amid failure?

LIGHT THOUGHTS
Luke 8:16-18

"No one lights a lamp and hides it under a lid or under a bed. Instead, you put the lamp on a table so that others can benefit from the light. Hidden truths will become clear. Nothing stays a secret for long. Pay attention to how you listen. Those who gain understanding will get more, and those who have little will lose even that."

+

Light separates: "Then God said, 'Let there be light,' and light appeared. God saw that the light was good; then God separated the light from the darkness" (Genesis 1:3-4).

Light brings confidence: "God is my light and my salvation; I have no fear" (Psalm 27:1).

Light is given away: "I've given you as a blessing to the people, a light to the nations" (Isaiah 42:6b).

Light illumines the way for others: "Nations will come to your light, and rulers will see the brightness of your dawn" (Isaiah 60:3).

Light prevails: "Life was in Jesus, and that life was the light of everyone. The light shines in the darkness, and the darkness doesn't overcome it" (John 1:4-5).

Jesus is light: "I am the light of the world. Those who follow me will never walk in darkness but will have the light of life" (John 8:12).

We are light: "Once you were in darkness, but now in God, you are light. Live as children of light with fruit that is good and wholesome" (Ephesians 5:8-9).

God is light: "God is light, and in God there isn't any darkness. If we say that we're one with Christ while we walk in darkness, we lie and don't do what's true" (I John 1:5-6).

Light is forever: "The time is coming when night won't exist. People won't need lamps or the sun, for God will be their light, and they will live forever" (Revelation 22:5).

How will you be light this day?

128

THE NEW TRADITIONAL FAMILY
Luke 8:19-21

Jesus' mother and brothers were looking for him, but they couldn't get near him because of the crowd. Some people said to him, "Your mother and your brothers are here and they want to see you." Jesus replied, "My mother and my brothers are those who hear God's teachings and do them."

+

Considering how often the phrase "traditional family" is uttered by religious folks, Christian talk show hosts, and some politicians, one would think the Bible has a lot to say on the topic. It doesn't!

A traditional family, some say, consists of a man and a woman (gay couples not included), preferably in their first marriage (though no points are deducted if this isn't the case), along with their children (adopted children count). The husband is the head of the home. Oddly enough, it's nearly impossible to find a traditional family in the Bible.

I tested this out on Hebrews 11 where we find a spiritual Hall of Fame of fifteen biblical notables. I applied the following "anti-traditional family" filters: the person was part of a family where members murdered each other; the person murdered someone outside the family; the person got drunk and exposed himself to his children; the person offered his wife as a sexual partner to a world leader; the person was willing to sacrifice his son; the person had more than one wife (simultaneously), or one wife and many concubines (simultaneously), or many wives (simultaneously) and many concubines (simultaneously); the person was a prostitute; the person murdered his own daughter; the person was such a lousy father that God despised his sons.

After applying these "anti-traditional family" filters, only Enoch is left standing. We know little about Enoch other than that he "walked with God," and apparently didn't die a normal death (Genesis 5:24). If Enoch was married, you can bet he enjoyed the company of many concubines. The "anti-traditional family" filter would toss him out.

Jesus reminds us that the only family that ultimately counts is the community where the hearing and doing of the life-giving word is practiced. All other definitions are neither biblical nor moral.

How many family configurations exist in your circle of acquaintances?

129

STORM FRONT
Luke 8:22-24

One day, Jesus got into a boat with his disciples and said, "Let's cross to the other side of the lake." So they set out, and while they were sailing, Jesus slept. A gale-force wind swept down on the lake, and the boat started to take on water. Realizing the danger, the disciples woke Jesus and shouted, "Master, Master, we're going to die!" Jesus rebuked the storm and ordered it to stop. Just like that, all was calm.

+

God's presence in the world is hidden to those who can't or won't see, but revealed to those with eyes and ears open. Like a vulnerable seed hidden in the ground, God's transformational work starts small only to grow a hundred times over. God sheds light on the world, but one can easily hide it for a time if determined to do so.

Jesus' recent teachings emphasized the vulnerability of God's way in the world. His demonstration on the Sea of Galilee, however, emphasizes God's power over nature's forces. In ancient mythology, opposing gods often battled for superiority on the seas. In Hebrew literature, the sea was frequently the arena in the struggle between Satan and God.

With much at stake, including their own lives, the disciples' panic is understandable. They are about to die. But Jesus rebukes (literally, "muzzles" or "gags") the wind and the waves, taming the raging chaos in a manner reminiscent of God's spoken word in Genesis 1. The power of God, Luke wants his readers to know, resides in Jesus.

We learn some lessons in places we'd just as soon leave—on hospital beds, in unemployment lines, at gravesides, in places that remind us of our brokenness. Storms always arise. Whether or not Jesus stills all our storms, who can say? The miracle is that we never ultimately perish.

What was your last storm front?

130

MAKING CONNECTIONS
Luke 8:25

After Jesus calmed the storm, he said to the frightened disciples, "Where's your faith?" Afraid and amazed, they said to each other, "Who is this who gives orders to the winds and the waves, and they obey him?"

+

Which poses the greater fear for the disciples: the winds and the waves or the one whom the winds and the waves obey? In either case, the calming of the chaos outside the boat does nothing to calm the chaos within the disciples. The incident that begins in terror ends there.

"Where's your faith?" Likely caught in their throats or lodged in their stomachs. Jesus isn't suggesting that if they had faith, they could do what he did. Rather, he's questioning their fear.

It's curious that the disciples ask, "Who is this?" By Luke's count, Jesus already has performed seven miracles: Peter's mother-in-law healed; a miraculous catch of fish netted; leprous flesh cleansed; paralysis conquered; a misshapen hand restored; a centurion's dead servant raised; and a Nain corpse revived. Most of those miracles didn't leave the disciples wondering about Jesus' identity. Why now do they react differently?

Their question suggests not that they're without a clue, as if wondering aloud, "We have no idea who this man is!" Rather, it's a question asked with the Psalms ringing in their ears. "God, who is as mighty as you? . . . You rule the raging sea" (Psalm 89:8-9). "Then they cried to God in their trouble, and God delivered them from their distress and stilled the storm, and the sea was hushed" (Psalm 107:28-29).

The disciples make a connection—a connection they don't fully comprehend. Amazed and afraid, another Psalm comes to life: "God rebuked the Red Sea" (Psalm 106:9). This one, who a moment ago was sound asleep, has a connection to God like no other person.

When did an event make you both afraid and amazed?

TOMB DWELLER
Luke 8:26-27

Then Jesus and his disciples sailed across the Sea of Galilee to the non-Jewish region of the Gerasenes. When Jesus stepped out of the boat, a demon-possessed man met him. He was naked and lived in the burial tombs.

+

The region of the Gerasenes, located southeast of the Sea of Galilee, included ten major cities built by Alexander the Great nearly three hundred years before the time of Jesus. The Romans later rebuilt them.

Jesus is in a foreign land, a land of pagan worship and unclean practices. Having demonstrated his power over the winds and the waves, Jesus now battles demonic forces inhabiting this non-Jewish region. A naked, demon-possessed man who lives in a tomb confronts him.

Though we imagine ourselves more sophisticated than those who believed in demon-possession, is it always wise to dismiss ancient assumptions? Granted, we've developed treatment procedures and medical prognoses for afflictions the ancients believed were caused by demons. Yet, is that the whole story? To date, there's no medical cure for gambling or lying or bigotry or a host of other destructive behaviors. Look deep enough and most of us have a thing or two we wish no longer plagued us, something we long to get rid of, something in need of . . . an exorcism.

I'm not aware of a dictionary definition of "demon-possession" that would satisfy both ancients and moderns, but I'll offer one: "any affliction of the mind or body that compels a person to live alone among the community of the walking dead." Most of us know what a tomb's interior looks like.

What would you identify as your demon?

132

TREATMENT FAILURES
Luke 8:28-29

When the demon-possessed man saw Jesus, he fell face down and shouted, "Why do you bother me, Jesus, Son of God? Stop tormenting me!" He said this because Jesus had just commanded the unclean spirit to come out. The demon had seized him so many times that he was kept under guard and bound with chains and shackles. Every time, however, he broke the restraints and fled to an uninhabited place.

+

The possessed man recognizes Jesus' authority. He has no doubt who will prevail. Time to negotiate: "Please, Son of the Most High God, go easy on me. I know you're going to win the match—no need to torment me."

Standard treatment protocols proved ineffective. Maximum-security measures failed. Containment strategies couldn't ensure the public's safety. Dark forces mocked any attempts to control him.

This is a community issue. This man's grave condition affects and infects others. Human affliction is seldom a solitary habitation; spouses, children, families, co-workers are drawn into the struggle. The lines separating the sick from the healthy get blurred. Treatment options that sound reasonable on paper don't always hold up in real time. Some play the role of victim. Others want to come to the rescue. Problem-solvers impose their untested solutions on the situation. Some point a finger of blame or internalize the shame. It's contagion by association and nothing is left untouched.

The phrase *total depravity* is much maligned (not always without warrant) in some theological circles. It doesn't mean we're filled with absolute evil and we always act malevolently. Rather, the phrase is a reminder that there is no pristine area of earth or humanity that's untainted or unstained by brokenness and sin. Every nook and cranny, every crack and crevice of this world is touched. To discover a treatment requires that we seek a solution in something or someone bigger than ourselves.

How do you define total depravity?

133

Chicago, IL

LEGION
Luke 8:30-31

Jesus asked the demon-infested man, "What's your name?"
He answered, "They call me Legion." Everyone knew he had
hordes of demons living in him. The demons begged Jesus
not to send them back into the abyss.

+

His name is Legion. We can be reasonably sure this isn't the name
his parents gave him. A legion was a division of five to six thousand Roman soldiers. That this man is inhabited by a swarm of demons, the number of which would stretch the storytelling talents of
most sci-fi writers, attests to his powerlessness to combat them.

Though we may sympathize with his madness, making a
connection to his demon world is no easy maneuver. However, the
fleshing-out of his demons may bring us closer to his world than we
care to admit or imagine.

> He's a slave to five thousand impulses,
> none of which he can control.
> He's a prisoner to five thousand urges,
> none of which he can direct.
> He's beholden to five thousand masters,
> none of whom he can please.
> He's a pawn of five thousand gods,
> none of whom he can satisfy.
> He's held to five thousand expectations,
> none of which he can meet.
> He hears five thousand voices,
> none of which he can identify.
> He's a nail to five thousand hammers,
> none of which he can escape.
> He sleeps in five thousand beds,
> none of which gives him rest.

With which of these demons do you identify?

COLLATERAL DAMAGE
Luke 8:32-35

Numerous pigs were feeding on a nearby hill. The demons begged Jesus to let them enter the herd. Jesus consented. When the demons entered the pigs, the animals rushed down the hill into the lake and drowned. The men in charge of the pigs witnessed this and immediately ran off and spread the news. People came out to see what had happened and found the healed man, clothed and calm. They were afraid.

+

It goes without saying: *Do Not Attempt This at Home!* Luke doesn't give us a pig count, but Mark puts the number at two thousand. The explanations offered by biblical commentators are almost as numerous as the death toll itself. Some say Jesus didn't cause the pigs to cascade down the cliff, but merely permitted the demons to take possession of them. Others conclude that the demons never actually entered the pigs; the stampede was caused by the shrieks of the man during the exorcism. Another line of reasoning concludes that the welfare of a person is more important than the happiness of pigs. The animal rights group PETA might have something to say about that. Who knows? Maybe the question is simply: Why do bad things happen to good pigs?

Jesus' display of power causes no little disruption and leads to a public relations nightmare. Somebody has to clean up the floating carcasses. Pig keepers find themselves suddenly unemployed. Bacon prices soar in the non-Jewish markets.

Once the curious see the man "clothed and calm," they're afraid. No awe-filled wonder. No inclination to worship. No offers to take the guy out for the meal of his life. Are they afraid of the sane man and how they might have to relate to him? Are they afraid of the power Jesus wields and what he'll expect of them? Are they afraid of the transformations Jesus brings and where such transformations might lead? Sometimes we're happier when certain people remain in their bondages and afflictions.

What do you fear most about change?

FEAR FACTOR
Luke 8:36-39

Word spread like wildfire about the man healed of his demons. Soon, all the people of that area asked Jesus to leave because they were afraid. So Jesus got into the boat and was ready to return to the other side. The healed man begged to go with Jesus, but Jesus sent him away, saying, "Go home and tell everyone what God has done for you." Eventually, he went on his way, reporting throughout the city everything that had happened to him.

+

That the man "had been healed" indicates in Greek more than the absence of demons. Literally, the man "had been saved," which suggests this miracle is as much about having a right relationship with the healer as about gaining release from afflictions. The town's reaction to the healing reminds us of the adage "No good deed ever goes unpunished." At least they were polite enough to *ask* Jesus to leave.

For the second time in this story, Luke mentions their fear. There's no indication here that anyone—not the pig farmers, not the townsfolk, not the mayor—doubts that a miracle actually occurred. No one questions whether the man is truly free from that which possessed him. No one grabs the rope or chains or shackles and attempts to bind him again. Guards don't keep a 24/7 watch on him. No one challenges the transformation of his condition. Their reaction isn't unbelief, disbelief, or doubt—it's fear.

The townsfolk redefine for us the nature of faith and of faith's opposite. We assume the opposite of faith is doubt or disbelief. This story, however, suggests that the opposite of faith is fear. Fear is the lack of faith. Fear trusts something or someone not worthy of one's trust. Fear is an anxious demon plaguing us with a past we can't undo, paralyzing the present, and creating a future we dare not face. Fear begs Jesus to leave. Fear prevents us from embracing wholeness.

The healed man can't help himself; he has to tell his story to anyone who will listen. Thanks to Jesus, he's a new person. He can't keep quiet, nor should he.

In what ways do you tell God to leave you alone?

137

WELL-GROUNDED
Luke 8:40-42

When Jesus returned to the other side of the lake, a crowd was there to greet him. A leader in the synagogue named Jairus knelt at Jesus' feet and begged him to come to his house. His only daughter, almost twelve years old, was dying.

+

Jesus returns from the Gentile territory of the Gerasenes to the region of Galilee, where an eager crowd welcomes him. Immediately there is a need: a father's daughter is dying.

As the leader or president of the local synagogue, Jairus is responsible for the daily administration and planning of public worship. The position is one of authority that has earned him the respect of the town's citizens.

However, more than being the leader of a local synagogue, Jairus is a hurting parent—his only daughter is dying. The twinkle in his eye is fading. The light of his life is dimming. Jairus needs help, and the synagogue president isn't so proud that he can't lie face down at Jesus' feet.

The Latin word *humus* means "ground" or "soil." The closest we come to it in English is the word *humility*, meaning "low" or "lowly." From its Latin origin, humility implies "living close to the ground."

Jairus does none of the things we teach our children to do when they meet people in social settings. Parents tell their kids, "Stand tall! Don't slouch! Hold your head up! Maintain eye contact! Offer a strong, firm handshake!" In other words, "Be politely confident!" The unspoken message that usually gets conveyed is "Don't be too humble!"

Jairus chooses to live close to the ground—face to soil, lips to dirt, hands grasping Jesus' feet. The proud, positioned, and well-respected leader of the synagogue, accustomed to others showing *him* homage, can't imagine showing Jesus respect any other way. Jairus knows there's more than one way to be well-grounded.

How do you practice humility?

STEALING A MIRACLE
Luke 8:43-44

Many people followed Jesus as he made his way to the home of Jairus. There was a woman in the crowd who, for twelve years, had been suffering from uncontrollable bleeding. Though she had spent a small fortune on doctors, none could cure her. She came up behind Jesus and touched the edge of his clothing, and immediately her bleeding stopped.

+

In the middle of one pressing need, Luke thrusts another. A woman with needs of her own interrupts the procession. She has multiple problems and a boatload of issues.

As a woman, she's a second-class citizen. She lives in a first-century culture where spiritually minded men wake up each day and pray, "God, I'm thankful that you didn't make me a woman."

In addition to her gender subordination, she suffers from a severe case of bleeding—twelve years of bleeding, constant bleeding, chronic bleeding. Her malady may have been a menstrual condition, a bleeding ulcer, cancer of the colon, or a dozen other possibilities. She hates the color red.

Her financial situation is every bit as dire as her health condition. Forced to run from doctors to specialists, from HMOs to PPOs, from quacks to quick cures, she's broke. No one will give her a loan. No one will buy her a lottery ticket.

Lastly, she's religiously unclean. Her medical condition, if publicly known, would have placed her outside the worshipping community as prescribed by the holiness laws found in Leviticus. She's damaged goods—a sinner.

On a downward spiral, fresh out of options, and as good as dead, she has nothing to lose and nothing to offer Jesus except her desperate touch. A nameless woman. One last hope. Just one touch. Can life get any worse?

What does desperation look like to you?

WHO TOUCHED ME?
Luke 8:45-48

Then Jesus asked, "Who touched me?" No one said anything. Eventually, Peter broke the silence: "Jesus, look at all the people surrounding you." Jesus replied, "Someone touched me and power left me." When the woman with the bleeding condition saw that she couldn't hide any longer, she became anxious. Finally, she stepped forward and told Jesus everything, including her healing. Jesus said to her, "Daughter, your faith in me has made you well. Go in peace."

+

If the woman hopes for a "touch 'n' run" healing to preserve her anonymity, it isn't going to happen. It's impossible to know the tone of Jesus' voice when he inquires, "Who touched me?" Is he upset that he hadn't been asked first? Is he annoyed that someone has taken advantage of him?

I wonder if the question "Who touched me?" reveals deeper relational elements. Is Jesus seeking a deeper connection? On one level, Jesus' question is a matter of pure physicality; by placing a hand on him, someone became spatially present. A body touched his body. A finger touched the fringe of his robe. His question seeks to identify that person.

On another level, though, Jesus' question has less to do with mass and matter than it does with the emotions of his heart. "Who touched me? Whose circumstances in life moved me to react instinctively with compassion? Whose situation was so desperate that touching me from behind was all the fearful heart would permit? Who sought in me what can't be found anywhere else? Who touched me?"

Jesus' question builds a relationship. The woman tells Jesus everything—the twelve years of pain, the isolation, the heartache, the whispers, the bills, the uncleanliness, the shame. She holds nothing back, and neither does Jesus. "Daughter, your faith in me has made you well." Jesus publicly commends her and acknowledges her faith. Jesus brings wholeness and, in the presence of all the witnesses, reminds her and the community that she belongs.

If the opportunity came along, what would you tell Jesus about your life?

NOT DEAD, JUST ASLEEP
Luke 8:49-53

While Jesus was still speaking to the crowd about the woman he had healed, someone came from the home of Jairus with the news, "Your daughter is dead; don't trouble the teacher any longer." Jesus replied, "Don't be afraid. Believe that she will be well." When he got to the house, he didn't allow anyone to accompany him, except Peter, John, and James, and the child's parents. Though everyone was weeping, Jesus said, "Don't weep. She's not dead, just asleep." And they laughed.

+

We return to Jairus and his daughter, a story that brackets the healing of the bleeding woman. Jesus' delay, though causing the healing of one, contributes to the death of another. Disregarding the messenger's news of her death, Jesus continues to Jairus's home and enters the room where the body of the young girl lies.

The grief in the room confirms the certainty of the girl's death. However, scholars remind us that evidence exists in ancient cultures of incidences when people were buried alive. A deep trance or a comatose state easily could appear as death and prompt loved ones to arrange a premature funeral.

Speaking above and against the lamenting affirmations of death, Jesus pronounces a life-affirming diagnosis: "She's not dead, just asleep." This could mean, as some suggest, that Jesus recognizes a trance-like state and detects a faint pulse that others have missed. More likely, Jesus is making a claim about God's power to prevail even in the face of death.

They scoff at his claim. "We're professional mourners, for God's sake! It's our business to recognize death when we see it! Even a third-rate amateur knows the difference between death and sleep!" So does Jesus, and that's why he points to God's power that challenges what we've long believed about the world. Death is not the ultimate power.

Where do you find your place in this story?

141

JUST ONCE
Luke 8:54-56

Jesus touched the girl's hand and said, "Child, get up!" Immediately, she was revived and got up. Then he told them to give her something to eat. Her parents were astounded, but he told them not to tell anyone what had happened.

+

We hear of many men and woman (mostly men, it seems) with names like "Pastor This" and "Reverend That" and "Dr. So and So" who run large ministry empires. Their worship services, praise gatherings, preaching crusades, and healing conventions regularly appear on television at all times of the day and night. Their ministries rake in millions of dollars, much of the revenue from viewers and listeners, $5, $10, $20 at a time.

The ministries that most amaze me are the ones that offer healing miracles. Sometimes these miracles are conveyed through prayer, as the host shares with his listeners that God told him someone with irritable bowel syndrome or carpal tunnel has just received healing. Other times, the host reads testimonial letters sent by listeners who've experienced healing because of the ministry. Always, always, God is praised.

Often these ministries book large venues. The faith-healing pastor invites audience members to come on stage and experience miraculous healing up close and personal. People always come forward. Some come with canes; some push aluminum walkers; some arrive on stage with a bulging spinal disc, a defective heart valve, or an inoperable brain tumor. Broken, sick, and maimed, they come to get healed.

Call me a doubter and a cynic, but I saw Steve Martin in the movie *A Leap of Faith* and I don't buy it. I don't believe in so-called faith healers. In response, I offer a modest proposal, a sure way to turn a doubter like me into a believer and maybe a financial backer. Just once, I'd like to see a coffined corpse (with a doctor nearby holding a signed death certificate) placed on center stage. Then, just once, I want to see the well-coiffed preacher/healer/miracle worker stand beside that stiff, lifeless corpse and say in a booming voice, "Boy/Girl/Man/Woman, get up!" I'd pay good money to see someone do the same.

How has your faith brought healing for someone?

SHARED MINISTRY
Luke 9:1-2

Then Jesus gathered the twelve and empowered them with
authority over all demons and diseases. He sent them out to
heal and to witness about all the good things God was doing.

+

The learners become doers. Those Jesus has called to follow him are
now instructed to walk down roads and enter towns Jesus has yet
to travel and visit. It would be reasonable to assume that the disciples
are elevated to active status because they've demonstrated fitness for
ministry by fulfilling requirements and passing competency exams.
However, it seems the opposite is the case. The disciples repeatedly
prove themselves slow learners, deficient in faith, and doubtful about
who Jesus is and what Jesus came to do. Yet, Jesus sends them out.

Jesus gives them power and authority, gifts without which they
would have neither impact nor influence. Their personality profiles and
temperament analyses are less important than the gifts Jesus bestows.

Jesus defines their threefold ministry: (1) By expelling demons,
they will challenge evil forces. (2) In curing diseases, they will restore
the marginalized to wholeness in the community. (3) As healers of
brokenness, they will point to the transforming work of God in the world.

Who they are and what they're called to do is for the benefit
of others. Their ministry programs are designed for the sake of those
not yet included in their community. Their ministry objectives don't
emerge from a survival mentality ("We've got to keep this organization
intact!") but from the call and mandate to give themselves to the world.

For those serious about taking to heart this notion of *call*, I
propose a modest definition of ministry, suitable for anyone
seeking to make a difference in life. It doesn't say everything that can
and should be said, but it seems a worthy starting place: Find
something you're passionate about doing—something that causes you
to lose all sense of time when you do it, something that gives you a
sense of fulfillment regardless of the money. Learn to do it well.
Then do it for vulnerable and marginalized people who will be
blessed by your presence, and who will never be able to repay you.

What are the ways you bless people by your presence in the world?

TRAVELING LIGHT
Luke 9:3-6

Jesus said to the twelve disciples, "Take nothing for the journey you're about to go on. Take no walking stick or bag, no bread or money, not even an extra coat. When you enter a house, stay there until it's time to move on. If they don't welcome you, walk away and shake the dust off your feet as a warning against them." They went through the villages, curing diseases and bringing the message of God's love.

+

Jesus doesn't woo his disciples with promises of a generous benefits package. They are to take nothing for the road. No walking stick—nothing with which to balance themselves. No bag—nothing with which to carry necessities. No bread—nothing by way of planned sustenance. No money—nothing with which they can meet their own needs. No extra coat—nothing to get them through emergencies.

Lean and light is Jesus' way. Vulnerability is the only possession. The disciples must rely on the grace of God that will come through the hospitality of others. They're not to shop around for the best accommodations, but to accept whatever offers come their way.

Not everyone will be receptive to their ministry and offer them a warm welcome. Nevertheless, failure shouldn't inhibit them from doing what Jesus calls them to do. What will matter most is remaining faithful in using their gifts of power and authority.

The twelve won't be able to hedge their bets by playing it safe in some things and playing loose in other things. Traveling light, without clinging to the usual security handles, will powerfully witness to the God who calls them.

I've preached scores of stewardship sermons and never have I challenged a congregation to recklessly give away its endowment or deplete its savings down to zero just to travel lightly. Had I done so, the more cantankerous church members would have expressed their appreciation by telling me not to let the door hit me in the rear end as I left the premises . . . forever. Take nothing for your journey. The implications haunt me. Some days, I wish I could take the risk.

What stops you from traveling light?

HEROD'S PERPLEXITY
Luke 9:7-9

When the ruler Herod heard about Jesus' ministry, he was perplexed. Rumors were swirling that John had been raised from the dead, that Elijah had appeared, and that one of the ancient prophets had come back to life. Herod said to his advisors, "I beheaded John, so who's this everyone is talking about?" From that day on, he tried to meet Jesus.

+

Herod was interested in all things associated with power. Rome was a powerful empire. Caesar was a powerful emperor. Herod Antipas came from a powerful family. When a powerful one hears about another powerful one, perplexing questions surface: "Who is this new power? Is he the reincarnation of a past power? The slayer of 450 prophets of Baal hasn't reappeared, has he? Could he be another Amos or Jeremiah, a version of Nathan come to taunt yet another king? A beheaded prophet can't come back from the dead, can he? I myself ordered John's death. I saw with my own eyes his bloodied head, severed from his body. He's *got* to be dead. Somebody tell me, who is this going around my kingdom doing such powerful things?"

Herod's perplexity is understandable—a powerful upstart rabbi with twelve underlings in Herod's backyard and no one will give him a straight answer. And all the rumors! If there's one thing an insecure ruler doesn't need, it's more rumors.

So Herod clears his appointment book, sets aside imperial business, and makes repeated efforts to see Jesus. The Greek suggests that Herod "tried to get to know Jesus." Galilee's king wants to get to know Galilee's King. Who can blame him? Perplexity makes a lousy bedmate.

It's likely that Jesus learns of Herod's desire to meet him. Why he feels no compulsion to attend the monthly prayer breakfasts in Herod's White House we'll never know. Maybe some ministries are more important than sipping coffee with the powers that be.

What area of faithfulness in your life might trouble a person in power?

YOU DO IT
Luke 9:10-13a

When they returned from their ministry campaign, the disciples told Jesus everything they had done. Then Jesus took them to the town of Bethsaida. The crowds followed him and he turned no one away. He cared for the sick, and spoke how God was changing the world for the better. Late in the day, the disciples came to Jesus and said, "This is a remote place; send the people into the villages to get something to eat." Jesus replied, "You give them something to eat."

+

Fresh from their mission projects, the disciples report back to Jesus the accounts of their healings and proclamations. Knowing from his own experiences the draining demands of ministry, Jesus immediately takes the twelve on a much-needed vacation to a Bethsaida retreat center. But before they can unwind, the crowd interrupts their downtime. For the rest of the day, Jesus preaches and tends to the sick.

Later, the disciples implore Jesus to send the people off to find food and shelter. We shouldn't conclude that the twelve are insensitive to the crowd; the sun is setting, this is a remote place, and people are hungry. If Jesus doesn't dismiss the crowd soon, people will miss the opportunity to take care of their own needs.

With pointed emphasis, Jesus responds, "You give them something to eat." In response to their notions that these people should take care of themselves, he reminds the twelve of their calling to offer the complete message to broken and hungry people in order to restore wholeness. Feeding people in Bethsaida is as much a ministry as the expulsion of demons and the preaching of sermons.

Let's hear Jesus' words again: "You give them something to eat; if you're too spiritually minded, you're of little use to the world. You give them something to eat; don't imagine ministry tasks beneath your dignity to do. You give them something to eat; so what if they haven't yet grasped the truths you have? You give them something to eat; I don't make distinctions between soul needs and stomach needs. You give them something to eat; that's why I gave you power and authority."

What unique power and authority is for you to use?

146

SCARCITY MYTH
Luke 9:13b-17

The disciples said, "All we have are five loaves and two fish. We can't possibly buy enough food for all these people." The crowd numbered about five thousand, not including women and children. Jesus instructed the disciples, "Tell them to sit down in groups of about fifty each." After they did this, Jesus blessed the five loaves and the two fish, broke them, and gave them to the disciples to give to the crowd. Everyone had enough. The remaining leftovers filled twelve baskets.

+

This is the only miracle story recorded in all four gospels. Is it a miracle more significant than other miracles? This miracle parallels the story of God's feeding of the Israelites in the wilderness in Exodus 16. Jesus provides bread and fish as God provided manna and quail. The twelve tribes of Israel gathered and ate each day; the twelve disciples distribute until the people eat their fill, and then collect twelve baskets of leftovers. The obvious connections would have caused Jesus' audience to wonder: Since Jesus did what God once did, might he have a relationship to the Divine in ways that others do not?

Interpretations abound as to what actually happened to the five loaves and two fish. Some scholars suggest that a physical feeding didn't happen; the crowd was spiritually fed while sitting in Jesus' presence. Others contend that the disciples' altruistic sharing inspired people to dig into their own pockets and share what they had. Some interpreters see in this story a sacramental theme where community and fullness are experienced whenever Holy Communion is celebrated.

There are multiple ways to understand and receive biblical stories. This story finds its place in the tapestry of God's generous dealings with creation. In the midst of apparent scarcity, God creates abundance. From infertility, God makes possible an Isaac, a Samuel, a John the Baptist. From a nation least among the powers of the world, God forms a people. From twelve disciples, God gathers a church. From a handful of bread and a couple fish, Jesus fills a need. Scarcity is nothing more than God's opportunity to provide.

What experiences do you have of scarcity turning to abundance?

OPINION POLL
Luke 9:18-19

Once after a time of prayer, Jesus asked his disciples, "Who do people say I am?" They answered, "Some say you're John the Baptist; others think you're Elijah; and there are those convinced you're one of the prophets raised from the dead."

+

Who do people say I am? Strange that Jesus frames the question this way. A popular public figure never asks, "Who do people say I am?" The assumption that one's identity is already known would lead one to ask, "What do people think of me?" or "Do they like what I'm doing?" or "Do they approve of my agenda?"

Who do people say I am? Jesus knows the rumors. He has inklings of what others say about him. When he asks the twelve for the word on the street concerning his identity, perhaps he does so more for the disciples' edification than his own.

Who do people say I am? Jesus asks the question while riding the crest of public approval. Who raises crucial queries about self-identity when at the top of his or her game?

Who do people say I am? It's an easy question. The disciples merely repeat what they've heard: "Some say John, some say Elijah, and some say one of the prophets." We could add, "Some say a great physician, a rabbit's foot redeemer, a social revolutionary, an American patriot, my best friend, a WASP Savior, a lucky charm, a quarterback's secret weapon."

Who do people say I am? Considering the multiple and perverse ways we fashion Jesus to fit our petty agendas, being mistaken for John the Baptist, Elijah, or one of the prophets must not have been nearly as disheartening for Jesus as the roles laid on him by opportunistic politicians, greedy economic systems, and preachers who proclaim to gullible audiences that "Jesus wants you to be wealthy just like me!"

Who is Jesus to your circle of acquaintances?

GETTING PERSONAL
Luke 9:20

Then Jesus asked his disciples, "But who do you say I am?"
Peter replied, "You're the anointed one of God."

+

Clearly, this is the real question Jesus wants to ask. You can bet he puts added emphasis on the word *you*. Repeating what others have said risks nothing, but answering for oneself requires a personal investment.

Peter answers for himself and, no doubt, for the rest of the disciples. *Anointed one* is translated "Messiah" in Hebrew and "Christ" in Greek. Peter is saying, "You're not merely another prophet, or Elijah coming back to life, or John the Baptist; you're the one who embodies the hopes of our people, the long-expected one."

Luke doesn't tell us how Peter comes to this awareness. Maybe it was a flash of insight or a conviction shaped after months of arduous struggle. Perhaps it became real for Peter while watching Jesus deal compassionately with the sick, or in quiet conversation with Jesus at the end of a day. However it happened, Peter is the first of the twelve to speak aloud what he feels, knows, and sees demonstrated on a daily basis.

As we've already witnessed and will continue to experience throughout Luke's gospel, the designation "Messiah" is packed with multi-layered implications. Depending on where one gazed along Israel's horizon, the anointed Messiah of God would usher in everything from hyper-obedience to the fulfillment of the law of Moses, to ascetic holiness, to a resurgence of nationalism, to armed liberation from the Roman oppressors, to radical forgiveness.

"But who do you say that I am?" That Peter answers correctly is testimony to the Spirit's inner stirrings. That his understanding of Jesus will undergo future reformations, revisions, and realignments is evidence of every human being's imperfect grasp of who Jesus is.

How do you answer Jesus' question?

SHHH!
Luke 9:21-22

Jesus warned them not to tell anyone. "I [The Son of Man] must endure much suffering. I will be rejected by the religious leaders who will plot my death, but on the third day I will arise."

+

Theologians and biblical scholars call it the "messianic secret." Jesus commands his disciples to keep from the public his true identity as the anointed of God, the Messiah.

Jesus has reasons for issuing this gag order. There were as many opinions then about the role of a coming messiah as there are opinions today about the role of the federal government in our daily lives. Jesus refuses to contribute to the rabid speculation. Some enthusiasts hoped Jesus would rival Roman rulers—a threat Rome would not tolerate.

The title "Son of Man" has a rich Hebrew tradition. The prophet Daniel foresaw the day when the Son of Man would come to bring judgment on earth. "Son of man" (with a lowercase *m*) is also a generic designation for human beings, as we discover in Psalm 8:4: "What are human beings, the sons of man, that you care for them?"

Many scholars believe the "Son of Man" title was added by Luke rather than used by Jesus himself. This is a reasonable explanation. How awkward for Jesus to talk about himself in the third person. Regardless of whether it's original or inserted, this title is paired with his future suffering, death, and resurrection. This may suggest another reason for silencing the disciples. Though many expected the Messiah, no one expected the Messiah to suffer at the hands of Roman occupiers.

Jesus knows his suffering and death are part of his mission. He must do this, not because his enemies will bring it about, but because of the implications of the calling to which he is uniquely committed—a calling to bring light to darkness, voice to the voiceless, wholeness to the broken, and God's truth to the powerful ones.

Luke doesn't indicate whether the disciples understand this. Matthew and Mark suggest they don't. There is grace yet to come from the God who patiently waits for the truth of divine ways to sink in.

How would knowledge of your imminent death affect you?

150

TOUGH TALK
Luke 9:23-27

Then Jesus said, "If you want to follow me, give up certain things and take up a daily cross. Those who try to save their lives will not obtain a deeper life, but those willing to lose the lives they have will find true life. What's the advantage of gaining the whole world while destroying yourself in the process? If people are ashamed of me and my teachings, then I'll be ashamed of them when I come into the presence of the Father and the holy angels. Listen, some standing here right now will see the full glory of God revealed before they die."

+

I offer a congregational mission statement suitable for church bulletins, newsletters, websites, and Facebook pages.

THIS IS WHO WE ARE . . . We are cross bearers with Jesus. We know you're looking for a "friendly church" filled with nice people. We're not inhospitable; it's just that we believe God calls us into *true* community. The cross we invite you to carry isn't the same as a physical affliction or emotional distress. We all get headaches. We all put up with annoying relatives. These are life's annoyances, not crosses. We believe Jesus calls us to carry burdens of the world we never before considered carrying. We invite you to lose your life, to give yourself to the one who gave his life to show us a more godly way of living. This is serious business. We don't care about your felt needs. Jesus didn't live and die for felt needs. He was executed because he cared too much for victims of unfair treatment, who were overlooked and underrepresented. This church isn't a therapeutic center. Even though you expect church to make you feel good, sometimes you'll leave feeling a lot worse than when you arrived. The gospel cuts deep. Get over it! By all means, we welcome you. However, if you decide that our community isn't for you, we understand. Not everybody looks good nailed to wood.

What would you add to or delete from this mission statement?

151

ALTERED STATES
Luke 9:28-31

A few days after these sayings, Jesus took Peter, John, and James up a mountain to pray. While he was praying, the appearance of his face changed and his clothes became luminous. At the same time, the disciples saw Moses and Elijah, who appeared like Jesus. They were talking with him about his impending death in Jerusalem.

+

Some things are experienced and believed but never fully explained. The event known as the Transfiguration is one of those things—a bizarre mystery wrapped around an enigma and shrouded in ambiguity. Matthew, Mark, and Luke all record this event. Each writer places the incident shortly after Jesus makes the first prediction of his impending suffering in Jerusalem. Of the twelve disciples, Peter, John, and James are the only ones to witness it.

Mountains played pivotal roles in Hebrew history. On Mount Sinai, Moses received the Ten Commandments, and his face shined brightly after speaking to the Holy One (Exodus 34). On Mount Horeb, the prophet Elijah received a revelation from God in a still small voice (1 Kings 19). Israel's leaders communed with God on mountaintops.

On this mountain, Jesus undergoes an altered state. His face glows; his clothes are transformed. Moses, Israel's lawgiver, and Elijah, Israel's greatest prophet, speak with Jesus about his departure (or "exodus"—meaning his death), an event yet to happen in Jerusalem. Luke wants his readers to know that this nighttime mystery is an affirmation of Jesus by two great Hebrew leaders. Imagine a presidential candidate receiving the endorsement of Washington and Lincoln!

For the three disciples, for Luke's first-century readers, and for the early church, this event served as a reminder that Jesus was worthy of devotion and commitment. This night of altered appearance is a foreshadowing of the day when altered lives will acknowledge the transformational power of Jesus.

What do transfiguring moments look like to you?

PRESERVING THE MOMENT
Luke 9:32-33

Even though Peter, John, and James were struggling to stay awake, they saw Jesus' glory, and Moses and Elijah standing near. When the two men left, Peter impulsively said to Jesus, "Master, it's good that we are here. Let's make three memorials—one for you, one for Moses, and one for Elijah."

+

Peter speaks for himself, and probably for most of us.
"Master, it's good that we are here."
       Was it the mystic glory of the moment
       Or the grogginess of sleeplessness
       That prompted Peter to gush forth on the mountaintop?
       In hopes of building upon "You are the anointed one of God"
       Maybe Peter sensed here another occasion
       To vault himself above the others.
       It's not every day that past heroes
       Come around for a visit.
       Who could say when Moses and Elijah again would appear?
"Let's make three memorials."
       How else are we to mark important events
       If not by erecting dwellings of stone and wood,
       Testifying to what's taken place?
       Speaking for James and John, Peter
       Was ready to roll up his sleeves to save Jesus from
       Unnecessary suffering and loss.
       Peter knew opportunity when it came knocking.
"One for you, one for Moses, and one for Elijah."
       All for one and one for all,
       Three houses of equal size and trinitarian proportions.
       Each commemorating why we are here:
       To preserve that which might be taken from us.
       To save that which might be stripped away.
       To protect that which might get exposed to the world.

What do you recall about a holy moment experience?

REAL WORLD
Luke 9:34-37

After Peter spoke, a cloud covered them and the disciples were scared. A voice spoke from the cloud: "Listen to my son, my chosen!" Then they saw Jesus alone. They didn't tell anyone what they had experienced. The next day, when they came down the mountain, a great crowd met Jesus.

+

Clouds, like mountains, have a rich history in the Hebrew tradition. In the book of Exodus, a pillar of cloud led the former slaves through the desert. Mount Sinai was enveloped with the cloud of God's presence when Moses received the Ten Commandments. When the desert tabernacle was erected, a "cloud covered the tent of meeting, and God's glory filled the place" (Exodus 40:34).

The cloud housed the presence of God. The cloud was synonymous with God's glory. In the cloud, God was pleased to dwell. Small wonder the disciples were terrified as they entered the cloud. Who could say what would happen next?

This night, the cloud speaks, and the voice of God repeats what was spoken at Jesus' baptism. The voice confirms Jesus' identity: "my son . . . my chosen." The voice gives Jesus an authority greater than that of any lawgiver or prophet: "Listen to my son." The voice reminds Jesus that he is filled with God's approval.

Jesus will need this assurance when he descends the Mountain of Transfiguration and makes his way through the valley of human need. This is the source into which Jesus will tap when he agonizes in Gethsemane's garden and when he climbs crucifixion's hill.

This won't be the last time Jesus will need reminders of his identity and chosenness. The world of brokenness and need, of cruelty and despair, will test his resolve and require further reassurances.

The world Jesus enters when he descends from the mountain is the world the church is tempted to avoid. It's messy and unpredictable, dangerous and risky, often unfriendly, and sometimes hostile. Rather than remain in the high elevations of retreat, Jesus walks straight into the world of human need—a world that will require of him everything.

What need of the world is calling for your attention?

BUT THEY COULDN'T
Luke 9:38-40

A man shouted to Jesus, "Teacher, please take a look at my son, my only child. An evil spirit takes control, causing him to scream and foam at the mouth. It attacks him and won't leave him alone. I begged your disciples to intervene, but they couldn't do anything."

+

Whatever relief and retreat the Mountain of Transfiguration provided for Jesus and his closest disciples, their renewed vigor for ministry is immediately put to the test. Demonic forces and evil's many faces are busy in their destructive work. The next day, a crowd seeks out Jesus and human need calls for his intervention.

Desperation is everywhere. A father's son, his only child, is not only ill but also possessed by an evil spirit. What we would call epilepsy was viewed in the ancient world as another manifestation of demonic habitation. The boy is helpless in the struggle. All muscular coordination is lost. Speech is impossible when the mouth foams. The spirit mauls him (literally, "rips him apart") and wears him out.

Even the disciples, given power and authority over all demons and diseases, prove impotent. What's gone wrong? What happened to their power? If they had power before, how did they come to lose it? Was it their lack of faith? Had they grown arrogant and overconfident? Was this demon out of their league? Luke leaves us wondering.

If the disciples have wandered away from the Source of their power, only to rely on their own best practices, it won't be the last time the disciples or pastors or churches or religious institutions, initially called and empowered by Jesus, will come to see themselves as the "ends" rather than the "means."

What did you do, the last time you were unable to fix a situation?

DIVINE IMPATIENCE
Luke 9:41-43a

Jesus said to them "You unbelieving and perverse people, how much longer can I put up with you? Bring the boy here." At that moment, the boy fell to the ground in convulsions. Jesus ordered the spirit to be quiet. Then he healed the boy, and gave him back to his father. Everyone was astonished and awestruck at the power of God present in Jesus.

+

We want God to be patient with our failings and accommodating of our uncanny ability to get things wrong. We prefer God to be long-suffering, "slow to anger and ready with abundant love" (Psalm 103:8).

Jesus' sharp reply takes us by surprise, and we can't be entirely sure to whom his words are directed. Is Jesus speaking to the father of the boy and chiding the parent for his lack of faith in the power the disciples had? Is Jesus speaking to the disciples, reprimanding them for their diminished power to heal and cure? Or is Jesus speaking in a general way to the gathered crowd, lamenting their faith deficiencies?

And what is the perversity of which Jesus speaks? The Greek suggests that the word *perverse* can also be understood as "twisting." Truth and reality are often twisted to suit our preferences. The mission of Jesus to reveal the life-giving ways of God is easily twisted into programs that bear no resemblance to that for which he was willing to give his life.

We are people hard to please, and since the time of Genesis, we've regularly tested God's patience. If the biblical God isn't to our liking, we don't hesitate to enlist the services of other available products at the "Gods R Us" store.

Jesus restores wholeness to an epileptic—this is the miracle Luke tells. That Jesus continues to be with us and put up with us may be a greater miracle still.

In what ways are you spiritually impatient?

156

PARADOXICAL POWER
Luke 9:43b-45

Jesus said to his disciples, "Listen carefully to what I'm saying: I will be betrayed into people's hands." The disciples, however, didn't understand what he was talking about, because the meaning was hidden and they couldn't grasp it. They were afraid to admit this to Jesus.

+

Jesus pulls his disciples aside to remind them again of the paradoxical nature of power. His power, the same power he conferred on them, the power that prevails against the manifold faces of evil, one day will appear to the world as ultimate powerlessness. "I will be betrayed into people's hands."

The one who gives life, whose voice prevails over destructive forces, will have his own life snuffed out by those determined to silence him. Given the absence here of any resurrection prediction, Jesus' words come with dire heaviness.

Understandably, the disciples are confused; they have exalted notions of what a messiah is supposed to do. Betrayed into human hands? How's it possible for power and powerlessness to exist side by side? How does one win by losing? Nothing in their personal experiences and nothing in their Hebrew traditions help them to make sense of a messiah whose power comes disguised in powerlessness.

Three times Luke describes their confusion: "They didn't understand . . . the meaning was hidden . . . they couldn't grasp it." Seeking explanations, perhaps they wonder to themselves if there is an easier way. Yet, they're afraid to admit this to Jesus. Perhaps they fear the worst. Have they given up their lives and livelihoods for a defeated cause?

Maybe the disciples' inability to perceive is our inability too—their fear, our fear as well. The easier way, the way of dominant power, the way of "might makes right," is always the attractive way for individuals, for corporations, for nations. Surely, God must see things our way, right?

What does submissive power look like for you?

157

CHILD LESSONS
Luke 9:46-48

As the disciples argued about which one of them was the most important, Jesus took a child and said, "When you welcome a child, you welcome me; when you welcome me, you welcome the one who sent me. The least of you is the most important."

+

Leave it to the disciples to miss Jesus' point. Pecking order? Really? Welcoming a child, showing hospitality to the least, embracing the insignificant ones—these are God's intentions for the world.

In a sermon entitled "Dreams to Tell," the late R. Maurice Boyd reminds us of the daily choices between following the path of conventional wisdom and following the path Jesus chose to walk.

If what you are after is power, you had better forget about love; it is very difficult to be after both. If you put self at the center, you had better be prepared to find your outer limits there; and that can be very lonely. If you believe only in justice, and not in mercy, you'd better not make any mistakes. If you are a gossip, don't look for confidences. If you believe life is a rat race, you mustn't hope to find any dignity in it. If your basic stance is confrontation, don't expect people to knock on your door when what they need is tenderness. If you are ruthless on the way up, you shouldn't look for sympathy on the way down. If you never forgive, you must never offend. If your work is life, you had better keep one eye on your relationships. If you are a materialist, don't consult us gurus about spiritual values; there is little we have to say to you and even less that you will understand. If you believe that life is purely quantitative, you had better keep your averages up. If you spread yourself thin, you mustn't expect to go deep. And if you move in the fast lane, don't set your heart on anything that takes time. If you decide to live by the sword, then, by God, you had better carry one.

What part of the above quote speaks to you?

158

Western Wall, Jerusalem

NOT ONE OF US
Luke 9:49-50

The disciple John said to Jesus, "Someone was expelling demons in your name, and we tried to stop him because he wasn't one of us." But Jesus insisted, "Don't stop him; whoever isn't against you is on your side."

+

The disciples are on a roll. Not only have they demonstrated an inability to confront evil by harnessing the power and authority granted them by Jesus; not only have they failed to grasp Jesus' own predictions about his future suffering; not only have they revealed their true stripes by jostling for positions of greatness. Now they raise an objection that outsiders have performed works they themselves are unable to do. It's religious paranoia of the worst kind!

Rather than celebrate healing and transformation wherever and whenever it is evident, the disciples object on grounds of territorial concerns, as if to say, "We get your point about welcoming a little child, but make those people stop, Jesus—they're not with us!"

In infinite ways, this sentiment is repeated. We see evidence that God is at work in the world; it's just too bad our competitors down the street are doing it. The sermon was thoughtful, biblical, and challenging; too bad it was preached by a woman. He's gifted for ministry and she's experienced a call to seminary, but we don't recognize gays and lesbians in leadership positions. Gandhi and Mohammad were worthy men, but God's heart has no room for Hindus and Muslims. We see your Spirit's effectiveness, Jesus, but we don't approve; they're not like us and certainly not our kind. Put a halt to it now! We've got purity issues to consider!

Does anyone, any group, any sect, any tradition, any religion, or any nationality have a monopoly on God? So what if they're not one of us! If they're making lives better by alleviating pain, knocking down barriers, fighting against injustices, and working toward wholeness for the world, isn't that a God-thing and shouldn't we celebrate it? If we can't bring ourselves to embrace it when we see it, do we have to tear them down while they're doing good things?

What raises your suspicions about someone else's good deeds?

160

FACE-SETTING
Luke 9:51-53

As Jesus left the area of Galilee, he set his face toward Jerusalem and sent messengers ahead to make preparations in a village in the region of Samaria. However, the village didn't receive him because he was heading toward Jerusalem.

+

We witness here in Luke's gospel a geographical shift. Up to this point, Jesus' ministry has occurred in the northern Galilean region. With few exceptions, his ministry has received praise from the crowds and criticism from certain religious leaders. In the next ten chapters, Jesus makes his way to Jerusalem where suffering awaits him.

Jesus "set his face toward Jerusalem." His face-setting is reminiscent of earlier Hebrew prophets who did the same. "Therefore, I've set my face like a flint, and I won't be shamed, for the God who calls me is near" (Isaiah 50:7). "God said to me, 'Mortal, set your face toward Jerusalem and preach against the sanctuaries'" (Ezekiel 21:1-2).

To "set one's face" suggests resolve, and focus. Athletes call it being in the zone. Jaw set. Eyes ablaze. Shoulders square. Jesus won't be a victim of anything or anyone. Suffering will come—death, too—but Jesus knows he is part of a purpose larger than himself.

This journey begins with rejection in Samaria, just as it began with rejection at the synagogue in Nazareth. The Samaritan villagers want nothing to do with Jesus, so they reject his messengers. Jews and Samaritans harbored mutual hostilities that dated back hundreds of years. Now the Samaritans reject Jesus upon finding out he is on his way to Jerusalem. Because they rejected Jerusalem as the center of worship, for them to reject a popular Jewish rabbi intent on taking his message there was no surprise.

The one who reaches out to Jew and Gentile, to clean and unclean, to native sons and foreign daughters, experiences rejection even from those he loves like no other. Lest we imagine that the pursuit of holiness is a journey of ease and comfort, nourished by daily supplements of the world's accolades, Jesus' face-setting is a reminder of the hostilities that await today's followers, too.

Toward what goals and aspirations is your face set?

FRY 'EM!
Luke 9:54-56

When the disciples James and John realized that the Samaritan villagers would not welcome them, they said to Jesus, "Do you want us to annihilate them with fire from heaven?" Jesus refused to feed their hunger for violence. So they went to another village.

+

I wonder if Jesus gave half a thought to responding to the disciples' bravado with: "Yeah, sure. Go on! I'd like to see you invoke fire from anywhere. Give us some sparks. Let's see if your 'might makes right' can light even a match."

At least the hawkish disciples have precedent on their side. Centuries before, Elijah the Tishbite did exactly that to a few hundred false prophets of Baal on Mt. Carmel. But Jesus isn't about nuking his enemies.

In most Bibles, a footnote appears in this passage after Jesus rebukes the disciples. Some ancient manuscripts of Luke's gospel include this addition: "You don't know what spirit you're of, for the Son of Man hasn't come to destroy lives but to save them." Some scholars argue for the inclusion of this omitted verse, reasoning that it's consistent with Luke's understanding of Jesus. Others argue against the inclusion, claiming that, though reflective of Jesus, it's an example of a later editorial addition.

Regardless, few lessons are harder to fit into a mindset. Even those who oppose what we stand for deserve our hospitality. We spend lifetimes protecting our self-interests and guarding our rights. Some days we think we see the world so clearly: those who are for us, those who are against us; friends of God, enemies of God; those in the right, those in the wrong; the good, the evil. Why is Jesus more content than we are to shrug his shoulders and leave the sorting for another time and place? Like these power-hungry disciples intent on protecting Jesus and themselves, sometimes our egos are part of the problem.

Whom do you hate more than God does?

162

DEFECTIVE DISCIPLESHIP
Luke 9:57-62

As a crowd was traveling with Jesus, someone said, "I'll follow you wherever you go." Jesus replied, "Foxes have holes to live in and birds have nests, but I've no place to lay my head." Jesus said to another, "Follow me." The person replied, "I will, but I must first bury my father." But Jesus responded, "Let the dead take care of themselves; it's up to you to point to the transforming presence of God in the world." Another said, "I'll follow you, but I must first say goodbye to my family." Jesus replied, "Those who start a commitment, only to wish they were doing something else, aren't fit for God's work."

+

Disciple wannabees and eager prospects. The first one volunteers, the second is recruited, the third steps forward with conditions. This trio of "almost" disciples piques the curiosity of many preachers. Sermons probe their motives, question their sincerity, and suggest their secret ambitions.

That Jesus dampens their enthusiasm to follow him and raises the discipleship stakes isn't unrelated to his face-setting posture toward Jerusalem. Following Jesus doesn't guarantee displays of power and plentiful picnics of loaves and fish on serene Galilean hillsides. Discipleship will bring hostilities and rejections, making the recent Samaritan discourtesies pale in comparison.

In the days ahead, Jesus' followers won't have the securities of home and livelihoods on which to rely. Following Jesus will mean a shift in priorities. Noble causes that once centered on family will give way to deeper loyalties. Choices have to be made between what's good and what's better, between what's better and what's best. It's a wonder any follow Jesus at all, or make serious inquiries about doing so.

We prefer Jesus on our terms, asking little of us and demanding even less, custom-designed for what we think we need, want, and desire. That makes for a high attrition rate when things don't go our way.

What's the best excuse you have?

SEVENTY
Luke 10:1

Jesus chose seventy followers and sent them in pairs to places he intended to go.

+

In addition to the twelve disciples/apostles Jesus appointed in the
previous chapter, seventy others are commissioned to go to locales
he will later visit.

The symbolic significance of the number seventy offers some
clues to Jesus' understanding of his mission and to Luke's theological
particularities. Seventy is the number of Noah's descendants who were
scattered over the earth after the flood (Genesis 10:32). After the
patriarch Joseph's death in Egypt, we read of the numerical growth of
the Hebrew nation: "Jacob had seventy descendants" (Exodus 1:5).
Moses appointed seventy elders to assist him in leadership (Numbers 11).

The number seventy suggests outward growth in ever-expanding
circles. Though his face is set toward Jerusalem, Jesus' message is not
proclaimed to Jewish hearers alone. Universal in his inclusion, Jesus is
determined to bring the healing and justice of God's rule to nations.

Luke's language has a royal feel to it. In Roman political and
military protocol, officials selected and appointed envoys who were
sent ahead to announce a dignitary's arrival. Jesus sent the apostles in
pairs for companionship and mutual support, but also to ensure that
testimony to him received the confirmation of two representatives.

Though suffering awaits Jesus in Jerusalem, his journey there is
not one of concession to that reality. The appointing and commissioning
of seventy ambassadors is not the behavior of one who feels his cause
lost, his life wasted, his hopes abandoned, his future jeopardized, or his
way a dead end.

Living as Jesus lived isn't a cerebral exercise that requires us
to master information that we dispense at any given moment. At its
core, it is a lifestyle, and those who walk it become practitioners of a
radical love-giving, justice-seeking movement that reflects the heart
of God. Such a way of being can be a solo effort, but to walk it
with another means instant support and ongoing accountability.

Who provides you with support and accountability?

164

REALITY CHECK
Luke 10:2-3

Jesus said to his closest disciples, "The needs of the world are huge, but the workers are few; therefore, ask God to send workers into the harvest. Go on your way and know that I'm sending you out like lambs among wolves."

+

Specific realities await the disciples, and Jesus uses this opportunity as a teaching moment.

"The needs of the world are huge, but the workers are few." The reality of the world's needs is great, but the harvest of God's transformational work is greater. Don't let the enormity of the need paralyze you. Focus on what God is able to do. Don't dwell on what you don't have.

"Therefore, ask God to send workers into the harvest." There is a necessary way to go about this. You have your job and I have mine. It's not up to you to draft the workers needed. I'll call whom I'll call. Don't arm-twist others. Don't use guilt as a motivational tool. Ask me and I'll raise up more partners than you'll know what to do with.

"Go on your way." Be mobile. Don't sulk over the hugeness of the task. *Go* on your way.

Don't worry how others go on *their* way. Go on *your* way.

It's a journey, not a program; a lifestyle, not a weekend stint. Go on your *way*.

"See, I'm sending you out." This is *my* doing, not yours. *I'm* the one who calls and equips. You don't call and equip yourself. Without the call, nothing is accomplished, no matter how hard you try. When will you start seeing this from my perspective?

"Like lambs among wolves." Don't get it reversed; you're lambs, not wolves. The world is full of wolfish behavior; don't imitate it. If vulnerability isn't your thing, then think twice about walking my way. Remember, I'm the Lamb of God who absorbs the pain of the world.

What's the most daunting thing you have faced?

TRAVELING INSTRUCTIONS
Luke 10:4-12

"Take no purses, bags, or sandals. Greet no one on the road. When you enter a house, say, 'May peace abide here!' Your peace will reside with those who share that peace, but if peace isn't there, it will return to you. Eat and drink whatever is provided; you deserve these things. Stay in the same house. Whenever people welcome you, eat what's offered. Cure the sick and say, 'God's wholeness is meant for you.' But if people don't welcome you, go into the streets and say, 'We shake this town's dust from our feet as a warning to you. Know that God's intentions for the world are becoming visible.' Listen, on that day it will be better for Sodom than for that town."

+

These thirty-five pairs of missionaries will be totally reliant on God and the hospitality of others. Traveling lean and light, they'll know what few of us ever learn about keeping God as the source of life. Trivial conversations will serve only to distract them from their calling.

They'll eat what others provide; that may mean eating food at Gentile tables thought to be unclean by Jewish standards. And eat they will, for God's work is more important than the dietary laws of their tradition.

Jesus includes a harsh prediction for the towns and villages that don't show hospitality to the seventy. The ancient city of Sodom, destroyed for ignoring the needs of the poor (Ezekiel 16:49), will receive more divine leniency than populations that reject these messengers.

A side note: If judgment comes, it will be God's doing, and not the job of these messengers to invoke it. Maybe there's a lesson here for messengers today.

How have you experienced hospitality?

FIVE-CITY TOUR
Luke 10:13-15

"Watch out, Chorazin! Watch out, Bethsaida! If the powerful miracles done in your cities had been done in Tyre and Sidon, they would have repented long ago in sackcloth and ashes. The future will be more tolerable for Tyre and Sidon than for you. Listen up, Capernaum; do you think you'll find a place in heaven? Think again—you'll end up in the depths of the earth."

+

Continuing the dire forecast, Jesus identifies five cities—three Jewish (Chorazin, Bethsaida, and Capernaum) and two non-Jewish (Tyre and Sidon)—that will experience harsh judgment.

The Bible says nothing about the town of Chorazin, likely located at the northern tip of the Sea of Galilee near the towns of Bethsaida and Capernaum. Bethsaida was the setting for the feeding of the five thousand. Capernaum had the high privilege of serving as the background for many of Jesus' synagogue appearances and miracles. That its residents failed to honor Jesus is evidenced in his condemnation.

On the Mediterranean coast, the towns of Tyre and Sidon were located beyond the borders of ancient Israel. Their pagan practices and opposition to God's people are well documented in the accounts of Isaiah, Jeremiah, Ezekiel, Joel, and Amos. Jesus uses them as examples of two cities that, had they witnessed his signs and wonders, would have responded with greater receptivity than the Galilean villages that witnessed him but rejected his message.

Multiple lessons emerge from Jesus' warnings: With divine favor come weighty responsibilities. What we do with what we are given matters. Reception or refusal move us outside the territory of neutral consequences. As Martin Luther King Jr. reminded us, "to remain neutral is to side with evil." Choices are required. Times of reckoning arrive daily. It's not a harsh and heartless God who condemns; we condemn ourselves. God's purposes won't be frustrated forever. Failure is as much a part of life as is success. God asks from us faithfulness, period. Eventually, a last word will be spoken, and the last word will be God's.

What concerns do you have about the place where you live?

ANY WAY YOU READ IT
Luke 10:16

"People who listen to you also listen to me. Those who reject you also reject me. Whoever rejects me also rejects the one who sent me."

+

H ere's a sampling of other translations of this verse:

"Whoever listens to you listens to me, and whoever disregards you disregards me, and whoever disregards me disregards him who sent me" (*American Translation*).

"He that heareth you heareth me; and he that despiseth you despiseth me; and he that despiseth me despiseth him that sent me" (*King James Version*).

"He who listens to you, listens to me; and he who sets no value on you, sets no value on me; and he who sets no value on me, sets no value on him that sent me" (William Barclay's translation, *The Daily Study Bible*).

Whether one's favorite Bible is Old English, the King's English, or contemporary English, the inseparable relationship is evident. When people see and hear Jesus' disciples, they see and hear Jesus. When people accept or reject Jesus' disciples, they accept or reject the one who embodies God's intentions for the world.

This disciple-Jesus connection is as inseparable as the Jesus-God connection. C. S. Lewis (*Mere Christianity*) goes as far as to suggest that we become "little Christs." But the sandals are too big! The role is larger than our ability to fill it!

I know the thoughts that race through my mind when a car displaying a religious bumper sticker speeds through a red light or turns right at a no-right-turn corner. Actually, that's pretty tame compared to *my* indiscretions! Little Christs? We're mere amateurs! All the more amazing that God still desires to have an intimate connection with us.

What do you hope people see of God in you?

PROGRESS REPORT
Luke 10:17-20

The seventy disciples returned with glowing reports: "Jesus, in your name, demons obeyed us!" Jesus replied, "I watched Satan fall from heaven like a flash of lightning. I've given you authority to tread on snakes and scorpions, and defeat all kinds of evil. Nothing will hurt you. However, don't rejoice in all this, but rejoice that your names are written in heaven."

+

During my three decades of parish ministry, I often imagined standing before Jesus to share monthly highlights of my ministerial activities. Here's one such report.

Yes, Jesus, it's good to be with you again. As you know, we observed Holy Week and Easter. I wrote five liturgies and prepared five sermons. I attended the meeting of the Church Board. We narrowly managed a quorum. People are busy.

I met with Property, Christian Education, Missions, and Worship committees. An elder and I served communion to three homebound members. I guided the repairman into the bowels of the heating system. I made five hospital calls. Excuse me? No, I wasn't able to cure anyone.

I conducted the funeral of Glenn; as you know, he died of cancer at forty-two. The sanctuary was packed. No, I wasn't able to raise him from the dead.

I counseled Lois; she's chronically depressed. I called the lawn care service and got them to stop cutting the grass on Sunday mornings. I started a Saturday morning Bible study for anyone interested—three folks showed up. I'm hopeful.

I bowled in the church league on the first Saturday night of the month. Excuse me? My best game was 185. Well, those are the highlights. I'll report back in another month.

Were demons expelled? Were snakes and scorpions stepped on? Were enemies overpowered? Did spirits submit? Of course!

What highlights would be in your report?

GOD'S HIDDEN THINGS
Luke 10:21-24

Inspired by the Holy Spirit, Jesus prayed, "I thank you, God of heaven and earth, because you've hidden these things from people who are wise and smart and revealed them to infants and children. You're so gracious! You've given me all things. No one knows me like you do, and no one knows you like I do and those who accompany me." Then privately Jesus said to the disciples, "Blessed are those who see the world as you see it! Many prophets and kings desired to see and hear all that you do, but didn't."

+

Threaded through these verses is the strangeness of God's ways. God hides things from the wise but reveals them to infants. No one knows what God is up to except those to whom God chooses to reveal such things. Not even prophets and kings have seen and heard what the disciples have seen and heard.

We've seen this hidden strangeness in Jesus' life. Those once blind, with newfound sight see what those who've never lost their vision can't. Little children are held up as examples of what the rest of us should strive to become. The last will be first. The meek will inherit the earth. To gain our lives, we give our lives away. The unschooled grasp truths the religious pros fail to understand. The weak of the world stare down the evil one.

None of it makes sense. St. Paul says as much: "For God's folly is wiser than human wisdom, and God's weakness is stronger than human might" (I Corinthians 1:25). What we grasp of God isn't a result of crunching the numbers or maneuvering our way through a celestial organizational chart. We don't work through the God textbook and wave a diploma on graduation day. God chooses to reveal the hidden things, and when the hidden is perceived, we have no one but God to thank.

In shorthand, that which meets the eye isn't all there is to see. Modern-day disciples—storytellers, artists, and the deeply spiritual—get it.

Is God more or less "hidden" from you these days?

LEGALESE
Luke 10:25-28

A legal expert tested Jesus with a question: "Teacher, what do I have to do to get eternal life?" Jesus answered, "What does the law say?" The legal expert replied, "Love God with all your heart and mind, and your neighbor as yourself." Jesus congratulated him, "Well done! Do this and you'll get what you're looking for."

+

The legal expert knows never to ask a question without first knowing the answer. He knows Moses and the law. He knows what's required. If by testing Jesus he hopes to out-maneuver an inferior opponent, Jesus wholeheartedly agrees with the lawyer's own understanding of what the tradition says. Quoting from Deuteronomy 6:5 and Leviticus 19:18, the lawyer repeats life's requirements: Love God totally and your neighbor as yourself.

Jesus now evaluates the expert's own test-taking ability: "Your theology is sound. You answered correctly. You passed your own test. Now, put it into practice. Continually do this and you'll get what you're looking for." Jesus not only accepts the starting place of the expert's own question ("What do I have to do?") but reinforces it without suggesting that keeping the law is beyond even the best of us.

Jesus could have pulled out the heavy artillery and blasted the legal expert out of the water. "I don't care what you think you know about getting the eternal-life payoff. What you need to do is believe in me." The omission of an evangelical response is evidence of Jesus' winsome way of keeping a conversation going; he uses the lawyer's own answers to engage him without shutting him down.

Not every religious debate needs winning in the first two minutes, or at all. That doesn't weaken the life of faith; it just widens the circle of inclusion. And if we aren't about inclusion, then we're living the kind of life Jesus wasn't interested in living.

How would you frame life's most important question?

A DEFINITION, PLEASE
Luke 10:29

Not satisfied with Jesus' answer, the legal expert asked, "Who's my neighbor?"

+

Not content to end the discussion with his own understanding of eternal life affirmed, the questioner seeks clarification regarding a proper definition of "neighbor." An odd inquiry. If you don't know your neighbor, just walk outside and look around. Cross the street or hallway. Knock on a door. Attend the next block party. Invite a few people to your home next Friday night. We know who our neighbor is, and we know where our neighbor lives.

The expert's follow-up question is directly related to his need to get closure. He has no issues with the "loving God" part of the commandment; it's the "loving your neighbor" that requires a clearer definition. He expects an answer along the lines of, "Your neighbor is your family member, relative, friend, one of your own—an Israelite." That's what the tradition taught, and he hopes Jesus will affirm this common understanding. If his neighbor can be defined within those parameters, then there's no compelling reason (religious or otherwise) for him to love as a neighbor anyone who falls outside that definition. The legal scholar seeks limits.

Who can blame him for wanting to reduce the size of his neighborhood? The world is a complex and scary place. The farther out one goes, the greater the dangers. There's good reason why early cartographers drew dragons on the distant edges of their world maps.

If I can't control everything in the world, at least I can strive to create a community of like-minded people; a circle of acquaintances just like me; an intimate gathering of folks who are, if not my closest friends, at least easy to like.

What type of person is most difficult for you to love?

172

ROAD RAGE
Luke 10:30

Jesus responded with this story: "A man, traveling from Jeru-salem to Jericho, was brutally assaulted by robbers. They stripped him, beat him, and left him half dead."

+

Jesus tells a story involving a random act of violence. Those within earshot of Jesus probably sense something foreboding when he sets the scene on a seventeen-mile stretch of road, descending more than three thousand feet. It was a known haven for highway robbers. The perpetrators in the story are never caught; the victim is never named.

Though we would prefer that Jesus pin the violence on some probable cause, he offers no answers to questions such as: Why was the victim traveling alone? Was the victim wearing jewelry? Did the victim put up a fight? Were the perpetrators minorities? Was it a failure of the educational system? Was this incident yet another sign of the deteriora-tion of the family? Is this what happens when social cuts are made to balance the budget? Jesus' silence pleases neither liberals nor conserva-tives. Blame isn't assigned. Reasons aren't given.

Here is an ancient tale of road rage, a senseless act of violence, meaningless and all too common. We've numbed ourselves to stories about anonymous victims left for dead along roadsides, hillsides, and bedsides. Violent gun crime reduction in American cities makes big news. Headlines rejoice when the annual gun crime rate in Chicago dips below 2,500. It's seen as progress when fewer than fifty citizens are victimized each week. The weapon of choice? A handgun, often purchased outside the city.

I'm not a criminologist or a sociologist, and I don't easily make sense of statistical data. Yet, several realities are apparent. If an American city experienced an outbreak of polio affecting 2,500 victims, you can bet public outcry would demand that health care professionals, public officials, and city and state legislators pool whatever resources necessary to bring that number down to zero. In no time, we would eliminate the disease. The tragedy is that more than thirty thousand gun deaths occur each year in America because the vast majority of us don't care enough to do anything about it.

What do you see as the solution to such violence?

173

REASONS TO PASS BY
Luke 10:31-32

"A member of the clergy, traveling on the same road, came upon the bleeding victim; instead of helping, he continued on his journey. A short time later, another religious leader also saw the victim; he did nothing and passed by."

+

The good things we could have done but didn't are a source of much regret. William Sloane Coffin (*Collected Sermons*) lamented that it's not the lives we lived, but our unlived lives, that stand out and poison our existence.

We miss the spiritual thrust of Jesus' story if we insist on seeing the two religious figures as bad guys, guilty of behaviors we would never dream of enacting. Rather, these religious leaders have many good reasons to pass by.

Who knows what traps are set for unsuspecting folks; a body on this road could easily be a plant. I'm at risk if I contaminate myself by touching the dead; who knows how many people I might infect? There's no right or wrong here; sometimes faithfulness to one's tradition is more important than responding to human need. He seems dead, he looks dead, he must be dead; someone more qualified to tend to the dead will come along. I've got nothing with me to help—no oils, no bandages, no way to transport him to safety; the best I can do is find help when I get to Jericho. I'm not going to put it off any longer—the Jericho Highway Commission is going to hear from me. There but for the grace of God go I; sometimes others get what they deserve. Soon he'll be in the heavenly arms of God; that's a far better place anyway.

We can spend a lifetime passing by, negotiating around the world's victims, and stoically accepting the world's violence. We tell ourselves we can't change much about that, but at least we can manage to keep ourselves safe. The tragedy of unlived lives is an epidemic.

Who was the last victim you passed by?

174

THE GODLY SAMARITAN
Luke 10:33-35

"While traveling the same road, a Samaritan saw the victim and was deeply moved. He went to him, poured oil and wine on the wounds, and bandaged them. Then he put the victim on his own animal, brought him to an inn, and took care of him. The next day he paid the manager and said, 'Take care of him. I'll pay you the rest when I come back.'"

+

Jesus doesn't speculate on the causes behind the violent act or the reasons why the two travelers refused to get involved. Neither does Jesus probe the motives of the Samaritan. The Samaritan's response speaks for itself. He acts without hesitation.

He's moved with pity and compassion—words which in Greek suggest "innards." The Samaritan's insides are affected. He feels for the victim. He's moved by the victim's plight. His stomach churns. His pulse quickens. Once he sees the victim in need, he can't rest.

The Samaritan's compassionate response recalls earlier incidences of God's own saving action. Moses stands at the burning bush as God calls, "I've heard the cries of my people because of their taskmasters. I know their suffering, and I've come to deliver them" (Exodus 3:7). God "will heal us . . . will bind us up . . . will revive us and . . . raise us up . . . as robbers wait to attack someone" (Hosea 6:1-2, 6).

The hero is a Samaritan—a detail no Jewish listener in the crowd would fail to notice. There's the shock value. The animosities between Jews and Samaritans were centuries old, and now Jesus tells a story in which the despised one acts better than the religious professionals do.

Let's retell the story: A person is shot on Main Street, USA. A Catholic priest passes by without stopping to help. A Protestant minister also passes by without lending a hand. Then a person, later identified as a member of the Muslim faith community, stops and gives life-saving assistance. At great risk (someone might link him to the crime), he transports the victim to the emergency room of the nearest hospital.

Jesus calls him a hero and lifts him up as the only one of the three who did the godly thing.

How do you feel about the new parable?

175

WHO IS A NEIGHBOR?
Luke 10:36-37

Jesus asked the legal expert, "Who was a neighbor to the one beaten by the robbers?" The man answered, "The merciful one." Jesus replied, "Live like that."

+

The legal scholar seeks a definition of *neighbor*, but Jesus refuses to play a game of pick 'n' choose. Instead, Jesus turns the tables and asks, "Who acted like a neighbor?" By answering correctly, the expert again proves himself an able test-taker. Jesus agrees and sends him off to do the same.

Does the legal expert leave satisfied? Does he concur with Jesus and eventually do the same? Does this story change him in profound ways? Or does he perceive Jesus' command as a burden for which he has neither the energy nor the will? For that matter, which of us truly has the stamina to "live like that" on the thousands of roads between our Jerusalems and Jerichos? It doesn't take long before compassion fatigue sets in.

Maybe in hopes of believing our own advice, we tell ourselves that it's wiser to travel safer paths through communities where victims and needy strangers are less visible and less likely to capture our attention. If they do catch our eye, most of us can out-reason altruistic logic any day of the week.

Rather than give specifics, Jesus leaves to us the task of working out the details. "Live like that." How am I to be a neighbor? Is mercy one-size-fits-all? The answers for each of us won't be the same. This much is certain: Like Jesus, we live by dying. We find our lives by losing them. Freedom comes when we give up control. We descend into greatness. When we do so for the least of these, we imitate Jesus. By showing mercy, we expand the ever-widening circle of God's great compassion.

What would it mean for you this week to "live like that"?

Agra, India

UNPRODUCTIVE ATTENTION
Luke 10:38-42

Later, Jesus and the disciples entered the home of a woman named Martha. Her sister Mary sat at Jesus' feet and listened to his teachings while Martha was busy in the kitchen. Frustrated, Martha said to Jesus, "Don't you care that my sister has left me with all this work? Tell her to help me." Jesus replied, "Martha, Martha, you're preoccupied and worried with many things; there's only one important thing here. Mary has chosen the better part, which won't be taken away from her."

+

Everything Jesus held up as a worthy example in the Good Samaritan story seems dismissed in the home of Martha and Mary. Though Martha is the hospitable host, it's the passive, inactive Mary who receives Jesus' praise. Martha tends to the needs of her guest; Mary sits and listens. Not unlike the Samaritan, Martha chooses action; Mary chooses meditation. One is productive; the other is less so.

Most of us can empathize with Martha's frustration. Food needs preparing. A table needs setting. If discipleship is both word and deed, why does Jesus praise Mary's hearing but not Martha's doing?

One interpretation suggests that Jesus is critical of Martha's attitude. She's anxious and wrapped up in multi-tasking. Some point out that the "many things" and the "one important thing" is Jesus' way of saying, "I'd prefer a simple meal to a seven-course dinner."

Perhaps this isn't an either/or but a both/and situation. Each posture finds a place in the balanced life; keeping them balanced requires vigilance. Those who serve, and let you know at every opportunity that they're not pleased when others don't follow their lead, fail to recognize the virtue of the reflective life. Those who commit their lives to meditation and spiritual introspection, while remaining oblivious to a hungry world, fail to be the hands and feet of Jesus. Discerning the proper time for each is a daily exercise.

I love St. Augustine's take on this biblical scene: "What Martha was doing, that we are now. What Mary was doing, that we hope for. Let us do the first well, that we may have the second fully."

With whom do you most identify in this story?

178

TEACH US
Luke 11:1

One time after Jesus finished praying, a disciple said, "Jesus, teach us to pray like John the Baptist taught his disciples to pray."

+

We often ask experts to teach us their craft. "Teach me how to fly-fish . . . Teach me the proper golf swing . . . Teach me how to speak in front of people without sweating bullets . . . Teach me how to navigate through the maze of investment options." When we see something done well and want to learn to do the same, we tap an expert on the shoulder.

The disciples aren't uninformed about how to pray. From early youth, they have heard prayers uttered by their parents at home and by rabbis in the synagogues. They already know many prayers, including the Psalms, from memory. They're Jews, and because they are, prayer isn't optional but standard equipment. Why, then, do they ask Jesus to teach them something they already know?

Like many first-century religious sects, a group's prayer was also the group's definition of who they were. As a leader of a desert community, John the Baptist, as implied by Jesus' disciples, taught his followers a distinctive prayer that reinforced their mission.

Likewise, other groups had their own prayers. If one's religious community sought a military overthrow of Roman occupiers, or longed for the purification of the temple, then one's prayers would reflect such longings. A community's prayer functioned like an organization's mission statement that clarified purpose and vision.

By asking Jesus to teach them to pray, the disciples aren't admitting that they don't know how or that they lack a technique. Rather, they're looking to Jesus for a clearer definition of who they are and what they are to be about. The disciples remind us that prayer, at least on the level Jesus taught, doesn't come naturally. As we will soon see, we're not innately inclined to seek the things that Jesus would have us seek. Let the learning begin.

To whom would you turn for advice on prayer?

TERM OF ENDEARMENT
Luke 11:2a

Jesus said to the disciples, "When you pray, say, Father . . ."

+

Jesus answers the disciples' request by responding with what we know as The Lord's Prayer. Luke's version of the prayer is considerably shorter than the one found in the sixth chapter of Matthew (the more familiar version). Both versions, however, begin by addressing the object of our praying as "Father." Jesus used the Aramaic word *Abba*, which is translated as "Daddy." Whatever else is prayed in this prayer, whatever else follows, the spirit of this prayer emerges from the intimate relationship God has established with us.

We're invited to address the Creator of the sun, moon, and stars in the most endearing way, like a child calling out to a parent: "Daddy." Let's admit it here—to add "Mommy" isn't only appropriate; it deeply enriches the relationship. The issue, though, isn't God's masculinity or femininity, but that God cares for us in parental ways. The prayer doesn't start with God's power or majesty, nor with God's justice or authority. The prayer of Jesus begins where our lives begin: in the deepest, most intimate relationship—with God.

Jesus is reminding his disciples and us that we begin with God and God begins with us. We don't work our way into God's heart. No need to scrape together enough good merits and gold medals to get God to look kindly on us. We're already there and have been even before we came to that realization. We can claim it now, without waiting for a future acknowledgment from God. Jesus teaches us to begin this prayer with boldness, confidently addressing God in terms of parental love.

Daddy, Mommy, Parent . . . what emotional weight do these words have for you?

NAME HALLOWING
Luke 11:2b

"Hallowed be your name."

+

Years ago, the Xerox Corporation committed itself to an advertising blitz, discouraging the general public from using the word *Xerox* as a generic term for copying done on other brands of copiers. The manufacturing giant had a point. How many times haven't you said, "I'm going to Xerox these papers," even if the work is done on a Canon copier?

Xerox wanted to communicate to the world that its name stands for something in particular and not for everything in general. The company sought to remind the public that the name Xerox is "set apart" from other copier companies.

When we hallow something, we set it apart from other things. When something is set apart, it becomes sacred and holy. When we hallow God's name, we're saying something about who God is apart from who we are. God is otherness, and when we acknowledge that otherness, we honor God's name.

We have infinite ways to hallow or honor God's name. Every time we give thanks for another manifestation of God's grace, we hallow God's name. Whenever we acknowledge that all life belongs to God, we hallow God's name. When we confess that we aren't our own, but belong to God, we hallow God's name. When we see the Spirit of the God-life in others, we hallow God's name. When we point to the work of God in the world, we hallow God's name.

Likewise, there are plenty of ways to "dishallow" or dishonor God's name. The ease with which we attach God's name to political platforms, war efforts, and economic structures is ready evidence that, though we utter the words Jesus taught us to pray, we haven't yet learned how to make this prayer a reality.

The company had a point: not every copy is a Xerox. Not every God-reference is a hallowing act.

Where do you see God's name most abused?

CULTURE CHANGE
Luke 11:2c

"Your reign come."

+

A simple petition. A single plea. A focused request. Jesus teaches his disciples to pray for the reign of God. Most translations read, "Your kingdom come." I've chosen not to use the word *kingdom* throughout these reflections. *Kingdom* is neither a contemporary nor a relevant nor an inclusive word for most of us. If kings have kingdoms, do queens have queendoms? The only kingdom of which most Americans are aware is Disney's Magic Kingdom.

Yet the kingdom of God is a central concept in both the Hebrew and Christian scriptures, so what is the kingdom of God? What does God's reign and rule look like? How do we know it when we see it? What are its characteristics? Is it something ushered from beyond into our world? Is it a reality *we* bring into being? Is it another world altogether?

All these questions have their place, but one question above all others best gets at the nature and character of God's reign: What would the world look like if God were in charge?

That question was partially answered when, at the synagogue in Capernaum, Jesus read from Isaiah 61 and preached his inaugural sermon. When we add the vision of the poet in Psalm 146, the following markers of God's reign emerge: When God is in charge the needs of the poor are addressed; no one goes hungry; the bound and the captives experience release; the blind see new possibilities; oppressed ones receive justice; those bowed down are lifted up; strangers are welcomed in; those without parents, spouses, or partners know they belong; God's gracious favor falls on everyone.

Praying for God's reign, for God's dreams to become real, for God's intentions to take on flesh, is praying not for escape from this world, but for deeper involvement in it. Jesus instructs us to pray, "Your reign come."

Where do you see God's reign most evident?

TODAY'S BREAD
Luke 11:3

"Give us our daily bread."

+

If we're honest, regarding most things in life we really don't feel a need for God. Nowhere is this independence more evident than in our supply of food and daily sustenance. Most of us are quite able to provide for ourselves. What, then, does this prayer mean for people whose biggest concern is not whether we will eat, but what we will eat?

In Luke's abbreviated version of Jesus' prayer, we read the word *our* for the first time here. With the request for daily bread, the prayer shifts from a vertical orientation to a horizontal one, from our relationship with God to our relationships with others. We don't pray isolated from the needs of others, "Give *me my* daily bread." Jesus' prayer connects us to God and to humanity.

Praying this petition reminds us that God isn't inattentive to the physicality of our lives. Though this prayer begins with the hallowing of God's name and the request for God's new community to emerge, the petition for daily bread acknowledges that the God of the universe also cares about our hungers and thirsts.

The Greek word translated as "daily" is used nowhere else in the New Testament. Possible meanings include that which is necessary for one's existence, necessary for the present day, or necessary for a future day. This much is certain: the bread of the Jesus prayer isn't a spiritualized bread; it is food for each day, one meal at a time, for others and ourselves.

According to the United Nations, 25,000 people—mostly children—die every day from hunger-related causes. Over eighteen deaths every minute. A death every three seconds. Daily bread. Most of us never think twice about it, but nearly ten million people die each year for want of it.

What can you do to make daily bread possible for more people?

FORGIVE US
Luke 11:4a

"Forgive us, as we forgive others."

+

The stories are beyond comprehension. Pope John Paul II sitting with his would-be killer, Mehmet Ali Agca, and forgiving him. The Amish of Nickel Mines, Pennsylvania, forgiving Charles Roberts, who killed five of their children.

Forgiveness doesn't come naturally. We're born with the absence of a forgiveness gene. Though the notion of forgiveness lies at the heart of the world's great religions, the practice of forgiveness is a scarce commodity. Whether the wound is slight or severe, forgiveness is no easy thing to pull off.

Jesus doesn't teach us to pray, "Forgive our sins because we're sorry for them" . . . "Forgive us because we promise to do better next time" . . . "Forgive our sins because in spite of them, we're still nice people." We pray for God to forgive us *in the manner* in which we forgive others, *because* we forgive others, *like* we forgive others. C. S. Lewis (*The Weight of Glory*) takes this to its sobering conclusion: "We are to forgive them all, however spiteful, however mean, however often they are repeated. If we don't, we shall be forgiven none of our own."

What seemed to come with relative ease for Pope John Paul II and the Amish is far more difficult, perhaps, for the rest of us. Yet, we pray this prayer and, if we're open to its shaping influence in our lives, learn that forgiveness doesn't change what's been done; it changes the person who prays it. When all is said and prayed, the little word *as* can keep you up at night.

What's the name of the person you need to forgive?

184

TRIAL RELIEF
Luke 11:4b

"And lead us not into trying times."

+

The familiar rendering of this petition is, "Lead us not into temptation." Whether the Greek word *peirasmos* is translated as "temptation" or "adversity" or "trial," this petition is a troubling request.

Does God actually set the stage for temptations and design the
scenarios that bring adversities on us? Does God test our faithfulness
by creating obstacle courses of tribulation through which we must navigate? Or is this petition calling upon God to rescue and save us when
such trying times arise?

Perhaps the aim of this petition is less a matter of talking God out
of doing something that poses a threat to us, than one of leaning on
God when such occasions arise. The trying time to which we're most
susceptible is leaning upon ourselves, imagining we're on our own and
that it's all up to us.

This prayer in general and this petition in particular are a cry of
dependence. If we have any awareness at all of ourselves, this much we
know to be true: on our own, left to ourselves, empowered by what
little strength we're able to scrape together, we're prone to succumb to
failure and loss of nerve.

Realizing our limitations, we're invited to pray boldly, "Your
strength, O God, we seek, in times of trials and temptations. Don't let
us fail."

What trying times are you facing?

HOW CAN I SAY?

As earlier noted, Luke's inclusion of Jesus' prayer is a shortened version of the more familiar one found in Matthew. Let's visit this prayer one more time using the traditional wording many of us know by heart. I am thankful to countless unnamed people who have asked the questions this prayer raises.

How can I say *our* unless I make room for others who, in some ways or every way, are different from me?

How can I say *Father* unless I also acknowledge the feminine biblical qualities of God as a nursing mother and a protective hen who cares for her young?

How can I say *who art in heaven* unless I'm willing to believe in what I can't see or touch?

How can I say *hallowed be your name* unless I commit myself to respecting the life of every living creature?

How can I say *your kingdom come, your will be done* unless I'm willing to work toward that reality?

How can I say *on earth as it is in heaven* unless I believe that this world—here and now—is where God acts?

How can I say *give us this day our daily bread* unless I commit myself to improving the lives of those who don't have enough?

How can I say *forgive our sins as we forgive the sins of others* unless I make forgiveness a regular practice?

How can I say *lead us not into temptation* unless I'm willing to accept the leading of God to places I might not be willing to go?

How can I say *deliver us from evil* unless I'm willing to fight against evil in all its shadowy forms, including the evil that resides in me?

How can I say *for yours is the kingdom* unless I'm working to create God's new society for all people?

How can I say *and the power* unless I'm willing to acknowledge that all human powers, including my own, are submissive to God?

How can I say *and the glory* unless I'm willing to serve humbly without seeking glory for myself?

How can I say *forever* unless I truly believe that in God's hands, forever is held?

What part of this prayer is most difficult for you to live out?

186

KEEP AT IT
Luke 11:5-8

Jesus said, "Suppose you go to a neighbor's house at midnight and say, 'Please give me three loaves of bread; friends of mine arrived unannounced, and I've nothing to give them.' Your neighbor answers, 'Don't bother me; the house is locked up and my children are asleep. I can't help you.' Let me remind you, even though your neighbor is reluctant to help you out as a friend, because you won't take no for an answer, he'll get up and give you what you need."

+

In this story, one's hospitality is taxed to the max. The one imposed upon has three good reasons not to help: (1) the property has been locked up for the night; (2) the children are sound asleep; and (3) getting up would cause too much commotion. Since most Palestinian houses consisted of one room where the entire family slept, we can understand the neighbor's reluctance to offer assistance at this late hour. Yet, because of the persistent request, the neighbor will oblige.

Kenneth Bailey (*Poet and Peasant/Through Peasant Eyes*) suggests that the neighbor is moved to help so as to avoid the public shame of having it known in the village that he refused to give assistance to one in need. No doubt, the borrower is aware of this as well.

The Greek word translated as "persistence" can also be understood as "importunity" or "shamelessness." All three words suggest a nagging tenacity and a stubborn determination that refuses to give in or give up until the request is heeded. In short, the borrower is stubborn enough not to give up.

There are days, and we all have them, when the only thing we can do is to not give up, to hang in there until something happens. Blessed are those who keep at it.

What situation in your life requires persistent action?

187

ASK, SEARCH, KNOCK
Luke 11:9-10

Jesus reminded the disciples, "Ask, and you will get; search, and you will find; knock, and the door will open. Everyone who asks receives, everyone who searches finds, and everyone who knocks will find the door open."

+

If only it were so easy. If only it depended on our asking, our searching, and our knocking. If only we were persuasive enough to get that for which we pray.

One doesn't have to be a prayer veteran to realize that the promises of these verses don't always match life's experiences. We all have stories about asking until our voices weakened, searching until our eyes dimmed, knocking until our knuckles bled (at least figuratively). After all the praying and pleading, things only got worse: The cancer metastasized; the ALS worsened; a loved one died. Our requests fell on a deaf deity. Our arm-twisting couldn't get heaven to come around to our way of thinking. Our prayers failed.

Then comes the self-doubt, the nagging worry that we did something wrong, that our well-intended praying was flawed beyond effectiveness. Maybe we should have prayed harder, longer, more confidently, less selfishly, or upside down three days a week.

If asking, searching, and knocking were our idea, maybe we could dismiss the promise of answered prayer as nothing more than wishful thinking on our part. But it isn't. Jesus himself instructs his disciples and us to begin by asking, searching, and knocking.

Are the lessons here to keep at it, never to stop, to plead with God until God finally caves in to our requests? In a parable Jesus tells of a persistent widow (Luke 18:1-8), that seems to be the case. But maybe there's another lesson, a more basic reality at work here. Perhaps we simply need to start, to gather the courage, the strength, the awareness . . . to begin.

What keeps you from initiating prayer?

Managua, Nicaragua

MENU MIXUPS
Luke 11:11-13

"If your child asks for a fish, do you give him a snake instead? If your child asks for an egg, do you give her a scorpion? If you, who are capable of doing evil things, know how to give good gifts to your children, how much more will your Heavenly Parent give the Holy Spirit to those who ask!"

+

Jesus shifts from the neighbor at midnight to the parent/child relationship. Would a loving parent ever give a child something dangerous? A snake for a fish? A scorpion for an egg? Of course not! Though these pairings share a resemblance—an eely snake looks like a fish and a coiled scorpion looks like an egg—one is harmful; the other is healthy.

This section of Luke, beginning with the disciples' request for Jesus to teach them to pray, ends with God's willingness to give us the one needful thing—God's Spirit. Prayer's ultimate purpose brings us into communion with God. Prayer is the door through which we experience God's intimate dwelling. The most satisfying answer to our prayers is not necessarily the thing for which we pray, but God's self. When we are attentive to such a presence, whether or not we utter words to acknowledge it, we are in the midst of prayer.

Maybe our unanswered prayers will never find their answers. Maybe we'll never know the reason for not getting those things for which we persistently prayed. Maybe being completely and totally in the presence of God will be enough.

How do you deal with unanswered prayer?

NOT SATISFIED
Luke 11:14-16

One day, Jesus expelled a demon that was afflicting a person who could not speak. When the healed person finally spoke, the crowd was amazed. But some skeptics said, "He casts out demons by Beelzebul, the ruler of the demons." Others demanded that Jesus give a heavenly sign.

+

The response of the crowd receives more coverage than the healing itself. Jesus' powerful demonstration elicits from the witnesses multiple reactions: some are amazed, some accuse him of collaborating with the devil, and others, clearly not satisfied with what they've seen, demand a heavenly sign.

Nobody believes that the healing is a hoax. No one suggests that this is a fake demonstration. There's no denying that the mute is suddenly able to speak. The crowd is interested in one thing only: From where and from whom does this power originate? What's Jesus' source? Does he have the proper credentials to liberate people? If Jesus' critics can't disprove the healing, the next-best strategy is to find him guilty of unsavory associations.

Dark forces, it was believed, inhabit the world. Demons, devils, even Beelzebul (literally, "the Lord of the house") could manufacture powerful displays. Of course, we don't hold to such superstitions anymore, right? Have you ever wondered why many elevators in modern high-rise buildings are missing a thirteenth-floor button?

Some demand the confirmation of a heavenly sign. A voice from above? Angels circling the sky? What sign would suffice? Jesus gives voice to a mute man. How do you top that? Everything they need to know is standing in front of them—a healed man and a healed man's healer.

For some, it's not enough, and anything else offered won't prove enough either. A "never satisfied" posture some gladly choose. It's easier to define ourselves by what we stand against than by what we stand for. Some people just can't shake off their negative identity.

What are you waiting for God to prove?

FINGER OF GOD
Luke 11:17-23

Sensing their thoughts, Jesus said, "Every reality divided against itself becomes a desert, or a house collapsing on itself. You say that I'm in cahoots with Beelzebul, but if Satan is in an alliance with me, how will his reality stand? If I cast out the demons by the power of Beelzebul, by whom do your exorcists cast them out? Let them be your judges. Because I expel demons by the finger of God, God's reign has come to you. When a fully armed man guards his house, the property is safe. But when one stronger comes along and overpowers him, he takes away his trusted weapons and plunders the property. Those who are not with me are against me, and those who do not gather with me, scatter."

+

Jesus responds to his critics with a three-part answer. First, he rejects the accusation that he is a partner with Satan. Why would Satan work against himself and cast out one of his own demons? Not only would such collaboration prove counterproductive; it would ensure the total collapse of Satan's world.

Second, Jesus turns the question on his accusers. If you accuse me of working with the devil, with whom do your own exorcists work? Many Jewish exorcists were plying their trade throughout Palestine. If his critics insist on implicating Jesus with the devil, then those exorcists should be implicated as well.

Finally, Jesus draws the obvious connection between his work and God's work; they are one and the same. The finger of God that amazed even the magicians of the Pharaoh (Exodus 8:19), that metaphorically inscribed the stone tablets of the Ten Commandments (Exodus 31:18), and that caused the poet to marvel at the heavens (Psalm 8:3), is the same creative power at work in Jesus.

The systems and structures of evil that seem in charge are dealt a mortal blow by one stronger than the "strong man." Though the outcome is determined, skirmishes and clashes continue. Each day we decide with whom to stand.

Where is the most convincing evidence of God's finger at work in your world?

RE-HABITATION
Luke 11:24-26

"When an unclean spirit leaves a person, it wanders aimlessly looking for a suitable place. If none is found, it returns to the house it once inhabited. Though the house might be swept clean, the evil spirit brings seven other spirits—more evil than itself—to live there, making the person worse off."

+

Cleanliness might be next to godliness, but cleanliness left unattended is an open invitation to trouble. A plot of dirt cleared of weeds and left to itself is overrun in no time with a fresh crop of thistles, dandelions, and crab grass. A clean-swept house left unattended is a welcome space for critters, intruders, and, in some neighborhoods, drug dealers. We know the obvious lessons. It's not enough to clean it up and leave it at that; something needs to take up the vacancy—new sod, fresh plantings, occupants, and homeowners.

If talk of demons and evil spirits doesn't work for our modern senses, then let's change the terminology. Instead of evil spirits inhabiting the soul, think of destructive patterns of behavior. Imagine those attitudes and mindsets that have the capacity to dominate and control us. If Satan's activity doesn't register on your radar screen, how about the evil wrought by addictions and compulsions and impulses that are every bit as deadly? Maybe this passage has more to say to us than we imagine.

Jesus teaches an important lesson about emotional health and spiritual well-being, echoed in the Bob Dylan song "You Gotta Serve Somebody." That somebody might be yourself, your career, the corporate ladder, materialistic gods, even the devil itself—or God.

On the path to health, it's not enough to rid oneself of behaviors, attitudes, addictions, and compulsions that take us down Dead End Road and Despair Alley. We need to fill the vacancy left by their expulsion with a new master. Either we choose to live under God's transformation or we run the risk that former gods will return in supersized degrees of infestation. Every twelve-step program teaches that healing is a lifelong process that requires the supportive presence of others.

What space in your life is awaiting re-habitation?

HEARERS AND DOERS
Luke 11:27-28

As Jesus was talking, a woman in the crowd blurted out, "Blessed is the mother that birthed you and the woman who nursed you!" Jesus replied, "Blessed rather are those who hear God's teachings and obey them!"

+

The unidentified woman praises Jesus' mother Mary for the man he turned out to be. She honors Jesus' family of origin, then blesses the womb and breasts that carried and cared for him. This nameless woman is impressed with what she hears, and wants Jesus to know she appreciates his upbringing. Perhaps she's giving expression to her own regret for not having birthed a son like Jesus. A woman's worth, society maintained, was determined by her husband and the children (especially sons) she bore.

Though Jesus' reply seems like a mild rebuke, we shouldn't understand it as a denigration of the family, but as an expansion of it. Jesus isn't belittling motherhood, but exalting a woman's personhood. Her value isn't determined by her childbearing capacity, but through hearing and doing the word of God.

God's presence in Jesus redirects where we find our value, how we acquire our worth, and where we discover our status. The God who gives a voice to the mute and subdues the strong arm of the Evil One is the same God who gives welcome and blessing to those who, regardless of parentage, family, fortune, or misfortune, live the godly life. Blessed are they who hear these words and live them out.

Where have you experienced your value affirmed?

INSIDERS AND OUTSIDERS
Luke 11:29-32

As the crowds grew, Jesus continued to teach: "People today have evil intentions. They ask for a miraculous sign, but no sign will be given except the sign of Jonah. In the same way Jonah was a sign to the people of Nineveh, I will be a sign for people of this time. The queen of the South, who traveled a great distance to listen to King Solomon's wisdom, will rise and judge people of this time and condemn them. Listen to me, someone greater than Solomon is here! The people of Nineveh weren't nearly as wicked as people today. At least the city of Nineveh repented because of Jonah's preaching. Don't miss the point I'm making: someone greater than Jonah is here!"

+

Those demanding an additional sign from heaven get their answer: Jesus won't give an additional sign. The preaching of Jonah became a sign for the people of Nineveh to repent. Jesus also stands in a prophetic role before his people, but unlike the citizens of that ancient city, his own people refuse to hear the word of God.

King Solomon's wisdom attracted the attention of the queen of Sheba, the queen of the South (I Kings 10). Impressed with Solomon's wisdom, she offered a vast array of gifts and praised the God of Israel.

In both examples, outsiders to the promises of God become insiders when they accepted the truth proclaimed by God's messengers and representatives. Jesus' ministry exposes the insiders, the ones in possession of the traditions and ancient stories, who exercise stubborn unbelief.

What are we to make of this irony? Those who should embrace the good news proclaimed by Jesus refuse; those who seem unlikely to perceive God's presence in Jesus do. Those closest are farthest away; those far off are near. Pagan Nineveh is more responsive than pious Jerusalem. An Arabian queen is holier than the religious elite. Outsiders become insiders and insiders become outsiders. Abiding here are lessons, if we're willing to see them.

What "signs" are people hoping to see?

WIDE-EYED/SQUINTY-EYED
Luke 11:33-36

"No one lights a lamp and then covers it up. Instead, you set it on a table so that those in the room can see the light. Your eye is like a light for your body. If your eyes are open, your whole body is light-filled; but if your eyes are closed, your body is full of darkness. Be careful that the light in you doesn't grow dark. If your whole body is full of light, with no darkness, you will give off as much light as a lamp's brightness."

+

Sometimes a different translation opens new vistas of understanding. Consider Eugene Peterson's interpretive treatment of this passage in *The Message*: "If you live wide-eyed in wonder and belief, your body fills up with light. If you live squinty-eyed in greed and distrust, your body is a dank cellar."

The light is Jesus, who said, "I am the world's light. Whoever follows me won't walk in darkness but will have the light of life" (John 8:12). Though the light of Jesus is present in the world, whether or not one perceives the light depends on opening one's eyes.

Living with our eyes open allows Jesus' light to fill our presence. His light will illumine and expose even that which we hope remains hidden in a secret interior closet. But if health is the goal, the pain that comes with exposure is a necessary prescriptive step to spiritual wholeness. No pain, no gain.

However, we can choose to live in squinty-eyed littleness. What happens to our eyes when we grow suspicious of someone's motives? What happens to our eyes the moment we decide to plot a little revenge? Our eyes reduce to narrow slits through which anger vents. Not a pretty picture.

Maybe we should start each day checking our eyes. Are they opened wide to wonder's light or squinty slits of meanness?

What will your eyes convey today?

CUP CONCERNS
Luke 11:37-41

A respected religious leader invited Jesus to his house for a meal; Jesus accepted and took his place at the table. The host was amazed that Jesus didn't first wash before eating. Sensing the disapproval, Jesus said, "Why is it that some religious leaders clean the outside of the cup and the dish, but inside are full of greed and evil? Foolish people! Didn't the one who made the outside make the inside too? Give to others what's inside you, and you'll be clean through and through."

+

There's no suggestion that this religious person has ulterior motives in inviting Jesus to join him for dinner. Not everyone in the religious establishment opposed Jesus; some were sympathetic and willing to listen to what Jesus had to say.

In Jesus' day, one did not invite one's enemy to supper. The fact that Jesus accepts the invitation is evidence of the ease with which he interacts with all kinds of people—saints and sinners, the respected and despised, those in the center and those on the fringes.

Though the invitation comes as a friendly offer, the congeniality doesn't last. Jesus chooses to ignore the customary pre-dinner washing. Whether his hands were dirty or not isn't the point. The issue for the religious leader transcends hygiene: by failing to wash his hands, Jesus violates the ceremonial law and, in the opinion of the watchful host, renders himself unclean and sinful.

Jesus turns this episode into a teaching moment. As a cup can be clean on the outside but filthy on the inside, so it is with some spiritual leaders. What good is a clean exterior if the interior doesn't match up? What good is a well-scrubbed face if the heart is soiled? Since God is God of both, one shouldn't be satisfied with a public self that bears no resemblance to the private self. We might fool some, but not God.

Paying attention to our interior lives is as important as the attention we give to our exterior lives. Like the habit of giving offerings to the poor, attending to what resides within might be the best cleansing agent of all.

What in your interior or exterior life is ready for some cleaning up?

MULTIPLE WARNINGS
Luke 11:42-48

"Watch out if you think you're so religious! You give to God a tenth of your income but neglect fairness and don't show God's love. These things you ought to practice without neglecting the rest. Watch out, those of you who think you're so spiritual! You love the best seats in the houses of worship and all the adulation that comes your way in the marketplaces. Beware! You're like unmarked graves that people walk over without realizing it." One of the legal scholars objected, "Teacher, you insult us too when you say these things." Jesus replied, "The same goes for you! You burden people with impossible expectations and don't lift a finger to ease them. You're just as guilty! You build tombs for the prophets your ancestors killed. You're nothing more than collaborators."

+

Not satisfied with keeping the conversation on cups and dishes, Jesus issues five warnings.

Certain religious leaders tithe (give 10 percent), yet are guilty of ignoring the larger concerns of fairness to the poor and love for God.

Some holy-minded folks are driven by pride and seek the places that give them the best exposure.

Instead of being life-givers, certain pious ones are life-takers, seeking to indict people who inadvertently tread on graves. The reference to unmarked graves is an allusion to Numbers 19:16, "Whoever touches . . . a grave will be unclean for seven days."

That a legal expert should object is no reason for Jesus to tone down his rebukes. Certain lawyers are guilty of requiring of others what they don't require of themselves. Jesus compares them to their ancestors who killed the prophets because they didn't like the prophets' message. Building tombs for murdered prophets is no less an affront to God than holding the swords that slew them.

Some religious leaders in the community fail to encourage others and refuse to lift up the weary or walk alongside them. They speak a good line, but don't follow through.

Which warning hits closest to home for you?

KEY OF KNOWLEDGE
Luke 11:49-54

Jesus continued, "God wisely said, 'I'll send prophets and apostles, some of whom they will treat cruelly and kill.' People today will be guilty of the death of all prophets since the beginning of time, from Abel's death to Zechariah's, who died between the altar and the temple. Punishment will come. Consider this a warning. You've hidden the key of knowledge. Not only do you lack this knowledge; you hinder others from acquiring it." The religious leaders were furious and questioned him on many topics. Waiting for just the right moment, they baited Jesus to say something they could use against him.

+

These verses bring to a close Jesus' warnings to any who use religion to penalize others. Jesus doesn't question their orthodoxy. Their failure is evidenced in their chosen preferences. Rules take priority over relationships. One's exterior life conceals an inferior inner life. Those who don't measure up are excluded from the community of the faithful. All determinations are the domain of the professionals who understand truth as fixed and static for all time.

These preferences mean one thing. Instead of encouraging others to experience the life-giving reality of God, certain leaders have hindered others from acquiring it. They're not facilitators, but roadblocks. The guardians of the religious traditions do the opposite of Jesus. Though much about their lives is laudable, some have stripped religion of all intimacy with God.

Perhaps we have personal inclinations and preferences of our own: Am I better able to identify faults in others than the same faults in myself? Why is it easier for me to weep when others weep than to rejoice when others rejoice? Where did I get this notion that the evils I avoid excuse me from the good I should take up? Why is it that the sins I rank as most heinous are the ones that don't seem to tempt me? Why do I take no little satisfaction in seeing public figures caught in their indiscretions?

Any personal preferences of yours in need of deletion?

NO SECRETS
Luke 12:1-3

Huge crowds followed Jesus, prompting him to speak privately to his disciples. "Beware of the yeast within some who consider themselves more religiously pure than others. I'm talking about their hypocrisy. Hidden things will see the light of day, and nothing will remain a secret forever. Whatever you say in the dark will get heard in the light, and what you whisper behind closed doors will get shouted from rooftops."

+

Contrasting the growing opposition against Jesus is the growing acceptance of his ministry and work. With near rock-star popularity, Jesus attracts thousands (a literal translation of the Greek allows for "tens of thousands") of fans, curiosity seekers, and those looking for displays of power.

Amidst it all, Jesus comments to the intimate circle of his disciples about certain religious leaders. The "yeast" Jesus identifies within certain leaders suggests an influence and pervasiveness that remain subtly hidden while performing a corrupting work. What Jesus is referring to is not altogether clear, but the combination of "yeast" with "hypocrisy" suggests he is exposing the religious leaders' masquerade. Outwardly, they observe the practices of tithing and ceremonial cleanliness, but inwardly they harbor ill intentions.

Again, Jesus isn't commenting about all the religious leaders of his day, but on those whose behavior is insincere. Their external performances mask baser motives. Though their behavior (detailed in the previous chapter) suggests a sincere piety, such externals are mere cover-ups for what lies within their hearts.

Truth, however, will have the day. Light will expose motives. Displays of outer piety—no matter how Oscar-worthy—will not mask forever the inner reality. It's enough to make anyone antsy about harboring secrets. Either we come clean on our own, sooner, or get exposed, later.

How might you flush out hypocrisy in your life?

HAIRS AND SPARROWS
Luke 12:4-7

"Don't fear those who can kill your body; they can do nothing more to harm you. Rather, fear the one who can kill you and sentence you to hell. Even though five sparrows are sold for two cents, God does not forget any of them. God knows the number of hairs on your head. So, don't be afraid. You are far more valuable to God than many sparrows."

+

Jesus prepares his disciples for the future. Malevolent people and godless empires have the power to kill them. But death isn't the domain of earthly authorities only. God, too, can bring about death, but God's power reaches beyond this life.

The Greek word used here for "hell" is *Gehenna*. The name is traced to the Valley of Hinnon that served as a burning garbage dump outside the walls of Jerusalem. Those who will threaten the disciples, even with death, are not as powerful as God, who alone can cast the darkest forces into a figurative Gehenna.

If God's power to cast enemies aside is worthy of respect, how much more is God's desire to care for those who seek the justice of God's rule—a truth illustrated by sparrows and hairs. Two sparrows were sold in the market for a penny. For two cents, one could purchase four sparrows and get an extra thrown in for good measure. Even five sparrows—collectively worth only two cents—are valued by the Creator.

And head hairs counted by God? The Master Storyteller's way of reminding us that God's relationship with us is one of profound intimacy. Though this intimacy doesn't insulate us from danger and death, it does provide ultimate security. Says Jesus, "Don't fear what might or might not happen. Know who holds your life, in this world and beyond."

What does feeling secure look like to you?

AGAINST THE HOLY SPIRIT
Luke 12:8-12

"To those who witness to me before others, I will do the same before the angels of God. But those who deny me, I will deny before the angels of God. Whoever speaks against me will be forgiven; but whoever speaks against the Holy Spirit will not be forgiven. When they bring you before religious and political authorities, don't worry about making a defense. The Holy Spirit will give you the words."

+

Jesus' disciples need assurances in times of insecurity. When the disciples face persecution and are accused of crimes against the empire, acknowledging their commitment to God's reign will bring assurance that Jesus is acknowledging them before authorities greater than Rome. Who can harm the real you when the real you is embraced by the one who absorbed the world's pain?

There is little agreement regarding the unforgivable sin of speaking against the Holy Spirit. Nor is it clear why an affront to Jesus is forgivable, but not one against the Holy Spirit. Some scholars suggest that speaking against Jesus is a specific act of rejection, whereas speaking against the Holy Spirit is a continuous state of rebellion. Others suggest the sin against the Holy Spirit is the deliberate and defiant act of calling good evil, and right wrong.

Though speaking against the Holy Spirit may include elements of all these answers, I find the explanations unconvincing. I believe there is no sin that lies beyond God's desire to forgive and forget, yet some human responses inflict more self-damage than others do. As Greg Carey of Lancaster Theological Seminary noted in *The Huffington Post* (June 15, 2012): "When I see healing at work, but resentment and fear build up in my heart, I'm executing deep damage upon my own capacity to live by grace and hope. I'm bringing the power of death to my own soul." Choosing intentional obstinacy instead of God's healing and transformative work is the ultimate mystery. Perhaps an even greater mystery is heard from the cross when Jesus prays, "Father, forgive them. They don't know what they're doing."

What's been your greatest life-and-death struggle?

INHERITANCE HASSLES
Luke 12:13-15

Someone in the crowd said to Jesus, "Teacher, tell my brother to cooperate in dividing up the family property left to us." Jesus replied, "Why should I get involved with this dispute?" Then Jesus said to the crowd, "Look out! There are all kinds of greed. Life is not about how many possessions you have."

+

A nameless individual in the crowd looks to Jesus for help in settling a family squabble about inheritance. The person isn't looking for advice on how to handle the grief over a father's death, or how best to care for a surviving mother, or whether there's life after death. No concern is shown about patching up the ruptured relationship with a sibling. The issue in all its familial ugliness is: How do we divide the stuff so I get what's rightfully mine?

Regrettably, this post-funeral scenario is repeated in many families. Disagreements about who gets the good china and who lays claim to the diamond earrings can leave siblings with cold hearts and hot tempers, unwilling to communicate for years. Squabbles can turn into all-out war with siblings at each other's throats. Sometimes the relational damage is permanent.

That Jesus is aware of his tradition's inheritance laws already governing such family issues may be the reason for his sharp refusal to play the role of referee. Why should he get entangled in a family dispute when the law is already clear? Or perhaps Jesus is in no mood to judge which sibling's greed is greater. Either way, his rhetorical question— "Why should I get involved with this dispute?"—suggests at a deeper level that Jesus understands his mission as more significant than deciding who gets the silver tea set and who walks away with the power tools.

Issuing a warning about the predatory nature of greed, Jesus cautions, "Look out! Beware! The stuff we love and dedicate our lives to accumulating can stealthily hunt its prey like a wild beast waiting for the right moment to strike. When the creature attacks, life itself hangs in the balance."

What was your last family squabble about?

203

SURPLUS DILEMMA
Luke 12:16-18

Then Jesus told a story: "The land of a rich farmer produced a bumper crop. The landowner thought, 'What should I do, now that I've run out of space to store my crops?' After mulling it over, he came up with a plan. 'I'll pull down my barns and build bigger ones and store all my crops in them.'"

+

We'd be hard-pressed to find a parable with more all-American themes. The story begins as a capitalist's dream. Hard work, sound planning, fiscal prudence, favorable market conditions, and a little help from Mother Nature all combine to make a rich man even richer. He's what most Americans strive to become—successful.

But how will he manage his success? Such problems! His solution is both obvious and seemingly wise. By tearing down the old barns and constructing new ones, he will solve the dilemma of cramped quarters. More square footage, bigger storage capacity, and higher efficiency are necessary ingredients for running a better business. He wins; his employees win; his customers win. God, life is good!

This barn-razing/barn-raising strategy is one adopted by many faith communities, too. When the present building gets too cramped, the solution is to build an addition or construct a newer version altogether. When the last brick is mortared into place, we throw a huge dedication party to the glory of God.

I'm not suggesting there's anything wrong with that vision's strategic plan. I'm just not convinced it's always the best solution. Whether it's how to store a bumper crop of soybeans, what to do with a financial windfall, or where to seat all the people in worship, a shared fear gets exposed in the unasked question: How do we keep what we have?

The farmer's answer is to build bigger barns. Most church folks would offer a similar solution and build a bigger building. In the case of the latter, seldom is there any discussion about giving away a sizable number of congregants to another location or neighborhood and birthing another church or two. Adding to the square footage might be the way to go, but a case can be made for dividing in order to multiply.

Where's your largest surplus?

A CONVERSATION
Luke 12:19

"The farmer reasoned with himself, 'Soul, you've got plenty of goods stored up for many years. Relax, eat, and drink. Enjoy the good life.'"

+

Hey, soul! How fortunate we are! How far we've come since our early days of scratching out an existence—the meager two acres we once leased; the cramped, one-bedroom farmhouse; the second-hand equipment we duct-taped together.

It all seems like a long, long time ago. Who could have predicted our success? Yes, we've got plenty of goods to protect us from life's uncertainties.

Relax! We've worked hard and deserve this payoff. Earned everything we've got. Nobody handed us anything (except, of course, the perfect weather, tax credits, and farm subsidies). Self-made we are and proud of it. Our time has come, for sure. Around-the-clock leisure is what we're after now.

Eat? Drink? You bet we will—anything and everything! If we want it, we'll have it. Let's savor our good fortune as the aroma whets our appetite. May we never talk about hunger and thirst—our own or anyone else's. No reminders of distended bellies and flies in the eyes. No mention of bloated excess and shallow lives.

Enjoy the good life? Of course! Why would we try to do otherwise? After all, even at its longest, life is short. If you can't spend it laughing at the world and letting others know what you have, then what's the use in having it all?

Besides, if we can't be happy with all this, we'd be nothing but fools.

Which parts of this conversation describe you?

FOOL
Luke 12:20-21

"But God said to the rich man, 'You're such a fool! Your life will end tonight, and who will benefit from all the things you've kept for yourself?' That's what it will be like for those who hoard treasures on earth but aren't rich toward God."

+

God calls the rich man a fool, but there are many names he isn't called. He isn't called a crook, a scoundrel, or a thief. He isn't called a liar, a scam artist, or a cheat. He isn't guilty of bilking senior citizens out of their nest eggs. Never once, apparently, has he over-charged customers for his crops, even though he could have gotten away with it. He isn't accused of shredding documents before a pending IRS audit. He isn't the kind of employer who refuses to pay his share of workers' Social Security tax. He's not a sweatshop operator.

God doesn't call him a bad man or an evil man, just a foolish man. He's a fool for placing too much weight on the wrong things; a fool for thinking security can be measured down to the square foot; a fool for imagining that his material insulation could keep him from death's cold grip. His grave marker says it all:

He had lots of stuff. He built big barns.
His harvests were awesome. He knew how to spend.
So much potential. So many opportunities.
So little to show for it in the end.

The story begs a few questions: What people-investments did he make? Did he work to alleviate suffering? Were other lives better off because of him? Did he ever stop to think of the "have-nots" in his corner of the world, and what he could do to assist them?

If this were merely an ancient tale, we could easily forget about it and move on. However, it speaks to us today, prompting some personal inventory. For what will I be remembered? Whose life was touched because I was here? What in this world will be better because I lived?

What relationships in your life are in need of more investment?

THE ABUNDANT GOD
Luke 12:22-24

Jesus said to his disciples, "Listen, don't worry about what to eat and what to wear. Life isn't just about food and clothing. Learn from the birds. They don't plant or harvest. They don't have storehouses or barns. That's because God feeds them. You're much more valuable than birds!"

+

Don't worry. Don't get distracted. Don't get pulled in two directions. Either we trust God's care, or we don't.

We might wish it were that easy. Some people seem adept at pulling it off. Saints of past centuries—Francis of Assisi comes to mind—were able to live singularly focused on God. More recently was Mother Teresa, along with the Sisters of Mercy, in Calcutta. All those children. All that poverty. She lived as one under a magnifying glass on a cloudless day, burning with the intensity of God.

I imagine St. Francis and Mother Teresa thought about food and clothing only in the ways those necessities could help others. What they cared about, more than their next breath, was the God who breathed upon them. God wouldn't fail to clothe them. God would be the food to sustain them. Life starts and ends with God's abundance.

Where are these people today? Seminaries and theological schools don't offer courses on "The Imitation of St. Francis" or "Be Like Mother Teresa in Ten Days." In my thirty-plus years of working in the church, no one (not once!) ever sat in my office and anguished aloud, "How do I live as freely as the birds?" As far as my own track record is concerned, I'm quite sure I wouldn't have been able to point the way.

Saints perceive God's abundance. The rest of us focus on our scarcity.

What's keeping you from flying?

WORRYING LESS
Luke 12:25-28

"Can you add even a single hour to your life by worrying? Since you're not able to do a small thing like that, why do you worry about the rest? Take a lesson from the lilies. They don't toil or fret, yet wealthy King Solomon wasn't clothed as beautifully as one of them. But if God clothes field grass, which is alive today and gone tomorrow, imagine how much more God will clothe you, even when your faith isn't much!"

+

After the theological textbooks are shelved, the matter of faith inevitably comes down to our willingness or unwillingness to let go. Either we unclench our tight-fisted hold on life, or we don't. Either we live now what matters most or we accept some pale version of the good life. When we stop worrying about this and that, we let go of those things that have the capacity to debilitate and enslave us.

When it comes to worrying less, I certainly wouldn't hold up my own life as a model for anyone to follow. For most of my adult life, I've worn a night guard in my mouth to keep me from grinding my teeth. Teeth grinders have worry issues; we are subconscious fretters. Though I don't live worry-free, I have a strong notion of what worrying less looks like.

Worrying less means I can't control all of life's outcomes, even though I may think I'm in control.

Worrying less means I can't make others do what I think they should do, even though it might be in their best interest.

Worrying less means I can't always fix another's problem but I can be supportive in the struggle.

Worrying less means that the past is done, the future is out of my control, and the present is all I've got.

Worrying less means those who disagree with me aren't necessarily wrong, and because they disagree with me, I'm not necessarily right.

Though we can't add a single hour to our lives by worrying, I'm guessing we can extend our lives by worrying less. I'll take a lesson from the lilies, but I'll keep wearing my mouth guard at night.

What does worrying less look like to you?

208

STRIVING
Luke 12:29-31

"Don't get anxious about what you're going to eat or drink. Stop worrying. People obsessed with this world strive after all these things. God knows what you need. Instead, strive to live out God's intentions for the world. When you do that, the things you really need will be yours as well."

+

Ask a hundred people—churched or unchurched—what it means to strive for the things of God and you're likely to get a hundred different responses.

The late Gordon Cosby (founding pastor of The Church of the Saviour in Washington, D.C.) and Kayla McClurg offer a vision of the reign of God. In a booklet entitled "Becoming the Authentic Church," they articulate a radical mission statement, a portion of which is included here.

> Most churches claim to follow Jesus, but not all are following the authentic Jesus. Too often we fashion Jesus in our own image and then wonder why there is no radical world change . . . There is only one real Jesus into whose being we hope to abandon ourselves, dying to our false illusions and letting our true selves be resurrected in him, who is the world's hope. The authentic church will be a diverse body, inter-connected and interdependent. The diversity will be of every sort—race, gender, economics, sexual orientation, age, etc. . . . If we think Jesus excludes anyone, we haven't yet gone deep enough in discovering who Jesus is.

Striving for a world as God intends it suggests that we haven't yet attained the world God has in mind. Some days it is clear that we're moving toward it, more fully embracing and living it out. Other days, not so much. Always, we are works in progress and projects under construction.

Where are you doing your most active holy striving?

SELL . . . GIVE
Luke 12:32-34

"Don't be afraid, my friends, for God wants to give you all that God has. Sell your possessions and give to the poor. Make wallets and purses for yourselves that don't wear out, a lasting heavenly treasure, where nothing gets stolen or destroyed. Your heart is where your treasures are."

+

God is a vulnerable God who accepts the risk of giving us that which is dear to God's heart. Then comes the specific command to "sell" and "give." Though we try, we can't spiritualize this command or ignore its materialistic tone. Too bad Jesus doesn't say, "OK, now that you're recipients of the things of God, pray, sing hymns, chant, reflect, shout for joy, enjoy yoga, and be filled with wonder." Where do I sign up?

Jesus takes aim at those things we guard with our heaviest arsenal. "Sell your possessions and give to the poor." God knows how hard it is to disinvest ourselves of the things of this world. No wonder we get cramps in our hands from clinging so tightly. Is it significant that Jesus talks more about money and possessions than about any other topic? Maybe that's why he never settles in with one audience of listeners, but moves from town to town. Who can long endure such a message?

As some surveys have shown, Christians in America covet, hoard, and embrace their stuff with no less devotion than those who profess no faith at all. Like a narcotic with demonic influence, money grips us more than we're willing to admit. Our buying and spending habits confirm what we never confess on Sunday morning: our first allegiance is to a consumer-driven culture, and only secondarily to ushering in the kind of world God desires.

The remedy for our addiction, Jesus suggests, is a reiteration of the "hold loosely" attitude. What we give away returns to us. We gain those things we're willing to lose. All that we hold near and dear—whether close to our hearts or our checkbooks—reveals who we truly are.

What's your biggest challenge in handling money and possessions?

Pine Ridge, SD

ALERT LIVING
Luke 12:35-40

"Be ready and light your lamps. Be like those who wait for a homeowner to return from a wedding reception. When the homeowner arrives and knocks, they open the door. The homeowner will bless those who are alert and will get dressed for dinner, inviting them to sit down to eat, and will serve them. If the homeowner comes late at night or early in the morning and finds them ready, they'll be blessed. If the homeowner had known when the thief was ready to strike, the house would have been safe. So, be alert, you never know when the homeowner will arrive."

+

As a youngster, I was frightened by passages like this one, to the point of insomnia. I feared the "unexpected hour" might strike during the night, and what would be my fate if Jesus found me unprepared? Better to enter heaven tired, I reasoned, than miss my only opportunity while fast asleep. (Yes, I had issues involving a scary and unpredictable God!)

Jesus spends an inordinate amount of time, here and elsewhere in Luke, telling his disciples about his return—a return that will be unexpected, unannounced, and sudden. If, as some believe, "being alert" means checking the clouds for his descent or scanning the horizon for his arrival, then I find such futurist concerns a waste of time.

Alert living is keeping our eyes open to the present moment. It means enjoying the day's joys and feeling the day's pains. Alert living is witnessing to the signs of God's activities already breaking into the world. Buddhists call it being present to the now. Alert living is consciously choosing each moment that life gives. Choose to live this way and you're apt to sleep well.

What were your earliest mental pictures of God?

ABUSE OF POWER
Luke 12:41-48

Peter said, "Jesus, is this story for us only or for everyone?" Jesus replied, "Who is the faithful and wise supervisor the homeowner puts in charge of the workers, to give them food at the proper time? The supervisor who works until the homeowner arrives will be blessed and put in charge of everything. But if the supervisor thinks, 'The homeowner isn't coming back for a long time,' and then begins to mistreat other people and get drunk, the homeowner will make a surprise visit and give that supervisor a severe beating. But those who didn't know and deserved a beating will receive a mild punishment. With many blessings come many responsibilities and demands."

+

I count myself among those who would just as soon leave this passage alone and move on to one less violent. How difficult to read this parable and see any trace of good news in it. Then, of course, as we assign the roles, the homeowner ends up being God, and the troublesome nature of these verses is magnified. We often accuse the sacred writings of other faith traditions (The Koran, for example) of justifying violence. As residents in the Bible's glass house, perhaps we should refrain from throwing the first stone!

I'm left with this thought: Sloppy living, whether it's inattention to the present moment, the shirking of responsibilities, sheer laziness in doing the right thing, or any behavior where the strong abuse the weak, has no place in God's world. Those in leadership positions, the disciples among them, have a unique calling as God's stewards. Power comes with the job description and can be used for good or ill, to lift others up or bring the innocent down.

Religious systems and institutions that claim God's blessing are especially prone to power's misuse. The wake left by the abuse of the weak and vulnerable is wide, long, and deep.

Where do you see abuse of power in the church?

213

FIRE AND BAPTISM
Luke 12:49-50

"I came to set the world ablaze, and I wish it were already smoldering! I must undergo a baptism of suffering, and I'm under great stress until it is completed!"

+

Jesus teaches his disciples another lesson on the nature of his work and mission. If they imagine following him as an idyllic and serene exercise, such notions are abruptly dispelled.

Jesus' use of the fire image is reminiscent of the prophetic understanding of fire as a purifying agent. "God is like a refiner's fire and like fuller's soap, a purifier of silver, and God will purify the descendants of Levi and refine them like gold and silver" (Malachi 3:2-3).

Fire separates the pure from the alloyed, good from evil, and light from darkness. Like fire to metal, Jesus exposes our contrasting loyalties. Recall the prediction of Simeon, who, when holding the infant Jesus in his arms, said, "This child is destined for the falling and rising of many in Israel" (Luke 2:34). Jesus brings a crisis of choice.

The baptism of which Jesus speaks isn't a direct reference to the occasion of his baptism by John in the Jordan River, but refers to his impending suffering and death. These are the "baptismal waters" through which he must go and the cup of suffering from which he must drink. Soon, he'll be doused in them.

With his face still set toward Jerusalem, Jesus expresses the most human of cries: "I'm under great stress!" The weight he bears is heavy, and the future toward which he moves is threatening. Though he could, he doesn't turn back, but continues to live out his mission and calling.

What comfort is there knowing Jesus endured such hardships?

FAMILY DIVISION
Luke 12:51-53

"Do you think that I've come to usher in peace on earth? Think again—I've come to bring division! From now on, five people in one house will be divided, three against two and two against three. Father will be pitted against son and son against father, mother against daughter and daughter against mother, mother-in-law against daughter-in-law and daughter-in-law against mother-in-law."

+

Can you imagine a candidate running for political office, standing before microphones, making the claims Jesus does? "I'll split families apart. My agenda will include encouraging children to take positions against their parents, and parents against their children. Elect me and together we'll work to destroy the American family."

Much to the shock and dismay of his handlers, Jesus promises to be the reason for such divisions. It's enough to question a spiritual leader's FVQ, or "family values quotient."

Sometimes, the obvious needs to be said so we can work out the implications. Following Jesus will raise the level of conflict we experience. Sometimes our choices will be between good and evil, right and wrong; other times the choices will be between the good and that which is better than the good. Family loyalties might be weighed next to fulfilling one's calling. Egos could die, along with a sense of one's invincibility. Priorities could get shuffled faster than a deck of playing cards. Things we imagined securely anchored could get ripped up and set adrift.

The risks of following Jesus mean we're members of an expanded family, one not based on biological parentage but on Jesus' personhood.

How have you experienced any of these divisions?

WEATHER REPORT
Luke 12:54-56

Jesus said to the crowd, "When you see a cloud moving in from the west, you immediately say, 'It's going to rain soon,' and it happens. When you see the south wind blowing, you say, 'A heat wave is coming,' and it happens. You're nothing but hypocrites! You know how to interpret occurrences on the earth and in the sky, but you don't understand things that are occurring before your eyes."

+

Will it rain or shine? In Palestine, the coming weather is fairly easy to predict. Clouds from the west, off the Mediterranean Sea, will bring rain; winds from the desert in the south will bring heat. It doesn't take a seer or sage to observe nature's patterns and plan accordingly.

Jesus proceeds to chide the weather watchers who are adept at one thing but inept at another. They see the coming weather but refuse to see in Jesus' ministry the embodiment of God's purposes. They fail to interpret what God is doing, and it doesn't bother them in the least.

How would Jesus address an audience today? What would he notice about our ability to discern in some areas but not in others? What do we have an eye for? What are we blind to? I imagine Jesus saying to us: "You know how to read the prices on the New York Stock Exchange, but haven't a clue about eternal values. You know the standings of your favorite sports teams, but are blind to what the least and the last of this world most need. You're familiar with IRAs and deferred annuities, but show no aptitude for higher investments. You can't wait to read the latest tabloid gossip, but can't be bothered to study ancient wisdom. You're attentive to the needs of your pet, but don't know the needs of your neighbor."

Would he call us hypocrites, too . . . and fools . . . and idiots? What compels us to develop expertise in areas that are nothing more than trivial pursuits, and then play the slacker in matters of weighty importance? Do we imagine we have all the time in the world or that someday we'll get around to it? Jesus just shakes his head.

What one good thing have you been putting off doing?

216

OUT-OF-COURT SETTLEMENT
Luke 12:57-59

"Decide what's right. If someone takes you to court over money issues, try to settle things before you're dragged before a judge who might sentence you to a prison term. You'll never get out until you've paid every last cent."

+

Sometimes the choice is as simple as taking care of matters sooner rather than later. There's nothing particularly spiritual about that strategy; it's just good sense. Every homeowner knows the wisdom of paying attention to a slow drip in the attic roof while it's still a manageable and inexpensive repair.

Most of us would live better lives, more intentional lives, more focused lives, if we were constantly aware of our own mortality. When we're young and healthy, time seems to go on forever. We imagine our lives will never run out of tomorrows. That changes as we grow older. The older we get, the more we realize time is a depleting commodity.

I don't desire to know the number of days or weeks or years I have left to live. I imagine, though, the benefits of a warning system—general, yet just specific enough—to get me to discern the times and take care of matters sooner rather than later.

I'm thinking of a color-coded system. Every morning on the bathroom mirror a single colored dot—say, three inches in diameter—would magically appear with my current age. The appearance of a green dot would mean I have 0–40 years to live; a blue dot, 0–20 years; a yellow dot, 0–10 years; a red dot, 0–5 years; and an orange dot, reminding me I have less than a month.

I wouldn't know which dot to expect each day; it could be any of the five colors. I might have forty years to go, or four days. I wouldn't know whether the time frame was accurate. I'd be left wondering.

The morning dot ritual would teach me about the importance of discerning the times. I think I'd be less prone to put off what should be done sooner rather than later. Maybe I'd even settle the case, or the argument, or the misunderstanding *that day* rather than put it off to a future that's not guaranteed.

What do you need to tend to now?

217

SINGLED OUT?
Luke 13:1-5

Some people told Jesus about the Galileans whom Pilate killed and whose blood he then mixed with the blood of sacrificed animals. Jesus asked them, "Do you think this happened because those Galileans who died were worse sinners than other Galileans? Listen, if you don't repent, you'll perish as they did. Do you imagine that the eighteen people who were killed when the tower of Siloam fell on them were worse sinners than others living in Jerusalem at the time? Listen, if you don't repent, you'll suffer the same fate."

+

In response to murders orchestrated by an oppressive government and a power-hungry magistrate, Jesus offers no answer. In response to senseless deaths that resulted from a freak act of nature, Jesus offers no explanation. Those who look to Jesus for answers and explanations walk away disappointed this day.

Jesus doesn't concern himself with what precipitated the twin tragedies. He doesn't use these incidents as an opportunity to lecture on random acts of suffering or the bad hand we're sometimes dealt. Jesus shows no interest in getting into a debate about life's unfairness.

Instead, Jesus twice tells his listeners to repent. On those occasions when death comes suddenly because of ill treatment or because one is in the wrong place at the wrong time, the fragility of life should move us to examine the places where our trust resides.

Can we trust a God who didn't prevent Roman swords from severing Galilean heads? Can we put our faith in a God who didn't catch a falling tower before it smashed into eighteen bystanders? Can we follow a God who didn't take over the cockpit controls of four planes on September 11, 2001? Can we give our hearts to a God who didn't warn coastal residents of a tsunami's path?

Sooner or later, we all stand before death and before God. Proud or penitent? Haughty or humble? Confident in ourselves or confident in God alone? Give thanks to God when it doesn't take a sudden death or a horrific tragedy to get you to ponder the question.

What explanations for human suffering make sense to you?

218

FRUITFUL INTERCESSION
Luke 13:6-9

Jesus told another story: "A man planted a fig tree in his vineyard. Seasons later he came looking for fruit on it and found none. He said to the gardener, 'For three years I've come looking for fruit on this tree and haven't found any. Cut it down! Why should it waste good soil?' The gardener replied, 'Sir, let's give it another year. I'll till the ground and put manure on it. If it bears fruit next season, great; if not, then I'll cut it down.'"

+

God, Israel, fig trees, and vineyards form a common quartet in biblical stories. "Like grapes in the wilderness, I found Israel. Like the first fruit on the fig tree in its first season, I saw your ancestors" (Hosea 9:10). "When I went to gather the grapes and figs there weren't on the vine or on the tree; the leaves were withered" (Jeremiah 8:13).

Because a fig tree produces annual fruit, three years of non-production would cause a landowner concern. The non-bearing tree takes up space and depletes the soil of nutrients. In spite of its inability to produce, a fig tree still requires attention. There are weeds to pull, branches to prune, and roots to water. Logic would dictate to cut it down and plant another one.

But the gardener convinces the owner to give the tree another year. Who knows, he reasons, if the soil is aerated and some fertilizer added, a year could make the difference. Though the parable comes to an inconclusive end, we can assume the owner responds favorably to the gardener's intercession on behalf of the fig tree.

In many biblical stories, an intercessor appeals to God's patience in dealing with a third party. Abraham did on behalf of the people of Sodom. Moses did the same for the Israelites when they defied God by dancing around the golden calf. When describing God's attributes, theologians usually turn to words like *omnipotence* and *omniscience*, words that exalt God's capacity for power and knowledge. Perhaps a case should be made for the divine capacity for patience—a patience that waits for hearts to turn, however long it takes.

What types of people test your patience?

219

BENT OVER
Luke 13:10-11

As Jesus was teaching in a synagogue on the Sabbath, a woman appeared who for eighteen years had been afflicted by an evil spirit that crippled her. She was bent over and unable to stand up straight.

+

We're not told her name, only the details of her condition. Indeed, her name is her condition. Synagogue worshippers know her as the "Crippled Woman" and the "Bent Lady" and the "Hunchback." She has no personhood apart from her infirmity.

This is no casual affliction, like a temporary back spasm that can be cured with two aspirin, a heating pad, and a day of bed rest. For eighteen years, she has stood crooked, a contorted woman of diminished and ever-diminishing stature.

Luke blames her condition on a "spirit." Nefarious, underworld spirits were to the realm of ailments and sicknesses what organized crime families are to prostitution and loan-sharking. Both are nasty and you're best off not running into them.

This bent, nameless woman appears in the synagogue on a Sabbath day. I choose to believe she is there every Sabbath day. Faithful in attendance. Faithful in song. Faithful in prayer. Faithful in devotion. After eighteen years of stiffness and pain, she knows how to cope with anything life throws her way, and she doesn't require a miracle to remain faithful.

Every church, synagogue, or mosque has people like Luke's bent-over woman, people known only by their ailment or problem or disability or condition or orientation. He's the bipolar one. She's the lesbian. They've got the problem child. She's on her third marriage. It's another way—often unconsciously and unintentionally—that we inflict a few more wounds on the already wounded.

What labels most upset you?

SET FREE
Luke 13:12-13

Seeing the woman in pain, Jesus said to her, "Woman, you're free from your affliction." Then he touched her, and immediately she stood up straight and thanked God.

+

She doesn't ask for a miracle. She says nothing to Jesus about her needs. There's no litany of aches and pains. Without prompting, Jesus heals. Her spine straightens and her vertebrae realign. From the encounter, to the physical touch, to the healing, Jesus initiates everything.

Encounters such as this one produce what the gospel writers call miracles. Would we call them such today? I doubt it. Good doctors, competent therapists, and capable chiropractors can do what Jesus did. However, it's still a miracle if you think about it. Just a few generations ago, nobody got heart transplants or new livers. It's a miracle when these cures happen today—more so when one's health insurance picks up the tab. Of course, if you're one of the millions of Americans without insurance, you're on your own when it comes to miracles.

Two truths emerge, the first of which is obvious: Jesus has compassion for suffering people. Human need moves him. He identifies with people's pain, and he's never the least bit interested in assigning blame or finding fault.

The other certainty is more mysterious: Rarely are faithful and saintly people healed of anything in a manner close to the healings recorded in the gospels. For most, healing never comes—not from God, not from doctors, not from anyone. The sick and infirm never get better. Yet I've known scores of people who, in the prison cell of their suffering, have been set free. Such people have revealed to me the reality of miracles.

When have you experienced the miracle of being set free?

RIGHTEOUSLY INDIGNANT
Luke 13:14

The leader of the synagogue was upset because Jesus healed
on the Sabbath, so he said to the crowd, "There are six days
in a week when work ought to be done; come on those days
and be cured, but not on the Sabbath day."

+

Apparently, there's nothing worse than a formerly stooped-over
woman standing upright on the wrong day. After all, there's a time
and place for everything. If she has suffered for eighteen years, what's
one more day when there's a Sabbath day to observe? Not that anyone
is against helping people in need; it's just that there are proper ways to
go about doing it.

The synagogue leader reminds me of the busy minister I knew
who posted his office hours in the church newsletter with the following
reminder to his congregation: "The pastor is available for crisis counseling on Wednesday and Friday mornings." Yes, indeed, people should
have the social grace to plan their crises on appropriate days!

Rather than reprimand Jesus directly, the indignant leader chides
the crowd for cluttering up the Sabbath and ruining a perfectly good
occasion for teaching and worship. The full weight of Old Testament
Sabbath laws is there to back him up. Since curing could be categorized
as a form of work, Jesus is guilty of violating the Sabbath and breaking
the third commandment.

Rules are rules, put there for a reason. Sometimes, 20/20 vision
that focuses on requirements and regulations blinds us to what God is
doing outside the lines. That's enough to make *God* righteously indignant.

When was the last time you ignored the rules to carry out a greater good?

TIMELESS COMPASSION
Luke 13:15-17

Jesus responded to the criticism, "You're hypocrites! Don't all of you untie your ox or donkey and lead it to water on the Sabbath? Shouldn't this woman, a daughter of Abraham, a woman Satan has afflicted for eighteen long years, be set free on the Sabbath day, too?" His critics were ashamed and said nothing more. The rest of the crowd rejoiced at the wonderful things Jesus was doing.

+

Jesus wastes no time answering his critics. If a beast of burden could be untied and led to water on the Sabbath, shouldn't this woman, a daughter of Abraham—one of our own people, no less!—be set free from her bondage? Is it right for a tethered and thirsty animal to receive better treatment than a person? If evil's insidious work doesn't stop on the Sabbath, why should God's good work cease?

Religious forms and rituals have their place, but never are they an excuse to overlook or ignore human need. Compassion that alleviates suffering is always an appropriate response regardless of when or where it happens. If Sunday worship is disrupted, so be it. If coffee is spilled on the carpet while the homeless are fed, rent a carpet steamer.

Once again, Jesus breaks more than a few cherished rules. He heals on a day when healing is forbidden. He touches a woman in the holiness of the synagogue. He speaks to her in public as no male would. He refuses to blame the woman for her condition.

Jesus' critics leave worship that day shaking their heads and grumbling as they go. My guess is that some walk away complaining that honored traditions have been trashed. But most of the folks get it right and rejoice in the presence of God's liberating work.

What's the most unexpected intrusion you've experienced in a worship service?

ARTIST AND POET
Luke 13:18-21

Jesus said, "What is God's dream for the world? To what do I compare it? It's like a mustard seed planted in a garden; it grows and becomes a tree where birds make nests in its branches. Again, I ask you, how do God's best intentions for the world become real? It's like yeast that a woman mixes with large amounts of flour until all the dough rises."

+

What does God dream for the world?
  To capture it, what pictures would an artist paint?
To convey it, what rhymes would a poet pen?
A mustard seed might be the place to start.
A seed smaller, one may never find.
Planted in the ground, it's no longer seen.
In the dirt incubator—both safe and vulnerable—
It grows, quite without our involvement.
Tall and wide, it stretches into a treelike bush,
A haven for birds (or nations) to raise their young.

What's the dream of God for the world?
  What images best describe this dream?
A pinch of yeast mixed with large measures of flour
May seem insignificant to a kitchen stranger.
But a little goes a long way
When every bit of the dough is affected.
The yeast works its wonder apart from our influence.
In spite of our doubts and fears—and incompetency—
Its presence makes possible the wonder of leaven
So multitudes might take, eat, and be blessed.

What are we to make of God's dream
  If mustard seed and yeast are the tools of the trade?
Though oft hidden, God's dream is working to become reality,
And it matters little whether we see it or not.

When has God's dream for the world been most visible for you?

ENTRY DOOR
Luke 13:22-24

Jesus taught in many places on his way to Jerusalem. One day, someone asked him, "Will only a few people be saved?" He replied, "Try to enter through the narrow door, for many will try to enter but won't be able."

+

Maybe the questioner thought about it for so long he couldn't keep quiet any longer. Maybe this unnamed someone, reflecting on vineyards and fruitless fig trees, realized that heaven is not guaranteed, not even for those with proper credentials and family ties.

Whatever prompts the inquiry, the question attempts to pin Jesus down. How many will be saved? Who are they? Where do they live? What do they look like? Are we among them? If not Jews, then who? If only Jews, then what about the rest? If it's a few, can you give us a round number? More than a thousand? Less than a billion?

Jesus has no need to play a saved/unsaved numbers game. His answer, at best, is an indirect one. Salvation's door is narrow. Make every effort to enter it. Many will try. Many will fail.

In John's gospel, Jesus uses many images to describe himself: the good shepherd, the bread, the vine, and the door through which others will enter. In these verses in Luke, Jesus makes an indirect reference to himself. The "narrow door" is Jesus. And why is it that many who try to enter aren't able? Consider the scandal of Jesus. He challenges religious hypocrisy. He calls people to sell their possessions and give the proceeds to the poor. He tells those on life's margins that they're at the center of God's concern. He breaks tradition when tradition stands in the way of giving wholeness to those who need it most. He's no fan of nationalistic myopia.

What woman can put up with such a life? What man chooses to lose his life in order to find it? The narrow door of living like Jesus is a tight squeeze. Episcopal priest Robert Farrar Capon (*Kingdom, Grace, Judgment*) reminds us that the repulsiveness of the life Jesus calls us to live is hard to accept, especially when we're sure our own "Plan B" is a better one.

What's the hardest part of following Jesus for you?

East Congregational UCC, Grand Rapids, MI

REMEMBER US
Luke 13:25-27

"When the homeowner has locked the door, and you stand outside knocking and pleading to be let in, the homeowner will say, 'I don't know who you are or where you come from.' You might reply, 'We ate and drank with you when you taught in our streets.' But the homeowner will answer, 'I don't know who you are or where you come from. Go away; you're full of evil!'"

+

This parable is similar to the earlier parable of the neighbor at midnight (Luke 11:5-13). Both employ the images of a door, an urgent request, persistent knocking, an inconvenienced homeowner, and a conversation between the homeowner and those standing outside. In the earlier parable, the homeowner grants the request; in this parable, the request is denied.

Who are these evil somebodies (literally, "workers of iniquity")? Of what evils or iniquities are they guilty? Murder? Greed? Greater or lesser evils? Whatever those evils are, they aren't identified. Are those knocking on the door religious rogues?

These evildoers remind the owner of the house (Jesus?) that they've made some good choices. They lunched and supped with him, shared wine with him, and listened intently to what he had to teach.

Since their evils aren't identified nor their associations commended, it appears they're guilty of no more than inattentiveness to opportunities when they had a chance to respond. However sensible their reasons, they chose to delay entering through the narrow door until it was too late. Tardiness proves fatal. Lateness is their undoing.

Nobody reads this parable and nods, "Yeah, I really like this one." There's severity here, a harsh reality that reminds us that our choices, or lack of them, make a difference and bear consequences. Faithful living is serious business, and life really isn't an endless succession of tomorrows.

Where is your inattentiveness causing the most harm?

WEEPING AND GRINDING
Luke 13:28-30

"There will be weeping and teeth-grinding when you see Abraham, Isaac, Jacob, and all the prophets in the eternal community of God, and you aren't with them. People will come from all directions and eat in this community. Indeed, some who are last now will be first, and some who are first now will be last."

+

Jesus concludes the parable. Weeping implies more than sorrow; it's the regret of what might have been, of losing what one could have had. Teeth-grinding or gnashing is an expression of anger and deep hatred toward one's enemies as evidenced in Psalm 37:12: "The wicked plot against the righteous and gnash their teeth." Visceral responses will be triggered at the sight of the ancestral heroes of faith—Abraham, Isaac, Jacob, and the prophets—enjoying God's company.

In one sense, Jesus finally addresses the original question asked earlier, "Will only a few be saved?" He replies that people will come from every direction to eat at God's banquet, from lands familiar and unknown.

So, what's the answer? We have to have an answer, right? Things need to be nailed down and airtight. Is it a few or many? A number we can tally or every human being who ever lived? And how do we understand this parable in light of Jesus' words in John12:32, "By the way I live and die, I will draw all people to myself"?

Maybe we have a choice here. We can spend every active hour of the day making our own calculations of who's in and who's out until the ink runs dry in our desktop printers. Or we can leave it up to the God whose supply of ink cartridges is endless. This much is certain: surprises are in store, and no surprise will be greater than the last being first, and the first being last.

Wait a minute! If both the first *and* the last get in, doesn't that imply everyone?

What does the last-will-be-first reversal mean to you?

DETERMINED DESTINY
Luke 13:31-33

Some religious leaders warned Jesus, "Get out of here because Herod wants to kill you." Jesus replied, "Tell that fox that I'm casting out demons and healing people today and tomorrow, and on the third day I'll finish my work. Yet today, tomorrow, and the next day, I must be on my way, because a prophet is never killed anywhere except in Jerusalem."

+

Doesn't Jesus know with whom he's dealing? This is Herod Antipas, ruler of Galilee, the John-the-Baptist-killing despot, not some political upstart. Though the Pharisees' warning may be evidence of their concern for Jesus' safety, it might also be a way to protect their own self-interest. Nobody wants Herod flexing his muscles in the neighborhood.

Jesus' unflinching response is nothing short of a taunt. He calls Herod a fox, insinuating that the one who threatens him is deceitful, untrustworthy, and a predator with animalistic instincts. In the prophetic tradition, Jesus doesn't hesitate to speak truth to power. Herod might determine taxes and where his palace will be built, but he isn't going to determine the nature of Jesus' ministry or its duration. Jesus won't be diverted from his mission. He'll leave only when he's ready to leave, not because Herod has anything to say about it.

Though Jesus' today/tomorrow/third day reply seems to foreshadow his death, burial, and resurrection, it's more likely that Jesus is referring to the short period of time he will stay in this region.

Jesus chooses to remain focused on his mission of bringing people into the great community of God. He won't be swayed from his path; not even threats from an annoyed earthly ruler will force him to change his course. That course leads to Jerusalem, where many prophets met their demise. Jesus knows this, and continues on the way anyway.

How does Jesus' in-your-face response give you confidence in living?

DIVINE LAMENT
Luke 13:34-35

"Jerusalem, Jerusalem, you kill prophets and stone those sent to you! How often I've wanted to gather your children as a hen gathers her chicks under her wings, but you weren't willing! Your house is empty. Listen, you won't see me until the time when you say, 'Blessed is the one who comes in God's name.'"

+

Jesus shifts from thinking about his own destiny to lamenting the fate of Jerusalem. His pain is revealed with the double address, "Jerusalem, Jerusalem." The poignant language is reminiscent of God's tender love for the chosen people: "Like hovering birds, so will God protect Jerusalem" (Isaiah 31:5).

Though God reaches out in love, it's a love that knows rejection. "Hear and listen, heaven and earth! God speaks: I raised children and brought them up, but they rebelled against me. The ox knows its owner, and the donkey its master's house; but Israel doesn't know or understand" (Isaiah 1:2-3). The relational bonds that animals instinctively know, God's own people reject. From Genesis to Revelation, the notes of that refrain repeat themselves. The Lover loves; the beloved spurns.

Following Jesus' lament come predictions of Jerusalem's future: "Your house is empty." *House* can mean the city of Jerusalem itself or its inhabitants, but it likely refers to the temple, the destruction of which will take place at the hands of the Romans in the year 70.

Jesus also announces that the day will come when the people of Jerusalem will no longer see him until they say, "Blessed is the one who comes in God's name." Though this phrase appears to be a clear reference to Jesus' Palm Sunday entrance into Jerusalem, some scholars understand it as a reference to his second coming at the end of time.

Divine pathos runs deep. God isn't a stranger to grief. The God who creates and saves is not an unmoved deity. God feels. Rejections of heaven's love move God to tears.

How does God's grief help you in your times of grief?

230

UNDER SCRUTINY
Luke 14:1-4a

While Jesus was going to the house of one of the clergy to eat a Sabbath meal, some people watched him suspiciously. Jesus met a man who had dropsy. He asked the religious leaders, "Would I be breaking the law if I healed on the Sabbath?" They didn't answer.

+

This is the fourth occasion of a Sabbath healing in Luke's gospel. On previous Sabbaths, Jesus healed Simon's mother-in-law (4:38), a man with a misshapen hand (6:6), and the bent woman (13:13). Each healing sparked controversy and criticism from the religious watchdogs who objected to violations of the "No Work on the Sabbath Day" laws.

Jesus' critics regard him as a dangerous lawbreaker, a threat to the religious establishment, and one who needs close monitoring. Yet, not all religious leaders are antagonistic toward him. Jesus receives from one an invitation to Sabbath dinner, a meal that would have been prepared in advance on Friday. We shouldn't suspect motives here, at least not on the part of the host.

A man appears who has dropsy, a disease in which the body swells up as fluids form in the cavities and tissues. Is he sent there by those who want to see what Jesus will do? Is he an innocent plant used to entrap Jesus into defiling yet another Sabbath? Will Jesus keep the traditions or break the law?

Sensing their scrutiny, Jesus drops the gauntlet and poses a question: "Would I be breaking the law?" Is he goading them? Challenging them? Pushing them to see the priority of human need above tradition? Even though they don't answer, you can bet they have a lot to ponder.

What traditions today would Jesus most challenge?

Granada, Nicaragua

PEOPLE PRIORITY
Luke 14:4b-6

Jesus healed the man and sent him away. Then he asked the religious leaders, "If one of you has a child or an ox that has fallen into a well on the Sabbath day, won't you immediately pull it out?" They didn't say a thing.

+

Waiting for neither their answer nor their permission, Jesus performs the healing and sends the man away. Jesus then uses his (and their) tradition to emphasize the point. Jewish law forbade the Sabbath-rescuing of an animal that had fallen into a hole or well, though in some cases, rescue was allowed if no tool or implement was used. Jesus ups the ante by placing a child in the mix. The operative word in his example is "your." What if *your* child needs rescue? What if *your* ox falls into a well? Wouldn't you take immediate action to preserve and save life, Sabbath law or no Sabbath law?

In their silence, Jesus has them in a dilemma. A yes answer would brand them as law-breakers of their own tradition; saying no would expose them as heartless in the face of suffering. By not replying, they opt to neither push the issue nor directly confront Jesus. Ironically, no one questions Jesus' ability to heal, only the appropriateness of doing so on the Sabbath.

Our dangers aren't unlike theirs. Doctrine and dogma, traditions and tenets—the human scaffolding of religion—don't always reflect well on the God who is the object of our devotion. Jesus' lesson is obvious enough. If the priority isn't people, then the tradition is as good as dead. Daring to put the former before the latter, Jesus continues to set the direction of his ministry toward necessary rescue operations.

In what ways, today, does the religious community demonstrate misplaced priorities?

PARTY FAVORITES
Luke 14:7-11

Jesus noticed how some guests chose the best seats, so he shared a story: "When you're invited to a wedding reception, don't sit down at the best seats in case someone more important than you has been invited. The host might come to you and say, 'Give this person your seat.' Embarrassed, you'll have to move to a less desirable place. Instead, when you're invited, sit down at a less important place, so that when the host comes and says to you, 'Friend, move to a better seat,' you'll be honored in front of the guests. For all who try to make themselves great will be humbled; those who choose humility will be exalted."

+

First impressions might lead us to assume that Jesus is offering a personal improvement plan in three parts: (1) aim low, (2) get noticed for your humility, and (3) be ready to move up when opportunity calls. Instead, Jesus challenges our notions of status, power, and place.

The seating arrangement at major meals often functioned (not unlike at certain high-class events today) as a flowchart of who's who and who's not there yet. Seats of honor close to the host were given to persons of status, while less significant guests sat further down the table. The pecking order was visible for all to see.

But something deeper is going on here, something more profound than who gets the chair with armrests and who must sit on the footstool with a TV tray. Jesus is defining how God's family is to behave, how communal mindfulness trumps personal entitlements. The world keeps score. Floor plans and square footage are tallied. Job titles and net worth are added to the mix. Vehicles and vacations are tabulated, too. In the end, we know who's on top and who's, well, who cares where anybody else lands once it's determined who's on top.

The only place where empty-handedness is worth something is in the community God is intent on fashioning. True humility acknowledges that in spite of (rather than because of) who I am, God wouldn't think of throwing a party without me.

Why is humility so hard to put into practice?

HOST GRACES
Luke 14:12-14

Jesus said to the host, "When you throw a party, don't invite your friends or family or relatives or rich neighbors. Someday, they will return the favor and you'll be repaid. Instead, when you have a party, invite the poor, the disabled, the lame, and the blind. You'll be blessed because they can't repay you, and you'll find your reward when good people rise again from the dead."

+

Jesus' words to the host might be harder to digest than anything on the table. After all, who criticizes a host for inviting family, friends, and other interesting people to a dinner party? So what if others feel an obligation to return the favor; that's how our society functions.

More to the point, this is a parable about how we experience grace. We expect Jesus to say that "the poor, the disabled, the lame, and the blind" receive and experience grace when they're invited to tables from which they've been excluded. They're the obvious beneficiaries.

Jesus, however, deftly turns the tables (so to speak!). He doesn't identify the grace-receivers as the *guests*, but as the *host*. The one who includes "the poor, the disabled, the lame, and the blind" is the one blessed beyond anything life can offer. *We* experience grace (liberation from society's tit-for-tat exchange, the kind of exchange that requires meticulous bookkeeping skills and up-to-date records) when we include those who can offer absolutely nothing in return.

Luke's Jesus challenges us to expand our tables, to lengthen the diameters of our circles, and to extend our definition of who's in. Unfortunately, when religion makes headlines these days, the stories that follow usually are about tables made smaller, circles shrinking, or definitions expanded regarding who should be excluded.

There's more here than offering soup suppers and making entrances handicapped-accessible. Though these are a start, accommodation isn't the same as inclusion. The former is what we do to make life easier for some; the latter is what it means to be the family of God.

Do churches lean more toward accommodation or inclusion?

235

MEALS AND GOD
Luke 14:15

One of the dinner guests said to Jesus, "Blessed is anyone who will eat at the table God is preparing."

+

Three cheers for the guest who gets the point! "Say it again, sister!" Jesus might have replied. "I love ya, brother!" Jesus could have concurred. We don't have to look far or long in scripture to make a connection between food and God, between banquet feasts and God's reign. "You prepare a table before me in the presence of my enemies" (Psalm 23:5). "I'm the God who brought you out of Egypt; open your mouth wide and I'll fill it" (Psalm 81:10). "On this mountain God will make for all people a feast of rich and succulent food, served with the finest wines" (Isaiah 25:6).

God is offering and will continue to offer food that satisfies. Jews of Jesus' day looked forward to the era when God would re-establish the nation and prepare a sumptuous feast for the chosen ones. The prophet Isaiah, however, had expanded that vision to include all people and all nations.

In Luke's gospel, meals, banquets, and feasts serve as the back-drop for many of Jesus' teachings. Much of what Jesus says about so-called outsiders is meant for the religious insiders who control the entrance door above which is written: "No Gentiles Served Here."

An unidentified dinner guest seems to get the point: "Blessed is anyone who will eat at the table God is preparing." *Anyone*—a danger-ous word! Anyone is welcomed! Anyone can come! Anyone can find a place. Anyone can belong. How many communities of faith are willing to say: "We exist for ANYONE!"?

What keeps people from seeking out a faith community?

THANKS, BUT . . .
Luke 14:16-20

Jesus told another story: "Someone planned a great dinner and invited many people. On the day of the dinner, the host sent a servant to those who had been invited, saying, 'Come and eat! Everything is ready.' But they all made excuses. One said, 'I recently bought some land, and I must go and see it. Please accept my apologies.' Another said, 'I just bought five pair of oxen, and I need to try them out. Please excuse me.' Another said, 'I just got married; you can't expect me to come.'"

+

Here's another dinner situation for our consideration. Invitations are offered and some are declined. Some scholars suggest the excuses are outright lies and blatant rejections of the host's generosity. In ancient times, no one bought property without first seeing it. Likewise, a prospective buyer would never purchase farm animals without first inspecting them to determine whether they could work a field. The third excuse is framed in the past tense, suggesting that the wedding festivities are done and all the guests have gone home.

Maybe the excuses are lies, but each one has some legitimacy. Who can deny that real estate acquisitions, capital improvements to one's business, and spousal responsibilities are good, noble, and virtuous pursuits in and of themselves? Most of us agree that it makes sense to take care of the things that require our attention.

Jesus presents us with a crisis of choices. Our dilemmas are seldom between something obviously good and something blatantly evil. That's too easy! Most of our choices are between that which is good and that which is better. "I'll settle for dabbling in the things of God but not let God influence every aspect of my living. Whet my appetite but don't saturate it. I'll follow the Golden Rule of treating others as I'd like to be treated, but I can't be expected to take seriously a sacrificial lifestyle. What's mine is mine and you can't have it."

When is choosing the good thing the wrong choice? When choosing the good means failing to choose what's better.

What's your best excuse?

237

PLAN B
Luke 14:21-24

"So the servant returned and reported this to the host. Then the host became angry and said to the servant, 'Go into the streets and alleys, and bring the poor, the disabled, the blind, and the lame.' Later the servant said, 'I did what you told me to do, and there's still room.' Then the host said, 'Go into the streets and alleys, and urge people to come so that my house will be full. None of those first invited will eat at my table.'"

+

Jesus' parables frequently contain elements of surprise. Something happens that catches listeners off guard. The jolt of this parable comes only after several plot lines have played out. That three people make three excuses is no surprise. That the host then decides to add to the guest list is no surprise either. What gives this story its shock value is that the host doesn't replace the original guests with guests of the same social standing. He doesn't turn around and invite another property owner, another businessperson, and another newly married spouse, as the first-century audience expects he will. Instead, it's "the poor, the disabled, the blind, and the lame" who become recipients of the host's desire to fill the banquet hall. Nothing will stand in the way of the dinner-giver's generosity.

Notions of who's in and who's out are turned upside down. Those who shouldn't be there are. Those we wouldn't expect to turn up—minorities, undocumented immigrants, those who sleep under the overpass and smell terrible—get a seat at the table. Grace is nothing if not scandalous.

How are we expected to take this stuff seriously? It's as if those who insist on their own successful striving are likely to end up hungry, while those who have nothing to offer the host will get their fill. Go figure!

What offense do you find in the story?

238

DANGEROUS LOYALTY
Luke 14:25-27

Jesus said to the crowd that was following him, "Those who want to follow me and don't hate their parents, their spouses, their children, their siblings, even life itself, can't be my disciples. Whoever doesn't carry the cross and follow me can't be my disciple."

+

Most people looking for a church home carry a checklist by which to evaluate a congregation's suitability: Do the sermons keep my interest? Is the pastor warm and personable? Is the congregation friendly? Does the music stir me? Is the youth program strong? Is the parking adequate? Is it OK if I tithe? (Just kidding!)

Today's church shoppers are educated and discerning consumers. It's hard to imagine Jesus faring well. Jesus uses here the strongest language recorded in the gospels: "Unless you *hate* everything about house and home, don't even think about signing on with me." Though Luke doesn't include the tag line, perhaps he should have: "From that day on, the crowds thinned out."

Jesus is saying something important about our loyalties and the allegiance we give them. In a Hebraic sense, to hate something implies a detachment or a turning away from it. Jesus puts his finger on the network of loyalties that wrap around our lives, and dares to claim that he is not merely one among many, but *the* one who defines, shapes, and informs all others.

To live as Jesus lived puts all other loyalties in a new perspective. We don't get a Jesus-lite who dabbles somewhere on the fringes of our lives seeking to turn us from nice persons to even nicer persons. Following demands all—nothing short of everything.

In what ways do you want to live more detached?

COST COUNTING
Luke 14:28-33

"What person builds a tower without first sitting down to estimate the cost to see whether there is enough money to complete it? Otherwise, when the foundation is laid and the money is gone, all who see it will ridicule the builder, saying, 'How stupid to start a building and not finish it.' If a ruler is waging war, he must first decide if ten thousand troops are enough to defeat an opposing army of twenty thousand troops. If he realizes he can't, then before the battle begins, he'll send a delegation and negotiate peace. You can't become my disciple if you don't give up everything you have."

+

Jesus continues his discourse on discipleship, reminding us that the requirements don't get easier. Like a real estate developer launching an ambitious building project without doing a cost analysis, or a general preparing for war without considering the size of the opposing force, only a fool, Jesus reminds his followers, refuses to count the cost.

Counting the cost. Carrying the cross. Giving up possessions. Taking on burdens. Hating house and home. The first will be last. The last will be first. The exalted, humbled. The humbled, exalted. Am I the only one who's not looking for such disruptions in life?

I wonder if recovering alcoholics or those in therapy would say they're not looking for disruptions in their lives. My guess is, they've counted the cost and gladly welcome the price such a cost exacts.

The great paradox in Jesus' life and the life he invites us to live is that in giving up everything we have, we are offered everything we need. The exchange eludes all logic and defies all reason. Freedom comes when we consider the costs—what they will demand of us and where they will take us—and accept them anyway.

Thomas à Kempis, a fifteenth-century German Catholic, reminds us in *Imitation of Christ*, "Jesus has many who desire consolation, but few who care for adversity. He finds many to share his table, but few who will join him in fasting. Many will follow him as far as the breaking of bread, but few will remain to drink from his passion."

What's the hardest thing you have had to do when counting the cost?

SALT LESSONS
Luke 14:34-35

"Salt is good, but if salt loses its taste, the saltiness can't be restored. It isn't fit for the soil or for the manure pile. Throw it away. Use your ears and listen to what I'm saying!"

+

The inclusion of this salt saying seems an unnatural conclusion to the parables just told. However, the varied uses of salt in the ancient world open our eyes to possible connections to Jesus' teachings.

Salt served three primary functions: As a preservative, salt was able to do to meats what refrigeration does today, preserving freshness and acting as an inhibitor of the decaying process. Salt was also used, then as now, as a flavoring agent, bringing out flavors and tastes which otherwise would remain hidden. Finally, salt was used in agriculture as a fertilizer. At deep levels in the soil, when combined with potassium found at the Dead Sea, salt improved a crop's yield. Some note that salt was also used in ovens to catalyze the burning of dung for fuel.

Jesus clearly identifies salt's flavoring function and suggests that when salt's taste is lost, it can't be restored. It's good for nothing and thrown away. Heading toward Jerusalem, to heightened suffering, Jesus gives a reality check to those who would suggest that following him is a walk in the park and merely a way to get their needs met. Like salt that loses its taste, enthusiastic followers unable to bear the opposition of the day (and the days ahead) won't last long.

When the circumstances of our situations don't meet prior expectations, when the newness of a task we began eagerly evolves into a dull routine, when the stuff of life—good, bad, and otherwise—tugs for our time and attention, how do we maintain an attitude of sacred detachment from all that competes with the one important thing of making real God's intentions for the world?

Committed salty living seldom ends suddenly; over time, it simply fades away—a gradual, imperceptible diminishing. Got salt?

In the realm of the spiritual, where can you use more salt?

241

EATING WITH SINNERS
Luke 15:1-2

As tax collectors and sinners sought to be with Jesus, the religious leaders voiced their disapproval: "This Jesus welcomes sinners and eats with them."

+

Of the accusations levied against Jesus in the gospels, some are theological in nature: Jesus claims a relationship with God that his critics label as blasphemy. Other criticisms arise from political concerns: Jesus calls for a loyalty to God's work far greater than loyalty to any political system—Roman or otherwise.

A third charge levied against Jesus is his unguarded openness toward persons deemed unclean, unworthy, and unholy. Like bits of metal to a magnet, Jesus attracts those whom society casts off. Tax collectors and sinners are drawn to him in ways that suggest that in the presence of this preacher/healer/teacher/prophet, their lives count for something.

Tax collectors were a particularly despised lot. Selling out their own people, they hired themselves out to the Roman authorities, collecting from the Jews taxes owed while keeping a percentage (more accurately, an overcharge) for themselves. It made for a good living and a lonely profession.

That Jesus extends to such people a warm and hospitable welcome prompts the complaint, "This Jesus welcomes sinners and eats with them." If welcoming isn't scandalous enough, sitting at the same table—a sign of social acceptance—is more than the righteous observers can bear.

They despise Jesus for the company he keeps. It's guilt by association. The ceremonial laws establishing cleanliness and purity all said the same: Stay away from drunks, prostitutes, lepers, and anyone else who can make you unclean. Separateness is next to godliness!

Jesus knows and loves his tradition. However, he just can't stay away from those who have nothing worthy to offer.

What would befriending the wrong people look like for you?

INHERENT VALUE
Luke 15:3-5

In response to the criticism against him, Jesus told some stories: "Who of you, if you had a hundred sheep and lost one, wouldn't leave the ninety-nine in the field and look for the lost one until you found it? And when you found it, you would lay it on your shoulders and rejoice."

+

This chapter of Luke is often called "The Gospel within the Gospel." Jesus tells three stories—about sheep, coins, and sons—linked together by the themes of lostness and foundness. Jesus intends to teach his critics something about the life he is called to live and the world as God intends it.

Jesus begins the first parable with an assault on the religious leaders' assumptions. "Who of *you*, having a hundred sheep . . . ?" It's doubtful any of the religious leaders understand this hypothetical address as a compliment. The tending of sheep, though idealized in Christmas pageants and carols, was a socially inferior occupation, in large part because of its inherent uncleanliness. Essentially, Jesus begins with a touch of humor: "OK, folks, imagine yourselves as sweaty, dirty, unclean shepherds."

Out of a hundred sheep, one strays and is separated from the rest. It's a loss that cuts into the profit margin but doesn't bring economic disaster. Still, the shepherd feels a personal loss and leaves the ninety-nine to find the lone sheep. Once it is found, rather than teach the wayward animal a lesson from the blunt end of his stick, the shepherd lays the sheep on his shoulders and carries it back to the flock.

If Jesus tells this story in response to objections to his welcoming-of-sinners behavior, then what is he lifting up as the criterion for such welcoming? From the parable, what about the sheep prompts the shepherd to seek it out? Clearly, the sheep has value and worth. Whether the sheep is in the fold or lost in the backcountry, the value doesn't change. The sheep doesn't manufacture a survival plan to reestablish its value. The value is already there. Jesus instinctively knows this about people: good, bad, or lost—everyone has infinite value.

What does personal value mean to you?

243

REPENTANCE
Luke 15:6-7

"When the shepherd returns, he gathers with his friends and neighbors, saying, 'Let's have a party because I found my lost sheep.' Listen, there will be more celebration in heaven over one sinner who repents than over ninety-nine good people who don't need to repent."

+

Rescue is incomplete without restoration. When the shepherd finds the lost sheep, the entire community is invited to join the party. The toil of the search gives way to the joy of the recovery.

The end of this short parable, though, raises some questions regarding our understanding of repentance. The theme of repentance, threaded through this chapter, suggests a nuanced meaning. Typically, we think of repentance as a change of heart, a turning from, and a turning toward. In religious language, repentance is something we do when we turn away from sin.

This parable reveals, however, that the sheep does nothing to secure its own rescue. The sheep doesn't repent of anything. Put in penitential language, the sheep hasn't experienced a "change of heart" or a "turning from sin." The sheep is simply lost, and that lostness is enough to move the shepherd into rescue mode. Lostness, as Robert Farrar Capon (*Kingdom, Grace, Judgment*) points out, is all the sheep can claim.

Who can imagine the shepherd inquiring of the sheep whether it's sorry for the trouble it caused, or if it will promise never to get lost again? The shepherd doesn't raise a stick and let out a reprimanding "Bad sheep!" Repentance for the sheep is simply getting found, being back in the company of the shepherd whose love for the sheep was always there.

This parable is a reminder of God's risk-filled, limitless determination to move in our direction, even to enter our wildernesses, to seek us out in our most lost and lonely places, saying to us, "I'm here for you. I'm here with you."

When have you felt like a lost sheep?

244

HOUSECLEANING
Luke 15:8-10

Jesus told another story: "A woman has ten silver coins and loses one. Won't she light a lamp, sweep the house, and search until she finds it? Once she finds it, she'll gather with her friends and neighbors, saying, 'Let's celebrate! I found the lost coin.' Hear what I'm saying: there's joy among God's angels over one sinner whose life is turned around."

+

This story continues the themes of lostness and foundness. Again, Jesus challenges first-century cultural assumptions about class and distinctions. Here a woman shows us the lengths to which God is willing to go—yes, another example prompting us to balance our male-dominated images of God with female images: God, the female homeowner.

The misplaced coin represents a significant 10 percent loss for the owner. It's not one of a hundred sheep, but one-*tenth* of all she has. The coin, a silver drachma, was the equivalent of a day's labor. Its value is intensified by the thorough searching and multiplied by the resultant joy when it is found.

God searches for God's own, like a shepherd for a lost sheep and like a woman for a lost coin. The Maker of heaven and earth, one's Higher Power, the Ground of our being, the one Native Americans call the Great Spirit is restless until broken community is mended. The shepherd won't rest until the one sheep is restored to the ninety-nine; the housewife won't rest until the one coin is restored to the nine.

Remember, Jesus tells these stories in response to criticism that he "welcomes sinners and eats with them." Luke's Jesus doesn't rest until those who've been pushed away, pushed aside, and pushed down, or who've simply lost their way, are restored again to the community. The implications are sobering when you think about prisoners who've served their time, addicts who've gone through the twelve steps, or the one and a half million teenagers who run away from home every year in this country. In the world to which Jesus points, everyone has a place in the community.

Where do you experience broken community?

New Orleans, LA

HOME-LEAVING
Luke 15:11-13

Jesus shared a third story: "A man had two sons. The younger son said to his father, 'Give me my share of the inheritance.' The father divided his property and gave the younger son what he demanded. A few days later, the younger son gathered all he had and traveled to another country where he squandered his money on wild living."

+

Though most of us know this story as the "Parable of the Prodigal Son," neither the prodigal son nor his older brother is the main character. The father, rather than the sons, is the subject of the story. Jesus wants his listeners to understand something of God's heart, so he tells a story more aptly named the "Parable of the Loving Father."

For the younger son to demand his inheritance while his father was still alive was a serious insult in first-century Middle Eastern culture. The boy might just as well have said, "I wish you were dead, old man. I want what's coming to me, now!" The disrespected father has some options. The book of Deuteronomy offers a remedy for a smart-mouthed kid: Beat him until he learns his lesson; if that doesn't work, stone him to death. The father could also call upon the village to reprimand his boy in ways the kid will not forget.

The father doesn't contemplate these harsh options. Instead, he gives the kid what he wants. This is no small sacrifice; the younger son is entitled to a third of the estate. Did the father have to sell off part of his property so the boy could get his cash? What about running the family business minus this able-bodied son?

At a huge financial cost and at the price of being known as a man who lost his authority, the father gives his son the independence he demands. The kid walks away from the house where he was reared and turns his back on the community that shaped him. He leaves home with a fat wad of money in his pocket.

The younger son broke his parents' hearts that day. Both father and mother now knew the untamed nature of love, a love that can't be forced. I doubt they slept at all for many nights.

In what ways have you experienced home-leaving?

CUTTING DEALS
Luke 15:14-19

"When the younger son ran out of money, a severe famine swept through the country, and he was desperate. He was forced to get a job on a farm, feeding pigs in the field. He was so hungry that he would gladly have eaten the pods the pigs were eating but no one gave him anything. Realizing his situation, he said, 'My father's servants have plenty to eat, but I'm dying of hunger! I'm going back to my father, and I'll say to him, 'I've made a mess of everything. I'm not worthy to be called your son; treat me like one of your servants.'"

+

The end of his rope. Rock bottom. The pits. Fresh out of options. His money gone. Party pals nowhere to be found. His stomach empty. Pigs everywhere. Home never looked so good.

If we think the prodigal son is the main character, then we're quick to conclude that the critical point of this parable swings on the son's confessional hinge. He wakes up in the pigsty and comes to his senses—contrite, repentant, and remorseful. Only thing is, he's not at all sincere about it. He has figured out how to get back into the good graces of his father. He scripts a speech, stands in front of a mirror, and rehearses it with just the right emotional appeal.

The boy heads for home, hitting the trail with newfound lightness in his step. With a fresh shot of confidence, he's sure his father will be moved by what he has to say. He's crafted a good speech because, after all, desperate situations demand desperate measures. This kid will make it happen. He's got it all planned out. Even with a heavy dose of remorse and regret, it's good to be in charge.

What does a pigsty look like to you?

ROBES AND RINGS
Luke 15:20-24

"While the son was traveling home, his father saw him in the distance, was filled with compassion, and ran out to meet him. When they met, the father threw his arms around his boy and showered him with kisses. Then the son said, 'Father, I've sinned and made a mess of my life. I don't deserve to be called your son.' But the father said to his servants, 'Hurry, get out the best robe and put it on him. Put a ring on his finger and sandals on his feet. Kill the best calf. Let's eat and celebrate. My son was dead but is alive. Once he was lost, but now he's found!' And the party began."

+

Did the father love his kid before the kid asked for his inheritance? Did the father love the son even when the boy left home? Did the father love the boy before his pigpen conversion? "Yes" to all those questions. The father, like any good parent, loved his child.

Was there ever a time in the son's life—pre-rebellion, full-throttle rebellion, or post-rebellion—when the father did not love him? Again, like any good parent, the father's love is always there and always present. That's why the father cuts off his son in mid-sentence, just as the kid is ready to launch into his I'm-not-worthy-to-be-called-your-son-take-me-back-as-a-hired-hand speech.

We tend to settle for the easy moralism. We reason that the son starts out in the father's good graces, becomes a deviant and falls from the father's good graces, arrives at his senses in a genuine act of repentance, and finally returns to the father's good graces. We think it's all about getting our repentance right, but as Amy-Jill Levine (*A Feminist Companion to Luke*) suggests, the son doesn't repent any more than the lost sheep or the lost coin repent. The radical truth about the father's love for his son is that the father's love never ceases, and nothing the kid does for good or evil changes that. The love is always there.

Do you see a connection here between the loving parent and God? Once loved, we're always loved. Much of life is simply coming to that awareness, regardless of the speeches we rehearse.

When have you felt most loved by God?

BOYCOTTING THE PARTY
Luke 15:25-28a

"The older son, who was working the field, approached the house and heard the music and dancing. He asked a servant what was going on. The servant replied, 'Your brother is back, and your father killed the best calf because he's safe and sound.' Then the older son became angry and refused to join the party."

+

The mood shifts. A somber, dark brooding infiltrates the festive mood. Enter the elder brother. If there exists an occasion for righteous anger, this son demonstrates it. We sense he knows what's going on even before asking the servant. His suspicions confirmed, he refuses to be drawn into the celebration. He stands on the outside looking in.

Finally, someone in this family whose attitude and actions make sense! We all understand where *this* kid is coming from. We know how he feels. We'd probably stand next to him and let him know his anger is justified. What's he to think? "A party for my delinquent brother? Where the heck does he get off? And what are my parents doing on the dance floor? Does anyone realize the crap I had to clean up after he skipped town? He broke my parents' hearts. I can't forget the pain he caused them. He never wrote. Never called. And now this?"

Some of us identify with the prodigal son who left home to sow his wild oats before his life turned around. But others more readily empathize with the older brother's anger. The party just isn't right. Sometimes you have to stand outside and seethe, even if it's raining cats and dogs.

When was the last time you were angry like this brother?

ELDER-SON RELIGION
Luke 15:28b-30

"The father came out and pleaded with his older boy. But the son would have none of it: 'Listen! For all these years, I've worked like a slave for you. Never once did I disobey you, yet you never gave me a goat so that I might party with my friends. But when this son of yours came back after blowing your money on prostitutes, you killed the best calf for him!'"

+

Elder siblings build civilizations. Corporations succeed because of elder siblings. Streets are cleaned, garbage is collected, and mail gets delivered because elder-sibling-type folks know their jobs and do them well. Even churches—small, medium, large, and extra-large—depend on the work ethic of dependable oldest sibling-like people.

Though he comes off as a joyless stick-in-the-mud, we get inside his skin because we identify with his resentment. No one enjoys being overlooked. No one likes being under-appreciated. No one feels good about being taken for granted. What's more miserable than doing all the right things and hating every minute of it?

However, deeper than the elder son's resentment is his anger at the father. The scales of justice are out of balance. Punishment hasn't been meted out. His good-for-nothing, come-what-may, fly-by-the-seat-of-his-pants brother has gotten off without even a slap on the wrist. The world doesn't operate on mega-doses of benevolence! The father is too gracious for the elder son's liking. Where's the justice?

Former pastor of The Riverside Church in New York City, Ernest Campbell, once remarked that the biggest problem with American Christianity is that we have a Loving Father gospel in an Elder Brother church. The lines are drawn with voracious clarity: we/they, us/them, good folks/bad folks, our flag/your flag. Elder-son attitudes, all!

The prodigal son broke his father's heart by leaving home and entering the far country. The elder son broke his father's heart by staying home and never leaving the far country of his own making. Saint Augustine observed, "A darkened heart is the far country, for it is not by our feet but by our affections that we either leave or return to God."

What reaction do you have to Campbell's comment?

ALWAYS . . . ALL
Luke 15:31-32

Then the father replied, "Son, you're always with me, and everything I have is yours. But we had to celebrate with a party, because your brother was dead and has come back to life. Once he was lost, and now he's found."

+

The most unpredictable and surprising character in this story isn't the prodigal son or the older brother, but the father, whose love is extravagantly liberal and excessively wasteful. The parent's love is more prodigal (recklessly lavish) than the one's loose living or the other's moral rectitude. Just as the father's love caused him to rush out of the house and run down the road to welcome his younger son, so again, it's the father's love that pulls him from the house to plead with his other son to join the celebration. The father seeks wholeness in the family, a wholeness that isn't complete until both children can celebrate.

The father is determined to express his love, revealing a heart that has room for both children. Like many of the parables Jesus tells, this isn't an either/or situation. The father doesn't say to one boy, "I'll love you only if you change your behavior." Nor does he say to the other, "I'll love you only if you change your attitude." Both children receive all that the father has, which is all they will ever need.

It's been said that there are at least two ways to get home: one is to go away and come back; the other is never to leave. Both are played out in each of us—the conflict of wanting to go and the resentment of staying. Simultaneously, each of us is the prodigal child and the resentful sibling. What remains constant—always and forever—is God's love that welcomes us when we return and reassures us when we stay.

How does this parable challenge your perceptions about God?

COOKING THE BOOKS
Luke 16:1-7

Jesus told another story to his disciples: "There was a rich man whose manager was accused of mishandling the rich man's business. The rich man summoned the manager and said, 'What's this I hear? Give me the accounting books because you can't work for me any longer.' Then the manager thought to himself, 'What will I do, now that I've been fired? I'm not strong enough to dig ditches, and I'm ashamed to beg. I'll have to come up with a plan so that people will befriend me.' So, calling on the people who were indebted to his master, he asked the first, 'How much do you owe my boss?' The person answered, 'A hundred jugs of olive oil.' He said to him, 'Take your bill and make it fifty.' Then he asked another debtor, 'How much do you owe?' She replied, 'A hundred containers of wheat.' He said to her, 'Take your bill and make it eighty.'"

+

This is the first half of a parable that has confounded people ever since Jesus told it. An irresponsible, thieving manager of a rich man's estate ingratiates himself to the owner's creditors by reducing their outstanding debts. One debt is slashed fifty percent; the other is cut twenty percent. Not only has the manager indebted them to him—he's shrewdly implicated them in his little scheme.

Some scholars suggest that he merely deducts his own cut from the bill and settles the accounts without taking his usual percentage. Others speculate that the landowner is a corrupt man who overcharges his customers. The manager, then, should be seen as an ancient-day Robin Hood who resets the scales of justice. Though these are creative explanations, they fail to capture the intent of the parable.

If we didn't know the ending to this story, we might expect one of the following conclusions: "Jesus condemned the manager for his unscrupulousness and restored to the rich man all that he had lost." Or, "Jesus condemned the manager for his deviousness and promised that on Judgment Day, he'll get what he deserves."

What ending do you come up with that would be satisfying?

HOLY SHREWDNESS
Luke 16:8-9

"The business owner congratulated the dishonest manager for being shrewd and clever. Often, worldly people are shrewder in dealing among themselves than spiritually minded people are. Listen, make friends by using the world's currency; when it's gone, people will keep you as a friend."

+

Fourth-century Roman emperor Julian the Apostate saw in this story an opportunity to discredit Christianity. It's not hard to understand why. The villain becomes the hero? The boss praises his underling in spite of the fact that he's out fifty jugs of olive oil and twenty containers of wheat?

What do we do with this one? Some scholars suggest the story ends as it does because it was reworked by many scribes. What we read in Luke, then, bears little resemblance to what Jesus actually said. Others claim that Jesus uses excessive hyperbole to arouse the attention of his hearers. Maybe or maybe not. In either case, this is the story we have, and as in stud poker, you gotta play the hand you're dealt.

Jesus praises the manager for acting shrewdly and suggests that children of God can learn something here. It's not hard to find shrewd people in all walks of life, people who are a step and a jump ahead of the crowd because they're singularly focused. What if holiness-seeking people had the same shrewd focus on living God-centered lives? What an unstoppable force for good we would be!

Jesus' use of the phrase "the world's currency" shouldn't be understood as dirty money retrieved through ill-gotten gain. Literally, the Greek means "the wealth of this unrighteous age"—not good money versus bad money, but the commerce of this world. Imagine if God-seeking people were as shrewd with their resources as the manager in this story. We'd challenge economic inequities and unfair playing fields where the wealthiest get the breaks and the poorest get the blame. If we used our money so shrewdly that the transformational light of God shined through the darkness, we just might change the world! And isn't that the point?

Where's a likely place for you to practice some holy shrewdness?

ENTRUSTMENT
Luke 16:10-12

"Those who are trustworthy in little things are also trustworthy in great things, but those who are dishonest with a little can't be trusted with a lot. If you can't be trusted with worldly wealth, then how can you be trusted with spiritual riches? And if you can't properly handle what belongs to someone else, how can you be trusted with what is your own?"

+

It's still not easy to identify who's the good guy in this story. The rich man? He owns the business and drives the luxury car, but Jesus doesn't have any praise for him. The dishonest employee? Even though the boss commends him in the end, he still operates from self-serving motives. The story defies any simplistic attempts to moralize, in part because the characters aren't all good or all bad. We want easy labels, but the labels don't stick here.

Yet, the dishonest employee does something worth imitating. He understands that the world's resources are a powerful influence on relationships. With these resources, he can build friendships or lose them; help people or hurt them. Take the theme of forgiveness. A loving parent understands that the relationship matters and welcomes home a selfish child who's wasted a small fortune. Do the disciples get it? Do the religious leaders practice it?

Savvy business folks understand and appreciate the creative ways relationships are established and maintained in up times and down. After all, it's not *what* you know but *whom* you know, and you never know when those you know can help you out. Do the disciples get it? Do the religious leaders practice it?

If we're not worldly-wise, street-smart, and ahead of the curve with the temporal stuff of the day, how are we ever going to manage the really important things in life, like healing racism, making the world safe from nuclear nightmares, caring for a fragile planet, and creating God's shalom?

What do you imagine God is waiting to entrust to you?

255

IN GOD WE TRUST?
Luke 16:13

"You can't serve two bosses. You will either hate one and love the other, or be devoted to one and despise the other. You can't serve God and wealth."

+

Though we can't serve two bosses,
    it's awfully tough to leave one behind.
Though we can't serve both God and wealth,
    we spend a lifetime trying.
Though we can't serve both God and money,
    we kill ourselves trying to prove Jesus wrong.
Though we can't serve both God and possessions,
    we know we're nothing without the things we own.
Though we can't serve both God and materialism,
    maybe God's the one who's got to give a little.
Though we can't serve both God and stuff,
    one can't ever have enough stuff, and that's a fact.
Though we can't serve both God and capitalism,
    we're absolutely certain our God is a free-market deity.
Though we can't serve both God and our IRAs,
    we can't depend on heaven's handouts in later years.
Though we can't serve both God and work,
    we are what our job titles say we are.
Though we can't serve both God and job advancement,
    there are many more than two masters we serve.
Though we can't serve both God and a bloated war machine,
    our prayers aren't going to protect us on the next 9/11.
Though we can't serve two bosses,
    we secretly hold it against God for being a jealous God.

What is God forced to compete with in your life?

LOVERS OF MONEY
Luke 16:14-17

A few religious leaders who loved money ridiculed Jesus' attitude on the subject. Jesus responded, "You're the ones who pump yourselves up, but God knows your hearts. What people long for isn't necessarily what God longs for. The law of Moses and the writings of the prophets were in effect until John the Baptist came. Now, the good news of God's new community is being preached, and everyone tries to enter it by force. It's easier for the world to pass away than for one stroke of a letter in the law to be omitted."

+

To feel the full brunt of these verses, let's make a substitution. In the place of "religious leaders," let's insert "Americans" or "free-market capitalists" or "consumers." Now Jesus hits home. "You Americans who love money . . . You capitalists who worship wealth . . . You consumers who are never satisfied with what you have . . . You . . ."

The health-'n'-wealth gospel is flourishing today. The notion that God wants us to have it all and that there's no materialistic itch we shouldn't scratch is an enticing message. Where did this idea come from? Actually, from the Bible, in many places. Though Jesus warns us about trying to serve God and money, there are any number of biblical passages claiming wealth as a sure sign of God's favor and blessing.

Many psalms, a large chunk of the book of Deuteronomy, and not a few television preachers make an inseparable connection between God and money. The thumbnail summary is this simple: Do good, be blessed; do evil, be cursed. Though the "cursed" side of the adage is left more or less undefined, the "blessed" side is a limitless inclusion of health, wealth, good fortune, and strong white teeth.

The biblical prophets tempered this God-is-on-our-side assumption with clear commands about caring for the poor, the stranger in the land, and those without a voice. Most true prophets were run out of town, thrown in jail, or killed. No mama ever prayed that her child would grow up to be a prophet. That much hasn't changed about prophets, and neither has the truth of their message.

What's the hardest thing for you to hear in Jesus' words?

257

DIVORCE
Luke 16:18

"A man who divorces his wife in order to marry another woman commits adultery. A man who divorces his wife in order to marry a divorced woman also commits adultery."

+

In the middle of a discussion about money and wealth, why this aside on marriage, divorce, and adultery? Who, other than divorce lawyers, sees an immediate connection?

This verse relates to the preceding verses and particularly to Jesus' reference to the law and the prophets. The issue of divorce was one example where the religious leaders fudged to get their way. Here's how it worked: Deuteronomy 24:1 states that if a woman no longer pleases her husband, he may simply sign a certificate of divorce and send her away. Done deal. The law sides with the man every time.

Certain religious leaders (male, of course) in Jesus' day were fond of interpreting this law for their own benefit, making it possible to rotate through any number of wives, while trampling a woman's personhood. This they could do, they reasoned, because the stipulations of Moses were on their side.

Jesus comes along and turns the law into a more equitable instrument of justice. A man who divorces his wife (as the legal tradition permitted) with the intent of marrying another woman, whether she's never been married or is divorced from her husband, is guilty of adultery. The one with power and rights and privilege and status doesn't get *carte blanche* when it comes to the most intimate of human relationships. Jesus insists that, in God's eyes, men don't get a free pass anymore.

At the very least, Jesus' words are an indictment against the men in the crowd who would gladly lean on the law or interpret it to serve their own purposes, regardless of the wreckage left behind. Since the children of these adulterous marriages would have been considered illegitimate by Jewish law, Jesus wags his finger at the men and essentially says, "Don't drag women into your sleazy plans!"

You have to believe the women in the crowd grinned and nodded as they gave each other a silent "thumbs up."

Where do the greatest injustices between men and women occur in society?

RICH MAN, POOR MAN
Luke 16:19-21

Jesus told this story: "There was a rich man who wore purple clothing made of fine linen and ate well every day. At his gate lay a poor man named Lazarus, whose body was covered with sores. Hungry, he longed for any crumbs that fell from the rich man's table. Dogs even came and licked his sores."

+

Jesus paints a parable of extreme contrasts—rich man/poor man, clothed in purple/dressed in sores, sumptuous food/table scraps, the have/the have-not, top/bottom. The differences could not be more obvious.

Interestingly, the poor man rather than the rich man is named. This Lazarus (meaning "God has helped") shouldn't be confused with Mary and Martha's brother (John 11). Some translations name the rich man Dives, a Latin word translated as "rich." Also worth noting is the fact that Jesus doesn't portray the rich man as a white-collar criminal, nor is Lazarus idealized as a first-century Mother Teresa.

That which separates the two men isn't an ocean or a country mile or even a city block, but a simple gate. The gate is the access through which the rich man comes and goes. The gate is where the poor man lies helpless and destitute. Behind this gate, the rich man lives in safety and security. He's protected with alarm systems and insulated from an often unpleasant world. Like any good father and husband, he provides for his family.

Lazarus has no such options. Hungry dogs feast on what oozes from his open sores. Exposed to the elements, he must endure whatever treatment comes his way. He exists without a single safety net.

As with many parables, much is left unsaid and much can be read between the lines. The rich man has no anxieties; his days are sunny and his nights cool. If some claim that money can't buy happiness, maybe they just don't know where to shop. And you can bet every time the rich man passes through his gate and sees the fleas buzzing around Lazarus, he utters a little prayer of thanksgiving: "There but for the grace of God go I."

Where are the gates you pass through each day?

Lafayette Cemetery, New Orleans, LA

REVERSAL OF FORTUNES
Luke 16:22-24

"The poor man died, and angels carried him to be with Abraham. The rich man also died and was buried. Torment-ed in Hades, the place of the dead, he looked up and saw in the distance Abraham with Lazarus by his side. He called out, 'Father Abraham, show some mercy! Send Lazarus to dip his fingertip in water and cool my tongue. This heat is unbeara-ble!'"

+

Rich or poor, death plays no favorites. Both men die. However, something shocking happens after death; a great reversal occurs. The poor man, Lazarus, receives special treatment as he's ushered into a new community next to the Hebrew patriarch Abraham. The rich man ends up (or down) in Hades and is left without a friend. *Hades* is the Greek translation of the Hebrew word *Sheol*, an Old Testament reference often translated "the place of the dead."

At this point in the story, Jesus' listeners would have raised their eyebrows. Aren't riches a sure sign of God's blessing? Aren't poverty and sickness sure signs that one is experiencing God's displeasure?

As in many parables, the absence of certain details is worth pon-dering. Jesus makes no mention of either man's personal faith. There is no suggestion that Lazarus ends up in heaven because his piety is ro-bust and his belief system is strong. Lazarus is rewarded in the afterlife for another reason altogether. On earth, he was poor and hungry and sick and lonely and forgotten and abused and abandoned. On earth, he counted for nothing. Period. For all we know, Lazarus was not even Jewish—he could have been a Buddhist, a Hindu, or an early Muslim before the arrival of the prophet Muhammad some six centuries later. He's definitely not a Christian.

Similarly, the rich man's faith, piety, belief, and orthodoxy are nonfactors in determining where he ends up. He's where he is for one reason: during his earthly life, he regularly ignored the needs of Lazarus at his gate and of all the Lazaruses beyond his lot line.

Why do we seem to get hung up on right beliefs instead of right actions?

261

FIXED CHASM
Luke 16:25-26

"Abraham said to the rich man, 'During your life you received good things, but not Lazarus. He's comforted here, and you're in agony. Besides, there's a great gap between us, making it impossible to pass from one side to the other.'"

+

I once met with a young couple seeking a church home. We rendezvoused at the local Starbucks. It wasn't long before they asked me the question whose answer would determine for them whether the church I served was a suitable one: "Can you preach a good sermon on hell?" they wondered aloud.

I wisely stifled several responses that popped into my head, but I thought them nonetheless: "No, but I can preach a *bad* sermon on hell" and "Why? Do you have an annoying relative you hope ends up there?"

We talked about literalism and metaphor, about historical facts and mythical truths, about Adolf Hitler and Charles Manson, about really good people who profess no religion and religious people who carry out evil in God's name. After a few hours, we shook hands. I looked for them on Sunday, but they never showed up.

I think we make our own hells right here on earth. Some of our manufactured hells are short-term; others are here for the long haul. We do stupid things and make dumb decisions. We give in to self-destructive behaviors and at the end of the day have no one to blame for our personal hells but the person in the mirror.

Other times, hells are thrust on us through no fault of our own. Forces beyond us—an F5 tornado, a malevolent dictator, a faulty legal system, an ill-designed levee system, full-blown Alzheimer's disease—can bring on hell like nothing else.

The rich man makes his own hell. He creates the chasm that separates him from others, a chasm he created when Lazarus was lying at his gate too weak even to swat the fleas. The rich man could have done something. He could have participated in making God's dream for the world a reality in his corner of the neighborhood. But he didn't. Now he sits in the worst hell there is, the hell of "If only . . ."

What do you think motivates people to do the right thing?

CONVINCING SIGNS
Luke 16:27-31

"The rich man said, 'Father, I'm begging you, send Lazarus to my father's house where my five brothers live so that he can warn them not to end up in this God-forsaken place.' Abraham replied, 'They have Moses and the prophets to listen to.' He said, 'No, that's not enough, but if someone returns from the dead, they will have a change of heart.' Abraham replied, 'If they won't listen to Moses and the prophets, they won't listen to someone who comes back from the dead.'"

+

The rich man has a heart and five brothers he loves. Their futures concern him. He wants to do all he can to make sure his fate doesn't befall them. "Abraham, I'm no stranger to giving orders; send Lazarus on an errand of mercy to warn my brothers." The request is denied. "Since they didn't heed the warnings of Moses and the prophets to care for those who can't pull themselves up by their own bootstraps, then there's no reason to assume they will pay attention to anyone else—not even a dead man walking." The Jews listening to Jesus would not have failed to note the reference to Moses and the prophets.

We don't know what happened to the five brothers. Did they know enough to open their eyes to the human need around them, to open their hearts, and maybe their wallets too? We shouldn't speculate long on the five siblings; without saying it in so many words, Jesus' point is obvious enough—the five are us.

Every day we have choices: Choices to create chasms and gaps. Choices to narrow the chasms and bridge the gaps. Choices to see who lies near our gate. Choices to remain blind and indifferent to gate dwellers. Choices to use our resources for a better world. Choices to pad our retirement portfolios beyond what we'll ever need. Choices to accept the world as it is and do nothing. Choices to point the world in God's direction. Choices in favor of the status quo. Choices in favor of a spiritual revolution.

What choice can't you avoid any longer?

STUMBLING BLOCKS
Luke 17:1-2

Jesus continued to teach his disciples. "Times of sinful behavior are bound to happen, but it won't go well for the person who causes them! Better for a large grinding stone to be hung around that person's neck and for him to be thrown into the sea than to cause a little one to stumble."

+

Jesus gives his disciples basic training in the tactics and techniques of living in community. Though faith may be a personal matter, it is never private.

The first of four sayings recorded in this chapter is a warning to those who cause "little ones" to stumble into sin. The term seems an obvious reference to children, but probably refers to those spiritually weaker or less mature in their faith formation. Some scholars suggest that the term refers to the poor and the most vulnerable of the earth. The warning is severe, as the consequences are grave.

Disciples don't share the same level of maturity. Some come to the faith community later in life; others are bathed in the waters of faith from infancy. Some enter the circle of faith as recent converts; others come seeking and questioning. Some insist on seeing every issue in black and white; others are open to nuances of gray. Amid these differences and temperaments, how do we maintain community? As we strive to embody God's deepest longings for the world, how do we accommodate one person's strengths and another person's weaknesses?

Jesus is most critical of religious leaders who trample relationships for the sake of maintaining and protecting doctrinal purity. As Jesus relates to those within the circle of the twelve and to those beyond, relationships always trump religious requirements that cut off others from the community. Why does it seem we have it the other way around? It's enough to cause a little one to stumble and walk away from the faith community forever.

What experiences have soured you about the church?

FORGIVE AGAIN AND AGAIN
Luke 17:3-4

"If someone you know sins, you must confront the offender. If that person is truly sorry, you must forgive. If the same person sins against you seven times a day, and says to you seven times, 'I'm sorry,' you're obligated to forgive."

+

Continuing his training session with the disciples, Jesus instructs them about healthy ways to respond when wronged by others. His instructions read like a prescription: *When sinned against, confront the offender. When repentance is expressed, forgive the offender. Repeat said action as necessary.*

The honesty is bold and direct. Jesus isn't promoting guerilla tactics that hide in the camouflage of passive-aggressive behavior. Confronting another means to "speak seriously to" that person. Nursing our hurts, soothing our sores, reopening our wounds might convince us of our undeserved victimhood, but it does little to address the hurt, move toward reconciliation, and repair the relationship.

Regarding the problem or offense, Jesus tells his disciples to name it, identify it, and bring it to the offender. Without acknowledgment on the part of the person wronged, the healing cycle of forgiveness can't get out of neutral and move forward.

To forgive "seven times a day" is an obvious reference to the Jewish teaching that seven times is the maximum limit in forgiving an offender of the same offense. As we'll hear later in Luke's gospel, not even seven times will be the outer limit in God's beloved community.

As the disciples begin to understand, faith is something less than faith if it isn't lived out in the web of relationships. Theology and sociology are inseparably bound.

When was the last time you let a wound, inflicted on you by another, fester too long?

MUSTARD SEED FAITH
Luke 17:5-6

The disciples said to Jesus, "Give us more faith!" He replied, "Even if your faith is the size of a mere mustard seed, you could say to this mulberry tree, 'Be uprooted and go into the sea,' and it would do just that."

+

Who can blame the disciples for looking within and finding themselves wanting? To do what Jesus says in matters of conduct toward others is neither easy nor always desirable. Either way, it requires more faith than what we think we have at any given moment.

Jesus isn't chiding the disciples' lack of faith, but affirming and expanding the faith they already have. Lest the disciples find the earlier discipleship demands so daunting as to prompt them to take a pass on fulfilling them, Jesus reminds them that the meager faith they possess is faith enough.

So, what is this thing—this so-called faith—of which Jesus speaks? What is this faith that can rip up trees by their expansive roots? Is it the same as bedrock certainty in the church's teachings? Is it the ability to parse the three persons of the Trinity? Is faith nothing more and nothing less than confidence in one's own ability to get the job done? Is faith something we master, something we can define?

Perhaps faith is less something we engineer than something we're given. If so, then the emphasis should rest more on the Giver than on any raw material we might mine within ourselves. And maybe this takes the pressure off. Who can say what's possible or impossible? We live into our expectations.

When was the last time your faith surprised you?

SERVANT MATTERS
Luke 17:7-10

"Why would a homeowner say to a servant who has just returned from plowing or tending sheep in the field, 'Come here and take your place at the table'? Rather, a homeowner says, 'Put on an apron, prepare supper, and serve me while I eat. Later, it will be time for you to eat your meal.' Does one thank a servant for obeying orders? Likewise, when you've done all that you're ordered to do, say, 'We're just servants; we've done exactly what we were told to do!'"

+

Using rhetorical questions, Jesus imagines several master/servant interactions that shake the sensibilities of his first-century audience. Would a master ever invite a servant to sit at his table and enjoy food the master has prepared? Of course not. Would a master ever thank a servant for following orders? That would be the day! Jesus' listeners know acceptable practices. Servants prepare meals for their masters. After the master dines, then servants eat. Servants, not masters, follow orders.

A few modern-day examples: Does a teacher say "thank you" to students for doing homework? Does a doctor say "thank you" to patients for taking daily medications? Does a mail carrier say "thank you" to a customer for placing postage on an envelope? Of course not! Such actions are the duties and responsibilities of students, patients, and customers.

Jesus says to his disciples, "So also with you." Disciples serve with a servant's heart, expecting no repayment or recognition. Reciprocity isn't required or sought. Those who live in such a way, even with the smallest faith, become a light that dispels darkness, a voice among the noisy clamor, and a cooling shade that provides relief. Live that way long enough and people eventually ask, "Why do you do what you do?"

Who models servanthood for you?

267

AS THEY WENT
Luke 17:11-14

While heading toward Jerusalem, Jesus went through a region between Galilee and Samaria. As he entered a village, ten lepers approached him. Keeping their distance, they shouted, "Jesus, Master, have mercy on us!" He said to them, "Go and show yourselves to the priests." As they went on their way, they were healed.

+

Societal demands required that lepers announce their presence so approaching persons could step aside to avoid contamination. Unlike other diseases, leprosy isolated the victim from the world. Forced to exist outside the normal constructs of society, many lepers lived together in leprosy ghettos, communities of the walking dead.

Keeping their distance, ten lepers cry out. Their cry this day is more than a warning to steer clear; it's a plea for mercy. The mercy they long for may be a plea for simple acknowledgment of their plight, for an encouraging word, or for a contribution toward their next meal.

There's no indication that Jesus approaches them or lays his hands on them. The mercy he grants is the specific instruction to show themselves to the priest. It's his word "Go"—given before a miracle—that brings healing. The word alone is sufficient.

Jesus' command is an acknowledgment of Leviticus 14:2ff, which gives ritualistic instructions to the priest when a healed leper seeks readmission into the temple. The priest verifies the healing and certifies that the leper is clean. The victim's life is changed forever.

Yet, Jesus' command that the lepers show themselves to the priest is confusing, for Jesus hasn't pronounced them healed. Instead, he expects them to act *as if* they are healed already. Only later, somewhere between their encounter with Jesus and their visit to the local priest, are they cleansed. Luke notes that "as they went" they were made clean.

Sometimes Jesus heals immediately. Sometimes Jesus brings wholeness without requiring a faith expression. Sometimes Jesus restores without being asked to do so. And sometimes transformation arrives in stages, only after a demonstration of obedience.

What next step are you waiting to take?

268

CURED OR WHOLE?
Luke 17:15-19

One of the lepers, realizing his healing, turned back and loudly praised God. Then he knelt before Jesus and thanked him. He was a Samaritan. Jesus asked, "Didn't I heal ten? Where are the other nine? Is this foreigner the only one who has returned to thank God?" Then Jesus said to him, "Get up and go your way; because you believed, you found healing."

+

Ten are cured. One returns to give thanks. Luke uses different verbs to describe the nine who are "cleansed" and the one who is "healed." All ten victims receive a physical change to their condition—the skin affliction is gone—but only one, in addition to his cleansing, undergoes the transformation of his heart.

Soon, the nine will return to the normal life denied them in their previous leprous state. They will re-enter the marketplace, earn money, regain lost years, and reconnect in relationships. There is precious time to make up in order to live like normal people again.

Therein we find the key to this episode. Jesus offers his life-changing presence not so that we can return to a rehearsal of the ordinary or re-assume our place in a business-as-usual world. Jesus isn't interested in resuscitating the old; he comes resurrecting us to a new way of living. That newness means living in God's shalom and daily acknowledging the one from whom all blessings flow. The thankful, former leper—a Samaritan, no less, an outsider to the promises God made to Israel—is the only one of the ten who sees Jesus as God's gift.

Without the integration of gratitude in our lives, is it ever possible to know healing of mind, heart, or soul? Grateful people spin off all kinds of residual virtues. Grateful people are generous, less critical, other-directed, and less accusatory. Need I say more?

On a scale of 1 (low) to 10 (high), what's your gratitude level?

AMONG YOU
Luke 17:20-21

Some religious leaders asked Jesus when God's reign would appear. He answered, "God's reign is coming, but not necessarily in ways you can see with your eyes. People won't be able to say, 'Look, here it is!' or 'There it is!' That's because evidence of God's reign is already at work among you."

+

Jesus' life bore witness to God's deepest yearnings for the world. In his ministry among the least and the last, the lost and the lone, Jesus reveals the nature of the world God envisions for humanity and creation. As Hebrew poets and prophets declared, and Jesus himself reminded us in his first sermon, the reign and rule of God emerges when justice is established among the nations, when everyone has enough, when restoration rather than retribution is the norm, when wholeness and well-being are available to all persons and systems. The biblical writers call this God's shalom.

That the religious leaders have God's reign on their radar screen is evident in their question to Jesus. What form they imagine this reign to take, we can't be sure; but they (like many today) expect a specific and observable timetable to kick in. Rather than make predictions, Jesus points to God's works already here "among you." This means whenever we live out God's redemptive presence—through acts of forgiveness, in the pursuit of fairness and justice, by working for the elimination of poverty and hunger, and by forging peace—we are making visible, among us here and now, God's intentions for the world.

Though tempting it is to reduce faith to an individual and private concern (me and God/God and me), the concerns of the biblical God are never for the sake of individuals alone, but for the transformation of society and the world.

I can imagine Jesus taking the religious leaders aside and saying, "Look, either you're busy making God's redemptive presence known right now, or else you're stuck with your heads in the clouds. If you insist on the latter, you're not much use to God."

What is your deepest longing for the world?

270

AND BE REJECTED
Luke 17:22-25

Jesus said to his disciples, "The time is coming when you will long to see me again, but you won't. People will say to you, 'Look there!' or 'Look here!' Don't fall for those bogus claims. As lightning lights up the entire sky, so it will be with me. But first I must endure much suffering and be rejected by this generation."

+

Though God's reign is present in Jesus and actively revealed when Jesus' teachings are lived by his followers, there is a sense in which it is not fully enacted. We see snippets of God's intention lived out and present in the world. We preview glimpses of the kind of world God intends. We taste the appetizer of God's future feast. Theologians call this the "already/not yet" character of God's rule. Whenever lives are transformed or wholeness experienced in its varied manifestations, whenever oppressive chains of unfair systems are broken, we witness—here, now, in this life—signs of God's reign.

But the fullness of such transformations, the completion of God's intentions for this world, and the main course of God's grand banquet remain in the future. Though we're moving toward it, clearly it isn't here yet. Like an emerging weather pattern, we experience God's shalom as a frontal edge. Walk a hospital hallway, visit a prison, or spend time reading the headlines of any newspaper for proof that God's intentions are not yet realized.

Many voices entice us with "Look here" and "Look there." We're pressured to give our loyalties to a host of second-rate allegiances: the American Dream, Might Makes Right, an I-deserve-it-all attitude. Such claims are a sham, and the sooner we recognize them as such, calling them out for what they are and are not, the closer we align ourselves with God's relentless voice.

Again, Jesus predicts his suffering and rejection. He knows his fate, but doesn't turn from it. Jesus' generation, like our own, isn't kind to those who fearlessly expose the futility of following the status quo.

Where do you go to see evidence of God's deepest passions for the world?

271

Positano, Italy

SURPRISE VISIT
Luke 17:26-30

"When I return, it will be like Noah's time. In those days, people were eating, drinking, and getting married until Noah entered the ark. Then the flood came and killed everyone. It will be like the time of Lot, Abraham's nephew, when people were eating and drinking, buying and selling, planting and building. When Lot left the city of Sodom, it rained fire and sulfur from heaven and destroyed everything. That's how it's going to be when I come again."

+

Against the backdrop of the stories of Noah (Genesis 6) and Lot (Genesis 19), Jesus reminds us that God's fullness is arriving in surprising ways. In the midst of business as usual, as bills are paid, real estate deals transacted, and winter wheat sown, God's cosmic and universal transformations are emerging and will continue to break into our old way of being.

Everything about Jesus' predictions suggests the element of surprise. The arrival sneaks up when we're looking the other way, doing other tasks, and thinking about other things. At that moment, God's reign breaks through—at times imperceptibly, but it breaks through nonetheless. Peace comes to places where there is no peace, and reconciliation is birthed when hostilities rule the day. Arabs and Jews, blacks and whites, rival ethnicities, longtime enemies, and estranged friends embrace and seek the other's good. Wishful thinking? No, God's dream taking on flesh! Often it starts small, even hidden, before it reaches the tipping point.

Exploitation of terminator-type language runs rampant today. Some ministries exist to scare people into a coerced commitment to sign up with Jesus and, of course, to financially support the ministry. Jesus, however, talks in metaphors and images, not in the specificity of times and dates. When the edges of God's ways break into our world, the old ways are turned upside down and the former things are thrown into convulsions.

Where's the good news for you in these verses?

273

LEFT BEHIND?
Luke 17:31-33

"On that day, anyone on a roof who has possessions in the house shouldn't come down to get them. No one working in the field should return home. Remember what happened to Lot's wife who didn't escape because she longed to return to her home. Those who try to make their lives secure will lose them, but those who give their lives away will keep them."

+

End time prophets and religious futurists feast on these verses. Their claims vary but include at least four common beliefs.

One: This world isn't going to last long. Its destruction, predicted in the Bible and by Jesus himself, could come any time—today, tomorrow, or next week. Definitely sooner than later.

Two: Jesus will return to (a) claim his followers, (b) judge the wicked, and (c) set up his reign and rule. Other elements include an intense tribulation, the emergence of an anti-Christ figure, the rapture of the faithful, and a span of a thousand years of peace.

Three: Since our world is destined for destruction, "true" believers shouldn't support entities like international peace accords, the United Nations, NATO, or the European Union. In fact, these organizations actually work against the will of God who is just itching to pull the plug on this sick world.

Four: "True" believers shouldn't get involved in issues like climate change and pollution because these realities actually speed up planet earth's demise, which, as they claim, is a good thing.

Many legislators who embrace this end-times scenario also decide on foreign-policy issues. Is it any wonder that Christianity in all its aberrations has a serious public relations problem?

Is the current state of the world the one God had in mind from the beginning? Hardly seems likely. The world will succumb to God's loving embrace (John 3:16) and to those willing to lose their lives for the sake of the same world God so loves.

What's your understanding of the "end times"?

274

SEPARATION
Luke 17:34-37

Jesus continued, "On that night, there will be two people in one bed; one will be taken and the other left. There will be two women grinding grain together; one will be taken and the other left." Then they asked him, "Where will this happen, Lord?" Jesus replied, "Vultures flock to rotting corpses."

+

Jesus talks a lot about separation and sorting. Someday, good will be separated from evil, grain from chaff, and wheat from weeds. Traditional interpretations maintain that heaven awaits the righteous and hell, the unrighteous.

I wonder, though, about alternative views. I wonder if the impact of this passage is lessened when we assume that the only separation to occur will be among people. Isn't there also a separation *within* each of us? Parker Palmer (*Let Your Life Speak*) refers to it as living "divided no more." He suggests we can choose to live in ways where our public selves don't contradict the truth about our inner selves.

Here's how it works for me: I live this life as two persons, divided always, sometimes in conflict, but mostly just cautiously aware of the other's presence. Two of me go to bed each night. Two of me grind coffee beans. Two of me exist side by side. One of me is noble and strives for higher nobility; the other is base and heads down the stairs to greater baseness. Some days, I'm gracious to strangers but a jerk to the people I love. I trust my neighbors, but lock my doors and windows at night. A divided self I am—patient and impatient, generous and miserly, accepting and intolerant, color-blind and racist. I'm such an unmade bed!

Will the day arrive when my dual personhood finds separation? Will the day arrive when someone—a goodly and godly one—does the sorting necessary to make me the whole person I'm created to be? One day, only one of me will know the completeness God intends. The other me will be nothing but food for vultures. To that I say, "Good riddance!"

Where do you long for separation in your being?

275

ON NOT GIVING UP
Luke 18:1

Jesus told a parable about the need to keep praying and not give up.

+

It's been said that prayer doesn't change things; prayer changes people. Neither perspective is very comforting to hear. We expect prayer to change things, all manner of things, from reversal of misfortunes to the eradication of cancer-mutated cells. Nor does it appeal to the stubborn side of our natures to hear that prayer's main purpose is to change the one doing the praying. Most of us hate change. We love familiarity and dig in our heels when our lives are threatened by change. Who really wants to be outmuscled by God?

Whether it changes things or changes people, prayer is an activity Jesus encourages us to do. Pray always and don't lose heart. Kathleen Norris (*Amazing Grace: A Vocabulary of Faith*) suggests that true prayer is not asking for those things we're convinced we want and need, but opening ourselves to an unexpected future we can't quite imagine. We're able then to rejoice in what we've been given today and fear less what we think we lack for tomorrow.

Perhaps Jesus is saying something similar. Prayer's attrition rate is astounding. The roadside is littered with prayers never uttered by travelers too tired, discouraged, or cynical to make the effort. If we attempt prayer at all, we soon lose the will to continue if, after a day or two, our invocations seem to fall on a deaf deity.

Two questions: (1) Who has time for such futility? (2) Who but God knows what needful changes we miss or what blessings we never receive because we lose heart too soon?

Regarding prayer, are you one who doesn't lose heart or hasn't started?

276

BOTHERING VIRTUE
Luke 18:2-5

"There was a judge in town who neither respected God nor cared about people. A widow in that town kept pestering the judge, saying, 'I've been wronged by someone and I want justice!' For a time, the judge refused to do anything, but later thought, 'Though I don't respect God or care about people, I'll act justly for this annoying woman so she won't wear me out.'"

+

To reinforce his point that we should pray always and not lose heart, Jesus tells a story about a judge of dubious character who meets his match in a determined widow who refuses to give up before getting what she wants.

This woman is too poor to buy him off and too weak to threaten him. Though she's at his mercy, she's anything but passive, and demands her rights in a male-dominated world. She's not going to be disregarded. Her only weapon is to stand her ground and refuse to go away. With dogged persistence and an in-your-face attitude, she finally persuades the judge to act justly regarding the issue she brings before him. The Greek word translated as "justice" also carries a meaning closer to "vengeance," which would suggest this widow is out for blood. No one is going to tell *her* to sit in a rocking chair and mind her own business. In this courtroom battle of wills, the judge is the first to cry uncle.

Perhaps this story's hero—a woman who's a widow—reminds us of people we know who, in the face of adversity, hardship, injustice, prejudice, racism, and a host of other "isms," refuse to back down or give up or give in. They just keep at it, like a dog to a bone. They don't listen to the odds-makers. They don't heed the naysayers. They never doubt the rightness of their pursuit. Like the flower that grows in the crack of the sidewalk, they give off their sweet scent to the rest of us.

Who's been a persistent widow-influence in your life?

WILL HE DELAY LONG?
Luke 18:6-8

Jesus continued, "Listen to this unfair judge. Won't God act justly on behalf of the chosen ones who cry out continually? God will not delay long before acting in a fair way on their behalf. Yet, when God's reign breaks into the world, will anyone believe?"

+

This is one of the few parables in which a character makes a direct reference to God: "Though I don't respect God . . ." In hearing the widow's plea and eventually granting it, the unjust judge demonstrates God-like qualities. Perhaps more peculiar is the possibility that there are qualities of God that resemble the less-than-flattering qualities of this magistrate.

Some troubling implications arise: If only we nag God enough, God will give in to our requests just like the weary judge. There are times when God needs arm-twisting; if we're willing to apply the pressure, we'll get what we want. God delights in watching us grovel and beg as we plead for attention. Like this hard-hearted judge, God isn't predisposed to act in our favor. The sufferings and injustices we're called to endure in life exist in direct proportion to our ability to persist in prayer.

But let's not force this parable to say more than it intends to say. The parable answers an underlying question and concern of the people of God, especially for those facing persecution at the hands of the Roman Empire: Will God act in God's time, in God's way, on behalf of God's people? Is God trustworthy? The answer, evidenced in this parable, is a resounding "Yes." God will restore justice to those who, like this widow, have been denied it. God doesn't forget those who suffer. The fullness of God's reign may arrive sooner or later, but make no mistake—it will arrive. The promise-making God is also the promise-keeping God. Faith embraces such a hope.

What do you hope God will set right?

278

A MODERN PARABLE (PART 1)
Luke 18:9-12

Jesus told a story to those who trusted in their own goodness and looked down on others: "Two men entered the temple to pray—one, a deeply religious Pharisee and the other, a tax collector. The religious person stood alone and prayed, 'God, I thank you that I'm not like other people: thieves, leeches, adulterers, or even this tax collector. I fast twice a week and give a tenth of all my income.'"

+

Two worshippers enter the House of Religion, each needing some prayer time. One prayerful soul is a pious man, a religious power-house, a heavy user of spiritual steroids. A good man is he, respected by the community, and a lifelong member of the holiness society. Long before he could ride a bicycle without training wheels, he knew the stories of his ancestors Abraham, Isaac, and Jacob, Sarah, Rebekah, and Rachel. As a youth, he earned the coveted Sunday School Attendance Award. Blue ribbons and brass-plated trophies crowded his book-shelves.

Now as an adult, he's a hard-working member of the House of Religion. Always volunteering. Always helping out. Always dependable. Always there. He can repeat from memory the creeds: The Apostles', The Nicene, and The Athanasian. When the congregation sings the old familiar hymns, his eyes are the first to mist over, especially on the refrain of "How Great Thou Art."

All the people agree that he's one saintly man. Why, just to hear him pray is an inspirational event. "God, I thank you . . ." Perfect simplicity. Even God has to be pleased. No laundry list of needs. No chronic complaints. No bones to pick with the Almighty. For this man of prayer, every day is Thanksgiving Day. If only we fared as well.

As he prays, he stands alone—alone in his perfection, alone in his rightness, alone in his aloneness. Alone.

What's been your experience with fasting or giving away 10 percent?

A MODERN PARABLE (PART 2)
Luke 18:13-15

"But the tax collector, standing alone in the corner, wouldn't even look up. He beat his chest saying, 'God, have mercy! I'm nothing but a sinner!' I tell you, this man went home justified rather than the other. Those who are full of themselves will be humbled, and those who humble themselves will be made great."

+

Two worshippers enter the House of Religion, each needing some prayer time. One prayerful soul is a scoundrel by everyone's definition. A lifelong member of the pond-scum society, he's a traitor to his people, bilking them with schemes and then pocketing the exorbitant profits. He's rich, but no country club would accept him as a member.

Long before settling into his lucrative telemarketing profession, he learned the ropes playing Three-Card Monty on street corners. Now as an adult, he's a full-fledged scam artist, a trickle-down capitalist whose credo is "If you're willing to buy it, I'm selling it."

And sell it, he does: home security systems that feed the fear of neighbors; miracle water packets from the Jordan River; whole life insurance policies to octogenarians; used cemetery plots; auto paint jobs without the primer; watered-down concrete minus the re-bar. Oh, he's good! And always a step ahead of the Better Business Bureau.

Everyone wonders aloud, "What the hell is *he* doing in *our* House of Religion?" No matter, it wasn't much of a prayer anyway. "God, have mercy! I'm nothing but a sinner." No need to point out the incredibly obvious when the merely obvious will do. He gets it right—the whole mess about himself, and the whole truth about where to go. Looking only at his own wretched heart and nobody else's, he offers it.

Amy-Jill Levine (*A Feminist Companion to Luke*) suggests that in the line "this man went home justified rather than the other," "rather" is not the only translation of the Greek. It could be read that both men left the temple justified "side by side." The only problem with translations that portray God's heart having room for all kinds of broken souls is that we're slow in catching up to God's idea of grace.

How does your life look compared to this guy's?

CHILDREN ONLY
Luke 18:15-17

People brought infants and children to Jesus that he might touch them. When the disciples saw this, they told the parents to stop. But Jesus corrected his disciples: "I want little children to come to me; don't stop them. God has a place for children too. Whoever doesn't receive what God offers like a child will never experience it."

+

Through the centuries, these verses have been the inspiration of countless paintings depicting Jesus doting over little children, patting their heads and bouncing them on his knee. The disciples see the attention as a waste of Jesus' time.

What does Jesus see in infants and children that afford them unique access to the community of God? Several possibilities exist: Children by nature are given to curious bouts of wonder, seeing those things to which adults have grown blind. When was the last time you grabbed a handful of freshly mowed grass, pondered your reflection in a mud puddle, or explored the possibilities of an empty cardboard box?

Most of us would agree that children implicitly are more trusting than adults, more transparent with their emotions, and less able to surround themselves with fortified defense mechanisms. Some might even claim that little children possess a morally clean slate of innocence. Such people, of course, have never witnessed a toddler in the throes of a temper tantrum in the cereal aisle of a grocery store.

Maybe what Jesus sees in this underage population is childhood ignorance about the world of accomplishments and achievements, and the inability to present any moral trophies or blue-ribbon accomplishments thought to entice God's love.

To receive like a child is to be stripped down to an essential bareness. In our nakedness, with nothing to offer and even less on which to rely, we receive from God the hand of love.

What's your best childlike quality?

Western Wall, Jerusalem

Q & A
Luke 18:18-21

A leader in the community asked Jesus, "Good teacher, how do I get eternal life?" Jesus replied, "Why do you call me good? Only God is good. You know the commandments: Don't commit adultery. Don't murder. Don't steal. Don't lie. Honor your father and mother." The questioner replied, "I've lived that way my whole life."

+

Let's give the questioner a ton of credit. He prefers the direct approach and wants Jesus to know what's on his mind. Let's also applaud him for an apparent lack of sinister motives. He's not trying to trap Jesus into saying something that later can be used against him.

The question on his mind is a universal one for all who believe or have a hunch that something exists beyond this life. He asks the question which millions of people have thought: "If there's something beyond this life, how do I get it?"

However he understands eternal life, the afterlife, the next life, or the good life here and now, he supposes that getting it involves something he must *do*. Surely, there exists a list of boxes he can check off.

Just the opening Jesus needs! What an opportunity to dispel every misconception about obtaining eternal life! We might expect Jesus to say with evangelistic fervor, "Believe in me and the God who sent me." Or, "Worship me as the only way, the only truth, and the only life; then you'll be saved."

Jesus doesn't go that route. There's no "Come to Jesus" sermon here—no emotional altar call either. Instead, Jesus honors his own tradition and that of the inquirer and says, "Live a noble life. Keep the commandments. Be good and do good." Confidently comes the reply: "Amen, Good Teacher, that's what I've been doing my whole life."

I like where Jesus starts with this one. He acknowledges and respects what the inquirer already knows. Jesus doesn't discredit or dismantle the beliefs dearly held. The lesson? We could do worse than honor the traditions of others who seek, as we do, answers to life's most important questions.

How would you answer the question raised in these verses?

ONE THING LACKING
Luke 18:22-23

Jesus responded to the inquirer, "There's one thing you need to do. Sell everything you have and give the money to the poor; then you'll have eternal treasures. Once you've done that, follow me." But when the man heard this, he grew despondent, for he was very rich.

+

Maybe it's the seven rings on his fingers or the thousand-thread count of his Egyptian cotton robe that tips off Jesus to the man's wealth. Or maybe Jesus just has a hunch about the one thing he lacks. Either way, Jesus definitely nails it.

I've never preached a sermon on this passage, nor have I heard a sermon telling hearers to take Jesus' words literally. Never. Not once. I know of no TV evangelist or mega-minister mogul who's admitted, "The Lord laid this command on my heart and I obeyed it completely."

Here are a few ways we make this passage easier to swallow: (1) Jesus is speaking to a specific individual in a specific circumstance; it doesn't apply to everyone. (2) Jesus isn't implying that money and possessions are inherently bad, just that they have that potential. (3) Jesus' instructions are best followed when we remain "spiritually detached" from material things. (Yes, it's confusing and lame.)

Maybe each of these explanations deserves a hearing. Yet, I wonder what deeper experiences of God we miss when we assume that "Sell everything you own and give the money to the poor" doesn't apply to us. Why are we so concerned that the poor are that way because of their own character flaws, while Jesus seems more concerned with *our* flaws? What depths of faithfulness and what heights of freedom will we never know because we imagine Jesus' challenge is prescriptive for this questioner but not a tonic for our ailments?

Nobody talks about this passage. Nobody takes it at face value. Nobody strives to live it. Not even those who swear they take the Bible literally! That's because money is the true American idol.

If you took Jesus seriously, what would you give away tomorrow?

ENTRANCE DIFFICULTIES
Luke 18:24-27

Jesus went on to make a point: "How hard for the wealthy to experience the social transformations that God is bringing about. It's a lot easier for a camel to pass through a needle's eye than for the rich to receive what God wants to give." The disciples wondered aloud, "Then who can be saved?" Jesus replied, "What's impossible for humans is possible for God."

+

C'mon! Enough already! Doesn't Jesus talk about anything else? Yes, he does, but not nearly to the extent of money and wealth. Close to a third of his parables and half of everything he says deals with materialistic themes. Jesus has more to say about our relationship with things than he does about prayer, family, or sexuality (for those who need reminding, Jesus says nothing about homosexuality).

"How hard for the wealthy to experience the freedom of God's reign!" As North Americans—most of us wealthy by every global standard—how do we hear these words? Is it true that we're less concerned with things of God than the poor are? Because of our riches and privileges, are we more selfish and less altruistic? Does our "blessed" lot in life make us less receptive to Jesus' invitation to follow him?

Clearly, the disciples are surprised and frustrated at Jesus' statement about the hindrances of wealth: "Then who can be saved?" Behind that question is an Old Testament perspective best summed up in Deuteronomy 8:18: "God enables you to get wealth, so that the promises made to your ancestors will come true." These verses in Luke follow Jesus' encounter with the rich man who wasn't able to give up anything in exchange for true freedom. In that refusal, we discover wealth's inherent danger—once it's ours, we can't imagine life without it. Not even the freedom gained by walking away from its grip seems worth the sacrifice. Nevertheless, what seems impossible to us isn't so with God.

What's the most radical decision you've made about money?

FAMILY TIES
Luke 18:28-30

Peter reminded Jesus, "We've left everything to follow you." Jesus replied, "Listen, anyone who has left house or family for the sake of pursuing God will get back much more in this life and in the life to come."

+

Leave it to Peter to point out what Jesus seems to forget: namely, the sacrifices the disciples made in order to follow him. Some walked away from fishing businesses and inventories of nets. Most of them, at least for a time, left loved ones who had to figure out why following a traveling rabbi could be better than anything around hearth and home.

We might expect Jesus to say an encouraging word about the importance of family in the scheme of the community of God, to remind the twelve that the institution of the family is the primary manifestation of God's will for our birth relationships. Why not use this teaching moment to say something positive about his own family, or at least to remind us of the priority of family obligations?

The fact that Jesus says little about the blessedness of families, even good ones, is worth noting. For Jesus, one's natural family ties are secondary to the higher relationship of belonging to the family of God. In the family of God, we find our true "family values." When Jesus calls people to follow him, that call isn't only about the embracing of new commitments but about the lessening of some old ones. In this spiritual molting process, not even our earthly biological families are as significant as the community into which Jesus calls us.

If family ties are down-rated in the call to follow Jesus, it's no surprise that the invitation gladdens some hearts, but breaks others.

What are the implications for you of being called into God's family?

PASSION THOUGHTS
Luke 18:31-34

Jesus took the twelve aside and said, "We're going to Jerusalem, and everything that's written about me by the prophets
will happen. I'll be handed over to the Romans to be mocked
and insulted and spat upon. After they flog me, they will kill
me, and on the third day, I'll rise again." But the disciples had
no idea what Jesus was talking about.

+

With troubling specificity, Jesus details for his disciples the treatment awaiting him in Jerusalem: "Handed over . . . mocked . . .
insulted . . . spat upon . . . flog me . . . kill me." Jesus isn't unaware of
the trouble that awaits him, yet he doesn't turn away from heading
into the storm.

Jesus speaks openly and plainly enough about his impending suffering. There's no parable to decipher, no image to interpret, no hidden
meaning to decode. Jesus lays it out before them without hyperbole or
embellishment: suffering, death, new life.

That the disciples neither understand these things nor grasp the
implications isn't the first occasion of clouded thinking. How can the
twelve wrap their minds around these future events when understanding requires alterations of their notions of what a Messiah is supposed
to be and do? Spiritual leaders aren't handed over. Supreme teachers
aren't mocked. Kings aren't insulted. True messiahs aren't spat upon.
Saviors aren't flogged. Death doesn't come to God's appointed one.
Until now. Until Jesus.

The rich ruler in the preceding verses refuses to give up the one
thing necessary for his freedom—his wealth. The Ruler in these verses
knows what he'll have to give up for his freedom—his life. And Jesus
will.

What would be the hardest thing for you to give up?

BLIND SIGHTINGS
Luke 18:35-39

A blind man was begging along the roadside as Jesus neared the city of Jericho. Hearing a commotion coming from the crowd, the blind man asked what was happening. Someone told him, "Jesus of Nazareth is coming by." The blind man shouted, "Jesus, Son of David, have mercy on me!" People told him to be quiet, but the blind man shouted even louder, "Son of David, have mercy on me!"

+

In the gospels, blindness appears in many forms. Some religious leaders were blind because they refused to recognize God powerfully at work in Jesus. The disciples were blind when they failed to grasp Jesus' predictions about his own suffering and death.

Amid this blindness, Luke inserts the story of a physically blind beggar (identified in Mark's gospel as Bartimaeus). Told that Jesus is passing by, the blind man shouts, "Jesus, Son of David, have mercy on me!" Refusing to be silenced by those (the real blind ones?) who consider him an annoyance, he shouts even louder.

Son of David is a title given to Jesus that is both appropriate to his identity and problematic in its potential misuse by the crowds. Jesus stands in the lineage of Israel's greatest king, a leader after God's own heart. Jesus shares continuity with Israel's past and arrives as a present-day deliverer of the people. The methodology of that deliverance and its potential for nationalistic misinterpretation, however, is a reality against which Jesus remains vigilant.

But the blind man sees what seeing people don't see. This roadside resident, whose days are as dark as night, sees in Jesus the one who will notice his condition. He demands to be heard and won't be silenced until he is. He won't remain quiet in his lightless world. Akin to the tax collector in the temple, he prays a prayer this Son of David can't ignore: "Have mercy on me!" It's the prayer prayed by anyone—blind or not—who's fresh out of roadside options.

What do you think people are most blind to in the world?

REQUEST GRANTED
Luke 18:40-43

Jesus stopped and asked that the blind man be brought to him. When he came near, Jesus inquired, "What do you want me to do for you?" He answered, "I want to see again." Jesus said, "Well then, see again! Because you believe, you are healed." Immediately, the man could see, and he followed Jesus. Those who witnessed this praised God.

+

Jesus stops, and from that stationary posture, grace begins to flow. As often happens in the gospel record, amid the crowd and among the throng, while on his way from one place to another, with the implications of his future suffering still fresh in his mind, Jesus stops to acknowledge one who cries out for his attention.

The God who said to Moses "I've observed the misery of my people in Egypt; I've heard their cry because of their taskmasters. I know their sufferings and have come down to deliver them" (Exodus 3:7-8) is the same God who prompts Jesus to stop along a Jericho roadside.

The God about whom David wrote ". . . who forgives your sins, who heals your diseases, who rescues your life from destruction, who rewards you with steadfast love and mercy" (Psalm 103:3-4) is the same God who empowers Jesus to do the same.

The God who spoke through Isaiah—"Seek the God who can be found, call out to the God who is near; let the wicked turn from their wickedness, and the unrighteous from their wrongs. Return to the merciful God who forgives" (Isaiah 55:6-7)—is the same God who moves Jesus to respond to the blind man's plea, "I want to see again."

Years ago, J. B. Phillips (*Your God Is Too Small*) cautioned us against limiting God to our tiny boxes. God is bigger, the author maintained, than any ideas or images we might entertain. The opposite also is true: sometimes our mental images of God are too big, as when we perceive a vast and detached deity beyond earshot of roadside pleas.

That Jesus stops and stands still is good news. As the world turns around us, most are content to pass by.

What roadside plea might you utter?

BECAUSE OF THE CROWD
Luke 19:1-4

Jesus entered Jericho, where there was a wealthy man named Zacchaeus, a chief tax collector. He was trying to get a look at Jesus, but because he was a short man, he couldn't see above the crowd. Hoping for a better view, Zacchaeus climbed a sycamore tree.

+

The colorful character Zacchaeus is one to whom children are introduced early in their Sunday School formation. I still remember a stanza of the Zacchaeus Song, complete with hand motions: "Zacchaeus was a wee little man, a wee little man was he. He climbed up in the sycamore tree for the Lord he wanted to see."

Luke doesn't tell us in what specific way the crowd prevents Zacchaeus from seeing Jesus, but the most obvious explanation is that no one allowed him to stand in front for an unobstructed view.

I wonder, though, about the more overt attempts to hinder this rich tax collector's attempts to get a glimpse of Jesus. What about an elbow to the side of his head, or a concerted effort to block his path, or verbal threats should he push his luck? Maybe the crowd shares more culpability in denying Zacchaeus access to Jesus than Luke lets on.

There are no few ways religious institutions prevent people from getting close to Jesus. We might advertise that "All Are Welcome," but our actions often say something else. Can the physically disabled get in without having to depend on a helping hand? Does a stranger come and go without anyone saying hello? Would a visitor with tattoo-covered arms find anyone to talk to at the coffee hour?

What do we do with the unshaven Saturday night reveler who reeks of stale beer or a few too many gin and tonics? Do children know they belong? How many people are bewildered as they struggle through the maze of an unfamiliar liturgy and songs impossible to sing?

Like Zacchaeus, some beat the odds and find the resources (and the tree!) for a better view of Jesus. How many people, however, simply get lost in the crowd and, because of the crowd, are never noticed and never return? Not even a "Nice to see ya."

Based on your experience, how does the church block a person's view of Jesus?

HOUSE CALL
Luke 19:5-7

When Jesus came near, he looked up and said, "Zacchaeus, come down! I want to stay at your house today." Zacchaeus hurried down the tree and was happy to welcome Jesus. But the people who saw it grumbled and said, "He's going to a sinner's house."

+

Countless sermons have been preached exalting Zacchaeus' ingenuity and determination. A never-say-die attitude can go a long way for someone facing insurmountable odds. Perhaps Jesus notices this and feels compelled to invite himself to the plucky man's house.

That Jesus knows Zacchaeus' name, no doubt, is an indication that Jesus inquired of the crowd the tree climber's identity. Happy they were to oblige and point out what this devious fellow did for a living. Not only is he a tax collector, but the chief tax collector, who occupies the top perch on a dubious pyramid scheme. He knows the system and uses it to his full advantage. No wonder they grumble when Jesus goes home with him.

We shouldn't fail to note an absence of any faith expression from Zacchaeus. There's no "I'll follow you wherever you go, Jesus." All he displays is a hyper-curiosity about a popular rabbi passing through his town. Maybe that's all Jesus needs to see—a curiosity seeker who can't be held down.

Jesus heads for the home of the rich man. As we've seen numerous times that Jesus issued stern warnings about the dangers of wealth. On several occasions, he fired off warnings to those who found themselves with money to burn. On this occasion, however, he seeks out the company of someone known for his ill-gotten gains. We're left to wonder, is any person beyond the friendship of this traveler heading toward Jerusalem?

Whenever grace's hospitality extends beyond respectable limits, there's always a crowd ready to grumble.

What do you find most endearing or annoying about Zacchaeus?

REPAYMENT PLAN
Luke 19:8

Zacchaeus stood there and said to Jesus, "I'll give half of what I own to the poor. If I've defrauded anyone, I'll pay them back four times as much."

+

The rich man has something to say. For the first time, Zacchaeus speaks. Without a guilt-inducing sermon given till it hurts, and without someone shoving a pledge card in his hand, Zacchaeus offers up half his possessions to the poor and, for good measure, a fourfold return to anyone he's cheated. All this just because Jesus wants to be his houseguest!

How do we explain Zacchaeus's change of heart? Was it light-headedness from sitting on the highest branch in the tree? Why this impulsive promise to reform his cheating ways? Jesus doesn't command him to do this as he did the rich young ruler in the previous chapter. If there's no pressure, why does Zacchaeus make this promise?

Fifty percent and a fourfold repayment plan. No excuses. No back-pedaling. No vain attempts to explain the nuances of a trickle-down economy. No effort to teach Jesus the fine art of making it in a bull or bear market.

Fifty percent and a fourfold repayment plan. No rationalizing that it's a jungle out there. No sideward glances at other tax collectors who are just as unethical.

Fifty percent and a fourfold repayment plan. No attempts to convince Jesus that his childhood was tougher than most in his old neighborhood. No reminder to Jesus that he set up his folks in a lovely condo on the Sea of Galilee.

Fifty percent and a fourfold repayment plan. No correction of the public sentiment against him: "Look, Jesus, I know what they say about me, but you need to hear all the facts. I'm really not so bad once you see beyond the bling hanging from my neck."

Fifty percent and a fourfold repayment plan. It defies any reasonable explanation. Logical it isn't. Impulsive and rash, it's what some people do once they discover life as God intends it.

What's the most irrational thing you've done for the sake of a higher purpose?

HOUSEHOLD OF SALVATION
Luke 19:9-10

Then Jesus said to the people standing near, "Today, salvation has arrived at this house because this man is a son of Abraham, too. I've come to find the lost and save them."

+

Since Jesus has been talking directly to Zacchaeus, we might wonder why he doesn't say to the crowd, "Today salvation has come to this man." By saying "this house," Jesus declares that Zacchaeus isn't the only one to reap spiritual benefits; included are his wife, children, servants, and whatever pets might wander in and out.

Similar good fortune came to the prostitute Rahab in the book of Joshua. Because she showed kindness and offered protection to two Israelite spies, she "and her household" (Joshua 6:17) were spared when Jericho was destroyed.

In the book of Acts, a God-fearing woman named Lydia was moved by a sermon of the apostle Paul. She and "her entire household" (Acts 16:15) received baptism. Later in the same chapter, Paul and Silas, both prisoners at the time, assure their jailer that he "and his household" will be saved (Acts 16:31).

How's it possible that those merely related to someone who responds to God's initiative receive the same blessings? It begs the question: Can the benefits of responding to God be transferred to another without the recipient's awareness? Can a mother's embrace of God's generosity come to a son even without the son's active acceptance? Can a daughter's journey along faith's pathway make her father an unknowing beneficiary just because he lives under the same roof?

No and Yes. If one understands a personal response, a personal relationship, a personal connection to Jesus as the *only* valid entry into the fullness of God, then the answer is No. However, if God also chooses to work beyond individual responses, deep into the web of family and social systems, then the answer is Yes.

As for me and for the sake of my household, I'll never bet against the One who comes to seek the lost, and to transform the world by whatever means necessary. God's circle of inclusion never shrinks.

Where is your circle of inclusion resisting expansion?

A NOBLEMAN AND HIS SERVANTS
Luke 19:11-15

As Jesus got closer to Jerusalem, he told a story because some people supposed that the fullness of God's dream for the world was about to take place. He said, "A landowner was getting ready to be made a ruler. Before he left to attend the official coronation, he gave ten of his servants three months' worth of wages and said to them, 'Trade and invest with this money until I come back.' But people in the area hated him and sent a delegation to follow him, saying, 'We don't want this man to rule over us.' When the landowner returned, having received authority to rule, he ordered the servants to give an account of the profits they had made with the money he had given them."

+

Since many of Jesus' followers expected an imminent intervention of God that would expel Roman oppressors and restore the former glory of Israel, Jesus tells a parable to correct this popular misunderstanding.

The first half of the parable echoes an actual event that took place in first-century Palestine. After the death of Herod the Great, his ruthless son Archelaus traveled to Rome to receive authority to rule in his father's place. So severe was the public outcry that a Jewish contingency went to the Roman capital to protest. As a result, Archelaus's kingdom, which did not extend beyond the region of Judea, never equaled that of his father.

The second half of Jesus' parable shares similarities to the Parable of the Talents in Matthew 25. In both parables, servants are entrusted with a sizable sum of money and told to trade and make a profit.

In Luke's version, Jesus addresses two concerns. Clearly, he sees himself as the landowner who must receive his authority in the distant country where God dwells. The fullness of God's reign won't arrive with his entrance into Jerusalem, but will be revealed as history unfolds. In the meantime, those entrusted with the things of the owner (Jesus) are to use on his behalf the gifts he has given each of them.

What things of God are we expected to "do business with"?

RISKY ADVENTURE
Luke 19:16-19

"The first servant came forward and said, 'Master, your money has grown tenfold.' The landowner replied, 'Good job! Because you've been dependable, I'll give you responsibility over ten cities.' Then the second servant said, 'Sir, I've increased your money five times over.' The landowner said to him, 'Good work! You will rule over five cities.'"

+

The landowner comes off as a good capitalist who is pleased with the savvy business dealings of two employees. The boss backs up his praise by granting the first servant management over ten cities and the second, administration over five cities.

We shouldn't forget that this parable is about a nobleman and his servants—two parties of unequal rank, importance, and privilege. One has all the authority and power; the others have none. In addition to entrusting ten servants (though we'll only hear reports from three) with substantial portions of his wealth, the nobleman now trusts them enough to turn over to their command fifteen of his cities.

The landowner and two of his servants take risks. The former gives away a portion of his estate and trusts others to use it wisely and productively. With infinite ways to lose what they've been given, the servants accept appropriate risks to manage and eventually multiply what is theirs to use.

For the moment, let's forget about the moneymaking and business-mindedness of the parable. Such details are merely the storytelling props Jesus uses to make a deeper point. (Unless, of course, I'm wrong, and Jesus is teaching us how to make double-digit returns on our investments. But I don't think so.)

Why is Jesus so obsessed with risk? Let's not overlook that he's getting closer to the city of Jerusalem. Does he know exactly what will happen to him there? Enough to know it won't be pretty. And what will his disciples and followers need to do when he is gone from them? Withdraw, and protect what memories they have? Or launch into the world, empowered and emboldened by Jesus' life?

Where in your life might you take more risks?

"I WAS AFRAID"
Luke 19:20-23

"Then the third servant said, 'Sir, here's your money; I wrapped it in this cloth. I was afraid because you demand a lot. You take money that you don't deposit, and food that you don't produce.' The landowner replied, 'Your own words condemn you. I can't believe how wicked you are! You say I'm demanding. Why didn't you put my money in the bank? At least then you could have collected some interest.'"

+

Is there anyone who doesn't empathize with this third servant? Life is full of uncertainties. Sometimes it's best to play it safe. Who can predict what tomorrow will bring? Not even banks are beyond failing.

Yes, he's cautious. He doesn't toss his master's money in a trash bag, but carefully wraps it in a piece of cloth—a fine silk cloth, probably—and tucks it in a safe place. He knows his master has high expectations and even tougher performance reviews. He is also aware that ancient laws at times protected those who, by burying valuables entrusted to them, absolved themselves of liability. A wicked servant? Really? Nothing's been lost, wasted, or frittered away. The servant didn't steal from his boss or drain the fortune like an open faucet.

Lessons of all kinds poke through. Most suggest that we need to put to good use that which the Creator gives us. If one has a special talent or skill, don't hide it in the folds of a cloth, but use it in service to others and for the glory of God.

Preachers love to expound on these verses when the church budget needs promotion. The standard stewardship message reminds listeners that everything we have is a gift from God. As servants, we're responsible to return our offerings in proportion to what we've been given. Worthy lessons are there, which too quickly we forget.

At the heart of this story, however, is the servant's fear. Fear is the dominant component in his strategy. Fear is the well-guarded possession. Fear defines his relationship to the landowner. Who can blame the boss, especially after his earlier generosity and graciousness, for being incensed?

In what ways does a fear of God keep you from living more fully?

296

OUTRAGEOUS COMMANDS
Luke 19:24-27

"The landowner gave the order, 'Take the money and give it to the one who turned a tenfold profit.' They said to him, 'He's already been rewarded!' The owner replied, 'Those who do well will be given more; those who don't will lose what they have. Now, concerning my enemies who don't want me to rule over them, find them and kill them in my presence.'"

+

The cause of faithful living wouldn't be diminished if these verses were scratched out forever. To sum up: A real estate mogul has such high regard for his servants that he grants them managerial responsibilities over his estate. One servant exceeds the owner's expectations. Another also does quite well. One, however, gets an "F." The landowner calls him wicked and adds a few expletives not included in the dialogue. The one who merely keeps intact what he was given is stripped of all duties and demoted to cleaning out the cattle stalls. Then, the landowner threatens to slaughter those who challenge his right to rule. Just the kind of Bible story we want our children to hear.

How do we read a passage full of condemnation and executive orders to wipe out the competition faster than a hostile corporate takeover? As always, let's remember the context. Jesus tells this parable in response to the expectation that he's going to Jerusalem to establish an earthly rule that will include throwing out the Romans.

Yes, Jesus is headed to Jerusalem, but not to oust the sitting governor. Jesus' purpose is nonviolent resistance, a posture that will lead to his death. In his departure—his going away—his followers will continue to multiply his ministry by feeding the hungry, tending to the sick, seeking the lost, and befriending the lonely.

Some, though, will oppose the kind of world God intends by doing anything to snuff it out. Some will side with the strong, the privileged, and the dominant culture by embracing a might-makes-right attitude. Some will deny the reality of God that puts at risk all other realities. "Kill them in my presence." It's impossible to soften those words. Maybe such folks are already dead—from the heart up.

Where do you see the strongest opposition to God's intentions?

Kane County, IL

AHEAD AND UP
Luke 19:28

When it was time, Jesus went on ahead, up toward Jerusalem.

+

The next event in Jesus' life will be his entrance into Jerusalem, which begins his final week. The last six of Luke's twenty-four chapters are devoted to the events between Palm Sunday and Easter. In the four gospels, nearly a third of everything written about Jesus occurs in these final days known as Holy Week.

In most Bibles, this single verse forms its own paragraph, reading like a transition or pause before the coming storm. Does Jesus go on ahead in order to be alone with his thoughts? Is he seeking a deeper communion with his Divine Source? Is he losing patience with the disciples' continued inability to grasp what lies ahead?

We can only speculate what Jesus thinks and feels while going up to Jerusalem. One thing seems likely: he probably does what his ancestors once did—sing the Songs of Ascent while making his way up the higher elevation to the ancient city. "Who will ascend the hill of God and stand in God's holy place?" (Psalm 24:3). "I lift up my eyes to the hills; from where will my help come? My help comes from God, maker of heaven and earth" (Psalm 121:1-2). "I lift up my eyes to you, O God, for you live in the heavens!" (Psalm 123:1).

Songs have a powerful influence on the mind and soul—calming, steadying, soothing. It's not a stretch to imagine that Jesus knows he will need all that and more for what lies ahead.

What songs do you keep coming back to?

BORROWED TRANSPORTATION
Luke 19:29-31

Jesus came near Bethphage and Bethany to a place called the Mount of Olives and said to two of his disciples, "Go into the village, and you will find a donkey that's never been ridden. Untie it and bring it to me. If anyone asks you about this, just tell them I need it."

+

Jesus' entry into Jerusalem, recorded in all four gospels, is the occasion for Palm Sunday observances throughout the Christian world. Most church services on this day are festive, joyous, and parade-like, complete with children processing with palm branches.

The scene begins about two miles east of Jerusalem, close to the villages of Bethphage and Bethany, near a hill filled with olive trees. With thoughtful deliberation, Jesus scripts the event. He selects the village. He determines the mode of transportation. He sends his disciples to secure a donkey that's never been ridden.

Why a donkey and not a horse? Why not choose to be hoisted on the shoulders of his disciples and carried triumphantly into Jerusalem? The answer lies in Jesus' understanding of his mission. Warhorses and chariots were the transportation of choice for victorious conquerors and military leaders. Jesus refuses to allow his image to contribute to any nationalistic fervor. He won't be another incarnation of political clout measured in battalions of uniformed foot soldiers. This Messiah comes in humility, atop a beast most commonly associated with peace.

By riding a donkey, Jesus follows the example of the prophets Jeremiah and Ezekiel and offers himself as the humble Prince of Peace. The disciples, raised with the sacred writings, couldn't fail to hear echoes of yet another prophet, who testified, "Rejoice and shout, Jerusalem! Your king arrives triumphant and victorious, yet humble and riding on a donkey" (Zechariah 9:9).

Who's a humble leader today?

"JESUS NEEDS IT"
Luke 19:32-34

The two disciples left and found the donkey just as Jesus said they would. As they untied it, the owners asked them, "Why are you untying the colt?" They said, "Jesus needs it." Then they brought the donkey to Jesus and placed their garments on the colt's back, and Jesus sat on it.

+

Their mission, simple enough, is accomplished without a hitch. They find the village and the tethered donkey. Even the animal's owners are satisfied with their explanation, suggesting that perhaps they know the disciples and, more important, Jesus himself.

The explanation is enough: "Jesus needs it." No attempt to convince the owners of more than that. "Jesus needs it." Apparently, not even the young donkey requires coaxing. "Jesus needs it."

Theological libraries are filled with shelves of books weighing in on Jesus' divine and human natures. At different times in history, Jesus' divinity has taken center stage. To counter the belief that Jesus was merely human and nothing more, church councils and resulting doctrines have emphasized his divine nature by referring to Jesus as the Son of God and the second person of the Trinity.

I wonder, though, if we're more apt to miss seeing in Jesus the fully human one, the limited and finite one, the one who got weary and hungry and whose feet got sore. Besides fulfilling a tradition going back to the ancient prophets, perhaps Jesus rides a donkey into Jerusalem because he's flat-out tired. Maybe the couple miles to Jerusalem were two miles too many for an aching body that had spent too many weeks making the ninety-mile trek on foot from the northern hills of Galilee. "Boys, get me a donkey; I'm beat!"

I know I'm projecting far beyond Luke's intent, but I take no small comfort knowing that someone like Jesus one day needed the assistance of a donkey. In our weaker moments, his need convinces us that whatever we need is not foreign to him. And that's a good feeling.

What are your physical needs right now?

THEY GET IT RIGHT
Luke 19:35-38

As Jesus rode from the Mount of Olives to Jerusalem, people spread their garments on the road. All of Jesus' followers, including the twelve disciples, enthusiastically praised God for all the miracles they had seen: "Blessed is this one who comes in God's name! May peace and glory abound!"

+

Though we call it Palm Sunday and celebrate it in sanctuaries filled with palms, Luke makes no mention of people waving palms or placing palm branches along the way. (Mark and Matthew only say "branches"; John alone specifies "branches of palm trees.") Instead, here, they honor Jesus by placing clothing and garments along the road, a festive gesture reminiscent of honoring King Jehu (II Kings 9:13).

Also unlike the other gospel accounts of the entry into Jerusalem, Luke doesn't mention the large crowds that were visiting the city for Passover taking part in the processional celebration. Luke's scene is more intimate. Many disciples accompany Jesus—more than the twelve, but fewer than the thousands of observant Jews who were in Jerusalem during the festival.

Amazingly, the disciples seem to get it right. They aren't squabbling about their own importance. No puffed-up claims about who's in and who's out. No attempts to convince Jesus he's choosing the wrong path. Quoting Psalm 118:26, they honor Jesus with their praise and echo the angelic announcement heard by shepherds at his birth. They testify to his mighty deeds. All without rushing to place a crown on his head or to anoint him king of Judea. How unlike the regal, majestic, and militaristic procession that Governor Pilate would have made this same week to impress the Passover crowds.

Soon, the disciples will deny, betray, and desert Jesus, turning into a shadow of who they are on this day. Rather than the exception, though, theirs is the pattern for much of our living, too. One day we're faithful; the next day, fickle. One moment we walk with much confidence; the next, with total collapse. Maybe grace is nothing more than the gift of having the opportunity to start over again and again.

In the story, where do you find yourself as Jesus enters Jerusalem?

WITNESSING STONES
Luke 19:39-40

Some of the religious leaders said to Jesus, "Tell your disciples to stop saying these things." Jesus replied, "Listen, even if they were silent, the stones would shout."

+

It's impossible to know for certain what motivates the religious leaders to object. Maybe they're jealous of the attention Jesus receives. Perhaps they're upset that he decided to set up base in Jerusalem, their home turf. Maybe they object to the undignified tone of the occasion. "Stripping off clothing to make a pathway? What's next, liturgical dance? Enough already!"

Whatever their reasons, Jesus isn't about to squelch the moment. If the human voice is silenced, then other inhabitants of creation—living or not—will pick up the witness: the sun, the moon, olives trees, humpback whales, geckos, even a pile of rocks.

This day, the disciples speak the truth, shouting it with the ancient psalmist. In days ahead, women will give witness to an empty tomb. Later, a one-time murderous persecutor of the church will establish congregations throughout Turkey and Greece. Later still, the blood of martyrs will speak from the ground.

Can stones speak in ways that the human voice cannot? Stand in front of the Vietnam Veterans Memorial in Washington, D.C., and you'll hear the answer. No spoken words here. No audio prompts. No human voice. No one to explain what the eye sees and what the heart feels. Just a glossy, black stone wedge slicing the earth and inviting both the casual and the observant to come near and linger. It's nearly impossible to resist the stone's invitation to touch, to feel, to receive the witness. Stones really can speak for themselves.

When have you witnessed something profound, absent the human voice?

CITY TEARS
Luke 19:41-44

Seeing Jerusalem, Jesus wept and said, "If you had only recognized today the things that produce peace! But now they're hidden from you. The days will come when your enemies will set up a barricade and surround you. They will destroy all of you, and not a single stone will remain standing. This will happen because you didn't recognize the time when God visited you."

+

Two times, Jesus cries. On two occasions, Jesus weeps: at the death of Lazarus, his friend most dear, and now, beholding Jerusalem, he is overcome with tears.

We would understand, knowing what lies ahead—arrest, trial, sentence, and execution—if for himself Jesus sobbed.

Were he weeping now for the fate for which he was born, his tear-filled panorama would strike us as no less poignant.

Yet, not for himself does Jesus weep, nor for fear of his future or dread of his demise does he find reason to cry this day.

Rather, for the unknown and unnamed who call Jerusalem their home—City of David, City of Peace, the Golden City with milk and honey blessed.

Jerusalem, where tens of thousands come, the Passover to observe. With heart-skipping desire, they make their pilgrimage to behold the temple, and before God to bow and pray.

Seeing his own coming day, Jesus cannot help but weep at what is to come: enemies . . . barricade . . . surround . . . destroy.

Not one temple stone upon another left. Roman wrath in the year 70. Talk about rain on your parade!

Does anyone but Jesus cry for cities today?

Is there a place or region in the world for which you cry?

HOUSECLEANING
Luke 19:45-46

Then Jesus entered the temple and drove out the money ex-
changers and merchants, saying, "It's written in our tradition,
'God's house will be a house of prayer.' But you've cheap-
ened this holy place by turning it into a place of robbers."

+

The cleansing of the temple is an event that appears in all four gospels. Along with Matthew and Mark, Luke places this episode after
Jesus' triumphal entry into Jerusalem. John places the story early in the
gospel, at the beginning of Jesus' ministry.

We shouldn't imagine that Jesus stumbles upon a first-century flea
market or a temple garage sale. Certain business transactions were necessary for the continuity of temple life. Vendors sold various animals,
often at inflated prices, to worshippers who came to offer appropriate
sacrifices. Additionally, moneychangers exchanged Roman currency—
containing the blasphemous image that declared Caesar divine—for
acceptable Jewish coinage so temple taxes could be paid.

Two developments seem to be the impetus behind Jesus' temple-
cleansing action. At one time, the animal vendors and stalls were located beyond the temple grounds; eventually, they were relocated within
the temple itself near the Court of the Gentiles.

Furthermore, it's probable that the moneychangers weren't overly
concerned about giving worshippers the best exchange rates. Imagine
that! Since the temple was the only game in town and faced no competition, greedy entrepreneurs charged whatever the market could bear.
Those least able to afford the surcharge had no recourse but to pay the
exorbitant rate. The sacred house of worship left customers with the
same ill feeling that "cash advance" storefronts do today.

Jesus isn't one bit happy about it, and his reflex response points to
the merits of cleaning house from time to time. Is there anything that's
not susceptible to becoming a dull and dim mirror of what God intends, or, more seriously, a corruption of it? Even ecclesiastical traditions, solemn rites, and long-practiced rituals are susceptible. Those
who shake out the rugs are seldom welcomed with open arms.

Where do you see the need for some housecleaning?

305

THE CAMPS
Luke 19:47-48

As Jesus taught in the temple in Jerusalem, the religious leaders plotted to kill him. For the time being, they were stymied because the crowds hung on Jesus' every word.

+

Opposition against Jesus continues to mount, but it's not outsiders to the religious traditions, or enemies of the state, or insurrectionists or anarchists or atheists forming the front lines of the protest movement. Opposition comes from the respectable folks: the theological scholars, the guardians of orthodoxy, those with thick, dog-eared God-books on their library shelves. Jesus is confronted by the establishment.

It's one thing to disagree with someone, to disagree vehemently, even to disagree to the point of wishing the other pneumonia, but plotting murder? The Greek suggests they're looking to destroy him—not merely to shut him up, but to remove any evidence of what he has said. They want to erase his existence!

The common people, those with no degree initials after their names or special titles in front of them, can't get enough of Jesus. Spellbound, they hang on his every word. The only protest they offer up is when Jesus concludes his teachings with "That's all for today, folks."

Even though Luke doesn't describe the scene as such, I'm inclined to think there were other camps besides the Destroyers and the Spellbound. People like the Seekers, the Doubters, the Procrastinators, the Curious, the Cautious, and the Non-Committals.

If I hope to grasp the significance of this or any other biblical snippet, it's necessary to see myself in the scene. It's not enough, however, to place myself squarely in one camp or the other. It's never that black and white. I'm in every camp, and every camp is in me. I'm a mix of the best and the worst. The lover and the hater. The friend and the foe. Awed to the point of being star-struck, yet determined to erase the demands of Jesus' life on my own. Not a day goes by when there's rest from the struggle.

What are the camps within you?

LEGITIMACY QUESTIONS
Luke 20:1-2

One day as Jesus was teaching in the temple, the religious leaders asked him, "We want to know where your authority comes from. Who gave you this authority?"

+

It's one thing for Jesus to preach about God's intentions for the world and pay attention to those who have no clout and live at the margins. It's one thing for Jesus to gather a crowd on a Galilean hillside and speak winsomely about birds and flowers. It's quite another matter to enter Jerusalem and confront the clergy in charge of the religious life of the nation.

With the temple-cleansing hubbub fresh in their minds, and incensed that their religiosity has been challenged, a distinguished assortment of religious leaders seeks to investigate Jesus' credentials. Some of these leaders have a seat on the council of the Sanhedrin, the official court and ruling body of the Jews.

Their concern about Jesus is twofold: What's your authority, and who gave it to you? It's not a stretch to imagine a host of follow-up questions: Just who do you think you are? What gives you the right to question how the temple conducts its business? What are your credentials to teach? Nobody rides into Jerusalem on a donkey and disrupts religious commerce without proper explanation. Are you a prophet, a rabbi, or just a self-appointed agitator?

Do the religious leaders really want answers to their questions, or are their questions meant to serve as a subtle warning for Jesus to watch his step and bite his tongue? It's safe to say the mood is less and less safe, and increasingly antagonistic. The establishment—religious, financial, political, educational—is a sleeping bear that doesn't like to get poked.

How does your intolerance show up?

QUESTIONABLE ANSWER
Luke 20:3-7

Jesus replied to the leaders, "Did the baptism of John come from God or from another human being?" They discussed privately among themselves, "If we say, 'From God,' he'll say, 'Why didn't you believe him?' If we say, 'From another human being,' all the people will stone us because they're convinced that John was a prophet." So they said they weren't sure.

+

That Jesus refuses to give a direct answer to their question may be an indication that he knows the religious leaders aren't interested in hearing one. Instead, Jesus asks a question of his own, a question about the legitimacy of John the Baptist's ministry.

The ministries of Jesus and John shared commonalities. Both men emerged on the public scene without the kind of authority recognized by the established, religious community. Both Jesus and John received praise from the common people and criticism from the religious elite.

Jesus asks a simple either/or question: Was John's authority divine or human? Was it a thing of God, or not? If John's ministry was of divine origin, then the religious authorities would look foolish for not believing that John was a legitimate messenger of God. John, of course, had regarded Jesus as the long-awaited Messiah who would come baptizing "with the Holy Spirit and fire" (Luke 3:16). If the religious leaders denied that John had any godly authority, their job security would grow suddenly precarious and they would lose the respect of the people. On the other hand, to say Yes to John's divine authority was to say Yes to the legitimacy of Jesus.

Jesus presents them with a public relations nightmare, a question for which either answer will get them into trouble. By answering the John question, the religious leaders, in effect, would be answering their own Jesus question; hence the dilemma and their hesitancy.

That they admit they aren't sure may have seemed to them, if not an honest answer, at least an expedient one. In the name of self-preservation and self-interest, safer to leave the question hanging than to play one's hand in public.

What do you notice about the way Jesus engages in debate?

CHOSEN SILENCE
Luke 20:8

Jesus responded to their silence: "Then it's settled. Don't expect me to tell you where my authority comes from."

+

With his critics squirming, Jesus could have turned this into a memorable teaching moment. They ask him a testy question; he responds with a question of his own. His strategy forces them to feign ignorance. With nothing more to say, they're vulnerable. Heads drooping, they shift their weight from one leg to another.

Awkward moments are teachable moments. When jurors' defenses are down, seasoned lawyers are at their best. When a hostile crowd is momentarily disarmed, skilled negotiators take advantage of the breach in the wall. When accusations give way to silence, it's an opportunity to set one's accusers straight.

Jesus could have taken this occasion to explain his unique relationship to the source of his authority, reminding them of the dove-descending moment of his baptism. But he doesn't. He declines to answer their question. Having the upper hand, Jesus doesn't launch into a full-scale theological assault. Instead, he chooses silence: "Don't expect me to tell you."

Maybe Jesus has a hunch that any explanation will fall on deaf ears and closed minds. Though they ask Jesus the authority question, they aren't much interested in hearing his answer. Their minds are made up and no response, regardless of its persuasiveness, is about to change that.

It's not difficult to find people ready to debate various points of theology: Does God exist? Was Jesus divine? Is the world moving toward Armageddon? Is America a model for the rest of the world? Theological banter and healthy bull sessions have their rewards. But Jesus' silence is a reminder that not every question requires an answer, not every inquiry deserves a response, and not every indication to go deeper is a genuine desire to seek the truth.

What was your last theological conversation about?

VINEYARD, TENANTS, AND SERVANTS
Luke 20:9-12

Then Jesus told this story: "A landowner planted a vineyard, leased it to some tenants, and went on a long journey. After the grapes were picked, he sent a servant to the tenants to receive his share, but the tenants beat the servant and sent him away empty-handed. The owner sent another servant, but the tenants also beat him and sent him away empty-handed. A third was sent, and as with the others, the tenants assaulted him and threw him out."

+

Addressing the crowd rather than the religious leaders, Jesus tells a parable that indirectly sheds light on the previous discussion. Jesus' use of a vineyard setting echoes a common Old Testament image symbolizing the relationship of God with God's people. "For God's vineyard is the people of Israel, a delightful planting. Even though God expected justice and righteousness, God saw bloodshed and heard the cries of the abused" (Isaiah 5:7).

God made heavy investments in the vineyard, cultivating it with care and loving it completely. The vineyard is God's prized possession. The tenants, entrusted with the vineyard, are Israel's religious leaders and rulers (the same leaders with whom Jesus has just interacted). The tenants are expected to tend the vineyard with the same measure of care that God does.

The servants sent on behalf of God to the tenants represent the various Hebrew prophets, whose role was to call forth from the land fruits of justice and righteousness. Such cries, however, often resulted in ill treatment, abuse, and banishment of the prophetic messengers.

That God (the owner) would send many servants (prophets), even after repeated rejection, isn't merely a measure of the obstinacy of the tenants (the religious leaders . . . and every human heart) but an enduring testimony to the long-suffering patience of God.

How have you experienced God's patience?

310

DRASTIC MEASURES
Luke 20:13-16

"Then the vineyard owner said, 'I'll send my beloved son. Maybe they'll respect him.' But when the tenants saw the owner's son, they hatched a scheme: 'He's the heir to the vineyard. Let's kill him, and everything will be ours.' So they murdered him. What will the vineyard owner do? He will kill the tenants and give the vineyard to other tenants." When the people heard this, they said, "This will never happen!"

+

Undaunted and unwilling to give up on the vineyard, the owner opts for a drastic measure. If the tenants won't receive the vineyard owner's servants, maybe they will respect his beloved son. Not even the owner, however, can guarantee the son's safety.

As the owner fears, his own boy faces danger. The tenants call an impromptu meeting and decide to do away with the only heir to the vineyard. The beloved son is treated more harshly than the others were.

Luke places this parable here to remind his audience of God's story, witnessed through the Old Testament prophets (the servants) and culminating in the person of Jesus (the son of the vineyard owner). In the son's death, the vineyard is taken from one and given to another.

For some Christians today, the telling of this parable supports the claim that the church has replaced Israel as the new tenant of the vineyard. Because Jews didn't accept Jesus as the Messiah, God gave the vineyard to the church. If this is true, one wonders how happy God is with the new tenants these days.

There's much triumphalism in certain strands of Christianity. Imagining ourselves as God's "A-team" makes it nearly impossible to imagine there could be others, also, on the front edge of God's ongoing transformation of the world. Do we imagine that God approves of the ways we've used our tenant status to justify all forms of prejudice, bigotry, and acts of aggression on foreign soils?

"This will never happen!" the crowd exclaims when Jesus tells them that the vineyard changes hands. Who's to say it won't change hands again? Maybe the new tenants will speak Mandarin or Hindi.

What has been the Christian community's greatest shortcoming?

311

STONE WORK
Luke 20:17-19

Jesus continued, "What does this mean: 'The stone the build-
ers rejected has become the cornerstone'? Everyone who
falls on that stone will be broken to pieces, and those on
whom the stone falls will be crushed." When the religious
leaders realized Jesus was talking about them, they wanted to
seize him, but they were afraid of what the people might do.

+

That Jesus suddenly shifts from agriculture to architecture may indicate that later writers added these verses or that Luke attached this
saying to the parable of the vineyard. In either case, Jesus' cornerstone
reference is a direct quote from Psalm 118:22. The apostle Peter uses
the same Old Testament passage in a sermon to the Jerusalem Jews
(Acts 4:11) and again in his first epistle (I Peter 2:7). On both occasions, the cornerstone image is a direct reference to the resurrected
Christ. Though Jesus will face rejection, his life will be exalted by God.

A footnote often appears in the Bible at these verses, suggesting
"keystone" as an alternate reading for "cornerstone." As the center-
piece in a stone archway, the keystone is essential to the structure and,
like the cornerstone, completes the builder's work.

Luke reminds readers of the essential role Jesus plays in the story
of God's ongoing interaction with the world. That said, these verses
and the preceding ones have long been used as justification for Christians to engage in anti-Semitism. One of the ironies of the current ten-
sions in Jewish/Arab relations today is that, for most of their mutual
histories, Jews and Arabs lived in relative harmony, respecting each
other's faith. The same can't be said for the history of Christians and
Jews. Jews have suffered more at the hands of Christians than at the
hands of any other religious group.

The Jewish leaders want to seize Jesus and silence him once and
for all. In the two millennia since—as it concerns the Jews—Christians
have returned the abuse a thousand-fold.

What will it take to break down walls of religious hostility?

312

TAX TEST
Luke 20:20-22

The religious leaders sent spies to entrap Jesus so that they could turn him over to the Roman governor. They asked him, "Teacher, we know you're wise, and you don't back down to anyone as you teach the truths of God. Should we pay taxes to Caesar or not?"

+

Foiled in their attempts to intimidate Jesus, his critics now hope he will say something self-incriminating, causing the Roman authorities to step in. With the help of a few spies passing themselves off as curious intellectuals, the plot is set in motion. Feigning sincerity, they flatter Jesus with a string of compliments: "Teacher, you pass the orthodoxy test. Truth rings from all you say. You don't pull punches when you teach God's will. We admire that." Then they set the trap: "Tell us, O wise one, should we pay taxes to Caesar?"

The specific tax in question was the poll tax the emperor Caesar levied on every Jewish person between the ages of twelve and sixty-five. Though not a heavy burden, this tax incensed most Jews because it was yet another reminder of the oppressive reach of Rome's long tentacles. More important, it was a slap in the face to the Jewish belief that God, not a "deified" Caesar, deserved ultimate allegiance.

Asked as an either/or question, the query is a shrewd one. If Jesus answers No, he'll be labeled a traitor of the Roman Empire. If Jesus answers Yes, he'll be accused of unfaithfulness to the Jewish nation.

"Should we pay or not pay? Where do your loyalties reside, Jesus—with God or with Caesar?" Since either answer would spring the trap, they don't much care what answer he gives, just as long as he steps into it.

When was the last time you were lured into a conversational ambush?

Elkhart, IN

Jesus was onto them and said, "Whose name is on a Roman coin?" They said, "Caesar's." Jesus replied, "Then give Caesar the things that are Caesar's, and give God the things that are God's." Failing to get Jesus to take the bait, they silently walked away in frustration.

+

On one side of a Roman coin appeared the head of the emperor with the inscription: "Tiberius Caesar Augustus, son of the divine Augustus." Carrying this coin and using it in daily commerce reminded the user that Rome's sovereign authority was absolute.

Though Jesus leaves his critics speechless, his answer is far from an airtight conclusion. It's clear that he doesn't respond to their staged question with an either/or answer. Jesus refuses to be drawn into a debate about Rome's justification for exacting from its citizenry the taxes deemed necessary to run the empire. Instead, he deftly tiptoes through the minefield and ultimately gives them a both/and answer: Give Caesar what he deserves, and likewise, God.

Maybe that ends the discussion, but all kinds of questions are left hanging: What exactly belongs to Caesar (City Hall? the state? the federal government?), and what belongs to God? Who decides how the pie is sliced? Who holds the knife that cuts the pie? Do the domains of Caesar and God operate independently of each other, much like the CIA and the FBI? Is this a material versus spiritual matter where Caesar is in charge of the former and God the latter?

No wonder those who pose the question to Jesus leave speechless. How do you argue with someone who never gives a direct answer? Profoundly illusive, Jesus refuses to get into a debate on the issue. He turns the issue back on the questioners, forcing them to decide what Caesar gets to extract from them and what will be God's.

If we give our lives over to Caesar's currency, then we have no one but ourselves to blame when mindsets such as "Our Security First" and "Close Our Borders" and "Invade Even When Not Threatened" and "Tilt the Game in Favor of the 1%" come back to haunt us.

How do you decide what is "Caesar's" and what is God's?

SADDUCEES
Luke 20:27-33

Some Sadducees asked Jesus, "Teacher, Moses said that if a man's brother dies, leaving his wife childless, the surviving brother must marry the widow and raise children with her. Imagine there are seven brothers. The first brother marries, and dies childless; then the second marries, and he dies, also leaving her childless. Eventually, the other five brothers also marry her and each one dies, leaving her childless. Finally the woman dies. Since each of the seven brothers had been married to her, whose wife will she be in the next life?"

+

One of many groups constituting first-century Judaism, the Sadducees were part of the priestly class. They administered temple affairs and participated in the governance of Jewish matters and religious rites. Sadducees were theologically conservative and aristocratically wealthy. Hoping to maintain their elevated status, they were willing supporters of Rome's policies and benefited from them.

Unlike the Pharisees, who accepted as authoritative all the Hebrew scriptures, as well as the oral or interpretive traditions that developed from those writings, the Sadducees accepted only the first five books (Genesis through Deuteronomy). In addition, the Sadducees didn't believe in a resurrection from the dead or in the coming of a Messiah.

The Sadducees' question to Jesus is based on the levirate law of marriage found in Deuteronomy 25:6-10. This law spells out a man's obligation to marry the childless wife of his dead brother and have children with her. The Sadducees spin a story of seven brothers who marry a woman and leave her without children. Hoping to show the absurdity of resurrection theology, they ask Jesus, "Since she can't be married to all seven brothers at once in the afterlife, whose wife will she become?"

This is the third test put to Jesus in Luke 20. The Sadducees have no interest in being influenced by his answer. Edification isn't the goal. Some convoluted questions about religious matters are nothing more than a vain attempt to end discussion before it starts.

What "afterlife" questions are on your mind?

316

MARRIAGE MATTERS
Luke 20:34-36

Jesus answered the Sadducees, "People of this world get married all the time, but in the world of the resurrection, people won't marry. What's more, in the next life, death won't exist. People will be like angels and children of God, a resurrection people."

+

In more than thirty years of conducting weddings and funerals, I've never been asked by the bride and groom or a grieving spouse to include in the service a reading of these verses. In our best moments, we imagine our best relationships will go on forever. We hope the persons who love us most dearly in this life will relate to us in the same way in the next life.

Jesus' response to the Sadducees' manufactured scenario suggests that relationships in God's future community will be no mere continuation of what we experience in this life. In fact, if we're hearing Jesus correctly, marriage, as we know it, will go the way of 8-track tapes and telephone booths.

On one level, Jesus reminds the Sadducees that in the world of resurrected and transformed people, God will set right those relational systems that some have experienced as oppressive and unjust. The Sadducees want to know to whom the woman, married seven times on earth, will belong in the next life. Whose wife will she become? They don't ask whose husband each brother will become. The issue for the Sadducees is one of property and ownership. In the next life, which brother will get to claim her as his property?

Jesus' answer is a reminder that in God's realm—a realm already breaking into the present—there is emancipation from any earthbound systems that have stripped individuals of their God-given personhood. Basic human needs—identity, belonging, community—find their complete realization in relationships that transcend earthly marriage.

When are human relationships at their best?

GOD OF THE LIVING
Luke 20:37-40

"Even Moses attested to the fact that the dead are raised when he spoke at the burning bush of the God of Abraham, Isaac, and Jacob. God isn't God of the dead, but of the living. As God sees it, they're all alive." Some of the religious leaders concurred, "Teacher, you've answered well." From that point on, they didn't dare ask any more questions.

+

Jesus already has invalidated the Sadducees' objection to the possibility of the resurrection by reminding them that heaven is no mere continuation of earthly arrangements. Now, Jesus deftly employs the Sadducees' own scriptural tradition to reveal a corresponding truth about God.

Drawing from the third chapter of Exodus (one of the five books to which the Sadducees gave authoritative weight), Jesus recalls the encounter of Moses and God at the burning bush. If God spoke of God's relationship to the departed patriarchs in the present tense—"I am the God of your father, the God of Abraham, Isaac, and Jacob"—then it follows that their relationship to a covenantal God didn't cease at the point of death.

When life runs its course and death occurs, God doesn't abandon God's own. Not even death can permanently sever the intimate relationship God has with us. Jesus isn't teaching a notion of the immortality of the soul, as if our beings after death exist on their own momentum. Rather, God is the life-giving source who sustains, restores, and regenerates life. In the face of death, God remains in relationship with God's own. Death isn't a relationship breaker. Death wields no veto power over God's love. Death can't break the grip of God's embrace.

These are soothing words for an audience living in the latter half of the first century, a community facing daily persecution and the possibility of annihilation. For people today who fear death's capacity to bring their lives to permanent dead ends, Jesus' words are no less healing.

What does a life beyond this one look like to you?

DAVID'S SON
Luke 20:41-44

Then Jesus said, "How can it be said that the Messiah is David's son? David himself says in the Psalms, 'God said to my Lord, "Sit at my right hand, until I make your enemies your footstool."' David calls the Messiah 'Lord'; how can the Messiah be his son?"

+

As Jesus moves closer to the cross, he uses this opportunity to provide a correction on the "Son of David" title. Some Jews anticipated the coming Messiah—a descendant of David—arriving with all the political clout and military prowess of Israel's greatest king. Some anticipated that David's heir would thresh foreign oppressors from the land and restore Israel to its rightful place of dominance.

Criticized three times in this chapter, Jesus now turns to his questioners with an inquiry of his own. Quoting Psalm 110:1, Jesus ponders aloud how he could be called "David's son" if David referred to the "son" as "my Lord, my Master." It would have been culturally appropriate for David the father to respectfully bow to one of his ancestral fathers, but inappropriate for David to bow to one of his sons.

Though Jesus is called "Son of David" several times in the gospel accounts, he is far from comfortable with the designation. Jesus is determined to add yet another clarification to the understanding of this title or, at least, to soft-pedal it. His ministry won't be determined by the populist understanding of what God's representative is expected to be and do.

In the ancient world, idolatry was the sin of embracing other gods and replacing the biblical God with a host of lesser deities. These days, the topic of idolatry is about as commonplace as black-and-white TV sets. Maybe we've grown up or simply outgrown what, for the ancient world, was once a daily pursuit. However, no less idolatrous is turning Jesus into someone and something he never intended to be: "Jesus leads us into combat against our enemies." "Jesus blesses us with wealth and possessions" "Jesus helps those who help themselves." There's no end to the ways we fashion Jesus to suit our own agendas.

What distortions of Jesus produce in you the strongest reactions?

319

New Orleans, LA

LEADERSHIP WARNINGS
Luke 20:45-47

Within earshot of the crowd, Jesus said to his disciples, "Watch out for religious leaders who wear long robes and like to be greeted with respect in public. They get the most important seats in the synagogues and at dinners. However, they evict widows from their houses while reciting long prayers. They'll get what's coming to them."

+

It needs to be stated again: Jesus isn't critical of all religious leaders, but he has harsh words for spiritual leaders who succumb to the insidious dangers of pride, greed, condescension, and abuse of power.

Jesus singles out those religious leaders who are guilty of taking over ownership of widows' houses faster than lending institutions in an anemic economy. In New Testament times, certain members of the clergy served as legal administrators and executors of widows' affairs. Assigned to care for widows in need, some unscrupulous religious leaders, while soaking in the adulation of the public, took advantage of the opportunity to line their own pockets. Jesus is incensed and blasts them for it.

Since the time of Adam and Eve, religious piety has been a cloak with which we wrap ourselves: "Let me remind you, God, *you* created woman and *she* gave me the apple to eat." With voters in mind, office seekers won't hesitate to sprinkle their campaign rhetoric with language that gives evidence of religious piety. If it will increase the bottom line, advertisers will promote religious values to sell lawn mowers. Though the claim holds no historical truth, we hear it all the time that America is a Christian nation.

Parker Palmer (*Let Your Life Speak*) reminds us about the ability of leaders to cast either light or darkness, good or harm, on the people and organizations they serve. Unless we're willing to expose and confront our own demons—our "shadow sides"—we're bound to project them on others, robbing people of their own identities and depriving ourselves of the chance to opt for our better nature.

What personal "shadow sides" haunt you?

ALL SHE HAD
Luke 21:1-4

While in the temple, Jesus saw rich people put their money into the treasury box. He also saw a poor widow put in two small copper coins. He remarked, "This poor widow put in more than all the rest. What the rich gave they will never miss, but out of her poverty she gave all she had."

+

Sermons on this passage are preached whenever stewardship and budget matters roll around. The characters are clearly defined and ripe for sermonic picking—the rich and the poor, those awash in abundance and the one who exists on the edge of vulnerability.

Sunday messages usually reminds us that our giving is godly only when it's sacrificial, like the giving of the poor widow that encompasses everything she has. What God really cares about has less to do with the amount given than with the amount left behind. Good lessons to hear.

Now consider this. Professional fundraisers, not-for-profit leaders, college presidents, and every minister who has ever served a congregation know that survivability and thrive-ability depend on those who give out of their surplus and abundance. Heating systems wouldn't get replaced, leaky old roofs wouldn't get torn off, athletic facilities and libraries wouldn't get built, parking lots wouldn't get repaved, and academic chairs wouldn't get endowed were it not for the deep-pocket generosity of those who can afford to give out of their abundance. Thank God when wealthy donors participate in philanthropic good works, regardless of how much money remains in their pockets.

Perhaps in his praise of the widow (one of those whose houses were stolen by the unscrupulous religious leaders?) Jesus is making an indirect indictment of a flawed religious institution, one that takes advantage of the poor and those least able to subsist. Her economic condition is on life support, in large part because those in abundance have reaped the rewards of a system tilted in their favor. Yet this sole survivor gives all she has, expecting no praise, no blessing, and no payback. Jesus is impressed with the freedom she demonstrates, a freedom about which others in the temple that day can only dream.

How do you make decisions about how much money to give away?

322

BRICK AND MORTAR
Luke 21:5-6

One day, some of Jesus' disciples were speaking fondly about the beautiful temple stones and the furnishings dedicated to God. Jesus commented, "The day isn't far away when this temple will be destroyed and not one stone will be left in place."

+

Few structures in the biblical world were more impressive than the temple in Jerusalem. Built and expanded by Herod from the rubble of Solomon's temple and the later rebuilding effort of the Hebrews who returned from Babylonian captivity, the great stone platform surrounding the holy place comprises an area equal to two dozen football fields. Visitors today who stand at the Western (Wailing) Wall can see seven exposed layers of the great stones laid by Herod's workers.

Standing before this architectural masterpiece, Jesus predicts its total destruction. "Take a good look—one day nothing will remain." Not only is Jesus predicting the literal destruction of the temple that would occur nearly forty years later at the hands of the Romans, but he's alluding to the end of a religious system that had turned into a legal means to exploit the poor, misdirect its wealth, and drain rituals of their spiritual content.

No age, including and especially our own, is immune from the lure of beautiful stones and gifts dedicated to God. Sometimes it's the architecture, stained-glass windows, vaulted ceilings, high-tech sound systems, plush offices, or expansive parking lot that accommodates thousands of cars that captivates our attention. Such grandeur might cause one to ponder: What Would Jesus Build?

What if some catastrophe of nature or human invention destroyed it all, leaving behind no buildings or foundations, just people—the only body that Christ has today. Would the loss be debilitating or liberating? And how soon would the Property Committee call its first meeting?

What's the most impressive church building you've seen?

DON'T BE MISLED
Luke 21:7-8

The disciples asked Jesus, "Teacher, when will the temple be destroyed, and what will be the sign this is about to happen?" Jesus replied, "Make sure you aren't fooled. Many will come in my name and say, 'I'm the one! The end time is near!' Don't listen to them."

+

The twenty-first chapter of Luke contains what is called the apocalyptic discourse of Jesus. *Apocalypse* is a Greek-based word meaning "revelation" and generally refers to those passages that reveal events that will precede the end days or end times. The next nine reflections deal with apocalyptic themes.

With Jesus' prediction of the destruction of the temple (an event that took place in the year 70, around forty years after Jesus died), the disciples press Jesus into giving them specifics. They want a timetable, complete with details.

It's been two millennia since the disciples' question, plenty of time for a host of experts to supply answers. William Miller convinced thousands of his followers that the world would end in 1843. In the 1970s and 1980s, such end-time prognosticators as J. F. Walvoord (*Armageddon, Oil, and the Middle East Crisis*) and the hugely successful author Hal Lindsey (*The Late Great Planet Earth*) also had a go at nailing down end-time specifics. Translated into more than fifty languages, Lindsey's book has sold more than 35 million copies. (As the story goes, Lindsey was invited by President Reagan to speak to Pentagon war strategists concerning the biblical ramifications of the Soviet Union's arms buildup.) The hugely popular *Left Behind* series, co-authored by Tim LaHaye and Jerry Jenkins, is closing in on 100 million copies sold. Obviously, the disciples' curiosity is alive and well, and lucrative for some.

In the verses to come, Jesus will have more to say about cataclysmic events, but he never gets around to fully answering the disciples' question. Maybe that should serve as a clue. For Jesus, the end time is never as important as the present time.

Where do you think the world is headed?

DREADFUL WARNINGS
Luke 21:9-11

"Don't be afraid when you hear about wars and insurrections. These things will happen, but that doesn't mean the end is near. Nations will threaten nations and people will threaten people. There will be powerful earthquakes, famines, plagues, and plenty of other dreadful warnings and heavenly signs."

+

Wars. Insurrections. Earthquakes. Famines. Plagues. Let's update the list: Tornadoes. Hurricane Katrina. Tsunamis. 9/11. California mudslides. Flash fires. Nuclear meltdowns. Traffic jams on Chicago's Dan Ryan Expressway. Computer crashes.

Many who obsess over an end-of-the-world timetable tend to read these verses as a direct reference to our present age and a sign that the end is as close as next Tuesday. Yet, these "dreadful warnings" have reared their ugly heads for a long, long time. Genesis 4 carries the account of war's first casualty when Cain slew Abel and his blood cried out from the earth. The Old Testament books of Joshua and Judges chronicle nation against nation engaging in some of the bloodiest battles in history. Famines and plagues were no strangers to Egyptian Pharaohs or anybody else subject to harsh Middle Eastern climates.

This history causes me to wonder if Jesus is saying simply, "Look, wars, insurrections, earthquakes, famines, plagues, and all the other dreadful stuff are facts of life. We can't escape such things. It's the price of being human and the cost of being alive. Nobody gets a free pass. No one gets an exemption."

What's Jesus' advice when such tragedies strike? What wisdom does he share? Just this: "Don't be afraid." Maybe that's a shorthand reminder for "Don't be afraid, because what seems like the end isn't the end, and even if it is, the end isn't the end."

How would you explain horrific disasters to young children?

Holy Door, St. Peter's Basilica, Vatican City

TESTIFYING OPPORTUNITIES
Luke 21:12-15

"Before all this occurs, you will be arrested, persecuted, handed over to religious authorities, and thrown into prison. You will be brought before heads of state and governors because of your loyalty to me. This will be an opportunity for you to testify to your faith. So make up your minds not to prepare a verbal defense in advance. I will give you both the words and the wisdom that will confound your opponents."

+

Jesus continues to paint a picture of the future, and little of it for the disciples is promising. Not only will dreadful things occur in nature and among nations, but the disciples themselves will face threats.

What anxieties must have overcome them as they imagined these bleak pronouncements! Everything nailed down and secure will be dislodged. Long-honored traditions will be dismantled. Whatever benefits and dividends they fancied for having followed Jesus won't protect them from arrests and persecutions. How will they testify amid all this?

It's a timely question for us, too. How will we testify amid all this? Wars and nuclear arms buildup? Economic earthquakes? Millions of Americans with no health insurance? Part of any response includes testifying to the way Jesus befriended the least and the last, the lost and the lonely. We testify by speaking up for those whose voices aren't heard. We witness when we decry every attempt to trim budgets at the expense of those for whom life is already a burden too heavy to bear. Our verbal defense includes reminding a nation that spends more on war than all the nations of the world combined that the war god is the god of the godless.

Such "words and wisdom" won't fall lightly on ears unwilling to hear. Like his first disciples, we can expect our share of trouble for living out God's dreams for the world. Maybe that's just a sign of the times.

What are your greatest fears about the future of our planet?

ENDURANCE TEST
Luke 21:16-19

"Family members, relatives, and friends will betray you. Some of you will be killed. Everyone will hate you because you follow me, yet not a hair of your head will be harmed. By keeping faith you will gain your souls."

+

The paradox of these verses is impossible to ignore. The suffering will get personal. The disciples will witness family struggles resulting in divisions and betrayals, and some will face a martyr's death. How is it possible then that "not a hair of your head will be harmed"?

Some interpreters suggest that these verses imply that the God who controls all human events allows nothing to happen to the disciples without God's permission. We're left wondering: Does God prevent some events from happening while allowing others to run their courses? Does God permit ethnic cleansing in one country but stop it in another? Did the bullet from the gun of James Earl Ray find Martin Luther King Jr. because God refused to guide it off course? Such logic is as weird as weird can be.

It's more likely that Jesus is assuring his disciples that though they will suffer and die on account of his name, no harm will come to their core beings. Physical death won't bring spiritual death. Their essential beings will remain their essential beings. The world can't strip everything from us.

Endurance is the key. Rather than heroic acts of aggression, endurance is the mark of people committed to bringing God's future into the present. More active than passive, endurance has transforming powers. Those whose lives are marked by patient endurance know whose hands created them, whose hands hold them, and whose hands will never let them go. Suffering and affliction, persecution and death may befall them, but their soulful identities belong to God. Said Dr. King, who understood endurance as well as any martyr, "I have attempted to see my personal ordeals as an opportunity to transfigure myself and heal the people involved in the tragic situation."

What was your last endurance test?

JERUSALEM'S TRAVAIL
Luke 21:20-24

"When you see Jerusalem surrounded by armies, you'll know its demise is near. Those in the surrounding region must flee to the mountains, and people in the city must leave. Everyone in the countryside must stay away, for these will be terrible days. Too bad for women who are pregnant and for those nursing infants during this time! The struggle will be great and the wrath intense. People will die by the sword and be taken prisoner. Jerusalem will be trampled by foreigners until their demise is complete."

+

With chilling detail, Jesus describes the fall of Jerusalem, an event that will take place some forty years after his death and nearly twenty years before the compilation of Luke's gospel. According to the historian Josephus, Jerusalem's destruction at the hands of the Romans caused the death of a million Jews and forced the captivity of tens of thousands.

Because no one will be safe, Jesus warns residents to flee to remote regions. Pregnant women and nursing mothers with their young will make up the most vulnerable. If Josephus's accounts are accurate, the invaders even offered Jewish children as food to their gods.

As the stones toppled and the flames reached heavenward, we can imagine faithful Jews—dislocated individuals and grieving families—reciting snippets of beloved psalms. "God is my light and my salvation; I need not fear anyone" (Psalm 27:1). "Pray for Jerusalem's peace. May the people who love you prosper. Peace within your walls, and security within your towers" (Psalm 122:6-8). "As the mountains surround Jerusalem, so God surrounds God's people" (Psalm 125:2). "If I say, 'Surely the darkness will cover me, and the light around me become night,' even the darkness isn't dark to you; the night is as bright as the day" (Psalm 139:11-12).

Darkest moments give birth to life's deepest questions: Does God care? Can God be trusted? When I come to an end, is that the end? Who will have the last word?

What questions were raised for you in your last dark moment?

IN A CLOUD
Luke 21:25-28

"Signs will appear in the sun, moon, and stars. Nations will grow anxious and confused by the turbulence of the seas. People will fear what lies ahead; even the heavens will shake. Then they will see me coming in a cloud with power and glory. When these things happen, look up, because your redemption is near."

+

I bought a bag of charcoal the other day, heeding the warning that came with it: LIGHTING THIS CHARCOAL INSIDE YOUR HOUSE CAN KILL YOU! Nothing like getting your attention! No benign warning about being hazardous to your health. Nope. This stuff can do you in.

Eschatology refers to the study of the last things or the last days. For much of this chapter, Jesus has been in an eschatological state of mind. Like the warning on the charcoal, talk of the end days surely gets our attention.

Eschatology is a slippery theological endeavor, in part because the events Jesus talks about are ambiguous and open to wide latitudes of interpretation. With regard to the timing and sequence of these events, little is clear and even less is certain—except one thing: In a world of nightmarish dangers, God's determination to bring transformation and wholeness will prevail.

But who can endure this language of cosmic upheaval and the shaking of the universe? Not those in control, that's for certain. Not those who prefer that things stay the way they are. Not those who profit from the status quo. Not those on top. Not those who have everything that life offers. Not those who have it made. Not those who determine for others how things should be.

Jesus says, at that time "your redemption is near." What will arrive as good news for some will arrive as quite the opposite for others. It all depends on where you're standing.

What is good news in this for you? Bad news?

LEAF LESSONS
Luke 21:29-31

Jesus continued to teach: "Consider the fig tree and all the trees. When leaves sprout, you know that summer is near. In the same way, when you see this happening, you will know that God's transformation of the world is taking shape."

+

As if the disciples' heads aren't spinning enough, Jesus concludes his end-time tutorial with the example of the fig tree. Simple enough. Just as sprouting leaves announce the coming of summer, the events of which Jesus has spoken will announce the full fruition of God's passionate desires for the world.

Maybe the only way to make sense of what Jesus is saying about cosmic end times and last days is to put it in a smaller, more personal perspective. Annie Dillard (*The Writing Life*) offers a suggestion to authors: "Write as if you were dying. At the same time, assume you write for an audience consisting solely of terminal patients." With a slight tweak, I can choose to live as if I am dying. Why? Because I *am* dying, and have been since birth. The end will come when what's "me" will no longer exist. Sooner or later—this week or a few decades from now—I'll die. A hundred years from now nobody will remember that I lived or much care that I took up space on earth. I've a choice to live in full awareness that the DNA that makes me "me" won't go on forever.

I can choose to put myself at the top of the food chain. I can imagine myself the most important shrub in the landscape. I can grab and hoard, guard and protect, fending off every threat to my way of life. I can justify being an S.O.B. to anyone who gets in my way. I can choose the way I will live my life.

When I reduce all that Jesus says about macro-cosmic endings to a micro-personal level, the end times and the last days of "me" are like leaves on a tree, each with a message if I choose to see. Hold things more loosely. Make every day worth living. Turn a wrong into something right. Don't be so impressed with those who seek to impress. Make sure my corner of the world is a better place because I'm here. Embrace the life Jesus lived.

What do you have left to do while you still have time to do it?

THIS GENERATION
Luke 21:32-33

Jesus continued, "People of this generation won't die until all these things happen. Things on this earth and above won't go on forever, but my words will remain."

+

Opinions on Jesus' discourse are as contentious as congressional debates on tax cuts for the wealthy. Is Jesus talking about an end-of-the-world scenario yet to happen? Is Jesus merely describing events that have always occurred in the ebb and flow of human history? Did Jesus know any more about the future than we do? Did Jesus foresee the European Union or the rise of China as an economic power? Did Jesus believe he would return to earth and finish what he had started?

Now throw into the mix Jesus' reference that "this generation won't die until all these things have happened." What generation? The generation to which Jesus is speaking? One would think so, but not everybody does. Maybe "this generation" refers to the race of Jews, or the whole of humanity, or a future generation that will actually witness these things.

Here's what I take away from this reference (I readily concede that not all scholars and commentators stand in my corner): Jesus' main reference point throughout this chapter has been the disciples' initial awe regarding the majesty and permanence of the temple in Jerusalem. Jesus foresees the day when the temple and all it stands for will be destroyed. With Rome's imperial power dominating the world scene, Jesus' crystal ball didn't have to be very clear to foresee the inevitable. Indeed, "this generation"—including most of his disciples—witnessed the burning of the temple and the toppling of its majestic stones in the year 70, about forty years after Jesus spoke these words.

The point of all this? That Jesus predicted the future? No. That we're living in the last days? No—well, actually Yes—each of us has been living in our last days ever since the day of our birth. The point of all this is that God remains faithful, not just in beautiful sunsets but in earthquakes too; not only when you complete a 10K run, but when the cancer metastasizes.

How do you experience God when the worst things happen to you?

BE ALERT
Luke 21:34-36

"Make sure you're not into thoughtless living, drunkenness, and needless worry. If you are, then the day I'm talking about, which will surely come, will surprise you like a trap. Stay alert at all times, and pray that you have strength to escape these things so that you can stand before me."

+

I get the feeling Jesus speaks these words because he senses that his disciples are on overload. Maybe the anxiety is in their eyes or written on their furrowed brows. Maybe Jesus simply anticipates the question on their minds: "OK, Jesus, all this talk about the end of the world and last days—we get it, but really we don't. Can you make it practical? What do we need to take away from this lecture?"

Jesus obliges. "Be alert. Keep your wits. Live in the present. Ease up. Live simply." For all his cautions about future things, Jesus reminds his disciples that nothing is more important than deciding to live each moment. Knowing that our time on earth won't go on forever can sharpen our intent to bring our best to each day.

What might it mean to "be alert at all times"? On some occasions, it will mean giving my full attention to the person sitting across the table from me. Other times, it will mean that today, rather than someday, is the best day to take up the challenge. Why not pay attention to what I eat and drink today rather than wait for a medical crisis to wake me up? The kind of living Jesus applauds is living that weds one's passion to the world's deepest need. This means resisting the urge to save my gifts for a future that isn't promised.

Knowing that time ends, that life ends, that I will end heightens intentional living and purposeful activity. At the end of the day, how many reruns of my favorite sitcom do I really need to see?

What one thing will you do to be more alert in living this day?

DAY AND NIGHT
Luke 21:37-38

Jesus taught in the temple during the day and spent the nights on the Mount of Olives. Crowds got up early in the morning to listen to him teach.

+

These verses serve as a transition from Jesus' long discourse to the events that will occur in the last two days of his pre-resurrection life. In his final three chapters, Luke will move from Thursday's Last Supper to Friday's crucifixion to Sunday's resurrection.

As if preparing for his own cataclysmic end times, Jesus maintains a balanced rhythm between temple teaching in Jerusalem and nighttime solitude on the Mount of Olives just east of the city. Though Luke doesn't give us a psychological assessment of Jesus' state of mind, it's easy for us to sense that Jesus is a leader who is neither overrun by nor overwrought with anxiety. While connected to those who seek his instruction (and with some in the crowd who seek his destruction), Jesus is also connected to his Divine Source. His private and public personas aren't conflicted or contradictory; one is nightly enriched in order for the other to provide daily service. Jesus practices self-care so that his life will usher in God's transforming presence to others.

These verses that close the twenty-first chapter suggest again what's been true throughout Jesus' ministry: he doesn't move as a helpless victim into unfolding events. Jesus enters Jerusalem every day, fleeing neither the adulation bestowed on him nor the conspiracy mounting against him. He teaches to the end. He knows the arc of his life. He knows who and what he is. He stays connected. He remains himself. Authentic and genuine.

How do you maintain balance in life?

PASSOVER PLOT
Luke 22:1-2

It was close to the time for the Festival of Unleavened Bread, also called the Passover. The religious leaders were looking for a way to kill Jesus, but they feared what the people who followed him might do.

+

Passover, the greatest of the Jewish festivals, falls on the fifteenth of Nisan, typically around mid-April.

Passover is the time to remember God's deliverance and emancipation of the Hebrews from Egyptian bondage.

Passover refers to the angel of death passing over the homes of the Hebrew slaves whose doorposts were sprinkled with blood.

Passover meals require unleavened bread, commemorating the haste with which the Hebrews left Egypt on the night of the exodus.

Passover, along with Pentecost and Tabernacles, was one of three obligatory festivals every adult Jewish male within fifteen miles of Jerusalem was required to attend.

Passover pilgrims coming into Jerusalem from all parts of the ancient world totaled nearly two million.

Passover was observed by Jews in every land with the prayer that next year one would celebrate it in Jerusalem.

Passover blood from the slain lambs was left at the base of the temple altar for it belonged to God, the giver and taker of life.

Passover feasts were shared by at least ten people in homes after sundown on Thursday evening of Passover week.

Passover is the time to recall liberation from suffering and freedom from oppression through sacrifice and blood.

Passover week was filled with high drama and even higher emotions, causing Roman officials to be especially vigilant.

Passover presented a problem to Jesus' enemies: How might they arrest him without infuriating the people following him?

What are your special traditions during Holy Week?

SATAN WORKED ON JUDAS
Luke 22:3-6

Then Satan worked on Judas Iscariot, who was one of the twelve disciples. Immediately Judas sought out the religious leaders and temple police to discuss how he could deliver Jesus to them. Their curiosity was piqued, so they agreed to give him money. Judas was happy to take it and began to look for an opportunity to betray Jesus when no crowd was present.

+

There are good reasons why parents don't name their sons Judas. Other disciple names are fine—John, Peter, Andrew, James, even Thomas—but never Judas. Of the twelve disciples, two share the name Judas. They are distinguishable in that one is called Judas Iscariot.

It's hard to know whether Luke intends for his readers to understand that Satan overpowers Judas and deceives him into betraying Jesus, or whether Judas has a choice in the matter and opens the door for Satan to work on him.

It's also impossible to know the motivation behind the betrayal. Was Judas an evil man from the get-go? Did he not have the willpower to resist his inner stirrings? Was he disappointed in the kind of Messiah Jesus turned out to be? Did Judas feel betrayed that he wasn't part of the Peter-James-John inner circle of disciples closest to Jesus? Was it Judas's strategy to force Jesus to respond to his enemies with a show of force? Why doesn't Luke speculate as to what prompted Judas to initiate his plan?

I wonder if Jesus already knew that Judas would betray him. If so, how long had he known? What did Jesus first see in Judas that gave him sufficient reason to believe he would make a worthy disciple? How many times did Jesus and Judas have heart-to-heart talks about God's intentions for the world and the role the disciples would play? Did they debate armed insurrection versus nonviolent resistance? Is it possible that Jesus played the betrayal card and planted the seed in Judas to fulfill a higher purpose? Why doesn't Luke speculate about what role Jesus may have had in Judas's actions?

What's your opinion about Judas?

336

MAKING PREPARATIONS
Luke 22:7-13

On the Day of Unleavened Bread, when the Passover lamb was sacrificed, Jesus said to Peter and John, "Prepare the Passover meal for us to eat." They asked him, "Where should we prepare it?" Jesus said, "Listen carefully. When you enter Jerusalem, a man carrying a jar of water will meet you; follow him into the house he enters and say to the owner, 'Our teacher wants to know where the guest room is so he can eat the Passover with his disciples.' He'll show you a large furnished room upstairs. Prepare the meal there." They followed Jesus' instructions and found everything just as he said they would, and they prepared the Passover meal.

+

Jesus gives his disciples specific instructions about where to prepare the Passover meal. The place to eat is of his choosing. Preparing the Passover meal itself, however, didn't require additional instructions from Jesus. Peter and John—observant Jews—know from memory of what the meal consists and what each element symbolizes.

An unblemished lamb had to be killed in the temple courts, its blood left on the temple altar. The lamb's bones were not broken. There was unleavened bread, quickly prepared, reminding them of the hasty preparations made by their ancestors before fleeing Egypt. A bowl of salt water represented the salty tears of the Hebrews as they slaved under the whip of their Egyptian overlords and reminded them of the Red Sea that God parted for their escape. Included on the Passover table was a dish of bitter herbs with horseradish, reminders of the hard and bitter life they left behind in Egypt. A plate of mixed apples, nuts, and pomegranates recalled the mud their ancestors made that hardened into bricks. Sticks of cinnamon in the mixture represented the straw they were forced to gather for the mortar. Red wine was served to the guests four times during the meal.

Jesus the Jew and his Jewish disciples follow the ceremonial traditions, observing the customs they know from childhood. As death approaches, Jesus finds comfort in the familiarity of this religious meal.

What meals have brought you comfort when you needed it most?

337

DEEPEST DESIRE
Luke 22:14-18

When everything was ready, Jesus took his place at the table with the disciples. He said, "It's my deepest desire to eat this Passover with you before I suffer. I won't eat another one until God's full intentions for the world are realized." Then Jesus took a cup, and after giving thanks, he said, "Take this and share it among yourselves. I won't drink wine again until God's hopes for the world come true."

+

On his last night, hours before his arrest, what Jesus most desires is to share the Passover with his closest friends. A double emphasis appears in the Greek: "With desire I have desired to eat this Passover with you." More than anything else in the world, Jesus seeks the community of those he knows best.

What exactly does Jesus know about the ones with whom he shares this meal? That they will stick with him through thick and thin? That he will be able to depend on them in his hour of greatest need? That they will defend his honor when questioned by the Romans? That they will prevail during the night and in the days ahead, standing their ground because of him? That when he breathes his last, he won't die alone but in the company of those he trained to carry on his work?

On this night, Jesus knows enough about his chosen twelve to know they won't display to the world their best natures but something less. In spite of that knowledge about them, Jesus' love for them doesn't diminish. As the storm clouds gather and the distant thunder rumbles, Jesus sees all their shortcomings, failures, and cowardliness, their betrayals, denials, and desertions, and loves them still. Even Judas.

In spite of who they (and we) are, God's love—present in Jesus—prevails.

When did you experience love in spite of your failure?

"DO THIS"
Luke 22:19

Then Jesus took some bread and gave thanks. After breaking
it, he gave it to his disciples, saying, "This is my body, given
for you. Remember me when you do this."

+

Space doesn't allow for adequate explanations of the myriad ways
Jesus' words have been received, interpreted, debated, and fought
over. "This is my body." Literally or metaphorically? Factually or sym-
bolically? Physically or spiritually? Past tense or present time?

Personal understandings and church teachings on the meaning of
"This is my body" are far less important than the fact that Jesus instructs us to "do this"—to eat this meal in community with each other
and with him. The transforming power of this meal isn't in the words
but in the action.

On any given Sunday, on every continent of the world, Christians
enact Jesus' words to do this. In mud huts, urban storefronts, stained-
glass cathedrals, steepled sanctuaries, rented gymnasiums, living rooms,
jail cells, hospital wards, on beaches, and aboard cruise ships, people
continue to follow his command to do this.

Saints and sinners, the faithful and the faithless, critics and skeptics, those who believe it all and those who've lost reason to believe do
what Jesus does with his disciples. They receive the blessed and broken
bread. They eat and do this.

Catholics and Protestants, liberals and conservatives, high church
and low church, denominations of all stripes and sectarian groups on
the fringe, people at opposing ends of the political spectrum, if not
while sitting together, at least in the communal action of doing this,
mimic each other and the early disciples. They carry out Jesus' instruction to do this.

The bread might be soft or hard, store-bought or homemade,
white, wheat, or gluten-free. Crackers or wafers will do just fine, too.
Regardless of the recipe and texture, whenever communities of two or
three worshippers or five thousand do this, they re-enact what Jesus
does with his disciples.

What's been the most memorable setting of this meal for you?

POURED OUT
Luke 22:20

After supper, Jesus took the cup, saying, "This cup, poured out for you, is the new promise of my blood."

+

If you've sat through enough church services, you probably recognize the words Jesus uses as he breaks the bread and pours the cup. In the Christian tradition, this meal goes by many names: The Lord's Supper, The Last Supper, Holy Communion, The Eucharist, The Agape Feast. All these names attempt to label what the church through the centuries has struggled to understand about this sacrament.

Defining a sacrament isn't a simple task. The word *sacrament* derives from the Latin word meaning "a sacred or consecrated thing or act." Throughout history, the church has understood a sacrament as a rite or an act instituted by Jesus.

Protestants recognize two sacraments: Baptism and Holy Communion. Catholics also include these two, but recognize an additional five: Confirmation, Penance, Extreme Unction (Anointing of the Sick), Holy Orders (Rite of Ordination for Priests), and Marriage. St. Augustine defined the sacraments as "outward and visible signs of an inward and spiritual grace." As a sacrament, bread and wine stand for something more than just food and drink. In them, through them, and with them, the mystery of Jesus is represented, embraced, and imparted.

Frederick Buechner (*Wishful Thinking*) describes a sacrament as something that makes holiness happen, and says that where that happens may or may not be in a church service. Indeed! A few years back, I experienced the Sacrament of the Redwoods. North of San Francisco, in Humboldt County, my spouse, Jody, and I got out of our rental car. In the silence of the forest, we stood on opposite sides of a 1,500-year-old specimen as tall as a football field is long. We stretched our arms around it. Our fingertips were separated from each other's by at least ten feet. As my face pressed against tree bark a foot thick, I had no doubt I was experiencing what Augustine called "an outward sign of an inward grace." The grace-filled life of Jesus, lived out of God's abundance, is poured out in measures impossible to predict.

When have you experienced a "pouring out" moment?

THE BETRAYER'S HAND
Luke 22:21-23

Jesus said, "The one who will betray me is sitting at this table. I'm going forward to complete what God has called me to do, but the one who will betray me should see this as a warning!" The disciples wondered who among them would do such a thing.

+

Interesting differences occur at this point in the Passover meal. In Luke's version, Jesus announces that one will betray him, but he doesn't identify the betrayer. In John's gospel, Jesus identifies his betrayer by giving Judas a piece of bread dipped in the cup of wine. In Matthew, Judas asks if he's the one and Jesus concurs. In Luke and Matthew, Judas remains with Jesus through the meal and leaves with the rest of the disciples. In John, Judas leaves immediately after he receives the bread.

Other issues, ignored by the gospel writers, arise in the minds of readers. If the betrayal is a God-determined thing, is Judas responsible for the role he plays? What were the factors that led Judas to choose the betrayal option?

Whether or not those questions have an answer isn't nearly as significant in this story as the inclusion of Judas in the evening's activities.

Jesus reclines around the table with the disciples—Judas included.
Jesus shares his last meal with the disciples—Judas included.
Jesus offers bread and wine to the disciples—Judas included.
In John's gospel, Jesus washes the disciples' feet—Judas included.

It's clear that Jesus wants Judas on the inside, not the outside; a part of the beloved community, not estranged from it.

Perhaps Jesus' warning is less a denunciation and curse than an acknowledgment of the turmoil and anguish Judas won't be able to endure when he separates himself from his companions and the one who loves him dearly.

What empathy might you have toward Judas?

Grand Rapids, MI

GREAT AMBITIONS
Luke 22:24-27

The disciples argued among themselves about which of them was the most important. Jesus reminded them, "Worldly rulers seek to control others, and those in authority like to be thought of as benefactors. It will be different with you. The greatest among you must become the lowliest, and the leader like one who serves. Who is greater, the one who sits at the table to be served or the one who serves? Isn't it the one who sits at the table? But I'm a servant among you."

+

Though the disciples resemble siblings arguing over who's the favorite child, their spat is related to seating positions around the Passover table. The seating order (more likely the reclining arrangement) reflects positions of greater and lesser influence. At a U-shaped table, the host sits at the top center. On the host's right is the guest of highest honor, on the host's left the guest of second honor, and so forth around the table. Positions at the table reflect social rank.

Jesus, however, isn't interested in where the most important person sits, but in how leaders behave. Greatness isn't an ascent to power, but a descent into service. Jesus identifies two objectionable characteristics in the way rulers of the world operate. First, these leaders are into power and control; their leadership style is tyrannical. Second, they like to be thought of as "benefactors," which, as Jesus implies, is an inappropriate title bearing no resemblance to their leadership style.

"But *you*," Jesus says emphatically, "must not copy their example." Nothing in this moment suggests that the disciples understand the connection Jesus makes between greatness and service. Perhaps the lessons of servant leadership are better learned at Friday afternoon hilltops than at Thursday evening tabletops.

What does servant leadership look like in your life?

STANDING BY
Luke 22:28-30

"Because you've stood by me in tough times, you will have a part to play in my reign, just as my Father gave me a part. You will eat and drink at my table from now on. You will have special responsibilities as you lead the people of God."

+

The disciples have been arguing about positions of honor and importance. They believe, as society taught them, that authority derives from rank and status. The higher your position in the organization, the greater your authority. According to Jesus, true leadership is demonstrated in serving others.

As if reminding the disciples of something they've forgotten, Jesus now commends them for having stood by him in difficult times. Though his disciples often failed to grasp his teachings, they did what Jesus needed most—they stood by him. Regardless of what will happen later this evening, and knowing that they will falter on the day of his execution, Jesus loves them for having stood by him. Because of their faithfulness, they will receive honor in the fullness of God's reign.

Jesus doesn't say to his disciples, "You will obtain positions of honor because you've figured out the trinitarian formula of the Godhead . . . because your theology is properly orthodox . . . because you've mastered an end-of-days timetable . . ." Standing by, standing with, standing alongside is the only measure of true authority in God's world.

As we strive for a world that honors God, there are important questions to ask ourselves. Are we standing by the ones Jesus stood by? Are we seeking justice and equality for those who suffer because of their gender, their race, their disability? Are we seeking out those pushed to the margins of insignificance? Are we welcoming those discriminated against because of their sexual orientation? Are we honoring those who know God by a different name? Are we taking up the cause of those who subsist in occupied territories?

Maybe the most important question we'll ever be asked in this world or the next is: With whom did you stand in their trials?

With whom do you stand, and who stands with you?

344

SIFTED BY SATAN
Luke 22:31-32

"Peter, Peter, listen! Satan is determined to sift all of you like wheat, but I've prayed for you that your own faith won't fail. Once you've turned back to me, you will strengthen your brothers."

+

If the disciples imagine that reaching positions of honor will be a steady, uninterrupted ascent, Jesus shatters such notions. As Jesus once did battle with the devil in the wilderness, so too will his disciples.

Various interpretations exist regarding the intent of the "sifting" process. Is it a sifting that will determine true disciples from false disciples? Will it leave the weak lost to the winds and the strong even stronger? Will Satan mount a full and deadly assault against those who fail the test? Most likely, the sifting metaphor suggests that severe testing will come. No disciple will escape it. At points and places, all will falter and fall.

Though Satan will test, assault, and sift all the disciples, Jesus tells Peter in particular that he has already prayed that he won't fail. In light of Peter's denials of Jesus that will come later this night, we might conclude that Jesus' prayer was not answered. However, the verb translated "won't fail" can also mean "won't give out," or "won't disappear completely." Considering the leadership role Peter later assumes in the post-Easter church, Jesus' prayer was indeed answered completely.

The disciples aren't bulletproof. They won't be immune from dangers or pitfalls. They will be leaders, but wounded leaders, bearing the struggles and marks of Jesus. Maybe we expect too much of our leaders and too much of ourselves—perfect in faith, consistent in parenting, making daily improvements, living in ever healthier ways. Jesus reminds us that the struggle of the sifting will always be there. We can't change that. The failure isn't in the daily struggle, but in the refusal to struggle at all.

How is your struggle with the "sifting" sometimes a blessing?

THE PETER LIST
Luke 22:33-34

Peter said to Jesus, "I'm ready to go with you to prison, even if it means dying!" Jesus replied, "Listen to me, Peter. Before the rooster crows today, you will insist three times that you don't know me."

+

With the noblest intentions, Peter struts his stuff. So sure of things, he confidently believes he has a firm grasp on it all. No prayers need to be offered on *his* behalf! No need for preparations as far as *he's* concerned. Peter is ready *now*, even if his colleagues aren't. Who is Jesus to suggest otherwise?

Some leadership lessons emerge from this exchange, particularly relating to leadership in the church. Having gone through the ministerial calling process a few times, I've come to learn that church search committees have at least three criteria when evaluating pastoral candidates: (1) measurable growth (numerical success), (2) measurable inspiration (pulpit presence), and (3) measurable wisdom (seasoned experience). As lists go, it's as good as any. Lists of any kind are necessary. Lists help to organize, clarify, and analyze. Lists make sense of things (and persons) which otherwise might appear senseless.

I humbly offer churches and search committees an additional list to put before each candidate being considered for ministerial employment. With a few tweaks, it's useful in other circumstances too. I call it *The Peter List*.

Tell us about your biggest failure.
Recall a time when you overestimated your ability.
How does your strength become a weakness?
When did you make a promise you were unable to keep?
Of what do you still need to repent?
Share an experience you hope never becomes public.
When did your convictions put your life in jeopardy?
In what specific ways do you deny Jesus?
Peter heard a rooster and wept; what moves you to tears?

Which of these would you least want to answer?

ENOUGH!
Luke 22:35-38

Jesus said to the disciples, "When I sent you out without wallets, purses, bags, or sandals, did you lack anything?" They said, "No, not a thing." Jesus continued, "But now, if you have a purse or bag, you must take it with you. If you have no sword, sell your coat and buy one. This scripture applies to me: 'He was counted among the criminals.'" They said, "We brought two swords." Jesus replied, "Enough of this!"

+

This isn't an easy exchange to understand, so we need to stay alert to the context. Jesus is preparing his disciples for the tumult that will arise in just a few hours. He reminds them of an earlier time when they were sent out in pairs, ministering throughout Galilee (Luke 10). In those days, they took no personal resources but relied on the hospitality of others.

But on this night, Jesus prepares his disciples for the impending hostilities that will be directed not only at him but at them. Once, people graciously opened homes to them, but in the future, people will invade the disciples' homes seeking to harm them. As never before, the disciples will need to depend on their resources: wallets, purses, bags, footgear, and whatever else they can grab.

But swords? They will have to sell personal articles for swords? Is Jesus suggesting that his followers should wield weapons, that armed conflict should be part of his way? Jesus is making an exaggerated statement to underscore a point. The imminent danger won't be that they lack resources, but that their very existence will be threatened. The time will come to sacrifice the most necessary things (as when one sells something as necessary as a cloak in order to purchase a sword) so they can stand with vigilant resolve. Hardship and sacrifice await them.

That the disciples produce two swords is evidence they've come prepared; they anticipate a struggle that they imagine can be won at the blade's edge. Jesus doesn't see it that way. "Enough of this! Your swords aren't the weapons God uses in bringing about heaven's transformation of earth. Enough of this! Let's move on. Enough!"

What weapons help you imitate Jesus' life?

THE CUP
Luke 22:39-42

Jesus and his disciples left the house and went to the Mount of Olives. When he reached the place, he said to them, "Pray for the strength you will need when your faithfulness is tested." Then he walked on about a stone's throw away, knelt down, and prayed, "Father, if you're willing, remove this cup of suffering from me. Yet, may your will rather than my own be done."

+

Aware of the approaching storm, Jesus doesn't change his habits or alter his ways to elude those seeking to harm him. He goes to his regular prayer spot in the olive grove. Mark and Matthew identify the place as the Garden of Gethsemane.

Though it may seem a subtle point, it's an important one. To suggest that Jesus is subdued by his adversaries or that he falls a passive victim to their strategies is to alter the scene as Luke describes it. Jesus continues to move toward the storm—resolutely, purposefully, deliberately, and nonviolently.

The trials of which Jesus warned his disciples earlier this evening are now close enough at hand that he instructs them to pray for strength in facing them. Alone in prayer, Jesus pleads that this cup—this cup of suffering—be removed from him. Does Jesus have second thoughts about his mission to embody God's intentions for the world? Is he seeking a less painful way to accomplish his task? Does he want to live rather than die? Does he fear the brutality of the capital punishment imposed by the Romans? Of course! This is a human being in the prime of his life, facing a cause that will cost him everything. Who *wouldn't* wonder if there might be another way?

Yet he prays for the priority of God's will. This isn't fatalism embraced or hopelessness acknowledged. Jesus gives in to nothing other than pure submission to the Divine Source of his identity and mission.

What cup of suffering have you prayed to be removed?

348

THE ANGUISH
Luke 22:43-46

Then an angel appeared to Jesus and comforted him. In his anguish, he prayed even harder so that his sweat fell to the ground like drops of blood. When he got up from prayer, he found his disciples sleeping, overcome with grief. He said to them, "Why are you sleeping? Stay awake and pray that you won't face further testing."

+

The most familiar artwork depicting Jesus praying in the garden is by German painter Heinrich Hoffman. Some maintain that this 1890 work is the most copied painting of Jesus in the world. I hope not. A pale-faced, bearded Jesus kneels with his hands folded on a rock. A heavenly light illumines his upwardly turned face. Three disciples are sleeping in the dark background. The faint walls of Jerusalem are barely visible in the distance. This Caucasian Jesus is calm and unshaken, a kneeling tower of strength.

Luke paints a different picture. Jesus is a man in turmoil. Even though he's just prayed that God's will be done, the anguish doesn't subside. The Greek word for "anguish" often was used to describe the overwhelming fear felt by soldiers in battle. Jesus is shaken by the prospect of suffering crucifixion's agonizing death, a death he might have witnessed others suffering along roads when the Romans wanted to send a clear message to the Jews.

Like Elijah, who was given strength to go on by a ministering angel, Jesus finds strength in a reliable source beyond himself. The disciples cope as best they can; they will need their sleep for what's soon to come.

Hoffman's placid Jesus does nothing to move me. Luke's Jesus, anguishing in the garden, gives me hope when I face my own trials.

When has God seemed near to you during a personal anguish?

THE BETRAYAL
Luke 22:47-48

A small crowd led by Judas Iscariot approached Jesus. Judas came near to Jesus and was ready to kiss him, but Jesus said, "Judas, you're going to betray me with a kiss?"

+

This is the second time Judas is mentioned in this chapter. I've added "Iscariot" to his name as Luke does in an earlier reference. A scholarly industry has sprung up over the years regarding who Judas was, where he came from, and his possible motives in betraying Jesus.

The significance and meaning of "Iscariot" is uncertain. Some speculate that it's a derivation of "Kerioth," an ancient town. Another school of thought suggests that "Iscariot" identifies Judas as a member of an indigenous rebel group known as the "Sicarii" (literally, "dagger-bearers"). This armed militia was committed to throwing out the Romans by whatever means necessary.

Other explanations of "Iscariot" based on linguistic origins suggest that the name means "liar," "deliverer," or "constriction." This last possibility makes a direct connection to Judas's suicide by hanging, as recorded in Matthew's gospel. Interestingly, Luke records in the first chapter of Acts that Judas dies by falling on his sword, causing his guts to spill out. (People who don't sleep well at night unless all scriptural contradictions are resolved suggest that Judas first hanged himself, causing the rope to snap and his body to fall on the sword, which he thoughtfully placed upright in the ground before he hanged himself.)

Most people are unaware that there exists a gospel of Judas. Though you won't find it among the sixty-six books of the Bible, ancient manuscripts, dating to nearly three hundred years after Jesus, were discovered in Egypt during the 1970s. Written from Judas's point of view, these accounts offer a more sympathetic understanding of the betrayer: his action helped Jesus move toward death so that he could be released from his earthly body and assume a divine status.

A disciple. A kiss. A betrayal. We all operate with mixed motives and conflicted consciences. If we can't see a bit of Judas in ourselves, then we're not reading the story with honest eyes.

What school of thought best describes how you imagine Judas?

"NO!"
Luke 22:49-51

When the disciples saw what was about to happen, they asked, "Lord, should we use our swords?" At that moment, one of the disciples cut off the right ear of a servant who was standing with the religious leaders. But Jesus said, "No more of this!" Then he touched the ear and stopped the bleeding.

+

That the disciples carry swords to the garden and are prepared to use their weapons suggests they are not the cowards we're quick to make them out to be. They're ready for a late-night scuffle. Of the four gospel writers, John alone identifies Peter as the sword-wielding disciple and names Malchus as the victim. Only Luke records that Jesus heals the wound.

These former fishermen and one-time tax collector are ready to fight. If Jesus needs protection, they're up for the challenge. If they have to defend themselves, they'll do that, too. The disciples are willing to make Gethsemane their Gettysburg, to spill blood—likely their own—for the sake of standing by Jesus. There are worse ways to die than sacrificing your life for another human being.

Jesus isn't subtle about where he stands on the issue of violence in the face of violence. He won't fight his way out of trouble, and neither will he allow his disciples to do so. He refuses to opt for armed conflict as a defense strategy, regardless of how many weapons of mass destruction the Judas-led posse has at its disposal.

Do the disciples at this moment suddenly see the truth about the one they've followed for three years? If so, do they despair over how Jesus will accomplish anything if he doesn't defend himself against those seeking to destroy him?

Where has violence played a role in your life?

THE HOUR
Luke 22:52-53

Jesus said to the religious leaders and Jewish soldiers, "Are you armed with swords and clubs because you think I'm a criminal? When I was in the temple every day, you didn't lay a hand on me. But this is your hour; it is full of darkness!"

+

Though this incident occurs in the dark, Luke is careful to illuminate the details. Those carrying swords and clubs don't belong to the uneducated masses, the criminal element, or a group of anarchists. Those seeking to apprehend Jesus aren't irreligious, irreverent, or irresponsible. They are respected members steeped in the religious system.

Some of the religious leaders are chief priests who administer ceremonial affairs of the temple. Some are enforcers who serve as the eyes and ears of the security team. Others are scribes who interpret and guard the traditions. They're collaborators with the Roman domination system. As long as peace is maintained, the temple can carry on without interference. Jesus has threatened the status quo, and the clergy of the day will make him pay dearly.

These religious authorities, however, didn't represent the civil law of the land. Rome alone rules. Roman authority recognized the benefits of a peaceable, subjugated people who were free to observe the rituals of their religion. As long as Jews paid taxes and acknowledged Rome's authority to levy such taxes, they were permitted to follow their religious traditions, including disciplining their own who transgress religious law. Freedom to enforce religious discipline, however, didn't include carrying out a death penalty. Rome alone held that authority.

Those who confront Jesus this night aren't acting on behalf of Rome or as emissaries of any Roman official. Jesus has threatened the religious leaders who belong to the same religious tradition in which he was raised. And they will take any steps necessary to silence the one who challenges the status quo and their security.

Nighttime is the perfect opportunity. The daytime crowd is home. Jesus' countless Jewish admirers can't protect him now. This is the hour, and dark is its power.

How would you have protected Jesus?

THE DENIALS
Luke 22:54-60

Then the religious leaders brought Jesus to the high priest's house. Peter followed at a distance and eventually sat down with the others who had gathered around a fire in the courtyard. Eventually, a servant girl saw Peter's face in the fire's glow and said, "This man is with Jesus." But Peter denied it: "Woman, I don't know him." Later that night someone else said, "You're one of them." But Peter said, "Man, I'm not!" About an hour later, another insisted, "Surely he's one of them; he's from Galilee too." Peter insisted, "I have no idea what you're talking about!" Then the rooster crowed.

+

When we piece together the four gospel accounts of Jesus' arrest and trial, the cumulative picture is more detailed than the record offered by any single writer. According to Luke, Jesus is led from Gethsemane to the house of the high priest, identified in John's gospel as Annas. John also acknowledges Caiaphas as the high priest. The inconsistency is explained, in part, by the fact that Annas, who had been deposed by the Romans and replaced by his son-in-law Caiaphas, was still regarded by the Jews as an influential religious figure.

As if to make good on his promise to accompany Jesus to prison and to death, Peter follows at a distance. Yet, in three different conversations through the night, the disciple denies any association with Jesus.

Thousands of sermons have been preached exposing Peter's failure. Most of us can recall similar failures in our own lives that include loss of nerve, feet of clay, saving our own skin, looking out for our own interest. Yet, only hours earlier, Peter (as recorded in John's gospel) was the one who unsheathed his sword and led a one-man attack against the armed captors intent on arresting Jesus.

Is Peter a brave defender or a willing denier? Most likely, he's a mix of both. Peter is a living paradox of ambiguity. One moment he's confident, the next moment crushed. Early in the evening, he's courageously strong, but later that night he's weak enough to lie. Peter is you, me—everyone. The rooster crows for all of us.

What's been your most regretful failure?

THE LOOK
Luke 22:61-62

Jesus turned and looked at Peter. At that moment, Peter remembered what Jesus had said earlier: "Before the rooster crows today, three times you will say you don't know me." Then Peter left the courtyard and wept uncontrollably.

+

The look—how would one describe it? The look—can you imagine it? Is it a look of disgust, a reprimanding glare as if Jesus is thinking, "I told you so, Peter"? Or is it a look closer to dismay, a reaction from one who thought he could depend on someone else? Maybe it's a look of dejection or despair, conveying the deep pathos Jesus feels when he hears three denials from the disciple whose name means "rock." Is that a rock on which to stand, or one to throw?

What does Peter see in Jesus' face? An answer might be found in the Greek verb *emblepo*, which means "to look at" and appears several times in the gospels. In John 1:42, we read, "Andrew brought Simon to Jesus, who looked at him and said, 'You're Simon, son of John. From now on, you'll be called Cephas' (which is translated Peter)." In Mark 10:21, we encounter the rich man who inquired about inheriting eternal life: "Jesus, looking at him, loved him, and said, 'You lack one thing: Go, sell what you own, and give the money to the poor, then follow me.'"

The look Jesus gives in these incidences is a loving look, a look that deeply connects. The look may be difficult to describe, or even beyond words altogether, but we all know it when we see it. It's the look of love that pulls us closer instead of pushing us away.

What does it mean for the God of the universe to look at creation and love it? What does it mean for the Holy One to look behind the doors of our darkest closets, behind the drawn window shades of our private lives, into the secret places we choose to hide . . . and love us still? It's enough to make one go out and weep.

When was the last time you saw "the look"?

THE COUNCIL
Luke 22:63-66

The guards taunted and beat Jesus. They blindfolded him and mocked him, saying, "Tell us, who just hit you?" In the morning, the religious leaders and members of the clergy got together and brought Jesus to the Sanhedrin.

+

Jesus is held in the custody of the religious authorities throughout the night. Who can say what liberties those in control take with a defenseless prisoner when the world is fast asleep? In the morning, Jesus is brought to the Sanhedrin council headed by the high priest. The Sanhedrin was the religious supreme court of the Jews and consisted of seventy members. Membership included scribes, Pharisees, priests, Sadducees, and elders of the people.

The Sanhedrin exercised jurisdiction over every Jew. Historians note that the Sanhedrin sought to preserve the rights of individual Jews accused of crimes, including refusing to find a prisoner guilty without sufficient evidence of independent witnesses. During the time of Jewish independence prior to Roman occupation, the Sanhedrin held authority to impose the death penalty upon Jewish citizens found guilty of violating religious law. In Jesus' time, during Roman occupation, such authority no longer existed.

Jesus, the Jew, appears before the highest religious court of his day. Again, we shouldn't fail to note that Jesus stands before the educated and respected leaders and scholars of his community. These are the well-connected folks, whose religious and social sensibilities have been challenged by a Galilean from Nazareth.

Imagine someone today challenging the status quo and claiming, "Our materialism isn't a sign of God's favor. God's not in the business of blessing our wars. God doesn't love America more than the rest of the world. Our economic system is no friend of the poor, whom God loves. If that person persists, you can bet she or he will get roughed up, too.

What in the status quo needs to be challenged today?

THE INTERROGATION
Luke 22:67-69

The religious leaders said to Jesus, "Tell us if you're the Messiah." Jesus replied, "If I, the Son of Man, tell you, you won't believe me. If I ask you questions, you won't give me an honest answer. Your minds are already made up. From now on, I'll take my seat of power next to God."

+

Jesus' terse reply suggests that his accusers aren't interested in what he has to say since they've already formed their convictions about him. What's the use of a discussion if one party isn't willing to listen? The accusers have already made up their minds. Nothing Jesus says will change what they believe about him.

Throughout the gospel accounts, Jesus uses the self-designation "Son of Man" more than any other title. Occurring more than a hundred times in the Hebrew scriptures, Jesus use of the designation is most likely a reference to Daniel 7:13-14: "In my night, I saw the Son of Man coming like a human being in the clouds of heaven. He came to the Ancient One and was given authority, glory, and influence, so that all peoples, nations, and languages would serve him. His authority will never end or pass away, and his influence won't be destroyed."

Connected to his heavenly source, Jesus stands confidently before his accusers and predicts his ultimate triumph. "You may appear to have the upper hand, but the day will come when my way will be acknowledged. You think you're the judge of me, but the day will come when God's ways will be the desire of all people. You might be powerful now, but the day is nearing when God's reign will have no rivals. You think you can silence me, but the time is coming when not even death will keep me quiet. It might look like you're in control, but soon enough your influence will be forgotten forever."

Jesus stands before the council of the Sanhedrin, but we're left wondering: Who is interrogating whom?

What impresses you about Jesus' demeanor?

THE PROOF
Luke 22:70-71

The interrogators asked him, "Are you the Son of God?" Jesus answered, "Your words." Then they said, "What further evidence do we need? We've heard it from his own lips!"

+

Many Jews saw Jesus as the Messiah, the anointed one of God. Many Jews, from Galilee in the north to Jerusalem in the south, followed Jesus. Many Jews who accompanied Jesus were known as his disciples. Jews closest to Jesus, trained to carry on his ministry after his death, were known as his apostles. Some Jews supported Jesus and his disciples financially. Many Jews believed that Jesus was a prophet in the tradition of Elijah and Jeremiah—a high accolade. Many Jews believed that Jesus had healing powers far greater than other healers of the day. Many Jews were amazed at the authority with which he taught. Some Jewish leaders' respect for Jesus ran so deep that they invited him to their homes for supper and conversation. On one occasion, a Jewish leader named Nicodemus sought out Jesus for theological conversation (John 3). Another wealthy Jew, Joseph of Arimathea, soon would offer his tomb as a burial site for Jesus' crucified body.

Only a small number of Jews—certain leaders of the temple in Jerusalem and some members of the Sanhedrin—despised Jesus to the point of wishing him harm. He threatened a religious system where power and security and control took precedence over caring for the vulnerable, the weak, the widows, the poor—a system that had lost its prophetic voice in favor of ensuring its own survival.

The few, working for Jesus' demise, accuse him of claiming to be the Son of God. Neither denying nor confirming the claim, Jesus lets it be. His indirect answer is enough to seal his fate. Matthew records that the high priest tears his robe and exclaims, "Blasphemy!"

History's soil is soaked with the blood of Jews who were persecuted, tortured, and destroyed because Christians believed them to be Christ-killers. The Jews as a people didn't kill Jesus; the Romans, at the behest of a proportionately small group of Jewish leaders, killed him in the same barbaric way they executed thousands of troublemakers.

What's been your experience with anti-Semitic attitudes?

THE CHARGES
Luke 23:1-2

Then the members of the Sanhedrin brought Jesus before Pilate and said to the Roman governor, "We found this man subverting the nation. He told us to stop paying taxes to Caesar. He calls himself the Messiah, and claims to be a king."

+

What does it matter to the Roman governor Pilate that Jesus is guilty of blaspheming the God of the Jews? He couldn't care less. The Jews have their God and the Romans have their gods. In order to get Pilate's attention, the Sanhedrin think tank has to come up with a more convincing strategy.

To that end, they choose a three-pronged attack. First, they claim that Jesus is a threat to the empire; he subverts (literally, "misleads") the nation. Pilate is mildly interested in hearing more. Second, they claim that Jesus preaches against paying taxes to Rome. This claim, of course, is a blatant lie. Jesus actually said, "Give to Caesar the things that are Caesar's." No matter, now they have Pilate's full attention. Third, and most damaging, they inform the governor that Jesus claims to be a Messiah. In other words, "He's got his sights on being king." Pilate's territorial instincts kick into gear and he feels threatened.

The third charge is a brilliant element in the game plan because the Sanhedrin council knows that Rome doesn't crucify pickpockets, shoplifters, or jaywalkers. Rome does come down hard on revolutionaries who pose an imminent threat to the supremacy of the empire. The last thing Pilate's bosses in Rome want to hear is that there's a Jewish power play gaining momentum in Judea. If Pilate cares at all about moving up the political ladder, this is one charge he can't ignore.

What is the biggest lie being spread these days?

YOUR WORDS
Luke 23:3-5

Pilate asked Jesus, "Are you the King of the Jews?" Jesus replied, "Your words." Then Pilate said to the Sanhedrin members and the crowd, "Your charges against this man are baseless." But they wouldn't relent. "He incites people everywhere he goes, first in Galilee and now here."

+

It's the shortest cross-examination in history. Pilate asks one question. Jesus responds with a shoulder-shrug and a two-word answer. Pilate knows revolutionaries, and Jesus, he surmises, is no revolutionary. According to Luke, "Your words" is the only defense Jesus offers the Roman governor. However, when we combine the exchange found in John's gospel, an unmistakable picture of Jesus emerges.

Pilate: Are you the King of the Jews?
Jesus: Is this your question, or did others tell you?
Pilate: I'm not a Jew. Your own people handed you over to me. What have you done?
Jesus: My way isn't the world's way. If it were, my followers would be fighting for me this very moment.
Pilate: So, then, you *are* a king?
Jesus: My way is about pointing to God's work in the world, even if it offends. Anyone who speaks that truth is a traveler with me on the way.
Pilate: What's truth? And where are you from? Aren't you going to defend yourself? Don't you realize I have power over your life and death?
Jesus: Any power you have comes from God.

Who's in control—the governor or the condemned? Pilate or Jesus? Jesus isn't conducting himself like a helpless victim. He's not resentful, but resolved; not confused, but confident. "I lay down my life in order to take it up again. No one takes it from me. I lay it down on my own terms" (John 10:17-18).

When was the last time you had to defend yourself to someone in authority?

359

QUESTIONS, BUT NO ANSWERS
Luke 23:6-9

When Pilate found out that Jesus was from Galilee, where King Herod ruled, he sent Jesus to Herod, who happened to be in Jerusalem at the time. Herod was glad to meet Jesus, for he hoped to be entertained with some miraculous signs. Herod questioned him at length, but Jesus refused to speak.

+

Herod questions Jesus on a host of theological and political issues. Nothing is off limits. Herod probes and prods, inquires and interrogates, but Jesus isn't in the mood to entertain Herod's curiosity.

"Tell me where you get your powers to perform miracles."
    Jesus gives no answer.
"Is it a skill you learned or something you were given at birth?"
    Jesus gives no answer.
"How about a miracle right here, right now?"
    Jesus gives no answer.
"Don't you realize I can be of help to you?"
    Jesus gives no answer.
"If you really are a king, should I be worried?"
    Jesus gives no answer.
"What's your military objective? What's your exit strategy?"
    Jesus gives no answer
"What do you think about my administration's policies?"
    Jesus gives no answer.
"Do you miss your cousin John? I beheaded him, you know."
    Jesus gives no answer.
"If you have special powers, tell me what I'm thinking."
    Jesus gives no answer.
"Just between you and me, can I trust Pilate?"
    Jesus gives no answer.

Though Jesus had answers for the devil in the wilderness, he gives no answer to Herod. His defense is his ministry. Enough said.

When was the last time saying nothing proved to be the best option for you?

BEST FRIENDS FOREVER
Luke 23:10-12

The religious leaders continued to accuse Jesus. Even Herod and his soldiers ridiculed and mocked him. Finally, Herod put a kingly robe on Jesus and sent him back to Pilate. That day, Herod and Pilate, once longtime enemies, became friends.

+

Like two politicians from opposing parties who set aside hard feelings, Herod and Pilate bury the hatchet and forge a new friendship. In some strange way, Jesus brings them together, proving that even old antagonists will consolidate a fresh alliance when threatened by a mutual enemy.

Luke doesn't reveal the cause of the rift between the two rulers, but some speculate that the relationship may have headed south when Pilate indiscriminately murdered a group of Galileans—residents of Herod's jurisdiction. The incident receives a brief mention without details in Luke 13.

Historians have pieced together that when Pilate needed money to finance a new aqueduct project, he siphoned money from the temple treasury without seeking permission from the Jewish leaders. When word of the funding coup got out, the Jews were furious. An angry crowd gathered to protest and demonstrate at the temple, prompting Pilate to dispatch soldiers disguised in civilian attire. Instead of keeping the peace and merely dispersing the crowd, the soldiers used force so excessive that many Jews lost their lives. The casualties included Galilean citizens for whom Herod was responsible. Bad enough for Herod to be upstaged by another Roman ruler, but things could have gotten worse had he received a reprimand from his superiors in Rome for failing to keep a lid on Jewish unrest.

Since both rulers had a chance to interrogate this sorry Galilean claiming to be a king with no army, the two politicians are willing to let bygones be bygones. Old grudges and deep hatreds are tossed aside as they share a good laugh over a few goblets of wine. You'd have to be blind not to see the humor.

In what ways does Jesus threaten people today?

NOT GUILTY
Luke 23:13-17

Pilate tried to strike a deal with the religious leaders and the crowd. "You brought me this man, claiming he was subverting the nation. I've thoroughly examined him and haven't found him guilty of any of the charges. Neither has Herod, who sent him back to me. As far as I can tell, he's done nothing to deserve death. After I have him flogged, I'll release him."

+

Though he has the power, Pilate doesn't want to use it to issue the death penalty. For the second time, Pilate pronounces Jesus innocent. The Roman governor couldn't foresee the designation, but early church fathers, including Tertullian, regarded the Roman governor as the first Christian witness for having declared Jesus not guilty.

There is, however, the matter of keeping the peace, both with the public and with his Roman bosses. Not willing to give Jesus up to crucifixion or to cause further public unrest because of his unwillingness to do so, Pilate offers to flog Jesus and then release him. Though Luke doesn't record the actual flogging, it's clear from other gospel accounts that the soldiers zealously carry out Pilate's orders.

The word translated as "flogged" has nuanced meanings. In other contexts, it means to "educate" or "chasten." In its strongest usage, it implies the use of force to teach a troublemaker a lesson.

The Romans were skilled practitioners in the art of flogging. Typically, the victim was tied to a pillar, leaving him in a bent position with his back exposed. An alternative method left the criminal upright, strapped to a post, with arms and legs fully extended. The whip consisted of leather straps studded with pieces of metal or bone that ripped the flesh. Though flogging wasn't intended to kill a victim, it proved most reliable for breaking a prisoner's spirit.

As an aside, the gratuitously violent film *The Passion of the Christ* holds nothing back in this bloodiest of scenes. Filmmaker Mel Gibson succeeded in giving movie-goers what they paid to see—blood and more blood. The movie made more than $600 million.

What methods of breaking a prisoner's spirit do you approve of?

PREVAILING VOICES
Luke 23:18-25

Then the crowd shouted, "Kill this man and release Barabbas!" (Barabbas was in prison for committing murder during an insurrection.) Even though Pilate wanted to release Jesus, the crowd kept shouting, "Crucify him!" Pilate pleaded a third time, "What's he guilty of? He doesn't deserve death. I'll have him flogged and then release him." But they kept demanding that he be crucified. Eventually their voices prevailed. Pilate gave in to their demand. He released Barabbas and gave permission for Jesus to be crucified.

+

It was customary at Passover time for a Roman official to release a prisoner as a gesture of goodwill and as an insurance policy for keeping the masses compliant. In John's gospel, Pilate suggests that the crowd choose between releasing Jesus or freeing Barabbas. The crowd needs no time to mull it over. "Release Barabbas!"

Interpreters have probed Pilate's emotional and psychological motivations for appeasing the crowd. Some go as far as to suggest the Roman governor suffered from migraine headaches and turned Jesus over to the crowd to gain peace and quiet. If so, who could blame him?

Historically, the relationship of Pilate to the Jerusalem Jews was, at best, tumultuous. Pilate's indiscriminate killing of the Galileans at the temple and his looting of the temple treasury have already been mentioned. The Jewish historian Josephus also tells of the occasion when Pilate processed into Jerusalem as his soldiers carried replica busts of the divine Caesar on the end of long vertical poles—an affront to Jews, who viewed such images as a sacrilege and petitioned Pilate to remove them. Only when the Jewish leaders threatened to take their complaint to a higher Roman authority did Pilate relent.

Perhaps Pilate caves in now because he's not up for another confrontation and wants to ensure his own job security. Their voices prevail not because logic convinces him to change his mind, but because peace at any price is sometimes a cost readily borne by one for whom taking an unpopular stand demands more.

When was the last time you made a compromise against your better judgment?

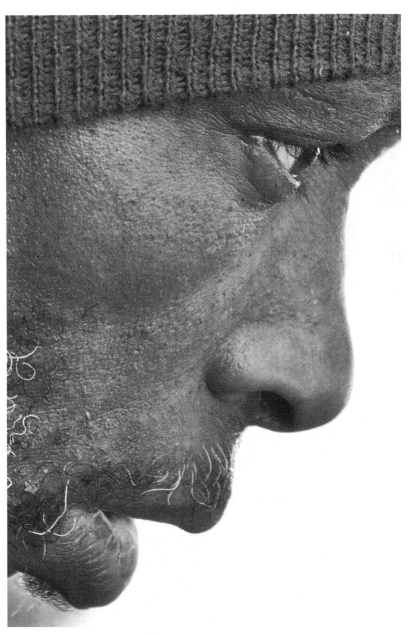

Union Station, Chicago, IL

INVOLUNTARY SERVICE
Luke 23:26

As the Roman soldiers led Jesus away, they stopped a man named Simon, who had arrived in Jerusalem from the city of Cyrene. They placed a piece of the cross on him and forced him to carry it behind Jesus.

+

Romans often forced condemned victims to carry the horizontal beam of their own cross. We can assume, because of the soldiers' severe flogging and mistreatment, that Jesus faltered under the weight of this timbered burden. With authority to draft a man into service, the soldiers choose an innocent bystander named Simon to shoulder Jesus' cross. Simon had traveled to Jerusalem from the North African town of Cyrene, the site of modern-day Tripoli, Libya.

The gospel writer Mark supplies the additional detail that Simon was the father of Alexander and Rufus. Some scholars believe that Rufus is the one St. Paul calls "chosen in the Lord" (Romans 16:13), thus supporting the claim that Simon became an early follower of Jesus because of his experience in Jerusalem.

Many scholars regard Simon as the first true disciple who literally carries a cross for the sake of Jesus. Others, noticing Simon's North African origins, proclaim him the first black disciple. Why not believe both claims? Simon's actions, involuntary as they are, speak a greater witness than anything he might have said. By sharing a burden, he silently eases another person's pain. If black, Simon isn't the first or the last of that continent to bear burdens imposed by harsh oppressors. The two cross bearers become brothers.

Since Jewish communities existed in North Africa at the time, we might suppose that Simon was a Jew; hence his reason for being in Jerusalem during the Passover. Perhaps, though, he's a non-Jew, a Gentile, a pagan merchant passing through the crossroads of Jerusalem, another outsider in Luke who becomes an insider. Whoever he was and whatever his origins, he reminds us that there's no limit to the power and influence Jesus' life has on others.

When was the last time being in the right place
became an opportunity for you to help another?

DON'T WEEP FOR ME
Luke 23:27-31

Many people followed Jesus, among them women who cried at the injustice of it all. Jesus turned to them and said, "Daughters of Jerusalem, don't weep for me, but weep for yourselves and for your children. For the days are near when some will say, 'Blessed are the childless, the wombs that never gave birth and the breasts that never nursed.' They will plead with the mountains, 'Fall on us!' and say to the hills, 'Cover us!' If they do this when the wood is green and full of life, what will happen when it is dead and dry?"

+

Again in Luke's gospel, devout women emerge among the crowd and don't go unnoticed by Jesus. This is the first time he speaks since the interrogation by Pilate, and what he says makes a connection with two Old Testament passages.

One reference is from Zechariah 12:10: "I will have compassion on David's descendants, the people of Jerusalem; when they look on the one whom they have pierced, they will mourn for him, like one weeping over the death of an only child or a firstborn."

The other reference is from Hosea 10:8: "Israel's high places, where sacrifices were offered to pagan gods, will be destroyed. Weeds and thorns will grow on their altars. They will say to the mountains, 'Cover us!' and to the hills, 'Fall on us!'"

It's hard to imagine, given his depleted physical state, Jesus suddenly quoting a large chunk of Hebrew scripture. More likely, Luke or the community that wrote Luke's gospel added these words. In either case, the warning is sobering. If Rome treats Jesus—an innocent man—with such harshness, how much worse will it be for Jerusalem, guilty of trying God's patience and ignoring the needs of the poor. Green wood burns slowly because of the moisture within; how much more quickly does old wood burn because it's dry.

For what people or population do you cry?

366

ANATOMY OF A CRUCIFIXION
Luke 23:32-33

Two criminals were led away with Jesus. When they came to the location called The Skull, they crucified Jesus between them.

+

Jesus and two criminals reach a location outside the city walls, a mound called Golgotha—"the Place of the Skull." There, the soldiers follow orders and carry out the execution.

This ancient form of capital punishment was never a private ordeal; by intent, crucifixions were carried out in full public view. The Romans reserved this death for runaway slaves and for those who subverted Roman law through insurrectionist activity. Crucifixions not only punished the guilty but also served as sobering deterrents for anyone who might challenge the absolute authority of the empire. The Jewish historian Josephus records that during one insurrection following the death of King Herod the Great, no fewer than two thousand crosses lined the roads in Galilee.

To die on a cross was to suffer a slow and painful death. Hands were tied or nailed to the horizontal beam. Feet were tied or nailed through the ankles to the upright beam. The weight of the victim was supported by a peg between the thighs or a wood support beneath the feet. The body of most victims hung close enough to the ground that wild animals could have their fill once death arrived and the spectators dispersed. Many victims were never buried because nothing remained of their ravaged bodies.

Death could take as long as two or three days. Beaten and abused even before the first nail was driven into his flesh, Jesus died in about six hours.

The word *excruciating* is an apt one to describe crucifixions. The Latin *excruciates* means "out of the cross." Out of the cross, Jesus—vulnerable and selfless—submits to the highest expression of love. The world witnesses no greater love than when one knows one will die for doing what's right, just, and godly—and does it anyway.

What circumstances would prompt you to die for someone you don't know?

INDISCRIMINATE FORGIVENESS
Luke 23:34a

Jesus said, "Father, forgive them. They don't know what they're doing."

+

The four gospel writers differ on how many times Jesus speaks and what he says while hanging from the cross. Luke and John record him speaking three times. In Matthew and Mark, Jesus speaks once. In all, seven different utterances are remembered.

Church tradition acknowledges that Jesus' prayer of forgiveness comprises the first words he speaks from the cross. On several levels, it's curious why Jesus prays "Father, forgive them" instead of saying "I forgive you." Because Jesus is the object and target of their abuses and taunts, it would seem *his* choice to forgive or not to forgive them. Recall also the incident (Luke 5:17-26) of the disabled man lowered through the roof by his four friends; on that occasion, Jesus announces, "Your sins are forgiven." Why not make the same announcement from the cross?

I don't know the answer or whether there is one, but I suspect there may be a relationship between Jesus' prayer, "Father, forgive them," and the lack of specificity in the word "them." Who is "them"? To whom is Jesus referring? The soldiers obeying orders? It would seem so, but does Jesus' prayer stop with the soldiers? Does "them" also include Pilate, who gave the order? And what about the array of religious leaders and temple thugs who plotted against him? What about the disciples who fled, and Peter who three times denied him, and Judas who betrayed him?

Where does "them" begin and where does "them" end? What's the limit? Might "them" include all those present that day, all those who had lived before that day, and even all those who have lived since that day? Does Jesus' prayer—vast in time and boundless in place—become a reality when the one universal God hears it? If so, is there anything or anyone who stands outside the scope of this prayer?

On a scale of 1 (low) to 10 (high), how large is your circle of "them"?

STRIPPED OF DIGNITY
Luke 23:34b

While Jesus was dying, the soldiers threw dice to divide his clothing among themselves.

+

As Jesus slowly dies, Roman soldiers determine his net worth by gambling for his last worldly possessions. Jewish men during the time typically wore clothing consisting of sandals, a head turban, an inner loincloth, an inner garment, an outer cloak, and a belt. Like all condemned men who were publicly crucified, Jesus is stripped of his clothing. For reasons of modesty, nearly all the paintings of the crucifixion show Jesus' waist wrapped with the inner loincloth. However, it's hard to imagine Roman soldiers allowing a condemned man his last shred of dignity. Jesus probably died as naked as the day he was born.

In the Gospel of John, the soldiers divide among themselves Jesus' articles of clothing like spoils of war collected by the victors. However, because Jesus' cloak or robe is a seamless garment, more valuable than one sewn together from two pieces, the soldiers opt to cast lots to determine who will win the prize.

By including this detail, the gospel writers establish a clear connection between Jesus and the lament of the psalmist, "I can count all my bones. They stare and gloat over me, dividing my clothing among themselves, and gambling for it" (Psalm 22:17-18).

The irony of misplaced value is obvious enough—soldiers gambling over Jesus' clothes while killing the person who once wore them. The irony of our misplaced values today, however, isn't always as obvious, or if it is, we choose to ignore it. How else do we explain the inordinate amount of time and energy we put into acquiring things we really don't need or want? What else could be the reason we as a nation are satisfied with substandard urban schools yet produce war weapons of the highest quality? How do we reconcile the fact that the rich and powerful divide up the wealth while the poor and the most vulnerable groan from their crosses? Are we any different from the Roman soldiers when we strip away the dignity of people of other sexual orientations, or of those who pray to the God they call Allah?

Who's most vulnerable to being stripped of their dignity today?

369

HE DID NOT SAVE HIMSELF
Luke 23:35-38

Bystanders watched while the religious leaders scoffed at Jesus, "He saved others. He should save himself if he's God's chosen Messiah!" The soldiers also mocked Jesus while offering him sour wine: "If you're the King of the Jews, save yourself!" An inscription attached to the cross above his head read, "This is the King of the Jews."

+

The taunting of Jesus is reminiscent of Satan's taunts in the wilderness. "If you're who you say you are, then why are you hanging on a cross? Messiahs don't get crucified! Chosen ones aren't nailed to wood! You say you're a king, but kings aren't treated like common criminals!" It isn't difficult to imagine Jesus going through long stretches of self-doubt as he drifts in and out of consciousness and slowly dies.

Actually, the scoffers, taunters, mockers, and ridiculers get it right. Up close, they're the first witnesses to the ultimate expression of Jesus' life and his approaching death. Honoring their unintended testimony, here's a ten-part summary of what they see.

The path to greatness is achieved through descent.
Leaders don't grasp power; they give it away.
Self-sacrifice is chosen over self-preservation.
This one seeks reconciliation rather than revenge.
Prayer is offered for those who inflict harm.
Nonviolence is the posture of resistance.
True power absorbs pain in order to mock the oppressor.
Minority voices are protected rather than silenced.
Losing one's life is not the ultimate loss.
A non-anxious presence conquers the chaos.

They get it as right as right can be. This chosen one of God, the one who lived his life to set others free, doesn't save himself.

Of the ten summary statements, which one most speaks to you?

ONE, BUT NOT THE OTHER
Luke 23:39-41

One of the criminals hanging next to Jesus kept ridiculing him, "I thought you were the Messiah. Save yourself and us!" But the other criminal admonished him, "You should respect God since you're getting the same punishment. We're criminals, and we deserve what we're getting, but this man's done nothing wrong."

+

The Romans could have made an example of Jesus by crucifying him alone—one cross, one victim, one silhouette against the Friday sky. There were other days for the two nameless criminals to die. But the Romans knew best how to terrorize an occupied land. *Take note, all you who pass by: this so-called king is no more special than these failed militiamen and their short-lived revolutions. Those who promise you a better life tomorrow only rob you of today. No one challenges the empire and gets away with it.*

That one of the criminals joins in bashing Jesus is no surprise; that the other criminal rebukes his comrade gives us reason to ponder. Why does one criminal give in to his lower nature and join in the ridicule, while his contemporary transcends all baseness and sees in Jesus the truth about himself? Both are eyewitnesses to the middle cross. Both hear Jesus' prayer, "Father, forgive them." Both behold the manner in which Jesus deals with his agony. Both watch as he suffers without cursing those responsible for it. Why don't both criminals have the same response?

At the end of the day, the question deflects all answers. Who can say why one antagonizes and the other acknowledges, why one rejects and another accepts? How's it possible that two children, raised by the same parents, shown equal amounts of love, told the same stories about God, arrive at opposite responses? Why a Cain and an Abel? Why an Esau and a Jacob? Why a prodigal son and a dutiful sibling? Why a Judas and a John?

Why is there within each of us a conflict of wills and ways? Maybe the question isn't why this is so, but which appetite and nature we will choose to feed.

What question can you imagine posing to God when death nears?

Bushnell, IL

REQUEST GRANTED
Luke 23:42-43

Then the criminal who defended Jesus said, "Jesus, remember me when you come into God's presence." Jesus replied, "Today, you will be with me in full communion with God."

+

The criminal's request is a modest one. Impressed by the dignity in Jesus' suffering, he voices a hope that Jesus will remember him. Many interpreters treat these words as an eleventh-hour confession; a guilty person face-to-face with death confesses a life of sin and looks to Jesus as Savior. Though such conversions regularly happen, that's not what happens here. This man makes no confession of sin and offers no remorse for past transgressions. He doesn't ask to be saved from anything or pardoned for the host of wrongs he's committed. He simply doesn't want his life to be forgotten. He just wants to be remembered.

At some level of understanding, he knows that the way Jesus has chosen will live on after death. He senses that the one hanging next to him has lived and now dies in a way that can be described only as godly. Knowing he doesn't deserve to accompany Jesus on the way to whatever the beyond holds, he clings to the hope that his life will be worth someone's remembrance.

If Jesus had said, "I'll be sure to remember you. I won't forget you," the man's modest request would have been granted. But Jesus exceeds the request: "I'll do more than remember you; I'll take you with me from this day forward." Another outsider, someone as far from sainthood as one can get, discards a two of clubs and receives an ace that trumps all else.

I'm left wondering, if such a modest request can get so much in return, is it possible that anyone—past, present, or future—exists beyond the remembrance and the accompaniment of the one on the middle cross? It wouldn't surprise me to discover that Jesus also turned to the other criminal, the one who had ridiculed him, and said, "I'll take you with me, too."

When was the last time your expectations were exceeded?

NOT JUST ABOUT ME
Luke 23:44-45

At noon, darkness covered the land for the next three hours. During that time, the curtain of the temple was torn in two.

+

A common understanding of Jesus' crucifixion and death has been around a long time, and it's as prevalent today as ever. The theme comes through many old hymns and contemporary praise songs. It's heard from pulpits in most denominational traditions and in independent megachurches, too. The message can be summed up in five words: "Jesus died for my sins." Depending on the church and the preacher, that theme might come through on every Sunday, in every sermon, with every prayer.

True enough! Jesus took on the weight of our sins—mine and yours included. But to begin there and end there is a bit like visiting our nation's capital and telling folks, "Washington, D.C. is all about Capitol Hill." Not a false statement, but hardly an adequate one.

Luke places Jesus' crucifixion in a context much grander in scope than just "my sins." Nature is affected as darkness covers the land (this could also imply the whole earth). Some biblical scholars maintain that a solar eclipse caused the darkness from noon to three. I doubt there's a meteorologist alive who could offer a reasonable explanation for a solar eclipse lasting more than three minutes, let alone three hours.

Luke is using symbolic language to convey that something of earthly and cosmic significance is happening in the death of the one on the middle cross. Nature itself recognizes and grieves the death of the one who showed the world the fullest way of living into God's reign.

In addition to the darkness, the curtain in the Jerusalem temple, separating the Holy Place from the Holy of Holies, where the Ark of the Covenant and the Divine Presence resided, is torn in two. A literal ripping of fabric? Again, this is symbolic language, making the point that in the life and death of Jesus, open and direct access to God is available to all, regardless of (sometimes in spite of) any dominant religious system that determines who's clean and who's unclean.

It's not just about me! Then again, it never was.

How are you closer to God because of Jesus' death?

INTO YOUR HANDS
Luke 23:46-47

A short time later, Jesus cried out, "Father, into your hands I entrust my spirit." Then he breathed his last breath and died.

+

Jesus knows the Psalms as well as any Hebrew of his day. He was born a Jew, raised a Jew, and died a Jew. As life slips from him, he quotes from Psalm 31, "Into your hands I entrust my spirit." To that quotation, Jesus adds the word "Father."

Jesus' last words from the cross, as recorded by Luke, are not a philosophical explanation of the mysteries of life. In his final moments, Jesus doesn't offer up a discourse of rarified wisdom to enlighten the minds of those nearby. Jesus essentially prays a prayer taught to him by his parents, a prayer Hebrew children of his day uttered to God at bedtime: "Into your hands I entrust my spirit."

On the slopes of Galilee, Jesus taught the crowds the ethics of the Sermon on the Mount. He taught his disciples a missional prayer beginning with "Our Father." But on the cross, he saves his best for last: "Father, into your hands I entrust my spirit." In his dying, Jesus does exactly what he did in his living—entrusts himself to the Divine Source of his being. Jesus surrenders to God.

For most of us, the idea of surrendering carries plenty of negative baggage. Losing in battle means surrendering to the victor. On election night, a losing candidate concedes defeat and surrenders to the voters' choice. To surrender one's car keys or driver's license is an experience no one wants to go through.

Jesus models for us a surrendering of self that leads to true freedom. In surrendering, we give up to take up. In giving, we find the fullness of living. The paradox is worth embracing. If in God's hands we're held, then, like Jesus, we're free to risk without concern, free to share without return, free to dare and not fear the loss, free to love and not count the cost.

In what area of your life are you least able to let go?

CENTURION CONFESSION
Luke 23:47-49

A Roman centurion standing near acknowledged, "This was an innocent man." After watching all this, the bystanders returned home, full of remorse. Those closest to Jesus, including the women who had followed him from Galilee, watched at a distance.

+

The centurion is a professional soldier, a career fighter, a battle-tough Roman who's seen many victims die. One doesn't ascend to the rank of centurion without growing callous to executions. Yet, this centurion, who obeyed the orders of Caesar, is the first to voice a verbal witness after Jesus dies. He sees in Jesus an innocent man. Mark's gospel suggests an even stronger confession from the centurion: "Truly, this man was God's son."

Was it the way Jesus died, or was it what Jesus said from the cross, that caused the centurion to utter his confession? Did the eerie darkness move him to behold light shining from the one hanging on the middle cross? What does the centurion's witness say about the Roman Empire and all empires past and present that have silenced truth-tellers?

Again, we're reminded that this death, like so many innocent deaths, was carried out by a sophisticated civilization led by efficient leaders who demanded respect. It took place in a city whose name means "peace," under the critical eye of religious leaders who were convinced they knew everything there was to know about God.

A pagan soldier stands near while Jesus' friends and acquaintances stand at a distance. The lines separating the insiders from the outsiders are blurred. Maybe those lines no longer exist. In the absence of such distinctions and judgments, we find the redeeming value of this death.

Where at the cross do you find yourself?

HE TOOK IT DOWN
Luke 23:50-53

There was a deeply religious person named Joseph who, even though he was a member of the Sanhedrin, had not agreed with the decision to condemn Jesus to death. He came from the town of Arimathea and was waiting for the fullness of God to appear. He went to Pilate and asked for the body of Jesus. After getting permission, he took down the corpse and wrapped it in a linen sheet. Then he placed the body in a cut-rock tomb that had never been used before.

+

Joseph of Arimathea is mentioned in all four gospels. Luke and Mark identify him as a member of the Sanhedrin; Matthew and John refer to him as a member of the wider group of disciples. The gospel writer John adds that Joseph is accompanied by Nicodemus, the Pharisee who once visited Jesus at night to inquire about matters of theology.

Typically, criminals weren't given proper burials but were thrown into mass graves or left on crosses as food for wild animals. Joseph faced a daunting task in removing Jesus' body from the cross. He had to climb a makeshift ladder, extract nails from the hands and feet, and then wrap his arms around Jesus' blood-splattered torso before carrying the limp body down the ladder. With a cart large enough to accommodate an adult corpse, Joseph had to negotiate the arduous journey down the hill, making his way to the tomb. If Nicodemus assisted Joseph, perhaps they carried the body, one holding Jesus' ankles while the other gripped his armpits.

Consider other risks. What if a member of the Sanhedrin recognizes Joseph? Would the charge of aiding and abetting the enemy stick? Though Joseph's quiet decency tends to get lost in the crucifixion story, I've come to see it as one of the most courageous acts in the Bible. Joseph takes a minority position against those who can do him harm. He knocks on Pilate's door and doesn't flinch. He absorbs the blood of the Innocent One on his own flesh. He accepts the likelihood of being ridiculed by those who don't understand. By such actions the world is saved.

What was your last Joseph act?

SABBATH KEEPING
Luke 23:53-56

Since it was late Friday afternoon, preparations for the Sabbath would begin at sundown. The women who accompanied Jesus from Galilee followed Joseph to the tomb and saw how Jesus' body was left. Then they returned home to prepare spices and ointments. On Saturday, the Sabbath, they rested according to their religious tradition.

+

Friday afternoon. Late. Slanted sunlight. Long shadows. Cool breezes. Crowds gone. Crosses bare. Minutes to six o'clock. Sabbath coming. Sundown near. Galilean women. Fresh tomb. Tortured body. Much to do. Much remains. Spices. Ointments. Oils. Perfumes. Proper burial. Linens. Cloths. No time. Rest now. Commandment kept.

It reads like a respectful tribute. The women, who supported Jesus in his ministry and remained at the cross, follow Joseph and the corpse to its final resting place. Friday sundown is near, and the work of a proper burial will have to wait. With the time remaining, they can only prepare the necessary burial spices that will be applied on Jesus' body when the holy day is over. Observant Jews, they rest on the Sabbath.

In one sense, it's an anticlimactic conclusion to a tumultuous day. What began with shouts—"Crucify him! Crucify him!"—ends with a handful of devoted followers quietly tending to the lifeless, bloodied body of their friend. They don't organize to protest the injustice done or occupy Pilate's residence. They simply observe the Sabbath.

Fred Craddock (*Luke, Interpretation*) reminds us that sometimes the best medicine is to re-engage with the common and ordinary routines of everyday life. What else is there to do when numbness sets in? They go home to observe the Sabbath. Even if they feel nothing in the rituals, they go through the motions of worship. If they no longer believe the words, at least they read the Psalms. Perhaps doubting the existence of a loving God, they still pray the prayers. Even if they aren't hungry, they eat what's in the house. Though body and mind resist, they rest.

When the world collapses and the sky falls, often it's the established habits and routines that bring back to us the first signs of sanity.

What routines have helped you deal with a particular tragedy?

THE SPICES
Luke 24:1

Early Sunday morning, the day after the Sabbath, the women came to the tomb carrying the spices they had prepared.

+

The gospel writers differ significantly on the details of Easter morning. They all agree, however, that none of the early morning visitors expect to find anything in the tomb but a two-day-old corpse. No one wakes up that Sunday humming Easter tunes. It's death, not life, that brings them out.

According to Luke, Mary Magdalene, Joanna, Mary (the mother of James), and other women leave their homes to finish what the crucifixion had started. Some of these women had financially supported Jesus' ministry. Mary Magdalene had experienced deliverance from dark bondage and an even darker past. Though the male disciples are huddled together fearing for their own safety, these faithful women refuse to leave Jesus' remains unattended. In his death as in his life, these women disciples remain near.

At Sunday's dawn, the women arrive as first-century undertakers to complete what Friday's sundown had prohibited. Carrying spices and ointments, perfumes and fragrances, they make their way to the cemetery to out-smell the smell of death. In a final show of respect, they hope to give their loved one a decent and proper burial. It's the least they can do for all he had done for them.

This female delegation arrives to acknowledge the finality of a Good Friday world—death is always one-for-one, and not even a good and godly man is going to beat those odds. Their spices are an affirmation that sooner or later death prevails. Their heavy hearts remind them that sometimes the preservation of mental well-being requires a simple acceptance of one's losses. The advice seems sound: the sooner we come to terms with life's tragedies, the sooner we can move on. Good advice on most days. But this day isn't like most days.

When was the last time your hopes were crushed?

PERPLEXITY AND TERROR
Luke 24:2-7

The women found the stone rolled away from the tomb's opening. They went in but didn't see Jesus' body. As they wondered about this, suddenly two men in luminous clothing stood beside them. Terrified, the women bowed to the ground. The two strangers said to them, "Why do you look for the living among the dead? He's not here; he's risen. He told you in Galilee he would be arrested and crucified, and on the third day, he would rise from the dead."

+

On Easter Sunday, churches and preachers, choirs and musicians pull out all the stops. The only way, it seems, to describe what happened that first Easter is to unleash words we've saved up a whole year to use, words like *triumphant . . . powerful . . . abundant.*

Different emotions, however, sweep over the visitors on the first Easter morning—not relief and joy, but perplexity and terror. There's no corpse, and standing in front of them are "two strangers in luminous clothing." The gospel accounts don't agree on these strangers. Matthew identifies a lone angel. Mark records the presence of a man. John counts two angels occupying the spot where Jesus' body had been placed. These discrepancies lead some to conclude that nothing happened on that morning because the accounts fail to agree on every detail.

Let's take that rationale and apply it to the assassination of John F. Kennedy. Conspiracy theories abound, speculations teem, and image-enhanced film from a handheld camera, played back in slow motion, raise more questions than answers. Yet, nobody denies the event that rocked the nation and the world on November 22, 1963.

"Why do you look for the living among the dead?" Is that a rebuke, an encouragement, or a rhetorical question? Perhaps it is a reminder by voices beyond ourselves that if we insist on seeing Jesus only in time-bound and earthly constraints, then his selfless life will appear nothing more than that of a good man who got a raw deal at the miscarriage of justice.

How do you reconcile the resurrection account with modern sensibilities?

FOOLISH TALK
Luke 24:8-11

The women recalled Jesus' earlier words and returned to the other disciples. It was Mary Magdalene, Joanna, Mary (the mother of James), and other women with them who told the disciples everything that had happened. The men, however, ridiculed the women and refused to believe a word of it. Foolish talk, they called it.

+

Understanding the Sunday challenge of connecting to an audience, most preachers take some comfort knowing that not even the first post-Easter message fell on open ears. "Foolish talk," the men call it. Silly ramblings by excitable women! If Jewish courts didn't admit the testimony of a woman, why should anyone think a woman's empty-tomb testimony could have the power to persuade a room of suspicious males?

Luke summarizes the men's response in a matter-of-fact way: They "refused to believe a word of it." They didn't believe because the news came from women? They didn't believe because there was no evidence in the flesh? They didn't believe because they were still overwhelmed by the events of Good Friday? Yes, to all these.

In the end, who knows for sure why they didn't believe? Who knows for any of us? Like a tug of war, one moment everything is up for grabs; the next, we cling securely to our theological support beams. Some days we seem to have everything strapped down tighter than bungee cords across a car's roof. Other days, we're on our hands and knees, grasping for scraps of our faith's debris strewn over the road.

How does anyone explain the path cut by the belief/unbelief tension? Who knows? Maybe belief takes its hesitating time in the disciples because to believe would mean that, even after his death, Jesus could still disrupt their lives and call them to places they would never consider going if he was still a corpse in a cool tomb, protected by an unrolled stone. Sometimes unbelief, requiring of us nothing, is the safest bet.

What about the Bible did you once believe but no longer do?

BUT PETER
Luke 24:12

But Peter had second thoughts and ran to the tomb. When he arrived, he bent down and looked in. Seeing the linen cloths but no body, he went home, wondering about it all.

+

A biblical footnote often appears at this verse, alerting us to the fact that numerous ancient manuscripts omit Peter's exploration. Scholars don't agree on whether this verse is original or a later addition, but it's similar to the resurrection account found in John's gospel.

Maybe Peter needs some fresh air. A weekend in hiding can make anyone claustrophobic. Perhaps he realizes there's something substantial beneath and beyond the women's "foolish talk" that prompts him to check it out on his own.

True to his character, Peter is the lone disciple to take action. With an economy of words, Luke describes this one-verse investigation: He "ran . . . bent down . . . looked in . . . went home, wondering." Unlike the women, who enter the tomb and look around for the body, Peter stays at the entrance, choosing instead to stoop and peer in. Near, but not inside. There, but not all the way.

Seeing the linen cloths, Peter neither shouts triumphantly nor shares the proclamation of his female counterparts. Neither does he return to the other disciples and confirm the women's earlier testimony. He leaves wondering; closer to the Greek, he leaves "puzzled."

Though the women serve as examples of faith ignited and belief embraced, I suspect most of us find ourselves closer to Peter, who hesitates at discovery's threshold. We hear the witness and, on occasion, even see the evidence, but we don't buy in immediately. We might not be in total denial or adamant unbelief, but neither have we found satisfying answers to all our questions.

Between the shedding of the old and embracing of the new, between the "tried and true" and the "not yet ready," is a place called liminal space. This is where the old answers no longer satisfy but the new ones aren't yet clear; a place where it's best to be open because you never know when you're going to be left wondering.

Where are the liminal spaces in your life?

INCOGNITO
Luke 24:13-16

Later that day, two disciples were on their way to a village called Emmaus, about seven miles from Jerusalem. While they were discussing the events of the weekend, Jesus walked with them, but they didn't recognize him.

+

Of the four evangelists, only Luke tells this story of the Emmaus road encounter between two disciples and Jesus. Though Luke identifies Emmaus as a village located seven miles from Jerusalem, other ancient manuscripts of the gospel identify Emmaus as located almost eighteen miles away. Today, the village of Amwas, about twenty miles from Jerusalem, is believed by many (especially savvy tour guides) to be the original location of Emmaus.

That the village of Emmaus eludes precise geographical coordinates is reason to imagine Emmaus being here, there, or anywhere. The road to getting there is the journey each of us walks.

As the two followers, part of the larger group of disciples, head home, Jesus appears, but they fail to recognize him (literally, "their eyes were prevented" from recognizing him). Some suggest that their grief over the crucifixion is so great that despondency prevents them from recognizing Jesus. Others, noting the time of day and the town's western locale, suggest their blindness is caused by the setting sun's glare. Whatever the reason, Jesus walks with them incognito.

If we lift this story from its first-century context and imagine that the road to Emmaus can be anywhere and everywhere, then a spiritual truth slowly emerges. We walk many circumstantial roads on which we're never fully aware that another presence walks with us. Sometimes such roads are paved with disappointment and discouragement—a tragedy sends us packing or a heartache blinds us to the companion walking alongside. Having eyes, we don't see. Sometimes all we can do and the best we can do is to keep walking.

When have you sensed a mysterious presence walking with you?

WE HAD HOPED
Luke 24:17-24

Jesus inquired, "What are you talking about?" They stopped walking because they were sad. Then the one named Cleopas said, "Are you the only one in Jerusalem who doesn't know the things that just happened there?" Jesus replied, "What things?" They answered, "About Jesus of Nazareth, a godly prophet who said and did powerful things. Our religious leaders turned him over to the Roman authorities, who crucified him. But we had hoped he was the one to free Israel. It's been three days since these things happened. Some women of our group surprised us when they said they were at the tomb early this morning. When they couldn't find his body, they came back and told us that they had seen a vision of angels who said he was alive. Some in our group went to the tomb and found it empty, just as the women had reported. But they didn't see Jesus either."

+

We're drawn to this story because it's a human story. High hopes, daring dreams, limitless possibilities, and then nothing. Rags to riches back to rags again.

We had hoped . . . and with that past-tense expectation, the implication we won't make the same mistake again.

We had hoped . . . and with that sentiment, the realization that hoping is dangerous business, and if you're not careful, it can chew you up and spit you out.

We had hoped . . . and with that sigh, the head hangs, shoulders droop, and the voice trails off down Resignation Road.

We had hoped he was the one . . . not just hope for the sake of hoping, not just hope for some nameless nobody to come on the scene, but hope for *him*.

We had hoped he was the one . . . not merely hope for the best within ourselves to come out of hiding, not merely hope that we might realize our full potentials, but hope for *him*.

We had hoped he was the one . . . not just hope for any run-of-the-mill, one-of-a-thousand messiahs to stake a claim, but hope for *him*.

We had hoped he was the one to free Israel . . . yes, the *goel*, a family member who has the right and responsibility to free you, to pay for your release should you fall on hard times, or be sold into slavery, or lose your land.

We had hoped he was the one to free Israel . . . to *free*, yes—like he read from the prophet Isaiah at his first sermon in Nazareth: good news to the poor, release for the captives, sight to the blind, freedom for the oppressed.

We had hoped he was the one to free Israel . . . to *free*, yes, our beloved land and the holy city from the Roman boot, to restore us to our rightful place among the nations, to make us shine as we once shined under King David.

We had hoped . . . he was the one . . . to free Israel.

What do you hope the Risen Christ will do?

Grand Rapids, MI

TEACHING TIME
Luke 24:25-27

Then Jesus said, "Don't be so slow to believe what the prophets spoke! Wasn't it necessary for the Messiah to suffer before being vindicated?" Then Jesus explained the writings of Moses and the prophets, showing them how he fit into their hopes.

+

We're not the first to have disagreements over the meaning and message of the Bible. The history of churches and denominations is pocked with episodes of scriptural wars and interpretive battles waged over particular passages. When it comes to the Bible, nothing is as simple as the bumper sticker suggests: "The Bible said it. I believe it. That settles it."

"New growth will sprout from the trunk of Jesse, and a branch will grow from his roots" (Isaiah 11:1). These two Jewish disciples aren't newcomers to the history and traditions of Israel. They know the stories, having heard them from their youth. They're at home with the ways of Moses, the Torah, the journeys of their forebears, the injunctions of the prophets, and all things religious.

"Your king arrives, triumphant and victorious, humble and riding on a donkey" (Zechariah 9:9). They, too, long for life to be different. Better. Holier. Less oppressive. The way God intends it. In their prayers, they invoke the Almighty to send the Messiah, one who will be charismatic to the core, a warrior beyond brave. Fearless.

"He was despised and rejected, one who suffered . . . Surely he carried our weaknesses and diseases . . . He was wounded for our waywardness, crushed for our iniquities . . ." (Isaiah 53:3-5). Yes, they know the traditions of hope. They aren't strangers to the stories. Each day was another day closer to the Coming One.

"They made his grave with the wicked and his tomb with the rich . . . He died following God's way . . . Out of his anguish he will see light" (Isaiah 53:9-11).

How do you respond to the bumper sticker's message?

GUEST AND HOST
Luke 24:28-31

As they entered Emmaus, Jesus walked on as if continuing his journey. But the two disciples urged him, "Stay with us; it's getting late." Jesus accepted their invitation. When they sat at the supper table, Jesus took bread, blessed and broke it, and gave it to them. At that moment, they recognized him. And suddenly, he disappeared.

+

The appearance of Jesus to the two disciples at Emmaus is sometimes called the "other" Easter story. No angels appear in dazzling white, no mysterious messengers pronounce resurrection realities, no anxious disciples hunt for a missing body. Rather, there's a homey comfortableness to this story—a supper table instead of a gravesite.

Easter isn't for everyone. The Risen One doesn't stroll into Pontius Pilate's office to prove that the governor's kangaroo court was just that. The Risen One doesn't give a repeat performance of the Palm Sunday procession, this time riding a hero's stallion rather than a lowly donkey. The resurrected Christ doesn't march into the temple or head back to the Nazareth synagogue to unroll Isaiah's scroll one more time and triumphantly claim, "What you've just heard is coming true." That's because Easter is an event of the willing heart more than it is a public spectacle.

Jesus chooses the intimacy of a kitchen table as the place to reveal his risen presence. In sacramental language: "Jesus took bread, blessed and broke it, and gave it to them." At that moment, recalling past meals with this teacher, rabbi, and friend, the scales from their hearts' eyes disappear. They experience the presence of one who lives. Beholding with the eyes of faith, they see what others fail to notice. They witness the resurrection.

If the Risen One is pleased to reveal himself in such company, aren't there other ordinary Emmauses where this is repeated? Any town will do. At any block, any house (crack and halfway, included), any table, any gathering, any time when Jesus' life is shared and the meal is given, the presence of the risen Christ is pleased to dwell.

Can you recall a time when a meal seemed surrounded by a resurrection presence?

DELAYED EFFECT
Luke 24:32-35

They said to each other, "Weren't our hearts on fire when he explained the scriptures to us while walking back to Emmaus?" Then they returned to Jerusalem and found the eleven disciples and the others together. The disciples said, "Jesus is alive! He appeared to Peter!" Then Cleopas and his companion told the others about their conversation with Jesus on the Emmaus road, and the moment they recognized him when they shared the meal.

+

What would you retrieve if you had only seconds to enter your burning house? There's a good chance your armful would include family photographs, picture albums, and the computer containing JPEG images. Nobody grabs the coffee maker or microwave.

It's the memory of the past, captured in images, that enables us to recognize, in depths not realized at the time, a particular moment's significance. Something similar happens when following the Risen One. Only when the two disciples look back on all that happened do they begin to understand. Not *at* the time, but sometime *after*. Remembrance sets in motion a delayed effect that leads to deeper recognition and understanding.

Faith's confirmations often occur when we look back on a period or specific event in our lives. At the time, while walking through the valley, or along the Emmaus road, or into the darkness, seldom are we certain or even aware of a transcendent presence with us. During such times, we tend to imagine just the opposite: that God has abandoned us to fend for ourselves. Later, however—sometimes years later—recalling that mental photograph, we see, as perhaps we've never seen before, the presence of one who was there with us in spite of our blindness to the company.

What "delayed effect" moments have you had in your life?

9th Ward, New Orleans, LA

PEACE TO YOU
Luke 24:36

While they continued to talk, Jesus mysteriously stood among them and said, "Peace to you."

+

This is the first post-resurrection experience of Jesus by the gathered disciples. Their last occasion together was three nights ago at Thursday's upper-room supper. Since then, there have been betrayals, denials, desertions, and huddled fear. Now, Jesus stands among them, returning to the very ones who had promised to remain loyal, returning to the ones who fled into the darkness and left him alone to die.

I can think of many things Jesus might have said: "How could you have done this to me? Where were you on Friday afternoon? You're all unbelievable failures! I've never been as disappointed as I am right now!"

Instead, standing in the midst of his disciples' fear and shame and regret, Jesus greets them with tender words: "Peace to you." With this gentle greeting, Jesus brings healing and makes it possible for every denier, deserter, and forsaker among them to experience again the relationship that's never been broken. Though they deserve the worst, Jesus makes all things well. "Peace to you." Knowing everything about their flaws and failures, Jesus loves them no less and all the more. "Peace to you."

In our own daily denials and desertions, in our own leanings toward laziness, the risen Christ doesn't wait for us to get our act together, or for us to get it right. Rather, he circumvents the doors we lock to protect our pride and hide from the truth, and stands with us in our broken humanity, saying at last the words we long to hear: "Peace to you." In the community of our brokenness, we experience the one who died and whose presence abides among us.

Where in your life are you waiting to hear "Peace to you"?

PLEASE HANDLE
Luke 24:37-40

The disciples were scared and thought they were seeing a
ghost. Jesus reassured them, "Why are you afraid and full of
doubts?" Then he showed them his scars. "Touch my hands
and feet. It's me. A ghost doesn't have flesh and bones like I
do."

+

They needed physical and touchable evidence. Skin to skin. Flesh to
flesh. Without saying as much, they needed to "kick the tires" for
themselves and shake off their unbelief. How else do you confirm the
presence of one who died?

In a manner that evidences his loving care for their slowness to
believe, Jesus offers his scarred hands and feet as proof that he stands
before them as no mere figment of their imaginations, nor as a ghostly
apparition of their troubled consciences. His presence is the real thing.

Luke wants the early church to know that the living presence of
the Risen One doesn't fit into old notions of soulful immortality. The
Greeks understood that after death the human soul—like an Eveready
battery—keeps going on and on. However, in the living presence of the
Risen One, something unique breaks into the world that is more than a
mere memory of him or recollection of his ethical ideal. His presence
comes with fresh wounds and all.

Rather than erase Good Friday, Easter confirms it. The suffering
way of Jesus now is the way for the church to engage the world. We
don't follow Jesus by merely stirring up fond memories of him and
offering up a sanitized devotion. We embody his presence when we
work for fairness and justice, when we relieve oppression and challenge
oppressive structures, when we give voice to those whose voice no one
cares to hear. We dream God's dreams for the world and live into
them.

To be a disciple of Jesus involves living the life he lived, being for
the world his wounded hands and scarred feet. When we dare to live
like this, we never see the world the same again.

Where do you see wounded hands and feet healing the world?

WHEN ALL ELSE FAILS
Luke 24:41-43

Tentatively joyous, the disciples weren't yet able to shake off their doubts and disbelief, so Jesus said, "Got anything to eat?" They gave him a piece of broiled fish, which he ate in front of them.

+

An empty tomb doesn't convince them. Word from the women informed by angels isn't enough. Peter's own substantiation fails to change their minds. Burning-heart testimony of the Emmaus travelers accomplishes little. The Risen One standing in their midst can't budge them. Wounded hands and feet offered for inspection fail to dispel their skepticism.

Disbelief and doubt haunt them still. Perhaps the disciples' emotional state is akin to what we feel when something is simply "too good to be true." Before giving ourselves to wholehearted belief, we check over our shoulder for a jokester to jump out and squirt us in the face with a Super Soaker.

When all the cajoling fails, Jesus pulls out the heavy artillery—proof that he's not a mere figment of their imagination. "Got anything to eat? . . . No, really, I mean it." Jesus eats with his disciples not only to satisfy his hunger, but also to satisfy their doubts. The one accused of eating with tax collectors and sinners is pleased to eat with those who now feel his presence but cannot fully understand it.

Perhaps they recalled the story of their ancestor Abraham who entertained God-like beings with curds and milk and calf meat (Genesis 18). Today, this mysterious one dines on broiled fish.

Who can predict the lengths to which God will go to get our attention, to shatter our illusions, and to dispel our doubts? Good things happen around meals.

Of what do you need to be convinced?

CONTINUITY WITH THE PAST
Luke 24:44-47

Then Jesus said, "I once explained to you everything that connects me to the writings of Moses, the prophets, and the psalms. It's written that the Messiah will suffer and rise from the dead on the third day, that lives will change, and forgiveness of sins will be preached in his name to all nations, beginning at Jerusalem."

+

This is the third time that Easter participants are instructed regarding the continuity of past prophetic announcements with the reality of the living presence of the Risen One. First, at the tomb, women are reminded by graveside messengers of what Jesus had said about the necessity for him to suffer, die, and rise again. Then in Emmaus, Jesus opens the Hebrew scriptures so his traveling companions can see for themselves all that to which Moses and the prophets pointed. Now with the gathered disciples, Jesus again opens their eyes to his connections to the traditions.

No new teaching here. No disconnect from the past. Previous revelations aren't disregarded and scrapped in favor of a new insight detached from history. Quite the opposite. Jesus wants his disciples (as Luke wants the early church) to know that his birth, life, ministry, suffering, death, and resurrection are a continuation of the purposes of God, a confirmation of everything God has spoken through the mouths of Israel's prophets, priests, and kings.

All this suggests that Jesus isn't God's emergency option inserted into the game like a ninth-inning pinch hitter. Into the tradition Jesus is born, in the tradition he is raised, and within the tradition he calls people to embody God's intentions for the world.

Living this way means the circles of inclusion expand beyond the impact of his earthly life. Like concentric ripples on a pond, God won't rest until all nations and all creatures are enveloped in the wave of heaven's grace.

Where do the circles of inclusion meet the most resistance in your life?

CLOTHED WITH POWER
Luke 24:48-49

"You are witnesses of all this. I will send you what my Father promised. Stay here in Jerusalem until you've been empowered by the Spirit."

+

To be called a witness is for the disciples both privilege and pressure. They're privileged to be firsthand recipients of Jesus' teachings, privileged to have witnessed his deeds of mercy and compassion, privileged to share in the work of his ministry.

But privilege also comes with pressure—the pressure of persecution, suffering, imprisonment, and death. As far as we know, none of the disciples died following complications of old age. Some suffered their own crucifixions; others died equally gruesome deaths.

Aware that the disciples are unable to walk into this future by their own strength, Jesus instructs them to remain in Jerusalem until the Spirit empowers them. To be called to a ministry, to a task, or to a specific path in life is only the beginning of a journey. Without empowerment beyond oneself, living the call will be ego-fueled and short-lived. Leaders aren't those who merely get others to follow; good leaders are those who inspire others to follow their God-given passions and to connect those passions to the world's deepest pain.

Scott Peck (*Golf and the Spirit*) distinguishes teachers from mentors by noting that the former usually are assigned to their pupils, while the latter choose their students. Mentors don't merely teach a body of information; they empower. Jesus' disciples, then and today, experience that power coming upon them as much as growing from within them.

When was the last time a power beyond yourself led you into a new venture?

ALL THINGS WELL
Luke 24:50-53

Then Jesus led his disciples to the village of Bethany. He raised his hands and blessed them, then went up to heaven. The disciples worshipped him, before joyously returning to Jerusalem, where they regularly met in the temple to praise God.

+

With few details, Luke describes Jesus' departure in an event that has come to be known as the ascension. Luke gives a fuller account of it in the opening chapter of the Acts of the Apostles.

How do we understand Jesus being lifted up into the sky? Clearly, this is language of a pre-scientific time. First-century notions of a three-storied world with a hell below earth and a heaven above it strike us as primitive, especially as we set our sights on sending humans to Mars.

Do we scrap the story because the physics is flawed? A better strategy is to ask: What did the ascension mean to the persecuted church in Luke's time? Among the answers is the testimony that a power greater than the powers of this world is in charge. For those facing death, Jesus' life, not Roman decree, is God's way. For those with no homeland, the City of God, not the city of Rome, determines citizenship.

Those caught in tragedy's despair, or finding no human ears to hear their cry can find confidence in the Ascended One, whose life was a testimony to God's deepest passion for the world. God was in Jesus making all things well. Julian of Norwich, a fourteenth-century mystic, may have been reflecting on Jesus' ascension when she wrote the words with which we end our study of Luke's gospel:

> Thus our good Lord answered to all the questions
> and doubts I might make, saying full comfortably,
> I may make all thing well, I can make all thing well,
> I will make all thing well, and I shall make all thing well,
> and thou shalt see thyself, all manner of thing shall be well.

Where in your life are you most well?

SOURCES

The following authors, some of whom I've quoted in these meditations, have significantly informed my understanding of Jesus. Without them, this book could not have come to life.

Bailey, Kenneth E. *Poet and Peasant* and *Through Peasant Eyes.* Grand Rapids, MI: Wm. B. Eerdmans, 1983.

_____. *Jesus Through Middle Eastern Eyes.* Downers Grove, IL: InterVarsity Press, 2008.

Barclay, William. *Daily Study Bible: The Gospel of Luke.* Philadelphia: The Westminster Press, 1975.

_____. *The Mind of Jesus.* New York: Harper & Row, 1960. Both resources by this New Testament scholar are dated, but the vast historical background he shares is rich and readable, especially for those with no theological training.

Borg, Marcus. *Jesus: Uncovering the Life, Teaching, and Relevance of a Religious Revolutionary.* San Francisco: Harper One, 2006. This is one of many books by Borg in my library. A progressive Christian, Borg believed the Bible is too important to be held captive by literalists and fundamentalists.

Buechner, Frederick. *Wishful Thinking: A Theological ABC.* New York: HarperOne, 1973. Whenever my faith supply is running on empty, I turn to Buechner. This is one of his numerous works worth reading.

Capon, Robert Farrar. *Kingdom, Grace, Judgment: Paradox, Outrage, and Vindication in the Parables of Jesus.* Grand Rapids, MI: Wm. B. Eerdmans, 2002. An Episcopal priest who opens up the parables of Jesus like no one else, Capon is irreverently witty and wickedly funny. In addition to being a prolific biblical scholar, he authored several cookbooks. He died in 2013; I count myself among the mourners.

Coffin, William Sloane. *The Collected Sermons of William Sloane Coffin, Vols. 1 & 2.* Philadelphia: Westminster John Knox Press, 2011. Former minister at The Riverside Church in New York City, Coffin was to America what the biblical prophets were to ancient Israel. A Coffin appetizer: "We are called not to mirror but to challenge culture, not to sustain but to upend the status quo, and if that to some sounds overly bold, isn't it true that God is always beckoning us toward horizons we aren't sure we want to reach?"

Cosby, Gordon and McClurg, Kayla. *Becoming the Authentic Church: A Guide Toward Being in Diverse, Healing Community Rooted in Reconciliation and Justice*. Washington, D.C.: Tell the Word, 2004. I recommend The Church of the Saviour's online resource (www.inwardoutward.org).

Craddock, Fred B. *Luke: Interpretation—A Bible Commentary for Teaching and Preaching*. Louisville: John Knox Press, 1990. If ever stranded on a deserted island with only one biblical commentary, I hope it's this one. Essential for preachers and accessible for all readers.

Crossan, John Dominic. *The Essential Jesus: What Jesus Really Taught*. San Francisco: HarperCollins, 1995.

Dillard, Annie. *A Writer's Life*. New York: Harper & Row, 1989.

Ellis, E. E. *The Gospel of Luke* (The New Century Bible). London: Nelson, 1966; Grand Rapids, MI: Wm. B. Eerdmans, 2nd edition, 1974. Dr. Ellis was my New Testament professor at New Brunswick Theological Seminary. Though I didn't know it at the time, he planted a seed that led to writing these reflections.

Levine, Amy-Jill (editor). *A Feminist Companion to Luke*. Cleveland: The Pilgrim Press, 2004. Along with her other New Testament commentaries, this is a resource all male clergy should read.

Lewis, C. S. *Mere Christianity*. New York: HarperCollins, 2001. This is one of several editions of the original 1952 broadcast.

_____. *The Weight of Glory*. New York: HarperCollins, 2001. A republication of the original 1949 addresses.

Marshall, I. Howard. *The Gospel of Luke*. Grand Rapids, MI: Wm. B. Eerdmans, 1978. Lots of valuable textual notes. Great if you're a Greek geek, or even if you're not.

Miles, Jack. *Christ: A Crisis in the Life of God*. New York: Alfred A. Knopf, Inc., 2001.

_____. *God: An Autobiography*. New York: Alfred A. Knopf, 1995. Trained as an Episcopal priest, Miles won a Pulitzer Prize for this title.

Norris, Kathleen. *Amazing Grace: A Vocabulary of Faith*. New York: Riverhead Books, 1998.

Palmer, Parker. *Let Your Life Speak: Listening for the Voice of Vocation*. San Francisco: John Wiley & Sons, 2000.

Peterson, Eugene H. *The Message: The Bible in Contemporary Language*. Colorado Springs: NavPress, 2002. A translation for today from the original Hebrew and Greek.

Rohr, Richard. *The Good News According to Luke*. New York: Crossroad, 1997.

_____. *Jesus' Plan for a New World: The Sermon on the Mount*. Cincinnati: St. Anthony's Messenger Press, 1996. I'm on the quest to read everything this Franciscan has written. Currently, he is the director of the Center for Action and Contemplation in Albuquerque, NM (www.cac.org).

Swanson, Richard W. *Provoking the Gospel of Luke*. Cleveland: The Pilgrim Press, 2006. This is an invaluable commentary for preachers and storytellers, highlighting all the Luke passages used in Year C of the Revised Common Lectionary.

Taylor, Barbara Brown. *Gospel Medicine*. Lanham, MD: Rowman and Littlefield, 1995. Everything she has written—and has yet to write—is a gift to the world.

Wink, Walter. *Engaging the Powers: Discernment and Resistance in a World of Domination*. Minneapolis: Fortress Press, 1992. The historical and scriptural basis for Christian nonviolence as practiced in the life of Jesus.

_____. *The Powers That Be*. New York: Galilee/Doubleday, 1998. A condensed treatment of the topics dealt with in *Engaging the Powers*.

ACKNOWLEDGMENTS

Many people encouraged me during the writing of these reflections and, though they could have refused, graciously agreed to read drafts of early manuscripts and offer their invaluable comments and insights. I wish to thank my spouse and partner Jody Betten, Mary and Norman Kansfield, Nancy and Allan Martling, Ada and David Kidd, Robert Anderson, Melissa Fore, and Barbara MacGregor for her early edits. I am deeply grateful for the Google search that led me to Heidi Mann of Final Touch Proofreading & Editing, who took my best efforts and made them better.

These reflections owe their existence to the insights and musings of countless theologians, pastors, preachers, biblical scholars, novelists, artists, poets, movie makers, musicians, bus drivers, pew sitters, street people, and bloggers who have shaped and reshaped my understanding of the Bible and my evolving awareness of Jesus. I owe a lifetime of thanks to all who continue to inspire me!

Made in the USA
Columbia, SC
06 April 2018